EU Higher Education Law

EUROPEAN MONOGRAPHS

Editor-in-chief Professor David O'Keeffe

In this series *European Monographs* this book. *EU Higher Education Law: The Bologna Process and Harmonization by Stealth* is the seventy-sixth title. *The titles published in this series are listed at the end of this volume.*

EU Higher Education Law

The Bologna
Process and Harmonization by Stealth

Sacha Garben

Wolters Kluwer
Law & Business

Published by:
Kluwer Law International
PO Box 316
2400 AH Alphen aan den Rijn
The Netherlands
Website: www.kluwerlaw.com

Sold and distributed in North, Central and South America by:
Aspen Publishers, Inc.
7201 McKinney Circle
Frederick, MD 21704
United States of America
Email: customer.serivce@aspenpublishers.com

Sold and distributed in all other countries by:
Turpin Distribution Services Ltd.
Stratton Business Park
Pegasus Drive, Biggleswade
Bedfordshire SG18 8TQ
United Kingdom
Email: kluwerlaw@turpin-distribution.com

Printed on acid-free paper.

ISBN 978-90-411-3365-6

Printed in Great Britain.

Table of Contents

About the Author

Sacha Garben (Ede, 1982) studied Dutch and European law at the University of Maastricht from 2001 to 2005 and obtained an LLM degree from the College of Europe in Bruges in 2006. She carried out her PhD research, on which this book is based, at the European University Institute in Florence. She successfully defended her thesis in June, 2010. In 2008, she spent a semester as a visiting researcher at the European Law Research Centre of Harvard Law School. She has published several articles on EU law and higher education and continues her research in this field, as well as in other areas of European law. Sacha Garben currently works at the European Court of Justice in Luxembourg.

The author can be contacted at: Sacha.Garben@EUI.eu

List of Abbreviations

BFUG	Bologna Follow Up Group
CRE	Confederation of EU Rectors' Conferences and the Association of European Universities
ECJ	European Court of Justice
ECTS	European Course Credit Transfer System
EHEA	European Higher Education Area
ENIC	European National Information Centre
ENQA	European Network for Quality Assurance
EQAR	European Register for Quality Assurance Agencies
EQF	European Qualifications Framework
ERASMUS	European Community Action Scheme for the Mobility of University Students
EU	European Union
FETAC	Further Education and Training Awards Council
HE	Higher Education
KIC	Knowledge and Innovation Community
LRU	Loi relative aux libertés et reponsabilités des universités
NARIC	National Academic Recognition Information Centre
OMC	Open Method of Coordination
PISA	Programme for International Student Assessment
TEU	Treaty on the European Union
TFEU	Treaty on the Functioning of the European Union
WTO	World Trade Organization

Preface

It is hard to imagine a more enjoyable place to write a PhD thesis than the European University Institute in Florence. The spectacular beauty of the place, the richness of its intellectual resources and the multicultural and interdisciplinary academic community all have contributed to a true once-in-a-lifetime experience, for which I am very grateful.

It is also hard to imagine a more appropriate place to conduct this research, as the European University Institute is a typical example of European cooperation in higher education. In the early days of what is now the EU, the Member States discussed creating a European University, for which a legal basis was explicitly provided by the Treaties. Due to the resistance of some of the Member States, the project was somewhat watered down. The European University Institute was created as a post-graduate institute on the basis of a separate Convention, denying it Community status. Nevertheless, it was and remains closely related to the EU institutional framework. The European University Institute operates in the intriguing twilight zone between EU and international cooperation, much like the Bologna Process. As a 1972 press release said: 'Like the Institute, European education can be either the product of intergovernmental cooperation or a function of the Community, the decision has yet to be made.' It seems that today, almost four decades later, the same still holds true.

Acknowledgements

It is because of the support of several people both within and outside the European University Institute that this research has come about.

First and foremost, I would like to thank my supervisor Professor Bruno de Witte for his invaluable support and guidance. Also Professor Marise Cremona deserves a special mention in this regard.

Furthermore, I am particularly indebted to Professor Hildegard Schneider, who has been there for me ever since the beginning of my academic life.

I would also like to mention Professor Michael Dougan and Professor Grainne de Burca, whose inspiring ideas have helped shape my own. Special thanks go out to the editorial team of Kluwer Law International, for helping me turn the PhD thesis into this book.

Last but not least, I would like to thank my family and my friends for their unconditional support and confidence.

Chapter 1

Introduction: A Surprising Evolution in European Higher Education

1. INTRODUCTION

A curious trend has emerged recently in the European educational landscape. European governments have embarked on an ambitious project to reform their higher-education systems so as to bring them in line with each other, in other words, to harmonize them with a view to creating a European Area of Higher Education. This revolutionary development is taking place under the name of the 'Bologna Process'. This process has been set in motion quite suddenly. It was initiated in 1998, when at an international Forum organized in connection with the celebration of the 800th anniversary of the Sorbonne University, the Ministers of education of France, Germany, Italy and the United Kingdom decided on a 'Joint Declaration on Harmonization of the Architecture of the European Higher Education System.' It was open for the other Member States of the European Union (EU) as well as for third countries to join. Belgium, Switzerland, Romania, Bulgaria and Denmark accepted and signed immediately. The Italian Minister for Education extended an invitation to fellow Ministers in other European countries to a follow-up conference, which was to take place in Bologna the following year.[1] This conference did indeed take place on June 1999, and it was on this occasion that no less than twenty-nine European countries agreed on a Declaration that would fundamentally influence the future of their higher-education systems.[2]

---

1. Hackl 2001, 21.
2. This is known as the 'Bologna Declaration'. Currently forty-six European countries take part in the process: Albania, Andorra, Armenia, Austria, Azerbaijan, Belgium (Flemish Community and French Community), Bosnia and Herzegovina, Bulgaria, Croatia, Cyprus, the Czech Republic, Denmark, Estonia, Finland, France, Georgia, Germany, Greece, the Holy See, Hungary, Iceland, Ireland, Italy, Kazakhstan, Latvia, Liechtenstein, Lithuania, Luxembourg, Malta, Moldova, the

This expeditious course of proceedings might give the impression that there was a great motivation and determination to Europeanize higher education. But was higher education not a highly controversial area in which the European countries were reluctant to yield national sovereignty? Had the same countries that now so willingly engaged in this far-reaching process not 'for decades praised the blessings of diversity, that is of system differences, across Europe'?[3] Reading the actual text of the Bologna Declaration, one cannot but be struck by the ambitious language it employs. The Declaration commences with the statement that 'the European process, thanks to the extraordinary achievements of the last few years, has become an increasingly concrete and relevant reality for the Union and its citizens'. Even more importantly, the Declaration continues to say: 'we are witnessing a growing awareness in large parts of the political and academic world and in public opinion of the need to establish a more complete and far-reaching Europe, in particular building upon and strengthening its intellectual, cultural social and scientific and technological dimensions'.

It seems difficult to imagine that these phrases stem from the same countries that have been keen on keeping higher education safely in the hands of the nation-state and forcefully resisting any kind of harmonization. Furthermore, the meaning of these phrases becomes quite ambiguous upon realizing that the Bologna enterprise is taking place outside the framework of the EU. While in words praising the achievements of the EU in the process of European integration and explicitly referring to the 'Union and its citizens' and the aim of 'consolidating European citizenship', the Declaration is in fact nothing more than a soft law instrument which envisaged practically no involvement of the EU. Its intergovernmental character, in addition to its extended membership that currently enables twenty non-Member States to take part, places the Bologna Process outside the EU's formal policy-making process.[4] Hackl points out that the developments concerning the Bologna Process seem to contradict the 'traditional resistance of the EU Member States to any harmonization policy in education and to increased Community competences'.[5] It is true that the pro-European integration wording and tone of the Bologna Declaration are in that respect remarkable. However, the fact that the Member States decided to tackle higher education issues in an intergovernmental manner actually illustrates their resistance against EU involvement and their desire to remain fully sovereign.

The zealous way in which the Member States guard their national educational autonomy is, in a way, understandable.[6] Education is closely connected to cultural identity, and seen as a traditional function of the nation-state. This is probably the reason why it was excluded from the original Treaty of Rome. Yet (higher)

Netherlands, Norway, Poland, Portugal, Romania, the Russian Federation, Serbia and Montenegro, the Slovak Republic, Slovenia, Spain, Sweden, Switzerland, 'the former Yugoslav Republic of Macedonia', Turkey, Ukraine and the United Kingdom. The European Commission is a voting member of the Follow-up Group.

3. Wächter 2004, 268.
4. Keeling 2006, 207.
5. Hackl 2004, 2.
6. Expression borrowed from Ryba 1992, 11.

education is an area where, in spite of the initial absence of explicit law-making competence, the EU has somehow managed to create law and policy. Both the European Commission and the European Court of Justice (ECJ) have played an important role in this development. It was in the landmark *Casagrande* case that the ECJ established that the Community could legitimately act in areas where it has not been expressly attributed with competence, if such is necessary for the achievement of Community aims.[7] Typically, *Casagrande* was an education case. Over the years, with its legislation on the mutual recognition of diplomas, the case law of the ECJ, and with its mobility programmes, in particular ERASMUS, the EU has established itself as an important player on the European educational field.[8] These developments have been criticized. According to Murphy, 'the fuzzy, blurred, and covert history of education policy in Europe does not contribute much to a sense of optimism regarding the strengthening of European democratic legitimacy, a key and indispensable component of any effective post-national form of citizenship'.[9] Leaving aside whether this criticism is entirely in place, the forgoing does create some understanding of the Member States' somewhat mistrustful attitude towards the EU when it comes to higher education.

It appears that with the Bologna Process the Member States have tried to avoid the growing influence on higher education by the EU. In this sense, the Bologna Process constitutes as much a *de-nationalization* (or Europeanization) of higher education, subjecting the national higher-education systems to European-level coordination, as a *re-nationalization*, by taking these matters of EU policy away from the European Organizations. It has been said that by deciding to proceed in this intergovernmental mode of European cooperation, the Bologna Declaration disowns the EU institutions of 'their role as drivers of European integration in higher education'.[10] This is certainly the case, although it is doubtful whether a driving role for the EU in this area was ever truly supported by the Member States. Traditionally, educational policy was perceived as 'an excellent subject for intergovernmental cooperation among the Member States in close connection with Community action, but could not be the subject of genuine Community action itself'.[11] Although the Maastricht Treaty included a legal basis for EU action in the educational field, it did so only reluctantly. The text of what is now Article 165 Treaty on the Functioning of the European Union (TFEU) – previously Article 149(1) EC – shows how limited the competence attributed:

> The Union shall contribute to the development of quality education by encouraging cooperation between Member States and, if necessary, by supporting and supplementing their action, while fully respecting the responsibility of the Member States for the content of teaching and the organisation of education systems and their cultural and linguistic diversity.

---

7. Case 9/74, *Donato Casagrande v. Landeshauptstadt München* [1974] ECR 773.
8. See Corbett 2003.
9. Murphy 2003, 560.
10. Wächter 2004, 270.
11. De Witte 1989.

Apart from this principle of national educational autonomy, Article 165 holds another restriction of EU competence, in that it prescribes that in the incentive measures that can be taken, harmonization of the laws of the Member States is prohibited. Nevertheless, the second paragraph of Article 165 TFEU does acknowledge a role for the EU in educational matters. It specifically mentions the promotion of mobility and in that context the (academic) recognition of diplomas and periods of study. Furthermore, the internal market competences can include a very real education dimension, such as in the case of the mutual recognition of diplomas for professional purposes. As we shall come to see in the following chapters, the EU has in fact been very active in these fields, to the extent that we can now speak of European higher education law. That means that the Bologna Process deals with matters that have become EU business over the years. This potential overlap between the Process and EU policies might be problematic.

One can theorize several possible explanations why the Member States decided to avoid the EU in adopting and operating the Bologna Process. It can be thought of as a kind of retribution, to punish the EU institutions for their intrusive efforts to force upon the Member States the Europeanization of higher education, to the detriment of their national educational autonomy. This would, however, neglect the fact that also the Member States themselves have supported and legitimized this action of the European Institutions, and that they in principle seem to support the aims of student and teacher mobility and the role of education in the European knowledge economy. A less polarized explanation would be that the Member States just wanted to be on the safe side with the Bologna Process, not as a punishment but rather as a precaution, knowing that involving the EU and its institutional framework could lead to unwanted spill-over and could run out of their control. A third explanation, which builds on the findings of political scientists that Bologna was inspired mainly by the national interests of national political actors, is that the Member States wanted to outmanoeuvre domestic constraints while at the same time avoiding the more democratically legitimate procedures of the EU's institutional framework. It might go far to qualify the Sorbonne and Bologna Declarations as deals done in smoke-filled rooms, but the truth might not be far from there. It could very well be that all these explanations, and perhaps even others, play their part. But as we shall come to see in the following chapters, it can be said that regardless the reasons for adopting the Bologna Process in an intergovernmental non-EU fashion, the Member States have in avoiding the EU framework opted for harmonization by less transparent, accountable, legitimate and democratic means. The Bologna Process amounts to harmonization by stealth.

2. CORE ISSUES

In order to determine how EU higher education law interrelates with the Bologna Process, and vice versa, it is firstly important to map the particular areas of overlap, and to assess its consequences. It could be that the course of proceedings in the Bologna Process actually worsens the picture as painted by Murphy, cited above.

As briefly pointed out above, the activities undertaken in the framework of the Bologna Process appear to overlap with already well-established EU policies, such as the Diploma Supplement, the European Credit Transfer System (the ECTS) and the promotion of teacher and student mobility through diploma recognition. The overlap between the EU's actions and the Bologna Process shall occupy a most central place, for this is where important legal questions – that remain unanswered in the otherwise blossoming academic literature on the Bologna Process as a policy phenomenon – present themselves. Should it be the case that the same activities in these areas are now pursued on two different planes, such could hardly be said to contribute to the needed transparency on the European level. Potential divergence and inconsistency could threaten the credibility of both the Bologna enterprise and the EU's educational policy. In a field where European action is on the one hand perceived necessary to meet the needs of contemporary societies but which is on the other hand so culturally sensitive and hard to sell to the stakeholders and the general public, one should arguably proceed with caution. This caution requires transparency more than anything. It is a fair point that having various actors acting in various capacities on various European levels does not foster intelligibility. At the same time, it could also be the case that the overlap leads to a fruitful alignment and mainstreaming of objectives, thereby achieving greater output than what would have been possible with a strict hard law EU approach. And perhaps the loss of transparency adds to a gain in effectiveness.

Furthermore, as the very existence of this overlap indicates, the EU possesses legal competence for various kinds of activities in the educational sector. The exact scope of this competence is however somewhat unclear. One of the most intriguing questions is whether the EU could have adopted the Bologna Declaration as a binding EU measure, such as a Directive, and – similarly – whether it would be legally sustainable to subsume the Bologna Process in the *acquis communautaire* in the future. The main focus in answering these competence questions shall be one of legal scope and interpretation, and not so much of political feasibility. The central question is what the limits are of the EU's competence in higher education matters, and how the prohibition of harmonization relates to competence to regulate the internal market. The yardstick against which the possibility to adopt the Bologna EU measure is tested, is what the European Court would be likely to uphold as legitimately adopted if challenged. Answering these questions is relevant for the understanding of the legal scope of action of the EU in general, and in higher education specifically, but also in the political context of the Bologna Process. After all, if the option existed to adopt Bologna as an EU measure, the decision to steer clear from the EU framework is all the more controversial. Furthermore, it is of practical relevance in that it could provide an option for future action, potentially incorporating the Bologna Process in the Union legal framework.

If the EU was indeed competent to adopt the Bologna Process as a binding measure within its institutional framework, the question that rears its head is whether it was lawful for the Member States to avoid the Union legal framework at will. It seems far-reaching to say that Member States have lost their ability to jointly arrange matters of higher education, which is an extremely sensitive policy area closely connected to state sovereignty, outside the framework of the EU in areas where the latter is competent. Not to forget, Article 5 Treaty on the European Union (TEU) (ex Article 5 EC) lays down the principle of subsidiarity, endorsing a preference of Member State action as opposed to EU action. But although higher education is a policy area that belongs primarily to the Member States, meaning that they have a large discretion to act on their own, it could be argued that Member States are not allowed to undermine the EU's *raison d'être* by adopting agreements involving all the EU Member States together on matters of EU competence, completely outside the EU framework with its inbuilt checks and balances designed to counterbalance the loss of democratic control inherent in international policy- and law-making. Member States are bound to their duty of loyal cooperation, as laid down in the so-called loyalty clause of Article 4 TEU (ex Article 10 EC).

Furthermore, regardless of legal competence questions, is the marginalization of the EU in the Bologna Process in itself regrettable? Paradoxically, the principle of democracy provides both opponents and proponents of this statement with valuable arguments in support of their point of view. The EU has since long been plagued by allegations concerning its so-called democratic deficit, but perhaps the intergovernmental mode can be said to be even less democratic. The EU could be dubbed bureaucratic and complex, but at the same time it does provide for a relatively transparent and democratic legislative process, with an increasingly important role for the European Parliament, representing the people of Europe, especially when compared with the public international soft law making that characterizes the Bologna Process. The intergovernmental process merely involves governmental officials and a limited number of higher education actors. It could be countered that these governmental officials benefit from a higher democratic legitimacy than European officials, but the merits of that argument are not certain. Another point is that contrary to the intergovernmental arena, in an EU context the ECJ is there to ensure respect for the rule of law and to safeguard the interests of the individual. But then again, the (democratic) legitimacy of the Court of Justice is at times doubtful, especially when it appears to surpass the intentions and sometimes even explicit stipulations of the Member States and European legislature. All the foregoing are important questions, going to the core of the European integration process and the relationship between the Member States and the EU, and linking into the debate on hard law versus soft law in European and international policy-making. Although the analyses of this book are confined to the European higher education sector, many considerations and conclusions deal with more fundamental and general questions of European law.

At this point it should be noted that the EU is not completely excluded from the Bologna Process. The European Commission is playing an increasingly influential role by means of funding and coordination, and arguably aims to gather and gain influence over the Bologna Process, so as to try to incorporate it into the EU framework, in particular the Lisbon strategy. Keeling argues that the Bologna Process has in fact significantly broadened the European Commission's basis for involvement in the higher education sector. In her opinion, 'the Commission's dynamic association of the Bologna university reforms with its Lisbon research agenda and its successful appropriation of these as European-level issues have placed its perspectives firmly at the heart of higher education policy debates in Europe'.[12] The increased involvement of the Commission has generally met with controversy. Some regard it as a positive development that might stimulate a better coordination of the various European-level initiatives, although from that point of view it is still regrettable that the most democratic organ of the EU, the European Parliament, remains practically excluded. Others are more mistrustful of the Commission, and regard the increased influence as a dangerous move in the direction of bureaucratization and 'Brussels-ization' of the Bologna Process. In addition to an increased influence of the Commission in the Bologna Process, the Bologna agenda has had a substantial impact on the higher education goals and policies of the EU. In response to the Bologna Process, the Commission's platform for action thus seems to have expanded not only outside the EU's framework but also within.

3. CONCEPTUALIZATION AND DEMARCATION

As Papatsiba sets out in a concise overview of the various conceptualizations of the Bologna Process offered by the plenitude of (political science) authors concerned with Bologna,[13] the Process is often analysed as a feature of Europeanization, either because it is perceived as focusing on the 'European' character of higher education in European countries,[14] because it is seen as an exemplary case of the new form of flexible European coordination aiming at European integration[15] or as a way of engaging universities in the process of making Europe.[16] In addition to Europeanization, as Papatsiba notes, there are other concepts, related but distinct, which are offered as frameworks of reference, such as Internationalization and Globalization.[17] In relation to the former concept, Teichler argues that the Bologna Process as a form of voluntary intergovernmental cooperation represents a paradigmatic shift of internationalization policies in higher education.[18] Globalization has been deemed relevant in the understanding of the Bologna Process either because it is seen as an extension of it, with its emphasis on the competitive and market-oriented aspects of higher education,[19] or because it is considered 'as a way of taking control of globalization and responding to its challenges' corresponding to a systemic effort at increasing the responsiveness of the higher education sector(s) to the globalization of societies, economy and labour

12. Keeling 2006, 203.
13. Papatsiba 2006, 96.
14. Enders 2004; Kwiek 2004; Teichler 2004.
15. Corbett 2004.
16. Abelson 2005.
17. Nokkala 2004; Papatsiba 2006, 96.
18. Teichler 2004.
19. Enders 2004; Teichler 2004.

markets.[20] Related to this is the idea that the Bologna Process amounts to a redefinition of the university as an institution, with a marked shift from a social institution to an industry.[21] In addition, Papatsiba notes another line of conceptualization, one that 'tends to mobilize a framework relating to governance issues and more specifically a framework of multi-actor, multilevel governance'.[22] Most of these various theories have a particular value in furthering the understanding of the Bologna Process and its impact. Although strictly speaking, none of the foregoing categorizations will be applied as an overarching theoretical framework, most conceptualizations will be referred to, sometimes explicitly and sometimes implicitly, in specific contexts when relevant for the core issues that are dealt with in this book. And, it should be noted, the concept that is most relevant for our purposes is the Europeanization of higher education.

What does the concept of Europeanization entail precisely? As is often the case with powerful catchwords, the term is as popular as it is ambiguous. In political and legal literature, one can find many different definitions and perhaps even more uses of the term.[23] For our purposes Europeanization shall be understood as *European-level action in a certain policy area that consequently affects the domestic systems in that area.* This definition requires some further explanation. First of all, it should be understood that both the European-level action in itself and its domestic consequences are important parts of Europeanization. Secondly, 'European level' is to be broadly interpreted, in that it does not necessarily imply involvement of the EU or (all) its Member States. Although many writers seem to see Europeanization as something intrinsically connected to the EU, and although the EU is undoubtedly a form of Europeanization as well as one of its sources, also the Council of Europe and other European Organizations can be regarded as (sources of) Europeanization. There are also intergovernmental projects, taking place on the European level, that do not involve European Organizations, but do involve Europeanization. The Bologna Process, aimed at creating a European Area of Higher Education, obviously constitutes such a project. Bilateral cooperation, by contrast, shall not be regarded as 'European-level action' for the purposes of this book. In third place it should be noted that the specific action taken at the European level can take many forms. It can *inter alia* concern an intergovernmental declaration, the creation of a European institution or the conclusion of a supranational Treaty. It can also take the form of a 'strategy' or a 'process', which indicates a series of actions or a policy plan to achieve a general aim. Fourthly, the action in question can be taken by a variety of actors, governmental or not.

20. Kälvemark & Van der Wende 1997.
21. Kwiek 2004; Meek 2002; Nokkala 2004.
22. Enders 2002; Mayntz 1998; Witte 2004.
23. In a landmark article, Olsen attempts to introduce some clarity in the field by summarizing and categorizing five ways in which Europeanization is used. According to Olsen, Europeanization is commonly used to denominate: (1) the territorial expansion of Europe's borders; (2) a process of European-level institutionalization; (3) the export of European institutions to the wider world; (4) the strengthening of the European integration project as a political ambition; (5) the domestic impact of European level institutions. See Olsen 2002.

Furthermore, it is important to realize that the effects that such action has on the domestic level can be manifold: social, political and legal. This book is mostly concerned with the legal consequences of Europeanization.

Although every topic will be primarily dealt with from a legal point of view, this is not to say that the political dimensions will be left entirely unaddressed, for they often interrelate in an important way with the legal questions. From two relatively short statements, the Bologna Process has grown into an enormous enterprise, involving a multitude of countries, stakeholders and generating an even greater amount of academic literature, especially in political science and higher education studies.[24] The ever-growing amount of excellent writing addresses the important questions what the Bologna Process entails,[25] where this powerful process suddenly came from[26] and how it has become so powerful,[27] and analyses the most important actors.[28] Also the relationship between the EU and the Process is extensively dealt with, but again solely from a political science perspective.[29] Where appropriate, this book intends to build on these findings, drawing the necessary information from it to embed the legal questions and analyses of the present book. For indeed, up until now, the legal implications of the Declarations and the Process, and their tense relationship with EU law, have been left almost entirely unexamined.[30] This work is intended to fill that void.

In order to grasp the entire scope of interaction between the EU's higher education policy and the Bologna Process, it is first necessary to delve into the exact scope of each. This means that the second chapter will be devoted to a discussion of the Bologna Process, its genesis, content and implementation. The latter dimension of the Process will be dealt with by means of a case study in three EU countries. The next step will be to map the EU's higher education policy landscape, which is surprisingly varied and at times complex. Two consecutive chapters will be devoted to this topic, dealing with general matters of competence, various modes of governance employed in this field and the case law of the ECJ. Although the accounts of the institutional features and legal content of both higher education policy forums should prove of value in themselves, their exhaustive discussion is not the primary aim of this work, for there already exists excellent literature on that dimension. The main focus will therefore lie on the most recent developments. These three chapters constitute the basis for the analyses in the following conclusive pair of chapters, dealing in turn with, first, the relationship between the European Organizations (*nota bene* including the Council of Europe) and the Bologna Process in terms of institutional interaction and material overlap and, second, with the most important legal questions in the context of this

---

24. See in general, Corbett 2006; Hoareau 2009; Ravinet 2008; Schriewer 2009; Witte 2006.
25. Terry 2008.
26. Racké 2007.
27. Ravinet 2008.
28. Charlier & Croché 2004.
29. Balzer & Rusconi 2007; Martens & Wolf 2009; Racké 2006.
30. The most notable exception can be found in the work of Verbruggen, who has written an excellent legal account of the Process. Verbruggen 2001.

relationship. A normative assessment shall constitute our end game, scrutinizing the Bologna Process on the basis of several important constitutional principles, such as democracy, transparency and accountability. In the conclusions, all the foregoing will be embedded in more general observations on the how's and why's of the Europeanization of higher education, the role of the EU, EU law and law in general in that context.

It should be pointed out that this book is limited to higher education. Higher education is commonly understood as education provided by universities, vocational universities and other collegial institutions that award academic degrees. Higher education is also often referred to, or described as, post-secondary or tertiary education. This refers to higher education being the third stage in the education process; the non-compulsory educational level following the completion of the secondary education level, such as high school, secondary school, or gymnasium. Higher education generally results in the conferral of certificates, diplomas or academic degrees. Although the concept of higher education remains, to a certain extent, imprecise, because 'nations do not define "higher" in the same way, just as they do not define "lower" education in the same way',[31] this does not pose any real problems for our purposes. The reason to confine ourselves to higher education, thereby excluding the areas of primary and secondary education, is firstly related to the fact that the Bologna Process is a project concerned with higher education only. The second justification is that the higher education sector constitutes a branch that is different from the other levels of education in many relevant ways. Most importantly, higher education is more closely connected to the labour market compared to primary and secondary education. Whereas the latter two can be described as primarily concerned with general/cultural formation, higher education (even general, non-job-specific education) by contrast is – to a certain extent – characterized by preparing students for their future profession. As the last steppingstone before entering the labour market, higher education has a different significance for society than lower education and is hence more likely to be the subject of European action. After all, as we shall come to see, European action is most readily undertaken in economically significant policy areas. This is not to say, however, that some matters of lower or secondary education will not be touched upon at all. When relevant, such as is – for instance – the case with the so-called European Schools dealt with in Chapter 4, lower and secondary education will be included in the discussion.

As a final preliminary note, it should be made clear that in accordance with the recent ratification of the Lisbon Treaty, reference shall be made to the new Article numbers, valid as of 1 December 2009, when describing the current state of the law. However, former numbers of Treaty articles will be used when specifically discussing the legal situation in the past. Similarly, reference to the EU will include areas that were previously designated as Community law, or the European Community. With reference to past events, however, the Community shall be named such, when appropriate.

31. Rothblatt & Wittrock 1993, 3.

Chapter 2
The Bologna Process

1. THE GENESIS OF THE BOLOGNA PROCESS

The Bologna Process, to be regarded as both the product and the continuation of a series of European conferences and a certain number of policy decisions,[1] had as its aim the creation of a so-called European Higher Education Area (EHEA) by the year 2010. Although the official launch of the Bologna Process took place in 1999, already in 1988 the very city of Bologna hosted an event that is generally considered to have constituted the catalyst for the recent momentum in the Europeanization of higher education. At the celebration of the 900 years of existence of one of the world's oldest universities, the so-called *Bologna Magna Carta Universitatum* was created. With this Magna Carta, the idea of restructuring the tertiary education systems in Europe was born. Ten years later, on the 25 May 1998, another prestigious University's anniversary took place. The Sorbonne University of Paris celebrated its 800th year of existence that day, and the ministers of higher education of France, Germany, the UK and Italy seized this opportunity to reach a non-binding agreement on the concrete future of their higher-education systems, adopting the so-called Sorbonne Declaration. This Declaration should be seen as the real starting point of what later became known as the Bologna Process, based on the follow-up Declaration that was signed one year later, back in Bologna this time. This chapter is concerned with the coming into being of the Sorbonne and Bologna Declarations, their content, political significance and legal status. It will also deal with the follow-up meetings that have taken place and that have significantly broadened the scope of the Bologna Process by adding objectives, follow-up mechanisms and participants. The process of adoption and the implementation of the aims set out in the Declarations into national law will be discussed by means of three case studies, focusing on France, Germany and the United Kingdom.

1. Eurydice Report 2003.

1.1. The Sorbonne Declaration

It was the French minister of education, Claude Allègre, who seized the opportunity of the Sorbonne's anniversary to organize a European colloquium with the idea to launch an important European initiative.[2] Allègre invited the Italian minister for public instruction, university and research Luigi Berlinguer, the UK junior minister for higher education Tessa Blackstone and Jürgen Rüttgers, the German minister for education, sciences, research and technology to the celebrations. They were to take part in the festivities as special guests and receive an honorary doctorate from the Sorbonne University. Perhaps the historical occasion facilitated reflections on the wandering scholars of medieval Europe, thereby inspiring the education ministers to contemplate on free movement of graduates in the post-modern age.[3] Others argue that the four ministers all had their own reasons, rooted rather in national concerns and aspirations than European ones, to embark on the project. In any event, Allègre's idea of a joint declaration on European higher education was readily accepted by the three other ministers. Duly acknowledging the longstanding autonomy of their universities, the ministers saw the time ripe to agree on some kind of convergence in higher education so as to promote mobility and competitiveness. The Declaration that was finally adopted bears a remarkably ambitious title: 'Joint Declaration on Harmonization of the Architecture of the European Higher Education System'. The other European countries showed reluctance towards joining the Sorbonne Declaration. After the UK, Germany, Italy and France had signed the Declaration, in which they called upon other states to join their initiative to create the European Area of Higher Education, the French had sent out individual invitations to other European countries.[4] However, most declined this invitation, allegedly because they felt dominated by the four big EU states.[5] Racké reports that especially the smaller countries strongly disapproved of the way the Sorbonne Declaration had come into being.[6] They felt excluded from the initiative, and were insulted that they had not been invited to sign the Declaration earlier, namely at the Sorbonne celebrations in Paris where some of them were in fact present. Apparently, the four initiators were mistaken in thinking that 'the rest of Europe' would easily accept and follow whatever they decided, or in Allègre's words: '*en matière d'éducation, si la France, l'Italie, l'Allemagne et la Grande-Bretagne sont pour, les autres suivront*'.[7] The countries that did decide to sign were Romania, Flanders and the German-speaking part of Belgium, Bulgaria, Switzerland, Denmark and the Czech Republic, making the official number of signatories eleven.

2. Racké 2007, 30.
3. Kirkwood-Tucker 2004, 54.
4. Racké 2007, 35.
5. Kirkwood-Tucker 2004, 54.
6. Racké 2007, 36.
7. Allègre 2000, 260.

Far from being empty rhetoric, the Declaration expresses desires, formulates aims and speaks of concrete measures to achieve those goals. The Sorbonne Declaration sets the stage by stressing the important role of universities in the development of a so-called Europe of Knowledge. Proudly stating that Europe is the birthplace of universities, it recalls the times of the past where students and academics would freely circulate and rapidly disseminate knowledge throughout Europe. The Declaration subsequently comes to mention its prime objective, being the increase of student mobility. Despite the various efforts made on the European level, substantial obstacles to student mobility remained. The problems, *for example* the only partial recognition of periods of study abroad, the continuing decrease of the ERASMUS grant and uneven student mobility,[8] became more and more clear due to the increasing demand for mobility from both students and employers.[9] In this context, the four Sorbonne signatories deemed renewed and further-reaching action necessary to enhance mobility. The Declaration mentions several objectives to be pursued by means of this increased mobility. Firstly, it is aimed at promoting employability, in essence an economic aim. This is phrased in terms of individual opportunity: 'we owe our students, and our society at large, a higher education system in which they are given the best opportunities to seek and find their own area of excellence'. Secondly, the Declaration refers to the 'international recognition and attractive potential' of European education systems, which it aims to improve. As Racké points out, the increasing internationalization of higher education and the desire to develop a knowledge-based economy made the international attractiveness of Europe's education systems a new priority.[10] The Sorbonne Declaration expresses the desire to boost Europe's external attractiveness by enhancing intra-European mobility, particularly through the improvement of internal readability. A third aim to be achieved through mobility is the strengthening of European integration. The Declaration speaks of 'ever closer cooperation' and the creation of the EHEA 'where national identities and common interests can interact and strengthen each other for the benefit of Europe'. According to the Declaration, to this end, barriers to mobility should be removed and an open European-wide framework for teaching and learning should be developed, whilst maintaining diversity. The achievement of the aims set out above is seen to be dependent on the external and internal readability of the systems. In a truly revolutionary way, in order to improve this readability, the Declaration proposes a structural harmonization, by introducing a system 'in which two main cycles, undergraduate and graduate, should be recognized for international comparison and equivalence'. The ECTS, the well-known system of credit transfer as developed in the EU context, is proposed as a flexibility tool, allowing for validation of

8. Uneven student mobility refers to the problem that some countries attract substantially more students than others. This is a concern to the countries that are overflooded by students, as they subsidize the studies of foreign students, as well as to the 'export' countries, that fear a brain drain and a lack of competitiveness. See Hackl 2001, 16.
9. Racké 2007, 31.
10. *Ibid.*

credits acquired abroad. The Declaration stresses that the international recognition of the first cycle, undergraduate degree as an appropriate level of qualification 'is important for the success of this endeavour, in which we wish to make our higher education schemes clear to all'. In the second *that is* graduate cycle there should be a choice between a shorter master's degree and a longer doctor's degree. The signatories envisaged this to be achieved through strengthening of already existing experience, joint diplomas, pilot initiatives and dialogue with all concerned.

The fact that the Sorbonne Declaration is a non-binding soft law instrument does not make it of less political importance. This significance lies in the first place in the fact that the Declaration constitutes the basis of the entire Bologna Process. The Sorbonne Declaration already contains almost all of the core elements of the Bologna Process as it mentions a two-cycle system, with an undergraduate cycle and a postgraduate cycle, the latter being divided into a shorter master's degree and a longer doctor's degree. This has led to the sweeping change of almost all higher-education systems in Europe, requiring major legislative reforms. Secondly, the Sorbonne Declaration is of importance as it marks a change of mentality. It has far-reaching ambitions and uses words that are normally highly charged, such as harmonization, with remarkable ease.[11] The use of this term in the Sorbonne Declaration has indeed been called the breaking of a taboo, and caused considerable controversy at the time.[12] The Sorbonne Declaration aims to establish the EHEA. This is a powerful image, conveying the same idea of disappearing borders as the European Economic Area and the Freedom, Security and Justice Area, even though the label as such has no actual content. The Declaration proclaims that Europe should become a Europe of Knowledge, and seeks to emphasize and develop Europe's intellectual, cultural and social dimensions. It does so to align with 'the Europe of the Euro, the banks and the economy'. This is to say the least a fundamental move away from the conservative attitude towards Europe's role in higher education. Clearly, however, it is not the EU that this role is attributed to. According to the Declaration, 'the progressive harmonization of the overall framework of degrees and cycles' is a role for the governments to play. The signatories plan to achieve such convergence 'through strengthening of already existing experience, joint diplomas, pilot initiatives, and dialogue with all concerned'. Whilst recognizing the EU legislative framework of mutual recognition of professional qualifications and encouraging 'the fast growing support of the EU for the mobility of students and teachers' which 'should be employed to the full', this Declaration sees Europe as something quite broader than only the EU. The four signatory states do invite 'other Member States of the Union' to participate in their idea, which might show that they feel, in a way, that they are acting in their capacity of a 'Member State of the Union'. But at the same time, they also invite other European countries to take part. By referring to the time where students and academics would circulate feely through Europe a quarter of a millennium ago,

11. The word harmonization is used in the title, as well as in the penultimate paragraph.
12. Racké 2007, 38.

the relatively recent enterprise of the EU is put into perspective. Furthermore, they offer a relatively bold statement in proclaiming that regardless of the achievements of the Council of Europe and the EU, 'our governments, nevertheless, continue to have a significant role to play to these ends'. It sounds somewhat like thanking the European Organizations for their efforts, adding the statements that the governments will take it from here. This remarkable combination of euro-ambition and euro-conservatism is representative of the entire Bologna Process.

1.2. THE BOLOGNA DECLARATION

Although the Sorbonne Declaration was only signed by a relatively small number of countries, it still sowed the seeds for major change. The countries that had refused to sign the Declaration had done this because they felt insulted, not because they disapproved of the content of the Declaration. On the contrary, the ideas fell on fertile ground, as most of the countries struggled with the same difficulties, these being described as the following:

> confronted with new demands involving contradictory expectations for equity and access on the one hand, and excellence on the other, and this, in a context of diversification of funding and decrease of public funding, globalization and knowledge society, quality assurance and accountability, entrepreneurial approaches, information-communication technologies and virtual universities, new providers and marketable knowledge, and finally competition for income from foreign students.[13]

In October 1998, under the Austrian presidency of the EU, an informal meeting of all the EU ministers of education took place, discussing the Sorbonne Declaration. It became clear that indeed many countries were eager to participate in the effort to Europeanize higher education, seeing potential benefits for their national systems as well as feeling fear of being left behind.[14] Since most of the states were not keen on joining the Sorbonne Declaration for the political reasons explained above, a new initiative was necessary. In order to facilitate this fresh start, a comparative study to map the existing structures of higher education in Europe was ordered.[15] A few days later, at a meeting of the Directors-General of Higher Education and the Chairman of Rector's Conference of the EU Member States, the Sorbonne Follow-Up Working Group was created. Apart from representatives from several countries, also the European Commission, the Confederation of European Union Rector's Conferences and the Association of European Universities took place in this working group. The group was responsible for the preparations of the Bologna conference that had already been planned.[16] On 19 June 1999, one year

13. Papatsiba 2006, 95.
14. Kirkwood-Tucker 2004, 54.
15. Hackl 2001, 22.
16. For interesting background comments on the four sessions of this working group, see Hackl 2001, 23–24.

after the Sorbonne Declaration, Ministers responsible for higher education from twenty-nine European countries signed the Bologna Declaration. They agreed on important joint objectives for the development of a coherent and cohesive EHEA by 2010.

The Bologna Declaration does not offer many surprising elements in terms of content. It builds on the Sorbonne Declaration and has the same aims: namely to enhance the employability of citizens through mobility and to increase the international competitiveness of European higher education ('we need to ensure that the European higher education system acquires a world-wide degree of attraction equal to our extraordinary cultural and scientific traditions'). Like the Sorbonne Declaration, it aims to achieve this ambition by the adoption of a common framework of readable and comparable degrees, the introduction of undergraduate and postgraduate levels in all countries and the ECTS-compatible credit systems. The Bologna Declaration adds a so-called 'European dimension in quality assurance', with comparable criteria and methods, and the elimination of remaining obstacles to the free mobility of students and teachers.[17] Although the Bologna Declaration now carefully avoids the use of the word 'harmonization', it does entail the structural harmonization of the higher-education systems of all of its participants. This structural harmonization entails the construction of a system of undergraduate studies followed by graduate studies, and comparable degrees. Access to the second cycle shall require successful completion of first cycle studies, lasting a minimum of three years, and the degree awarded after the first cycle shall also be relevant to the European labour market as an appropriate level of qualification. The second cycle should lead to the master and/or doctorate degree as in many European countries. The content of each course, however, remains to be determined by the different countries and their universities. The Bologna Declaration aims for structural comparability but content diversity.[18] It aims to fully respect 'the diversity of cultures, languages, national education systems and of University autonomy'. It states that to that end 'the ways of intergovernmental cooperation' will be pursued, 'together with those of non governmental European organizations with competence on higher education'. Remarkably, this excludes cooperation with governmental European Organizations such as the EU and the Council of Europe.

Twenty-nine ministers responsible for higher education in their respective European countries signed the Bologna Declaration immediately. In subsequent years, another seventeen have added their signatures. Currently an overwhelming number of forty-seven European countries take part: Albania, Andorra, Armenia, Austria, Azerbaijan, Belgium (Flemish Community and French Community), Bosnia and Herzegovina, Bulgaria, Croatia, Cyprus, the Czech Republic, Denmark, Estonia, Finland, France, Georgia, Germany, Greece, the Holy See, Hungary, Iceland, Ireland, Italy, Kazakhstan, Latvia, Liechtenstein, Lithuania, Luxembourg, Malta, Moldova, Montenegro, the Netherlands, Norway, Poland, Portugal,

17. Conference of European Rectors 1999, 4.
18. Vogel 2007, 132.

Romania, the Russian Federation, Serbia, the Slovak Republic, Slovenia, Spain, Sweden, Switzerland, the former Yugoslav Republic of Macedonia, Turkey, Ukraine and the United Kingdom. This extensive list of participating states is telling in several ways. In the first place it shows how far-reaching the project is. The Bologna Process has become a true pan-European project. It is also illustrative of the non-EU nature of the project as it extends well beyond EU territory. Most importantly, the number of participating countries shows that the support for European action in higher education was great, something which can be called surprising. In contrast with the traditional resistance to allow for or follow EU initiatives, the Bologna Declaration can count on the participation of all the Member States of the EU. That the Member States so readily agreed to the extensive reforms required by the Declaration in the very field where they had been consistently conservative in order to maintain system diversity and state sovereignty, is remarkable to say the least.

What is the precise significance of the Bologna Declaration when compared to its predecessor, the Sorbonne Declaration? The Bologna Declaration is not entirely new in terms of content, as it largely copies the main ideas of the Sorbonne Declaration. It does however constitute the clean slate which allowed the states to start again, after the Sorbonne Declaration had become tainted with controversy regarding its coming into being. That is exactly where its importance lies. It can be argued that without this new start, there would not have been a comparable pan-European higher education project, as it was clear that most states were not intending to join the Sorbonne Declaration. Forty-six states signed the Bologna Declaration, in contrast with a mere number of eleven signatories to Sorbonne. True, there was no need for the other states to sign the Sorbonne Declaration after the idea of Bologna was launched. It cannot be ruled out that in the absence of a new initiative, states would have changed their attitudes towards the Sorbonne Declaration and would have eventually participated even at the cost of their pride. The states did however make the effort to organize a new event so as to negotiate a new declaration, because it allowed them to renegotiate the content of the agreement and to be, or at least feel, involved on an equal footing.

This renegotiation might explain the watering down of the rigorous language as employed in the Sorbonne Declaration. The Bologna Declaration avoids the use of the word 'harmonization', unlike the Sorbonne Declaration where the word even appears in the very title. Indeed, this omission was deliberate. The use of the word constituted a contentious issue that had to be resolved before the Declaration could be signed.[19] There had already been discussion about the use of the term in the run-up to the conference. In a European law context, harmonization is generally taken to mean the approximation of national legislation in order to create one European standard, by means of legislation. Most of the participating countries deemed such standardization to be undesirable in the field of higher education. How does that relate to the fact that the Declaration does imply a certain extent of standardization? It seems that it is not the 'European standard' itself that states are

19. Kirkwood-Tucker 2004, 38.

afraid of. Rather, the states seem to oppose the supranational connotation of the concept, in that it is associated with undesired top-down imposition of European standards, limiting the liberty of states to organize their systems as they see fit. Although the French minister Claude Allègre tried to convince his colleagues that harmonization as used in the text of the Declaration was not to mean standardization in its unwanted sense, the majority of participants preferred to stay on the safe side and leave out the term. In that sense, Bologna appears much less radical than Sorbonne. Still, it is unlikely that the signatories to the Sorbonne Declaration actually ever intended harmonization to mean some kind of top-down standardization. The change of terminology is, therefore, not so much a change of content.

1.3. The Follow-Up Conferences

The Bologna Process is what can be called the product, or the follow-up, of the Sorbonne and Bologna Declarations. As said before, these two statements have turned into substantial enterprise, almost an institution in its own right, involving a multitude of countries, political actors and other stakeholders. The Process consists of a series of conferences held by the ministers of higher education of the signatory states, as well as the more numerous meetings of the working groups in between the ministerial meetings. It is in these working groups where all the preparation takes place, so where the content of the Bologna Process takes concrete shape. At the ministerial conferences, the progress of implementation is reviewed and additional objectives are formulated. At the end of each conference, ministers issue a collective Communiqué. Six follow-up conferences have taken place up until now, to wit in Prague, Berlin, Bergen, London, Louvain and Vienna/Budapest. The Bologna Process continues to grow, in terms of territorial as well as material scope. However, although the ministerial conferences have had a substantial impact, most notably by adding a third doctoral cycle, the core of the Process can still be identified as the introduction of a common system of degrees. Furthermore, most of the secondary objectives were already present from the start. The real value of the ministerial conferences therefore seems to lie in the high profile follow-up that they provide. National ministers discussing and comparing the progress made on the core and secondary objectives, the ministerial conferences help to make the non-binding declarations into a reality.

Two years after the Bologna Declaration, the first official ministerial meeting took place as planned in Prague. The Communiqué states that the choice of Prague to hold this meeting was a symbol of the will 'to involve the whole of Europe in the process in the light of enlargement of the European Union'. Three new members were welcomed. The admission of Croatia, Cyprus and Turkey made the total number of signatories into thirty-two. The ministers adopted the Prague Communiqué, in which they foremost reaffirmed their commitment to the objective of establishing the EHEA by 2010. The meeting addressed key issues like the development of a common framework of qualifications accompanied by coherent quality assurance and accreditation/certification mechanisms, the importance of lifelong learning, the importance of high-quality standards and the cooperation of higher education institutions, national authorities and the European Network of Quality Assurance in Higher Education.[20] Moreover, the Prague Communiqué for the first time set up a more formal structure for the follow-up work. A follow-up group and a preparatory group were created. The follow-up group was composed of representatives of all signatories, new participants and the European Commission, and chaired by the EU Presidency. The preparatory group was composed of representatives of the countries hosting the previous ministerial meetings and the next ministerial meeting, two EU Member States and two non-EU Member States; these latter four representatives being elected by the follow-up group. The EU Presidency at the time and the European Commission were to be part of the preparatory group. The preparatory group was to be chaired by the representative of the country hosting the next ministerial meeting. In addition, the European University Association (EUA), the European Association of Institutions in Higher Education (EURASHE), the National Unions of Students in Europe and the Council of Europe were to be consulted in the follow-up.

On 19 September 2003, the ministers of education from thirty-three European countries met in Berlin. The Communiqué that was adopted reaffirms the Bologna Declaration and the Prague Communiqué, and elaborates on the use of the ECTS in the framework of Bologna. The most important feature of the Berlin Communiqué is the explicit introduction of the third, doctorate cycle in the Bologna Process. The Communiqué states that:

> conscious of the need to promote closer links between the EHEA and the ERA in a Europe of Knowledge, and of the importance of research as an integral part of higher education across Europe, Ministers consider it necessary to go beyond the present focus on two main cycles of higher education to include the doctoral level as the third cycle in the Bologna Process. They emphasise the importance of research and research training and the promotion of interdisciplinarity in maintaining and improving the quality of higher education and in enhancing the competitiveness of European higher education more generally. Ministers call for increased mobility at the doctoral and postdoctoral levels and encourage the institutions concerned to increase their cooperation in doctoral studies and the training of young researchers.

Furthermore, in the Berlin Communiqué it was stated that: 'Ministers underline the importance of the Lisbon Recognition Convention, which should be ratified by all countries participating in the Bologna Process.' Regarding the follow-up procedure, the Berlin Communiqué introduced a Board and a Secretariat in addition to the existing structures. This Board, chaired by the EU Presidency, was given the responsibility to oversee the work between the meetings of the follow-up group. It was decided that it was to be composed of the chair, the next host country as vice-chair, the preceding and the following EU Presidencies, three participating countries elected by the follow-up group for one year, the European Commission

20. Kirkwood-Tucker 2004, 56.

and, as consultative members, the Council of Europe, the EUA, EURASHE and ESIB. The Secretariat supports the overall follow-up work and falls under the responsibility of the country hosting the next Ministerial Conference. In Berlin, the ministers also considered it necessary to adapt the clause in the Prague Communiqué on applications for membership:

> countries party to the European Cultural Convention shall be eligible for membership of the European Higher Education Area provided that they at the same time declare their willingness to pursue and implement the objectives of the Bologna Process in their own systems of higher education. Their applications should contain information on how they will implement the principles and objectives of the declaration.

It was decided to accept the requests for membership of Albania, Andorra, Bosnia and Herzegovina, Holy See, Russia, Serbia and Montenegro, and Macedonia. Thereby, the Process was expanded to include forty countries.

Since the Berlin conference, the pace of change increased considerably, both in terms of national reforms as well as in terms of administrative coordination.[21] The meeting in Bergen in 2005 constituted a mid-term review. At this conference, Armenia, Azerbaijan, Georgia, Moldova and Ukraine were welcomed. The ministers adopted a Communiqué taking note of progress made so far and confirming the three priorities defined at the Berlin meeting in September 2003: the degree system, quality assurance and recognition of qualifications and periods of studies. As further challenges and priorities, they identified higher education and research, the social dimension, mobility and the attractiveness of the EHEA and cooperation with other parts of the world. A new stocktaking exercise was announced to take place before the next Ministerial meeting in London in May 2007. Ministers in Bergen adopted the overarching framework for qualifications in the EHEA, comprising three cycles, generic descriptors for each cycle based on learning outcomes and competences, and credit ranges in the first and second cycles. They committed themselves to elaborate national frameworks for qualifications compatible with the overarching framework for qualifications in the EHEA by 2010, and to having started work on this by 2007. The Bergen Communiqué also provided another push to ratify the Lisbon Recognition Convention.

From 1 July 2005, the UK took over responsibility for the Secretariat, to the Bologna Follow Up Group (BFUG) and its Board. On 17 and 18 May 2007, the ministers met in London. At this conference, the 46th signatory was welcomed as Montenegro signed up as a state in its own right. The Communiqué that was adopted reviews the progress and formulates priorities for the coming years. The London Communiqué does not introduce any significant changes. One interesting point to note here is that the ministers call upon the Commission (Eurostat) 'to develop comparable and reliable indicators and data to measure progress towards the overall objective for the social dimension and student and staff mobility in all Bologna countries'. The ministers specified that 'a report should be submitted to our 2009

21. Furlong 2005, 55.

Ministerial conference'. Another two years later, the last pre-deadline Conference took place on 29 April 2009 at the Universities of Leuven and Louvain-la-Neuve (Belgium). Apart from the countries and organizations participating in the Bologna Process, a large number of non-European countries were represented: Australia, Brazil, Canada, China, Egypt, Ethiopia, Israel, Japan, Kazakhstan, Kyrgyzstan, Mexico, Morocco, New Zealand, Tunisia and the US, as well as the International Association of Universities. This illustrates the increased international attention that the Bologna Process is generating. The issues addressed included, among others, recognition of qualification, exchange of teachers, researchers, and students, and quality assurance. Although the Conference did not bring anything new in terms of content, it was the first time that the public at large seemed to take real notice. Student protests were scheduled, following massive demonstrations against the Bologna Process and higher education reforms in general in the preceding months, most notably in Spain and Greece.

At the most recent ministerial meeting to date, in Budapest and Vienna in March 2010, the EHEA was officially launched. At this anniversary conference, the EHEA was also expanded to forty-seven countries; the most recently admitted being Kazakhstan. Although it is difficult to establish whether and to what extent such a Higher Education Area has really come into existence, it is more than a symbolic image. The most tangible feature of the EHEA is, of course, the Bachelor-Master-Doctorate system now in place almost all over Europe. But indeed, as even the new EHEA website admits, this official launch 'in itself did not mean an achievement of all the objectives agreed upon by the ministers involved in the Bologna Process'.[22] Therefore, although 2010 was initially intended to be the deadline for the achievement of the Bologna objectives, and hence the Bologna Process, it has become clear that the Process won't really come to a halt now. The next ministerial conferences have already been planned, the first of which is to take place in Bucharest on 27–28 April 2012.[23] The Bologna Process has now entered a new phase, one of consolidation and operationalization, which was deemed necessary 'especially in light of the very different reactions to the Bologna Process implementation across Europe'.[24]

In a way, it was to be expected that the Bologna Process would not simply be discontinued after 2010. For one, as such things tend to turn out, the Bologna apparatus that has been created, with a Board and a Secretary and Follow-Up Groups and spin-off projects and experts and stakeholders, is not easy to shut down. Furthermore, like the Lisbon Strategy, which also designated 2010 as its deadline and in the context of which nevertheless new objectives have been formulated for the next decade, the general aim of the Bologna Process is so grand and ambitious that it merits a continuous effort, stretching beyond the original ten-year timeframe. Even if the Bologna Process is deemed to have been successful in creating an EHEA, one can imagine an endless amount of work that could still

22. <www.ehea.info/article-details.aspx?ArticleId=3>.
23. There is also talk of conferences in 2015, 2018 and 2020.
24. <www.ehea.info/article-details.aspx?ArticleId=3>.

be done in this context, if not to establish the EHEA, then to ameliorate its functioning. In other words, in light of such an expansive project, there is always a good reason to keep going. There are still plenty of Bologna action lines that can and perhaps should be further crystallized. In addition, it seems that an attractive new platform for European cooperation in higher education matters has been created, and it could very well be that Member States will continue to use this platform for matters not even specifically related to the original Bologna Process. Although the fact that the Bologna Process continues after 2010 does not stand in the way of it being subsumed in the frameworks of either the Council of Europe or the EU in the future, it does maintain for now the fragmented picture in European Higher Education that it has caused. An end of the Bologna Process would most likely have implied tasks and outstanding action lines to be transferred (back) to the European Organizations; a course of proceedings that has both strong opponents and proponents.

2. DISTINGUISHING CORE AIMS AND SECONDARY OBJECTIVES

Looking at the Bologna Process in its current shape, one is struck by the sheer magnitude of the enterprise. This is manifested in the number of participating countries, the ever-growing follow-up and its academic spin-off, the regular Bologna-themed meetings, conferences, colloquia and research projects left, right and centre, and perhaps most of all, in the expansive subject matter of the Process. The Bologna Process integrates several important aims and measures developed in the context of the European Organizations active in the field, to wit the Council of Europe and the EU, as it apparently intends to offer a comprehensive action plan for educational mobility through academic recognition in Europe. Its material scope thus includes *inter alia* student and teacher mobility, credit transfer, quality assurance and diploma recognition. On the one hand, dealing with a subject area such as student/teacher mobility in an inclusive and wide-ranging manner offers advantages. Since many of these areas are indeed closely related or even intertwined, they arguably merit a common approach. On the other hand, it seems that Bologna is unnecessarily doubling or taking over already well-established projects and measures, which are arguably better placed in the institutional frameworks they were developed in. This does not only harm the intelligibility of the European higher education scene, where it becomes increasingly difficult to locate the relevant projects and responsibilities as they become dispersed among various actors and institutional frameworks, it also harms the transparency of the Bologna Process itself. The Bologna scene is, at times, incomprehensible due to its comprehensiveness.

2.1. The Core Objective and Its Implementation

The Sorbonne and Bologna Declarations essentially introduced one core aim: the harmonization of Europe's higher-education system into a two-tier Bachelor-Master model, or in the words of the Sorbonne signatories: 'a system, in which two main cycles, undergraduate and graduate, should be recognized for international comparison and equivalence'. Accordingly, the Bologna Declaration prescribes the adoption:

> of a system essentially based on two main cycles, undergraduate and graduate. Access to the second cycle shall require successful completion of first cycle studies, lasting a minimum of three years. The degree awarded after the first cycle shall also be relevant to the European labour market as an appropriate level of qualification. The second cycle should lead to the master and/or doctorate degree as in many European countries.

This core aim was, and still is, the spearhead of the project, and it is its most straightforward as well as most far-reaching feature, and because of its visibility it is the best known. In Berlin, the two-cycle system was amended into a three-cycle one, including a third doctoral level. For the rest, this objective has remained unchanged. Although the aim is in essence straightforward, it has been rather ill defined. Initially, it was left almost entirely up to the participating states to figure out how and to what extent they would shape the new system. In terms of the length of the different cycles, one only finds the recommendation of a minimum of three years for the bachelor level, without a corresponding proposal for the master's degree. This lack of clear standards has been both applauded and criticized. On the one hand, it has allowed the participating countries to create the model that they felt was most appropriate for their higher-education system, and it is thereby respectful of European diversity. On the other hand, the result has been a heterogeneous implementation and therefore a lack of a true common structure.

Indeed, although the core aim of a two-tier structure at first face value benefits from a spectacular compliance record, with most participating countries having made legal accommodations for the Bachelor-Master system only within a few years after the Declarations, the lack of guidance and the absence of concrete descriptions of the characteristics of the Bachelor-Master system have led to different interpretations of the model in the various participating states. The fact that a considerable number of countries already had their own version of a two-tier structure in place before the Bologna Declaration makes the picture even more complex.[25] It turns out that two-tier systems come in many different colours. Furthermore, some countries are implementing the new system in parallel with the old one, like in Germany. The 2001 TRENDS Report observed a strong move

25. The 2003 Trends Report states: 'Around 40% of the ministries reported that there was a two-cycle structure in their national higher education systems even before the Bologna Declaration. This group spreads all across Europe and includes, apart from the UK, Ireland and Malta, for instance Bulgaria, the Czech Republic, Denmark, Latvia, Poland, Turkey and Greece.' 'Other ministries also indicated that their countries had two cycles before the beginning of the Bologna Process, but that they are now working to adjust them to the emerging consensus on degree structures in the EHEA, as expressed, for example, in the Helsinki seminars on Bachelors (in 2001) and Masters (in 2003). This is true for Belgium, Croatia, Finland, France, Norway, Portugal and Serbia.' See Reichert & Tauch 2003.

towards a two-tier system among the participating countries 'but not necessarily corresponding to the definitions used for the degree structure outlined in the Bologna Declaration'.[26] By 2003, 80% of the Bologna countries either had the legal possibility to offer two-tier structures or was introducing these, but various interpretations of the first and second cycle were found to exist. The Trends 2003 report identified an 'emerging standard' of 180 ECTS credits for first cycles, but 210 and 240 were also found. Several countries offered undergraduate programmes that were 'too long in comparison to the emerging norm': either because they carried more than 240 credits or because they were combined with long postgraduate degrees.[27] As to the Master level, a significant variety in duration and architecture was identified. At a Conference held in Helsinki on Master degrees in the context of the Bologna Follow-Up, it was proposed that Master degree programmes should normally carry 90 to 120 ECTS credits, with the minimum requirement of 60 ECTS. The opinion was that 'as the length and the content of Bachelor degrees vary' there was a need 'to have similar flexibility at the Master level'.[28] This illustrates that there is a tendency in the Bologna Follow-Up to formulate some outer limits, in order to compensate for the lack of precision in the Declarations, but that an enormous amount of diversity is still accepted. Even staying within these boundaries, one can follow Bachelor – Master tracks ranging from a minimum of $180 + 60 = 240$ ECTS (four years) to a maximum of $240 + 120 = 360$ ECTS (six years). The 2007 Trends Report states that:

> while diversity in thinking and culture is a great strength of European higher education, diversity in understanding and implementation of structures is likely to prove an obstacle to an effective European Higher Education Area. It seems as difficult in 2007 as in 1999 to find evidence that the 'European dimension' of higher education is becoming a tangible aspect of institutional reality. While the process may seem to be providing the same structural conditions for all, closer inspection reveals that some 'little differences' may confuse the picture.[29]

Could the diverse effectuation of the Bachelor-Master system jeopardize achieving the general Bologna goal, which is to have a common system so as to remove barriers to mobility? This begs the question whether the core Bologna aim is actually to have a tiered system, to have a common system or to have a common tiered system, as it turns out that these are not the same things. The text of the Declarations and the Communiqué's do not clarify this matter, so the answer must be sought in setting these options off against the ultimate goal of improving student and teacher mobility in an EHEA. A tiered system as opposed to a single-end-degree model, allows for more mobility. A student might obtain a bachelor degree in one

26. Haug & Tauch 2001, 1.
27. Reichert & Tauch 2003, 48.
28. *Conclusions and Recommendations of the Conference on Master-level degrees*, Helsinki 14–15 Mar. 2003, 5.
29. Crosier, Purser & Schmidt 2007, 21.

university, move to another to pursue master-level studies and subsequently will yet again have the possibility to relocate for the purpose of a doctoral degree. However, the success of this model depends on a factor closely related to the reason for having a common system: transferability through diploma recognition. If a bachelor degree is not recognized in another university for the purposes of accessing a master-level course, for example, because it is a three-year bachelor as opposed to the four-year one administered by that university, there is no value in having a tiered structure from the viewpoint of fostering mobility. The merit of having a common, harmonized system lies precisely in the fact that it will facilitate such recognition; for only the existence of differences justifies non-recognition. It therefore seems that in order to achieve the maximum level of mobility, a common and tiered model, that is with standardized cycle-lengths and possibilities for mobility in between cycles, is to be preferred. From this perspective, it is worrisome that the participants have focused more on the tiered aspect of the Bologna system, than on its common character.

The problem of divergent lengths of cycles can in theory be overcome by moving from an input-based approach to learning to an output-based one. The latter has been applied mostly in the UK, while most continental European countries have traditionally favoured the former. The ECTS tended to reflect the input-approach, by awarding credits on the basis of hours studied. Recent years have, however, seen a shift towards defining skills and competences, partially because of effective lobbying by the UK. The advantage of this approach is that it is more thorough and more substantive. It attempts to evaluate exactly that what one really wants to know for the purpose of recognition, namely what is the level/quality of a particular course, instead of using the artificial proxy of study hours. A disadvantage of this approach is that it is far more laborious, as it requires a detailed evaluation and comparison rather than a simple hour count. Consequently, it potentially affects the content of the educational courses, which is a controversial matter. If taken to its extreme, the outcome-based approach to recognition necessitates the establishment of minimum standards, that is the harmonization of the content of educational courses, something Europe has only seen in the context of the professional recognition of diplomas, relating to the regulated professions. Due to the difficulties in reaching agreements on these minimum standards, this approach was eventually abandoned and replaced by a mutual recognition strategy.[30] The spirit of the Bologna Process does not allow for such content harmonization, but due to its divergent implementation in terms of cycle-lengths, it does need to be accompanied by a certain output-evaluation mechanism.

The compromise has been to develop qualification frameworks, which determine a level of knowledge, competence and skill to be achieved in order to qualify for a certain qualification level. The most important example is the European Qualifications Framework (EQF), which has been developed in an EU context

30. Schneider & Claessens 2005. The already-harmonized curricula were left in place, and were integrated in the overall framework that applies mutual recognition as the fallback mechanism for the other curricula. See Ch. 3.

by the European Commission, but which integrates the Bologna cycles.[31] For instance, the sixth EQF level is equivalent to the Bologna Bachelor cycle, and specifies that the student possesses 'advanced knowledge of a field of work or study, involving a critical understanding of theories and principles', 'advanced skills, demonstrating mastery and innovation, required to solve complex and unpredictable problems in a specialized field of work or study' and can 'manage complex technical or professional activities or projects, taking responsibility for decision-making in unpredictable work or study contexts; take responsibility for managing professional development of individuals and groups'. Of course, countries and their higher education institutions might have very different interpretations of which 'theories and principles' should be 'critically understood' in order to have EQF level 6 knowledge of a certain field. This might not necessarily be a bad thing. To a certain extent, it seems to be an asset of diversity and creates a playing field for a healthy degree of competition between systems and institutions.

But important questions remain, such as how to accommodate the higher vocational institutions that have been included in the Bachelor-Master structure of some countries. The Prague Communiqué explicitly leaves open this possibility, by stating:

> It is important to note that in many countries bachelor's and master's degrees, or comparable two cycle degrees, can be obtained at universities as well as at other higher education institutions. Programmes leading to a degree may, and indeed should, have different orientations and various profiles in order to accommodate a diversity of individual, academic and labour market needs as concluded at the Helsinki seminar on bachelor level degrees (February 2001).

To a certain extent, the EQF description of the Bachelor level appears to allow for the often more practical approach of the vocational schools, when it offers the alternative 'field of *work* or study'.[32] This might, however, just as well be used as an argument to say that such descriptions are inherently vague and open for interpretation, and that they accordingly fail to set a reliable quality standard. Although in some countries, the vocational schools may not be regarded as a lower level of education compared to universities; in other counties they certainly are. Given the fact that in many countries several fields of study, such as communication, economics, law, management and psychology, can be studied both at the vocational level and the university level, the inclusion of vocational institutions in the system might lead to confusion and a potential dilution of the quality of studies. It could lead to a student having obtained a vocational-level Bachelor's in economics in one country, to apply for a university Master's course in economics in another country, without the latter institution being able to know (without thorough research) whether the student has obtained his or her Bachelor at a university or not. It weakens the signalling value of the degrees, and thereby threatens to undermine

31. The EQF will be further dealt with in Chs 3 and 6.
32. Emphasis added.

the common system. There have been discussions in some countries to create a parallel vocational Bachelor-Master track, trading the former confusion for a new kind. Remarkably, there is no real Bologna-level guidance on this important issue.

An important thing to keep in mind when assessing whether the Bologna recommendations for a common tiered structure contribute to mobility, and to what extent, is that there is no guarantee for recognition laid down in the Declarations. Nor has such an automatic recognition mechanism been developed in the context of the ensuing Process. This is to a certain extent related to the fact that the Declarations lack legal effect and cannot be relied on by individuals, but also in their non-binding capacity the Declarations could have encouraged the Member States to provide for (automatic) recognition of the new degrees. It could, for example, have been recommended to the participants to deem equivalent all bachelors in a certain field of study and hence to grant access to master courses in the same field. To make up for this deficiency, the Bologna Process has relied on yet another measure of one of the European Organizations, this time the Council of Europe. The Bologna members have sought to incorporate the Lisbon Recognition Convention into the Bologna Process. The Convention was created before the Bologna Process and operates separately, but as we shall come to see in Chapter 5, the Bologna Process has integrated the ratification of the Convention as one of its aims and has thereby raised its profile among the Bologna countries. The Convention provides in Article VI.1 that a Party is held to 'recognise the higher education qualifications conferred in another Party, unless a substantial difference can be shown between the qualification for which recognition is sought and the corresponding qualification in the Party in which recognition is sought'. The states are bound to subject foreign diplomas to a fair and transparent procedure. They do, however, remain free to reject recognition in case they find a substantial difference, which might not be too difficult a thing to do.[33]

Generally speaking, the qualifications frameworks might prove useful to counterbalance the negative effect of having divergent lengths of cycles and different inclusion criteria for higher education institutions among the participating countries, and the Lisbon Convention helps to give some bite to the objective of diploma recognition, which the Process lacks. In this sense, the fear of *double emploi* arguably proves less justified than one might have expected. The Declarations state that they intend to build upon the projects developed by the European Organizations, and in this sense, they indeed do. Nonetheless, it is curious that the Sorbonne and Bologna Declarations themselves do not provide a more specific outline of the structure they propose. Accepting for the sake of argumentation that this defect is not caused by indifference or a lack of commitment to truly achieve mobility on behalf of the member countries, this appears to be due to a constant tension between the aim to establish a common system and the aim to maintain diversity and to accommodate different approaches to the sensitive

33. Do note that the EU Member States are bound to examine qualifications on an individual basis, following the Morgenbesser case law. See Case C-313/01, *Christine Morgenbesser v. Consiglio dell'Ordine degli avvocati di Genova* [2003] ECR I-13467.

policy area that is higher education. One is left to wonder whether a messy compromise between these aims is an appropriate basis for a far-reaching overhaul of the European higher education sectors.[34] At times, the impression emerges that the feasibility of the core Bologna aim of a common tiered Bachelor-Master structure all over Europe was not sufficiently researched and contemplated before it was launched. The point is that it is very well possible that Europe is too diverse for such a common system, but in that case this core aim should perhaps have been abandoned altogether and the focus should have remained on the facilitating measures taken by the European Organizations. And if, on the contrary, a common system would have appeared feasible, its uniform implementation would have had to be guaranteed in order to do justice to the aim it serves.

2.2. Secondary Objectives and Ancillary Reforms

The foregoing goes to show that the apparently straightforward, albeit far-reaching, proposal to establish a common Bachelor-Master system, draws in several related areas in order to achieve its effective functioning. To briefly reiterate: the Bologna Declaration itself mentions five secondary objectives. Together with the core aim and four additional objectives developed in the Communiqué's, this makes for ten action lines. In essence, the aim of including research is merged with the core aim, as it adds the third doctoral cycle. The eight remaining secondary objectives are generally presented as the other pillars of the EHEA. None of them is new, as they are all taken over from the existing objectives and initiatives of the European Organizations.[35] The first secondary objective is to adopt 'a system of easily readable and comparable degrees, also through the implementation of the Diploma Supplement, in order to promote European citizens employability and the international competitiveness of the European higher education system'. This refers to the necessity of diploma recognition in the context of a well-functioning common higher-education system, and it has been used to rope in, apart from the explicitly mentioned Diploma Supplement, the Lisbon Recognition Convention. The second objective is a practical implementation of the first objective to promote academic recognition, as it entails the 'establishment of a system of credits, such as in the ECTS system, as a proper means of promoting the most widespread student mobility'. In the context of the Bologna Process the ECTS has been adapted so as to function as a credit accumulation system, allowing for the comparison of different Bachelor and Master programmes. Another necessary component of a common system is increased cooperation in quality assurance. The Bologna Declaration encourages the development of comparable criteria and methodologies. The fourth secondary objective of the Bologna Declaration is the 'promotion of mobility by overcoming obstacles to the effective exercise of free movement' of teachers and students, which does not add much by itself, just like the fifth promoting

34. This point shall be dealt with extensively in Ch. 6.
35. This particular observation shall be further explored in Ch. 5.

'the necessary European dimensions in higher education'. The Communiqué's have added lifelong learning, the partnership of higher education institutions and students and the attractiveness of the EHEA as dimensions to be taken into account when implementing Bologna.

The progress of implementation of most of the secondary aims is more difficult to measure when compared to the core objective, since they do not involve a concrete measure to be taken. Exceptions are the adoption of the Diploma Supplement and the ratification of the Lisbon Recognition Convention. To qualify these measures as part of the Bologna Process, however, would neglect their place within the institutional frameworks of the European Organizations. Rather, they should be regarded as benchmarks or indicators formulated by the Bologna Process to measure the progress towards the EHEA. The somewhat superfluous or vague secondary objectives are intended to embed the three-tier-reform into a larger scheme of rethinking of the role of higher education in contemporary societies and according changes. All the objectives taken together turn the Bologna Process into a comprehensive policy agenda for educational mobility, with 'the establishment of the EHEA' as an appealing overarching image. In the sense that this prevents tunnel vision and helps to promote admirable objectives such as lifelong learning, this holistic approach is a positive development. It does make the Bologna Process more difficult to grasp, though, and it allows the participating countries to read into the Process whatever they like. Indeed, this is a trend that most commentators and observers have noticed: an unrelenting tendency on the part of the policy-makers to focus on national priorities and reforms and using the Bologna Process as an inspiration or a leverage in that context, whilst often neglecting the common and European dimension of the project.

The same trend also includes the introduction of non-Bologna determined measures, implemented concurrently with other reforms, which have been attached as 'riders' to the implementation itself.[36] The complexity of the Bologna landscape makes it difficult to distinguish which reforms do belong to the Bologna agenda, and which do not. Sometimes this is because the national rhetoric differs substantially from the one at the European-level, even though they might be talking about the same thing. As Trends 2007 notes:

> It is important to highlight, however, that the mention of much of the terminology of the Bologna process – whether qualifications frameworks and learning outcomes, or to a lesser extent diploma supplements and ECTS – often met rather blank reactions. In many cases, further exploration revealed that a considerable amount of the content of reform takes place but using different local terminology. Meanwhile, the opposite phenomenon may also arise, as 'Bologna' terminology is applied locally in a manner which may not be immediately understood from outside the particular system. Implementation of what appears to be a single European process is thus altered by the variety of national contexts in which the reforms are taking place.

36. See <http://en.wikipedia.org/wiki/Bologna_process>.

It can also be that the national reform triggered by Bologna encompasses much more than only the ten action lines. According to some, this proves that governments are abusing the Bologna reform process to introduce separate unpopular reforms along the way. But many of such reforms, although strictly speaking, not introduced by Bologna, can't be entirely separated from the Bologna agenda either. This is inherent in Bologna's modus operandi, as it in fact encourages countries to rethink their entire higher education model, which necessarily leads to further reforms and further divergence in terms of those reforms.

An example is the merging of vocational schools and universities, which is not as such, a part of the Bologna Process, but which several countries have pursued in the framework of the Bologna reforms or are considering to do. Furthermore, the Bologna Process has often been linked to an increased focus on autonomy of the higher education institutions, which might be accompanied by a cut in government financing and a greater reliance on private sector funding. It seems that national measures can be qualified as rider-reforms when they have not been introduced by the Declarations or the Follow-Up, and when they do not (purport to) contribute to the Bologna aims in a broader, more general way either. When participation in Bologna is fuelled by a desire to shorten degrees and the amount of years students spend studying, this might be for reasons of competitiveness, but it might also be with a view to save money. Although shortening degrees in order to fit them into the recommended Bologna format does belong to the Bologna Process, restricting access to the Master's level studies and the discouraging of taking up a second study does not. It lies outside the scope of this book to map out all the different reforms that have taken place in Europe's higher education sectors over the past decade and to see if they were explicitly or implicitly linked to the Bologna Process or not, but it is without a doubt that Bologna has encompassed much more than the introduction of a three-tier system, and that there has been a large degree of variation in the national implementation. To a certain extent this is part of the open and all-inclusive character of the Bologna Process and the absence of clearly defined implementation measures. To another extent, it is caused by the national politicians who cherry-pick the Bologna objectives they would like to achieve for national reasons, interpret them in the way that is most beneficial to the national political context and disregard the ones that do not concur with their specific policy goals, or that have less short-term political win potential.

3. THREE IMPLEMENTATION NARRATIVES: FRANCE, GERMANY AND THE UK

The best way to grasp what the Bologna Process actually entails is to study it in its practical dimension; that is, how it has been adopted and implemented in the participating states. In the previous paragraph, we have already highlighted some of the implementing trends. It lies outside the scope of this book to inventory and elaborate on the entire implementation process in all the forty-seven signatory countries.[37] Detailed and up-to-date studies to that purpose are widely available, most notably in the form of the Trend reports, the depth and thoroughness of which could never be matched by this research.[38] Furthermore, the Bologna Secretariat's website contains all the national reports and other national documentation in relation to the Ministerial Conferences.[39] Instead, three small case studies will be conducted. The countries selected are three of the four initiators of the Bologna Process, to wit France, Germany and the UK.

Apart from the fact that they, as initiators, allow us to delve into the motives behind the Sorbonne-Bologna Process, they each constitute an interesting topic of study because of the different education models they represent. Furthermore, each country has its own particular Bologna narrative, it seems, and the following studies attempt to catch precisely that what the Bologna Process implies and means in three different national contexts. France shows us an example of how and to what extent national policy agenda has caused or at least facilitated the adoption of the Sorbonne Declaration and thereby the creation of the Process. Germany, with its Federal model, always has had a particularly sensitive position in relation to European level policy in educational matters. Often perceived as a reluctant participant in European-level action and trends in this area, it is remarkable to find it in the avant-garde of the most far-reaching reform project the European higher education sectors have ever seen. This applies to a similar extent to the United Kingdom. Furthermore, since it is generally believed to have been the 'model'-system, it is interesting to see whether the UK has adopted any real changes in its higher-education system in the context of the Bologna Process, or whether it has mainly regarded itself as automatically compatible with the requirements and has restricted itself to observing how the rest of Europe has adapted.

3.1. THE BOLOGNA PROCESS IN FRANCE

France has a special relationship with the Bologna Process, for it was host to the event that provided the Process' main trigger: the Sorbonne Conference. This was not coincidental. Claude Allègre, the French minister of higher education, had

37. The following paragraph concerning the legal status of the Declarations shall briefly identify the core national legislative measure taken to implement the Bologna aims in the EU countries, if there is such a legislative measure.
38. The Trends project is an initiative of the European University Association, 'designed to gather reliable information about how the European Higher Education and Research Areas are being developed across the continent'. Biannually a report is published, mostly based on survey results. The Reports can be found at: <www.eua.be/trends-in-european-higher-education/>.
39. Until 2010, the official website was operated by the host of the 2009 Leuven Ministerial Conference, the Benelux, and it integrates the previous Bologna Process websites of former host countries.

    See <www.ond.vlaanderen.be/hogeronderwijs/bologna/>. Although it is still in the air, it has now been replaced by the EHEA website: <www.ehea.info/>.

ambitious goals for his term. The once-so-prestigious French system had deteriorated over the years, due to a plethora of degrees, a much-debated division between the so-called *Grandes Ecoles* and the universities,[40] resulting in more inequality and a lack of international competitiveness. Allègre was committed to tackling these issues and aspired far-reaching reforms to that end. He decided to commission a study in order to identify problems and come up with some possible solutions. The Minister asked Jacques Attali, the former political advisor to President Mitterrand, to author the report. The influential study, known as the 'Attali report', although 'ill-received in large European capitals as some of them thought that France lacked the necessary moral leadership and scientific expertise to define a higher education model for Europe',[41] had its main ideas taken over in the Sorbonne initiative, which are now at the heart of the Bologna Process. In the report, Attali proposed new structures for academic degrees and for the general organization of higher education, allowing more mobility for students and more competitiveness of the French higher-education system in an international context.[42] He explicitly argued for the harmonization of the structures of higher education in Europe, proposing a 3-5-8 LMD System, consisting of Licence (Bachelor), Master and Doctorate degrees. He foresaw: '*Cela pourrait être à l'initiative de la France, un des grands chantiers de l'Union européenne pour la prochaine décennie*'.[43]

Although it is likely that the interest in finding a European solution for problems that seemed common also in many other European countries was genuine, and although it is not unlikely that France felt pride in taking up a leading role in a massive European reform project, it is also true that 'Europe' functioned as a pretext to analyse the French system and to change it.[44] This is illustrated by the fact that one of the main propositions of the report was the convergence of the French Universities and the *Grandes Ecoles.* In addition, the report proposed some fundamental changes in the organization of the governance of the French higher education institutions, with more autonomy and more 'openness'.[45] These changes would be very difficult to effectuate if not by means of the 'two-level game' that underlies the participation of many countries in the Bologna Process.[46] Based on a theory put forward by Moravcsik, this political strategy entails that international cooperation redistributes domestic power in favour of national executives by permitting them to loosen domestic constraints imposed by legislatures,

40. The *Grandes Ecoles* were created during the French Revolution, first known as *Ecoles Spéciales*, and were designed to train the best students for a specific profession. After the establishment of the initial four, the *Ecole des Ponts* of 1747, the *Ecole des Mines* of 1783, the *Ecole Polytechnique* and the *Ecole Normale Supérieure* of 1794, many more have followed and nowadays there exist over 300 *Grandes Ecoles* in France. See Attali 1998; Orivel 2008.
41. Charlier & Croché 2007, 12.
42. Belloc 2005, 4.
43. Attali 1998, 7.
44. Belloc 2005, 4.
45. *Ibid.*
46. Racké 2007, 32.

interest groups and other societal actors.[47] Moravcsik shows that this strategy is commonly used in European cooperation and identifies it as one of the main driving forces behind the European integration process.[48] Indeed, as Racké convincingly argues, this appears to have been exactly the strategy employed by Allègre in launching the Sorbonne initiative.[49] Allègre and Attali agreed that the best way to push the necessary reforms in the French higher education sector was to introduce them for 'European reasons' and thereby to force 'reluctant actors to accept a new scheme based on a European harmonization process'.[50] As Allègre phrased it himself: '*moderniser la trame en se servant de l'Europe*'.[51]

Allègre's subsequent invitation to his British, German and Italian counterparts to the Sorbonne summit was 'meant to launch a process toward reinforcing the position of French universities in the world',[52] partly by introducing the curricular reforms Attali had proposed, more or less distracted from national lobbies and stakeholders. It is not entirely clear why Allègre was so selective in his invitations. As we have seen, this choice created bad blood among the other European countries that felt unduly excluded from the initiative. This course of events eventually necessitated the fresh start in Bologna. If Allègre had launched a more inclusive project at the Sorbonne Conference, involving at least all the EU Member States, the Process would most probably have carried the name of the French university instead of the Italian one. In any event, taking Allègre's eagerness for reform into account, it is not surprising that in France the implementation commenced rather quickly, with the first serious discussions at the national level, taking place already before the Bologna Conference.[53] By the end of the next year, the one that saw the birth of the Bologna Declaration, France had taken preliminary measures on a large scale and even already had a two entirely new degrees in place.[54] Decree n°99-747 of 30 August 1999[55] created the *Mastaire* degree. The *Mastaire* was to be awarded on behalf of the State, received after five years counting from the student's high school diploma, the *Baccalaureate*, and to provide a single designation covering a range of diplomas and qualifications from both universities and *Grandes Ecoles*. By means of the Ministerial Act of 17 November 1999, Allègre himself established the professional *Licence* degree, the Bachelor, created to promote labour market integration and granted after three years of post-secondary education.[56] Furthermore, on the 4 October 1999,

47. Moravcsik 1994, 1.
48. *Ibid.*, 25–51.
49. Racké 2007, 32–35.
50. Orivel 2008, 125–126.
51. Allègre 2000, 263–264.
52. Charlier & Croché 2007, 12.
53. Belloc 2005, 6.
54. French Ministry of Youth, Education and Research, *National Report for the Prague Ministerial Conference*, 2001.
55. *Décret no 99-747 du 30 août 1999 relatif à la création du grade de mastaire, J.O. Numéro 203 du 2 Septembre 1999.*
56. Arrêté du 17 novembre 1999 relatif à la licence professionnelle, J.O. Numéro 272 du 24 Novembre 1999.

France ratified the Council of Europe/UNESCO Lisbon Recognition Convention, which introduced the Diploma Supplement.

The year after, in 2000, France took over the presidency of the EU. According to the French Ministry of Education, 'a strong commitment to mobility was developed under the French presidency', 'which resulted in the adoption, at the European Council in Nice in December 2000, of an Action Plan for Mobility'.[57] Also internally, the Presidency provided for some extra impetus, resulting in the completion of the French Action Plan for the implementation of the Bologna Process, by means of adopting the necessary 'accompanying measures', in foreign language training and support for student mobility.[58] Subsequently, in 2002, the Ministry decided to subject the French higher education sector to another reorganization, this time more comprehensive and intended to align more accurately with the Bologna Process requirements. The *Licence* and *Mastaire* that had been introduced in 1999 only applied to university training courses (except medical studies) and engineering schools, to which in 2001 management schools were added. Decree n°2002-482 of 8 April 2002[59] solidly (re-)established the LMD system.[60] The Decree stipulates that the French higher-education system is based on four degrees: the *Baccalauréat,* the *Licence*, the Master and the Doctorate. The fact that the *Baccalaureate,* the high school diploma granting access to 1st year University courses, is regarded as the first level is a particularity of the French system, but does not constitute a substantive deviation from the Bologna model.[61] The Decree also establishes the general use of the ECTS and the award of the Diploma Supplement. It modified the Decree of 30 August 1999, changing the name of the existing *Mastaire* to Master, in order to allow for its instant international readability. In that context it is odd, however, that the much more confusing term of *Licence* for Bachelor, has not been amended. The two kinds of Masters that were introduced, to wit the professional Master and the research Master, both require 120 credits after the *Licence*, amounting to a total of 300 credits after the *Baccalauréat,* corresponding to five years of post-secondary education. In 2003, political science institutes were included in the system, followed the next year by architecture schools and medical training institutions.

The implementation of the Bologna action lines falls under the responsibility of the Ministry of National Education, Higher Education and Research, although it is an inter-ministerial effort. However, in promoting the 2002 legislation, the Ministry awarded the higher education institutions a large amount of discretion

57. French Ministry of Youth, Education and Research, *National Report for the Berlin Ministerial Conference*, 2003.
58. French Ministry of Youth, Education and Research, *National Report for the Prague Ministerial Conference*, 2001.
59. *Décret n°2002-480 du 8 avril 2002 modifiant le décret n° 99-747 du 30 août 1999 relatif à la création du grade de mastaire et le décret n° 2001-295 du 4 avril 2001 portant création de la commission d'évaluation des formations et diplômes de gestion.*
60. L stands for *Licence*, M for Master, D for Doctorate.
61. French Ministry of Youth, Education and Research, *National Report for the Berlin Ministerial Conference*, 2003.

to propose the curricula for the new degrees.[62] This means that the government determines the general framework, but that the individual institutions can fill the framework in the way they see fit. Their projects are however subject to evaluation at the national level. They are presented in the National Council for Higher education and Research, which involves representatives of teachers, students and professionals. On the basis of the advice given by the Council, the government decides whether to accredit the institution, that is to allow the institution in question to award degrees for a limited period (four to six years) until the next national evaluation.[63] The institutions, however, have proved reluctant to reform their existing curricula in an innovative way, leading some authors to describe the success of the implementation a facade.[64] The majority of university departments have simply changed the names of their diplomas, without changing the content, and professors are teaching the same courses within a new architecture. Although the French government has acted swiftly by adopting legislative measures, opinions are divided over the question whether the reforms have really been a success. Especially the convergence of the universities and the *Grandes Ecoles* has met with criticism.[65]

In May 2007, another Decree was adopted, applicable to the two-year preparatory classes for the competitive entrance examinations to the *Grandes Ecoles*, worth 120 ECTS credits.[66] Another major reform took place in the same year with the *Loi relative aux libertés et responsabilités des universités* (Act on the freedoms and responsibilities of universities; LRU) dated 10 August 2007 (no. 2007-1119), which is part of a vast reform of higher education planned over the next five years.[67] LRU defines two new public service missions devolved to the universities: (1) participation in the construction of the European Higher Education and Research Area; (2) student guidance and professional integration. According to the Ministry:

> the LRU Act gives universities more room for manoeuvre, allowing them greater freedom of choice and the ability to interact with their environment. In this way, they can implement a development strategy tailored to their needs, demonstrate improved management and student support capabilities. The Act also adds to their appeal and heightens their profile at the European and international level.

Critics of the law, however, point out that the law empowers university presidents to the detriment of governing bodies, granting the former the mandate to reduce or

62. Belloc 2005, 6.
63. French Ministry of National Education, Higher Education and Research, *National Report for the Bergen Ministerial Conference*, 2005.
64. Orivel 2008, 145.
65. *Ibid.*, 146.
66. Decree n°. 2007-692 of 3 May 2007.
67. <www.legifrance.gouv.fr/initRechTexte.do>.

to double teaching hours at will.[68] Furthermore, it introduces a new mode of financing which depends more heavily on businesses.[69]

In recent years, some other European countries, most notably Spain and Greece, have seen massive protests by students and teachers against (further) higher education reforms, introduced most of the time under the header of the Bologna Process. In February 2009, French university staff and students followed suit and went on strike. The protests were mainly concerned with the LRU, but were phrased in general discontent with the Bologna Process. By now, almost all higher educational courses in French universities and higher institutions are established in the LMD system. As far as the medical and paramedical sectors are concerned, formerly excluded from the LMD scheme, negotiations are under way to enable their transition to the system as well. This means that on paper, the implementation of the Bologna Process has been a success. There does seem to exist, however, a general feeling among staff and students, that Bologna stands for more that increased intra-European mobility through transparency, standardization and recognition. The French main student union, UNEF, considers that the Bologna Process is used as a pretext 'to undermine the essential principles of higher education as a public service and the rights of students'.[70] It is the feeling that Bologna has been a pretext for cutbacks, for the introduction or the raising of tuition fees and for the privatization of higher education. And these concerns are increasingly vocalized.

3.2. The Bologna Process in Germany

The same criticism can from time to time be heard in Germany, where according to Ash it is 'an open secret' that financial concerns, among others, drive the Bologna Process.[71] Critics fearfully point out the incentive for the government, provided by the two-tier system, to limit financial assistance to students to the Bachelor degree only, leaving the Master level to be financed by the student himself or herself. This would allow the state support to be cut by one fourth, which can be seen as tempting in a time where the increasing number of students is not matched by an equal increase in resources.[72] As of yet, these fears have not materialized, but other financial measures have been taken. Although not an official part of the Bologna reforms, the matter of tuition fees has become a central discussion point in Germany, and it is often linked to the Bologna Process. In 2005, the *Bundesverfassunsgericht* issued an important judgment. Before 2005, no fees were charged for

68. Gaviano 2009.
69. *Ibid.*
70. *EurActiv*, 16 Aug. 2004, available at: <www.euractiv.com/en/education/eu-wide-students-protests-cuts-education-budget/article-114779>. See also *Euractiv*, 22 Jun. 2009, available at: <www.euractiv.com/en/innovation/creativity-ambassador-bologna-process-stifling-creative-thinking/article-183387>.
71. Ash 2006, 261.
72. Schüttemeyer 2007, 166.

study at Germany's higher education institutions up to the first academic degree qualifying for access to a profession.[73] A 2002 amendment of the Framework Act for Higher Education laid down a nationwide prohibition of tuition fees for Bachelor as well as Master studies.[74] The verdict of the *Bundesverfassunsgericht* however annulled the charge exemption, allowing the *Länder* to introduce tuition fees.[75] Since 2005, as Bevc notes, the *Länder* have had different approaches to the question whether or not to introduce such fees, the possibility for exemptions and the amount to be charged.[76] The *Bundesverfassunsgericht* did refer to a particular amount as a reasonable fee, to wit EUR 500, and all the *Länder* have kept to this ceiling.[77]

Apart from this development, several *Länder* have placed limits on the numbers of students allowed to proceed beyond the Bachelor cycle, thereby limiting potential claims on state support for second or third cycle programmes.[78] Although it is in accordance with Bologna aims to make the Bachelor degree relevant as a degree in itself, the German labour market (both in terms of supply and demand) will most probably take some time to get used to bachelor degrees. It should not be forgotten that up until recently, the German higher-education system hosted some of the longest degrees in Europe, meaning that it took students a relatively long time before they would enter the labour market. Although the new system might be an improvement for German students, who suffered a competitive disadvantage because of their long studies, they will most likely face some initial scepticism from employers should they decide not to proceed with a Master course after their Bachelor degree. In that light, it could be questioned whether it is equitable that students should be forced to discontinue their studies after the Bachelor, due to a limit amount of Master courses.[79] The move to restrict access to Master courses has met with fierce criticism of German students, according to whom this idea 'has

73. Eurybase 2007, 12.
74. Alesi et al. 2005, 55.
75. *Das Ziel, die Voraussetzungen für eine bundesweite Vertretung der Studierenden als Ansprechpartner der Bundesregierung in hochschulpolitischen Fragen zu schaffen, rechtfertigt eine bundesgesetzliche Regelung nicht. Denn es kann nicht angenommen werden, dass Bundesregierung und Bundesgesetzgeber ohne eine bundesweitinstitutionalisierte Interessenvertretung der Studierenden Gefahr liefen, Problemlagen und Sachgegebenheiten nicht angemessen zu erfassen und zu bewältigen. Die Nichtigkeit der Regelung über die Pflicht zur Bildung von Studierendenschaften erfasst auch die mit ihr untrennbar verbundene Bestimmung über deren Aufgaben und Verfassung.* Urteil vom 26. Jan. 2005 – 2 BvF 1/03.
76. Bevc 2008, 34.
77. Paragraph 72 of the judgment: *Soweit finanzielle Erwägungen danach bei der Wahl des Studienorts überhaupt eine Rolle spielen, ist zu beachten, dass Studiengebühren in der bislang diskutierten Größenordnung von 500 € je Semester im Vergleich zu den – von Ort zu Ort unterschiedlichen – Lebenshaltungskosten von nachrangiger Bedeutung sind.* The Bundesland Hessen in June 2008 decided to abolish the university tuition fees of EUR 500 per semester, introduced the year before.
78. *Ibid.*
79. 'For a large number of individual students, there are strong fears whether a Bachelor provides access to qualified jobs, relevant scientific education and access to Master programmes.' Freier Zusammenschluß von Studentinnenschaften 2003, 13.

been the driving force for two-tier systems in (Western) Germany since the 1960s. For many relevant actors, the Bologna Process is merely used as a pretext for realising this (old) idea'.[80]

Although it is not entirely certain whether there is such a clear agenda to strictly limit the amount of Masters' degrees at all cost, shortening the length of study courses in general was indeed one of the reasons for the Germans to participate in the Sorbonne initiative. In addition, Germany shared some of the problems that Attali and Allègre observed in relation to the French education system. Like his French colleague, Minister Jürgen Rüttgers' participation in the Sorbonne Declaration was partly motivated by a concern about the international attractiveness and competitiveness of German universities,[81] as well as 'the growing discrepancy between stagnating public resources for higher education and the explosive expansion of German universities that had turned them into mass institutions with high dropout rates [. . .] and a standing that increasingly suffered'.[82] The German Federal Government, keen to address the problems already in the mid-1990, was faced with a lack of sufficient competence to make the needed policy changes. Article 75 of the *Grundgesetz* stipulates that the responsibility for higher education resides with the sub-federal level of the *Länder* and not with the Federal Government (a principle that is referred to as *Kulturhoheit*). At that time, however, the latter was competent to propose changes to the *Hochschulrahmengesetz* (the Framework Act for Higher Education) to the Parliament, as well as to internationally represent German higher education jointly with the *Länder.*[83] The possibility to propose amendments to the Framework Act constituted a substantial power on behalf of the Federal Government.[84] Notwithstanding, any changes proposed by the Government could traditionally be expected to meet a fierce amount of resistance by the *Länder*, guarding their prerogatives jealously.

This was the background scene to which, as early as 1996, Rüttgers initiated a process to amend the Framework Act, aiming to institute more university autonomy as well as to promote a shorter duration of studies and higher completion rates.[85] Racké reports that, as was to be expected, Rüttgers' reform proposals met with opposition on the part of the *Länder* governments, as well as the higher education sector.[86] For that reason, as Martens and Wolf point out, the German government 'needed to mobilize international pressure for reforms in higher education to overcome the unwillingness and incapability of the individual *Länder* to agree on any substantial reforms'.[87] The Sorbonne initiative turned out to be very

80. *Ibid.*
81. Hackl 2001, 17.
82. Schriewer 2009, 36.
83. Witte 2006, 169.
84. In 2006, in the course of the modernization reform of the Federal system (the *Föderalismusreform*), 'the Federation's framework responsibility in the field of higher education has ceased to exist'. See Lohmar & Eckhardt 2009, 154.
85. Henkel 1997. Cited by Racké 2006, 5.
86. Racké 2006.
87. Martens & Wolf 2009, 10.

helpful in that respect. Martens and Wolf describe that by 'emphasizing the possibility that single courses or whole degrees could become recognized at the European level instead of the national level, reformists gained leverage'.[88] By pressuring domestic opposition, the Sorbonne-Bologna initiative 'brought together politicians' substantial short- and strategic long-term goals: outmanoeuvring domestic institutional barriers to specific education reform goals involved changing distribution of competencies for education in the long run'.[89] It furthermore allowed Rüttgers to strengthen his image to his benefit in the upcoming elections 'as a "European reformer" playing an important role on the international stage, who on top of that received an honorary doctorate from the Sorbonne'.[90]

The Federal Government and the *Länder* signed the Sorbonne Declaration jointly, politically committing themselves to reforming the German higher-education system within a European context.[91] Only a few months later, the *Hochschulrahmengesetz* was successfully amended. The 1998 amendment was to be the first in a line of many, and it created the legal possibility of the introduction of Bachelor and Master study programmes in Germany for a trial period.[92] The Bachelor phase was to last between three and four years, whereas Master programmes needed a length of at least one, and at most two years, in total not amounting to an entire study period over five years. The introduction of the new two-tier degree structure supplemented, rather than substituted, the traditional one-tier graduation system.[93] This meant that it was optional for the *Länder* to participate in the Bologna reforms. Although officially this initial 'pilot phase' came to an end in 2002, with the sixth amendment of the Framework Act in which Bachelor and Master programmes were defined as the standard, there has not been a clear decision on whether a nationwide introduction should be undertaken. This means that there still is no obligation to institute the Bologna reforms. Some *Länder* decided upon a rapid introduction, whereas others have been more reluctant.[94]

Accordingly, the introduction of the Bologna reforms in Germany has been gradual, flexible and to a certain extent rather un-coordinated. Depending on what the *Länder* provided in their legislation, some universities were already enthusiastically running Bachelor-Master courses from the start of the reform process, others took some more time to adapt to the new schemes, and 'still others are very reluctant to replace what is regarded as a traditional yet well-proven system of high quality with a degree structure which to many seems to be a pitiful goodbye to Humboldt's ideas of *universitas*'.[95] As of yet, the two systems are still running in parallel, but as Schüttemeyer notes, at some point it will be no longer feasible, for

---

88. *Ibid.*
89. *Ibid.*
90. Racké 2006, 5.
91. <www.bmbf.de/en/3336.php#history>.
92. Alesi et al. 2005, 49.
93. Germany, National Report to the Berlin Conference, 2003.
94. Alesi et al. 2005, 49.
95. Schüttemeyer 2007, 166.

political, practical and financial reasons, to maintain the traditional structures.[96] The Bachelor-Master system as introduced by the Sorbonne and Bologna Declarations will eventually become the one and only system, albeit relatively late in comparison with the other participating countries. Although Germany, as one of the Sorbonne initiators, was an early starter in the Bologna Process, it does take a long time to round up the reforms, which to a certain extent is a natural consequence of its complex Federal system. From one point of view, this shows the Bologna Process at its best. As a form of voluntary policy convergence without any top-down coordination by the Commission or any other (supranational) institution, it allows a Federal country like Germany, with an intricate system of competence division between the Federal and the State level, to participate in a European reform project in a way that is suitable and respectful to its national characteristics.

At the same time, it also shows the dangers of Bologna. In an extremely critical 2005 report, the National Union of Students in Germany stated to be 'deeply concerned with the incoherent implementation of the Bologna Process in Germany'.[97] They noted that the quality and speed of the implementation differed greatly among higher education institutions and the different *Länder* and that out of all the Bologna aims and goals, only a few were given the appropriate amount of attention. Only the introduction of a two-tier system had indeed taken place more or less in accordance with Bologna requirements, but the result was merely to 'cut programmes into pieces' rather than to qualitatively reform them. This tendency to 'fill old wine into new bottles' has been identified in the Bologna implementation of several other countries as well, such as France.[98] Furthermore, other Bologna aims such as lifelong learning have not received any attention at all, according to the report. The Student Union noted that this was not surprising, considering that:

> the main motivation for the Federal and *Länder* governments to sign the Sorbonne and Bologna Declarations has been mainly to create external pressure on the higher education system to introduce a two-tier system and shorten the effective duration of studies. The Bologna Process is not seen as a goal in itself, but as a pretext for other changes in the higher education system.[99]

A different tone is struck in the national reports, submitted in the context of the follow-up ministerial conferences, which state that 'despite the great challenges involved in implementing the reforms', the Bologna Process has contributed towards the successful modernization of German higher education. Although, compared to other European countries, there are still large numbers of students not enrolled in the Bachelor-Master system, the conversion has been picking up speed in recent years. In the 2007/2008 academic year, over 30% of all students

96. *Ibid.*
97. Freier Zusammenschluß von Studentinnenschaften 2003, 9.
98. Expression borrowed from Schüttemeyer 2007. See previous section on France.
99. *Ibid.*, 12.

were enrolled in Bachelor-Master courses and just under two-thirds of first year students enrolled in courses which had been converted. In 2007, 14.3% of students graduated in the new system. By the beginning of the 2008/2009-year, 75% of all study courses at German institutions of higher education had been converted.[100]

3.3. The Bologna Process in the United Kingdom

Compared to the self-perceived dire state of Germany's and France's higher-education system, matters were quite different in the United Kingdom. Whereas at the end of the last century other European countries were struggling with the faltering influence and standing of their once so glorious universities, and accordingly with the decreasing attractiveness of their higher-education systems, the only problem the UK had in attracting foreign students was that there were too many applicants from all over the world, eager to study at the UK's universities, either because these are still regarded as world-class and state-of-the-art by today's scientific standards,[101] or because of the opportunity for students to develop their English-language skills.[102] Accordingly, 'the UK's strong position in European higher education raises questions about why it needs to be involved in the Bologna Process, what it has to gain, and why the UK should help other countries in the EHEA to modernise if that is going to risk its competitive advantage'.[103] For indeed, the model towards which convergence is proposed in the Sorbonne and Bologna Declarations, closely resembles the UK bachelor-master system, which could mean that other countries would be copying the aspects of the UK's higher-education system that are considered to be responsible for its success. Thereby the UK's advantageous position could be diminished, without any additional benefits for the UK itself. Why indeed then, one could ask, is the UK one of the four founding members of the Bologna Process?

The initiative for the Declaration surely came from the French, Italian and German ministers more than from its fourth signatory, the UK junior minister Baroness Tessa Blackstone. The other three ministers already knew each other, and had been discussing some of the issues already well before the Sorbonne event.[104] Hoareau reports that only 'once France, Germany and Italy had agreed

100. German Federal Ministry of Education and Research Website, *The Bologna Process*, available at: <www.bmbf.de/en/3336.php>.
101. According to the authoritative Times Higher Education Supplement Ranking, the UK has more high-ranking universities than any other EHEA country. See: *Times Higher Education*, World University Rankings 2009, available at: <www.timeshighereducation.co.uk/hybrid.asp?typeCode=438>.
102. Furlong 2005, 60.
103. House of Commons Education and Skills Committee 2007a, 6.
104. The three ministers from France, Germany and Italy had 'come to know and esteem one another in the context of a virtually unknown international organization, sometimes called the "G8 of research", the largely informal grouping of the ministers for research in the key industrialized countries of the world established by the Carnegie Commission on Science,

on the principle of a reform of degrees establishing an undergraduate degree in three years, and two postgraduate levels in two and eight years' they 'contacted the British minister'.[105] The three initiators were well aware that for the Declaration to have an optimum impact, they needed the UK onboard, 'in light of the political clout the UK has as one of the "larger" EU Member States'.[106] Blackstone agreed to participate, probably because of the idea that the Bologna Process only proposed convergence towards the UK model. Indeed, Blackstone stated that signing the Sorbonne Declaration 'was a riskier action' for the other three signatories than for her:[107]

> They were committing their own systems of higher education to much greater change than I. The Anglo-Saxon model that was proposed that day in May 1998 was essentially the one that prevailed in the United Kingdom as well as North America. We in Britain had to make relatively few adaptations. In France, Germany and Italy more change was required following the Declaration.

Together with this idea that no reforms would be required, it was important for Blackstone that the project would be a strictly intergovernmental one, without any binding agreement, and for that reason she was keen to keep the EU and the European Commission out.

It is reported that when Blackstone returned from the Sorbonne meeting, she did face some 'criticism for signing something so "European" as a declaration on a common European Higher Education Area'.[108] But contrary to what one might expect from Britain's eurosceptic public and government, it seems that there was no real controversy or even a heated public debate about the UK's participation in (creating) the EHEA. Blackstone's justification for her signature, stressing that the agreement only implied that Britain's system would be introduced elsewhere,[109] was apparently convincing enough. The government, the higher education sector and the public were all more or less on the same side, because UK government did not have an agenda to participate in the Bologna Process to push national reforms in the same sense many of the governments of the other participating countries had. In contrast to the governmental rhetoric in those other countries, UK officials were eager to water down the importance of the Declaration, stressing that no reforms would be necessary as the UK was the model country anyway. Indeed, its higher education sector was not subjected to the massive and sometimes painful reorganizations that their colleagues on mainland Europe faced. This might have contributed to the fact that a large part of the reactions in the UK have consisted of

Technology and Government'. Tessa Blackstone, as a junior minister, was not in charge of research and had therefore not been a part of these conferences. Schriewer 2009, 35.

105. Hoareau 2009.

106. Schriewer 2009, 37.

107. T. Blackstone, *Education and Training in the Europe of Knowledge*, available at: <www.uniroma3.it/downloads/297_Lezione%20Blackstone.doc>.

108. Martens & Wolf 2009, 10.

109. *Ibid.*

'complacency, based on the view that much of this amounts to catch-up by other European countries'[110] combined with a sort of indifference to the ins and outs of the Process.

This is not to say that the UK was not actively involved in the Process from the beginning. Seminars and meetings were organized on a relatively frequent basis already a few years after the signing of the Declarations. The national Quality Assurance Agency launched a national framework for higher education qualifications 'with careful descriptions of bachelors and masters degree qualifications' in 2000.[111] In 2003, the UK Government ratified the Lisbon Recognition. A survey of UK higher education institutions by the Europe Unit in 2005 indicated considerable awareness and engagement with the Bologna Process among those institutions. But it can be said that it was only in 2006, when the House of Commons Education and Skills Committee launched an inquiry focusing on the Bologna Process and its impact on UK higher education, that a substantive debate really materialized. The inquiry was undertaken in the immediate run-up to the London Ministerial Summit of May 2007 'in order to facilitate broad discussion of the UK position' 'with the intention of making a constructive contribution to the negotiations at the 2007 Summit and beyond'.[112] The Report thoroughly addressed the question why the UK should join in on the Bologna Process, stating that 'as a European leader in higher education, the benefits of engagement in the Bologna Process might not be as immediately obvious for the UK as they are for other signatory countries in the EHEA'.[113] As a minimum case for membership, it was argued that in the rapidly developing global market for higher education, the UK could simply not afford not to be involved in the Bologna Process. 'The modernization of European higher education would continue to take place regardless of UK involvement and could have implications for the recognition of UK courses and competitive position.'[114] It would therefore be better to participate and attempt to influence and steer the Process from the inside.[115] The Report made it clear that a sense of complacency had to be avoided, and identified the pressure that the convergence process put on the UK's higher-education system. The competitive advantage in attracting overseas students, traditionally a particular focus of the UK's higher education policy, could be reduced if 'comparability and compatibility would develop apace across the EHEA without efforts from the UK to keep up',

110. Furlong 2005, 60.
111. Cowen 2008, 58.
112. House of Commons Education and Skills Committee 2007a, 3.
113. *Ibid.*, 25.
114. *Ibid.*
115. In the words of UK Minister: 'The problem is that they [mainland Europe] will get on with it, they will continue with this process and, given the competitive pressures that exist, over time for some of our institutions, I think that could hit them competitively in that they have ended up in a situation where a system of comparability and compatibility is developed elsewhere in the broader Europe [and] we are not a part of it [. . .] that is why I think the process is happening, we need to embrace it and we need to influence it in our national interest.' See House of Commons, Education and Skills Committee 2007a, 25.

forcing the UK to take steps to ensure that its qualifications would be recognized within this broader area.

Beyond the minimum case for membership, the Report identified some significant benefits for the UK in active Bologna participation. The Committee found government and the organizations representing higher education to be in agreement about the advantages of active involvement, supported by student organizations as well as university leaders and academic staff involved in implementing the Bologna principles and action lines in practice. Engagement in the Process could provide some economic advantages, such as increased employment and productivity. Furthermore, involvement could increase the competitiveness of the UK higher education sector through promoting the attractiveness and international reputation of the EHEA at large. Apart from these advantages, the Report pointed out that UK students could profit from increased mobility and employment opportunities. With regard to UK universities, active Bologna membership could guarantee an increased market for both EU and international students within the EHEA, increased mobility of staff, sharing of best practice and expertise in a broad range of areas, and increased opportunities for research collaboration across the European Research Area. All these considerations led the Committee to conclude that there were not only significant dangers for the UK not to be actively involved in the Bologna Process, but that there were also some significant advantages to be gained from membership, with the Bologna action lines increasingly reflecting the policy priorities in the UK. This settled the question of the desirability of the UK's membership of the Bologna Process, albeit almost ten years after it had helped create it.

The prevalent perspective was, and still is, that Bologna's main features were already a traditional and integral part of the UK system, and that the UK 'has not therefore had any need to alter current structural arrangements as these are broadly in line with Bologna recommendations'.[116] Nevertheless, some inconsistencies do appear to exist between the Bologna requirements and the UK higher-education system. Two main issues are commonly identified as potentially problematic. Firstly, the five-year two-cycle system is most commonly being implemented in the Bologna countries as the norm, while the UK has – generally speaking – a four-year two-cycle system. Second cycle programmes in full time mode in many Bologna Process participating countries last for two years, following a three-year bachelor, while in the UK many last for one year. Some argue 'that one-year Masters programmes are "lightweight" in terms of hours studied and might be incompatible with Bologna requirements', with as a result that UK graduates 'are experiencing difficulties in gaining recognition of one-year Masters programmes for further study and employment elsewhere in Europe and beyond'.[117] The UK is not the only country with a four-year system, as, for example, also the Netherlands accommodates several four-year Bachelor-Master programmes. These differences can indeed

116. UK National Report on the implementation of the Bologna Process, 2004, 3.
117. United Kingdom Higher Education Europe Unit 2006, 2.

become an impediment to a well-functioning EHEA. They flow directly from the fact that the Bologna Process does not stipulate the length of the Masters cycle, only that it is to be shorter than the first cycle. The UK has argued for a recognition based on outcomes of study rather than input of hours, which would add substantial work to the required assessment for recognition but would potentially solve the problem of divergence in length of studies. Furthermore, the UK Higher Education Europe Unit has defended the one-year master as 'successful among European and international students and employers alike' and therefore in line with the Bologna aims.[118]

The second area of potential friction is that of quality assurance and credit recognition. In the UK, credit is generally seen as a 'useful tool to measure the volume and level of learning that a student has acquired, rather than as an end in itself'.[119] As was noted above, greater emphasis is placed on learning outcomes. Furlong puts it as follows: 'the UK has a highly developed and complex system of reporting and inspection of teaching and learning output, whereas the predominant approach elsewhere in Europe is input-based, relying on measurement of student learning hours and staff teaching hours'.[120] Although it is not easy to reconcile these two systems, this is what the UK government is actively pursuing in the Bologna negotiations. The Government's main view is that credit transfer has to be about recognition of learning outcomes, meaning that a clearer link between credit and learning outcomes is necessary.[121] Sharing the concerns of the Education and Skills Committee, and the UK higher education sector at large, that the ECTS is not underpinned by the learning outcomes approach and retains a strong focus on workload, the UK has therefore lobbied within the Process to stress the importance of learning outcomes and has managed to achieve some agreement on the issue. The Government has in fact taken up the issue with the European Commission, who is the administrator of the ECTS, arguing for revisiting the underlying approach of the system. The Government however aims for 'a better balance between learning outcomes, workload and levels so that the ECTS is better able to function as an accumulation system' rather than the complete transposition of the UK's outcome-based approach in the Bologna Process.[122]

As Furlong points out, there are some additional areas of concern, such as divergent European views on fees and university autonomy, the relatively limited use of the ECTS in the UK and the inconsistencies between the Diploma Supplement and the British equivalent, the Progress File.[123] It seems, however, that the UK is content with negotiating its position on these issues within the Bologna Process and that it does not perceive these possible tensions or inconsistencies to be a reason to hold back on Bologna participation. The UK's only real concern is increased involvement of the European Commission and a development towards

118. *Ibid.*, 3.
119. UK National Report on the implementation of the Bologna Process, 2004, 4.
120. Furlong 2005, 60.
121. House of Commons Education and Skills Committee 2007b, 10.
122. *Ibid.*
123. Furlong 2005, 60.

more bureaucratization of Bologna. The House of Commons inquiry mentioned this as one of the main points of critique, recommending that 'the Government be increasingly vigilant in guarding against a move towards bureaucratic, top-down, detailed agreements', in order to maintain national determination of education policy.[124] In its reaction to the inquiry, the UK government stressed that it totally agreed it to be 'vital that the process should remain on a basis of voluntary participation' and accordingly that the Secretary of State for Education and Skills and the Minister of State for Lifelong Learning, Further and Higher Education had 'emphasized this point at the London conference on 17–18 May 2007, and it is reflected in the London communiqué'.[125] The Committee also expressed concern about the use of the Open Method of Coordination (OMC), finding that apparently 'the absence of a Treaty base poses little constraint on what the European Commission and Member States may do voluntarily in the area of education, and more specifically higher education'.[126] The Government responded by stressing that the OMC was not strictly speaking relevant to the Bologna Process, and that it did support the OMC's commitment to 'spreading good practice and building sustainable partnerships across Europe to ensure universities make their full contribution to the Lisbon strategy'. The Government assured the Committee that Article 149(1) EC (now Article 165 TFEU) places 'clear limits to how far the European Commission can get involved in higher education'. Regardless the merit of that statement, it is clear that the UK would fiercely resist the Bologna Process to be subsumed in the *acquis communautaire.*

4. THE LEGAL DIMENSION OF THE DECLARATIONS AND OF THE BOLOGNA PROCESS

The signatories of the Declarations ambitiously speak of 'committing' themselves and, in the Sorbonne Declaration, of 'the progressive harmonization' of their higher-education systems. This should not, however, lead one to think that the Declarations are legally binding. They are political statements of intent, important ones at that, but they do not have the status of a Treaty, binding under international law, or of a Directive or Regulation, binding under European law. They cannot be enforced in court. Nevertheless, to leave the discussion of their legal status at this would neglect the fact that the Declarations can, even in their non-binding capacity, produce both practical and legal effects. The Sorbonne and Bologna Declarations do not explicitly propose the enactment of legislative measures to implement their goals and aims, but the fact that in most countries the 'overall framework for degrees and cycles' is laid down in legislation means that a faithful effectuation of the Declarations would almost always imply the adoption of legal implementing measures under national law. Education acts would have to be

124. United Kingdom Higher Education Europe Unit 2006, 3.
125. House of Commons Education and Skills Committee 2007b, 2.
126. United Kingdom Higher Education Europe Unit 2006, 32.

amended, or entirely new ones would have to be adopted, at least in order to provide for the new structures and degrees. Other Bologna aims, such as the ratification of the Lisbon Recognition Convention, also require legal action. Indeed, in almost all Bologna countries, the Declarations have led to such legislative action. We have seen this in the case of two of the initiators: Germany amended its *Hochschulrahmengesetz* (the Framework Act for Higher Education) to allow for the Bologna structure and ensuing degrees to be applied and France adopted several Decrees, most notably n°2002-482 of 8 April 2002[127] which solidly established the Bachelor-Master-Doctor system. Also Italy, the fourth original Sorbonne country, implements 'the principles of the Bologna Process through national Laws and regulations which are valid and compulsory for all Higher Education Institutions'[128] such as Ministerial Decree 509/1999 concerning the reform of the Higher-Education system. Only in the UK no major legislative measures were adopted to implement the Declarations, which follows from the fact that it already had the envisaged higher education model in place and that contrary to many Continental countries its higher education structure is not laid down in an overarching legislative act. Some action, however, has been taken in relation to other Bologna goals, such as the ratification of the Lisbon Recognition Convention and the adoption of the national qualifications framework.[129]

127. *Décret n°2002-480 du 8 avril 2002 modifiant le décret n° 99-747 du 30 août 1999 relatif à la création du grade de mastaire et le décret n° 2001-295 du 4 avril 2001 portant création de la commission d'évaluation des formations et diplômes de gestion.*
128. Italy National Report on the implementation of the Bologna Process, 2004–2005, 3.
129. To briefly mention the other EU countries: In *Austria*, the University Act 2002 provided the legal framework for the implementation of the Bologna objectives. *Bulgaria* amended its 1995 Law on Higher Education in 2004, considerably changing the structure of Bulgarian higher education by introducing the Bologna degree system. Since in *Belgium* education is not a federal matter, the French and Flemish communities are separate members of the Bologna Process. The latter has accommodated the Bologna Process through, *inter alia*, the 2003 Decree on the structure of higher education, whereas the former adopted the so-called 'Bologna Act', by its 'Decree of March 31st, 2004 defining higher education in the French Community, favoring its integration into the European space for higher education, and refinancing its universities.' The *Czech Republic* implemented the principles of the Bologna Declaration by means of Act No. 111/1998 (Higher Education Act) and its Amendment No. 147/2001. *Denmark* had set out to introduce a Bachelor Degree in university programmes already in 1993 and following the Bologna Declaration this was made statutory in Act No. 403/2003 on universities. In addition, executive orders on Bachelor/Master programmes were issued in relation to specific fields of study. In *Estonia*, in 1999, extensive reform with regard to curricula and transition to a new system of stages of studies commenced in universities, firstly applied in the academic year 2002/2003 after the amendments to the Universities Act and related acts were passed by the Parliament in June 2002. The *Finnish* Universities Act (645/1997) was amended on 30 Jul. 2004. The amendment (715/2004) enacted a Bologna-compatible two-tier degree structure, with an obligatory Bachelor's level degree before Master's level degree in all fields except medicine and dentistry. The new Act made it possible for universities to award official English degrees and degree titles. *Greece*'s higher education system had been organized in two-tier levels (four year first cycle, one or two years second cycle) already since 1982, and it therefore did not amend its structures after the Declarations. In November 2005, *Hungary*'s Parliament passed the Higher Education Act, which launched the multi-cycle course structure

The foregoing goes to show how a non-binding international declaration can trigger tangible effects if the national competent authorities decide to implement its aims into national law. Thereby, the Declarations surely have deserved their label of public international soft law.[130] Soft law lacks features such as uniformity, justiciability and sanctions. Snyder defined it as 'rules of conduct which in principle have no legally binding force but which nevertheless may have practical effects'.[131] It has both been appreciated and criticized for these characteristics that make soft law flexible, but at the same time elusive. Something most of the authors agree on is that the practical importance of soft law should not be underestimated. One may even dispute whether soft law measures only produce practical effects. Some commentators have argued that soft law measures may be considered to have legal force, either directly or indirectly.[132] The Sorbonne and Bologna Declarations could certainly be argued to constitute an example of powerful soft law with indirect legal force. Compared to the average soft law policy document, outlining some non-binding aims for the future, the Declarations have had a much larger impact. Their implementation has triggered a vast amount of legislative measures across Europe. Of course, it should be kept in mind that the legal source of the ensuing provisions, with potential rights and obligations for individuals, is the

---

in the entire Higher Education system. *Ireland*'s system generally fitted within the Bologna framework. It did enact the Qualifications (Education and Training) Act 1999, establishing the National Qualifications Authority of Ireland (NQAI), Higher Education and Training Awards Council (HETAC) and the Further Education and Training Awards Council (FETAC). In *Latvia*, the Bologna process did not initiate higher education reforms, since the Bachelor-master structure had already been introduced in Latvia independently from the Bologna Process several years before. Other changes in Latvia that coincided with the start of Bologna process, such as changes in professional higher education brought by the law on Professional education in 1999, had also already been planned earlier. In the *Netherlands*, the 'Law amending the Law on Higher Education and Scientific Research and the Law on Study Finance 2000 in relation to the introduction of the Bachelor-Master system in Higher Education' was adopted on the 6 Jun. 2002. In *Poland*, the 'Act of 27 July 2005 – The Law on Higher Education', in conjunction with some implementing regulations, provided the legal basis for the establishment of the Bologna three-cycle structure on a compulsory basis in all higher education institutions. In *Portugal*, Law No. 49/2005 introduced changes in the Comprehensive Law of the Education System in order to allow for the changes in the legal framework leading to the implementation of the Bologna process. Subsequently, Decree-Law No. 74/2006 approved the three-cycle degree system, adopting the Bologna generic descriptors for each cycle based on learning outcomes and competences, and credit ranges for the first and second cycles. In *Sweden*, the Government bill 2004/05:162, New world – new university was adopted in February 2006, accommodated the three Bologna cycles, and the Higher Education Act and Higher Education Ordinance were amended accordingly. In *Spain*, Royal Decree 56/2005 and 1393/2007 served to implement the Bologna changes. The *Slovak Republic* enacted Act No. 131/2002 on Higher Education on the 21 Feb. 2002, in which all the principles of the Bologna Declaration are contained.

130. Hackl 2001, 28.
131. Snyder 1994, 198. Many authors have worked on the meaning and implications of the concept and its specific application in EU law. See for an overview of this academic literature as well as an extensive discussion of the topic itself, Senden 2005.
132. Van Crayenest 1989.

national law, and not the Declarations, which are and remain devoid of legal effect. The force is therefore indirect. The national governments are entirely free to ignore the commonly agreed measures, to implement them only partially or in a different way, or to reverse them later. Furthermore, although the national implementing legislation might make the Bologna-inspired measures judicially enforceable in a purely national context, there is no way to enforce the Sorbonne and Bologna Declarations directly in a national or European court.

Indeed, seen in this light, the fact that almost all the signatories have largely complied with the Bologna aims, by subjecting their higher-education systems to sometimes far-reaching reforms, is remarkable. Several explanations can be offered for this curious phenomenon. For one, the Sorbonne and Bologna Declarations are not the average non-binding policy documents, vague and phrased in general terms and abstract long-term goals, as they propose a relatively concrete measure: the enactment of a two-tier Bachelor-Master system (with later on an additional third doctoral cycle). Although, as we have seen, one can detect more than a few disparities in the implementation by the participating countries, which can to a certain extent be attributed to the fact that, for example, the exact length of the two tiers is not prescribed, the proposed model apparently provides a precise enough handle to allow for some kind of national implementation, albeit divergent. Furthermore, the very fact that Bologna is a non-binding instrument can be regarded as part of the reason why states were prepared to embark on the project in the first place, and why they decided to go along with it as it took shape. Since the states are the ones to own the project, in the absence of a supranational supervisor, it is up to them to make or break it, and arguably, this empowerment has provided them with an incentive to make the best out of it.

Moreover, the Declarations do not stand alone, but are the basis for a large-scale follow-up process, with an increasingly institutionalized structure and regular meetings of the competent national agents. It is fair to say that the Bologna Process has almost turned into a European Institution itself, with its secretariat and the follow-up mechanisms, formally separate from all other previously established European frameworks for governmental cooperation. For the biannual ministerial conferences, participating states are expected to prepare a country report, based on a standardized questionnaire, in which rather detailed information is requested on the status of implementation.[133] This has turned out to be an effective way to

133. For example, the 2004–2005 national report required information on the following questions: (1) Give a brief description of important developments, including legislative reforms. (2.1) Give a short description of the structure of public authorities responsible for higher education, the main agencies/bodies in higher education and their competencies. (2.2) Give a short description of the institutional structure. (2.3) Give a brief description of the structure which oversees the implementation of the Bologna Process in your country. (3.1) National quality assurance systems should include a definition of the responsibilities of the bodies and institutions involved. Please specify the responsibilities of the bodies and institutions involved. (3.2) National quality assurance systems should include a system of accreditation, certification or comparable procedures. Describe the system of accreditation, certification or comparable procedures, if any. (3.3) National quality assurance systems should include international participation, cooperation and networking. Are international peers included in the governing

exploit peer pressure mechanisms and to encourage best-practice exchange. Although the characteristics of the process such as benchmarking and peer review are similar to those of the so-called OMC in an EU context,[134] the Bologna Process is still a phenomenon sui generis, taking place outside the EU's institutional framework. It is not an international organization, nor is it an OMC, but at the same time it is much more than a set of non-binding declarations. There is no legal basis for the Process, and since it does not produce any binding measures as such, this has been rather undisputed. Nevertheless, one could argue that powerful policy mechanisms such as this should in fact rest on firmer legal ground, something that is supported by the fact that the Lisbon Treaty has introduced explicit legal bases for the use of the OMC in several policy fields.[135] Although one can certainly

---

board(s) of the quality assurance agency(ies)? (4) The two-cycle degree system is covered by the stocktaking exercise. Please add any comments, reflections and/or explanations to the stocktaking report. (5) Recognition of degrees and periods of study is covered by the stocktaking exercise. Please add any comments, reflections and/or explanations to the stocktaking report. (6.1) Give a short description of the organization of third cycle studies (e.g., direct access from the bachelor level, balance between organized courses, independent study and thesis). (6.2) What are the links between HE and research in your country? (e.g., what percentage of publicly funded research is conducted within HE institutions?) (7.1) Describe the main factors influencing mobility of students from as well as to your country (for instance funds devoted to mobility schemes, portability of student loans and grants, visa problems). (7.2) Describe any special measures taken in your country to improve mobility of students from as well as to your country. (7.3) Describe the main factors influencing mobility of teachers and staff from as well as to your country (for instance tenure of appointment, grant schemes, social security, visa problems). (7.4) Describe any special measures taken in your country to improve mobility of academic teachers and staff from as well as to your country. (8.1) Describe aspects of autonomy of higher education institutions. Is autonomy determined/defined by law? To what extent can higher education institutions decide on internal organization, staffing, new study programmes and financing? (8.2) Describe actions taken to ensure active participation from all partners in the process. (8.3) How do students participate in and influence the organization and content of education at universities and other higher education institutions and at the national level? (e.g., participation in University Governing Bodies, Academic Councils, etc.) (9.1) Describe measures which promote equality of access to higher education. (10.1) What measures have been taken by your country to encourage higher education institutions in developing lifelong learning paths? (10.2) Describe any procedures at the national level for recognition of prior learning/flexible learning paths. (11.1) Describe any legal obstacles identified by your country and any progress made in removing legal obstacles to the establishment and recognition of joint degrees and/or joint study programmes. (11.1.1) Describe the extent of integrated study programmes leading to joint degrees or double degrees. (11.1.2) How have these programmes been organized? (joint admissions, mobility of students, joint exams, etc.) (11.2) Describe any transnational cooperation that contributes to the European dimension in higher education. (11.3) Describe how curriculum development reflects the European dimension (for instance foreign language courses, European themes, orientation towards the European labour market). (12.1) Describe actions taken by your country to promote the attractiveness of the EHEA. (13.1) Give a description of your national Bologna strategies. (13.2) Give an indication of the main challenges ahead for your country.

134. See the following chapter for a discussion of the OMC.

135. Remarkably, the Lisbon Treaty fails to grant such an explicit legal basis for an OMC in education, even though the Lisbon Strategy has already launched an education OMC. This does not invalidate the existing education OMC, but it is curious nonetheless.

question the quality of the answers provided and the level of scrutiny applied, it does seem to have helped spur the required changes.

Nevertheless, although the foregoing explanations all play their part in explaining the high compliance rates of the non-binding Bologna Process, it seems that an important part of the picture is still missing. Of course, the concrete phrasing of the Declarations might facilitate implementation, the absence of a supranational supervisor might prevent recalcitrance and resistance, and the forceful follow-up mechanism might provide for the necessary peer pressure and best-practise exchange, but in addition there must have been a strong incentive for the Member States to embark on the Process and to rapidly implement its aims. Although shared concerns about the international competitiveness of their higher-education systems and recognition of the potential of student mobility might have fuelled the Bologna project, the only satisfactory explanation lies in the national interests that the actors had in the Bologna Process. Indeed, most Bologna commentators, both in political science and in public debate,[136] agree that apart from certain possibly genuine European reasons, at least an important part of most national politicians' participation in the Process was to push national reforms under the pretext of European obligations. The Bologna Process has enabled the governments to implement national reforms that were at least to a certain extent already contemplated before the ministers for education met in Paris. As Davies puts it: 'Bologna owes its origins in the Sorbonne Declaration of 1998 – to the fact that the French and Italian education ministers Allègre and Berlinguer resorted to inter-governmental action *in order to deploy the weight of Europe for domestic purposes.*'[137] As Papatsiba states, through the Bologna Process national governments were able to 'advocate the "Bologna" context to introduce long-standing unwelcome national reforms'. As she mentions, the latter phenomenon has been referred to as 'externalization'.[138] The same mechanism has been described as 'a two-level game', following Racké's application of Moravcsik's theory to the Bologna Process.[139] This political strategy entails that international cooperation redistributes domestic power in favour of national executives by permitting them to loosen domestic constraints imposed by legislatures, interest groups and other societal actors.

The pretext of European obligations suffers from one defect in the Bologna context, however, and that is that the Declarations do not contain any obligations. It thus appears that in some way, the governmental players have succeeded in manipulating the Bologna objectives and to use them 'as leverage and justification for reforms, even though they are not unilaterally obliged to implement these objectives'.[140] To a certain extent, they might have done so by fostering the myth that the Bologna Declaration was in fact a binding legal instrument. Ravinet explains:

136. See, for example, *The Economist*, May 2009, 'Another reason why some governments embraced Bologna was to give cover for reforms they wanted anyway.'
137. Davies*, 6. Emphasis added.
138. Papatsiba 2006, 96.
139. Moravcsik 1994, 1. Racké 2007.
140. Ravinet 2008a, 353.

> The Bologna Process seems to have an element of juridicity (Pitseys, 2004), in that it appears to be legally binding in nature, especially when participating countries misinterpret their commitments as requiring conformity to superior and legally binding European policies. This lack of clarity can be used as a means to legitimise national reforms. This misconception is reinforced when Bologna declarations and communiqués are presented as texts of quasi-legal value, even though initially the Bologna Process did not have any official legal status.[141]

The Bologna objectives arguably derive their authority and importance from the overlap between the Bologna aims and EU initiatives, programmes and legislation, partly explaining why they are surrounded by such 'a sense of bindingness'.[142] In this line, several authors argue that the use of the knowledge-economy rhetoric, coinciding with the Lisbon Strategy of the EU, has contributed to the increasing sense of 'being bound' to the Bologna objectives by the signatories themselves. Fejes concurs, stating that 'planetspeak rhetoric such as the ideas of the knowledge society, employability, lifelong learning, quality assurance and mobility [...] constitute a way of thinking that makes participation in the Bologna process and the implementation of its objectives a rational way to act'.[143] In that sense, one can say that the Process has begun to lead its own life, once the 'soft' and flexible product of informal intergovernmental cooperation, now turning into something that 'needs to be done' without anyone knowing exactly why, or having different reasons to think so. This partly explains the surprising force of this voluntary project of policy convergence. All the actors appear to have their own objectives, which can be located in some common rhetoric and therewith a powerful platform for action is created. These considerations will be reiterated and further elaborated in Chapter 6.

5. CONCLUDING REMARKS

Not many commentators or politicians will have expected the enormous impact that the two ambitious but relatively low-profile Declarations have had. Even though there were pressing concerns, both of national and international character, in many of the higher education sectors in Europe, it could not have been anticipated that countries would engage in such a far-reaching European-level process so willingly. And even after the coming into being of the Declarations, the effects would still have to be seen, and many were sceptical about the eventual implementation of the non-binding declarations of 'good intentions'. Now, a decade later, the overwhelming success of the Declarations, at least in terms of the subsequent reforms they have spurred, is undisputed. To a large extent, this

141. *Ibid.*
142. Ravinet 2008a, 357.
143. Fejes 2005, 219.

high policy output can be explained by the fact that most of the participating officials have used the Bologna Process as a catalyst, leverage or pretext for national reforms. We have seen this most clearly in the cases of France and Germany, and it is generally accepted that it also counts for Italy, the fourth initiator, as well as many of the other participants. The UK seems to be an exception in this perspective, whose participation can be attributed to having at the same time not much to lose in participating, and a lot to lose in not participating. It goes to show how powerful a dynamic the cooperation of a certain number of European countries can be, more or less forcing the others to converge.

The fact that national interests played, and still play, a dominant role, also means that the Bologna Process takes different shapes and forms in every participating country. Most of the participating states have their own Bologna narrative, with their own actors, interests and discussion points, and their own reforms. This colourful landscape of forty-eight mini-Bologna Processes does the diversity of Europe and its higher-education systems justice. At the same time, it is illustrative of the defects of the Bologna Process. The Process lacks an architect. In many countries, it seems that a true European vision for an EHEA is lacking, and many of the national reforms *alla Bolognese* do not properly fit within a European framework. Even if one accepts that in European-level policy-making national concerns always play an important – if not decisive – role in whether or not a certain project is embarked upon, and in which way it is executed, and if one accepts this as a sort of occupational hazard in European governance, it is still a fair point that regardless of all the different national specificities connected to the European project, it needs to be executed in a way at least respectful towards the European objectives it purports to attempt to achieve. In the case of the Bologna Process, officially its main aim is to introduce more mobility through better credit and diploma recognition. It is to this end that the common system is proposed. The fact that this system is a two-tier (now three-tier) Bachelor-Master system is important, but not as important as that it is supposed to be a *common* system. Otherwise, the very mobility with a view to which all the reforms are proposed will not be achieved. In that sense it is therefore disturbing that there is, for example, no agreement on how long the two-cycles are supposed to last, each and in total. It is very true that it would be necessary to accommodate national contexts, and it might therefore not be desirable to impose a common standard at all. That is, a question, however, that should have been addressed more extensively before the Sorbonne and Bologna Declarations and the ensuing rollercoaster-ride that the Process has turned out to be.

The Bologna Process' increasing international popularity among governments might distract one from the fact that it is a European project, curiously enacted outside the scope of the two European Organizations that have been key players on the European Higher Education stage: the Council of Europe and the EU. As this chapter has shown, the character of the Bologna Process is very intergovernmental. The Process has almost turned into a European Institution itself, with its secretariat and the follow-up mechanisms, formally separate from all other previously established European frameworks for governmental cooperation. The Bologna Process is very much a phenomenon sui generis. But the same time, it does have close links to both the aforementioned European actors, both with regard to its content and its way of functioning. There is overlap, interaction, cooperation and friction. It is this relationship, in all its complexity, that shall constitute a most central element of the following chapters. The material overlap as well as the institutional interaction between the EU and the Bologna Process shall occupy the central place, but also the Council of Europe shall be taken into account, especially in Chapter 5. In Chapter 6, we shall return to many of the findings and consideration of this chapter, to embed them in a European law analysis of the Bologna Process and to draw some critical conclusions.

Chapter 3
EU Higher Education Law I: Legal Competence and Modes of Governance

1. INTRODUCTION

Education is a highly sensitive policy area. This is partly due to its double-sided nature. On the one hand, education is the process 'whereby, in any society, adults endeavour to transmit their beliefs, culture and other values to the young'.[1] Being closely linked to national identity and touching the core of state sovereignty, education is perceived as a national prerogative. At the same time, education is of increasingly important economic value in the upcoming knowledge-based societies and, as it prepares students for their future profession, it can be seen as closely connected to the labour market. Every government will have different views and priorities concerning both the organization and content of higher education, and its purposes. Many new governments will have an interest in reforming this rich and versatile policy field according to their political convictions. But the sector is notoriously difficult to reform, because the strong views and interests of influential educational institutions, which often enjoy extensive autonomy, as well as those of the public at large, are also to be taken into account. Thus one often finds that in the national arena, politicians are at the same time eager and reluctant to push reforms.

This difficult deadlock situation might be a push-factor for governments to embark on European-level cooperation, as it allows them to pursue their reform agenda without too much internal resistance. For after all, as Moravcsik has established, international cooperation redistributes domestic power in favour of national executives by permitting them to loosen domestic constraints imposed by

---

1. European Court of Human Rights, Case *Campbell and Cosans v. The United Kingdom*, Series A No. 48 1982.

legislatures, interest groups and other societal actors.[2] The most prominent possibility at the governments' disposal is cooperation within the context of the EU. Further advantages include practical and institutional facilities, thanks to existing and relatively well-functioning structures and decision-making processes. Furthermore, the involvement of the EU can be justified as appropriate due to the aforementioned economic significance of higher education. Not only is higher education significant for the single market, it is increasingly linked to international economic competitiveness and therefore arguably merits a common European approach. The EU institutions themselves can be expected to stimulate such a development, perhaps due to a general pro-integration bias. Indeed, the fact that the EU has become one of the most important European actors in the field of higher education can be explained by reference to both the Member States' initiatives to tackle educational issues within an EU context and the enthusiastic European Institutions, which eagerly seized upon this and have continuously sought to strengthen the EU's role in education affairs.

Although it is in part due to their own doing, the Member States are not unequivocally enthusiastic about this development. The importance and relevance of European cooperation in educational matters is often acknowledged, but Member States are still keen on guarding their national educational autonomy, mostly because of education's imperative socio-cultural value. These difficulties find illustration in the constant competence struggle between the EU and its Member States. As is often the case in sensitive policy areas, it has been the ECJ to carry the difficult task to referee in this power struggle. We shall come to see that the ECJ has found it hard to grant Member States much room for restrictive behaviour under the – admittedly somewhat vague – flag of national educational interest, and has practically ignored the paradigm of Member State autonomy as laid down in Article 165(1) TFEU (ex Article 149(1) EC). Although the ECJ is expected to make judgments that are sometimes unpopular with the politicians but that are supposed to be in their common interest in the long run, it could be said that the Member States have less and less reason to see the Court in these matters as a true impartial referee rather than just another EU Institution favouring an extension of the scope of EU influence. To a certain extent, this development could be argued to have caused Member States to feel so threatened in their sovereignty that they have become reluctant to embark on legally binding projects within the EU framework.

To another extent, Member States might be pushed away from the EU legal system because of the fact that the aforementioned benefits of European-level action in escaping national parliamentary scrutiny have diminished. In certain cases, the international level can constitute an efficient 'smokescreen' for governments to pass unpopular reforms, as the conferences and conventions where the deals done between governmental officials are largely distracted from national parliamentary scrutiny. But the EU legal framework provides for such a complex system of checks and balances in order to counterbalance the loss of parliamentary control at the national level, that a convenient smokescreen can perhaps better be

2. Moravcsik 1994, 1.

created by means of non-EU intergovernmental cooperation. And to yet another extent, the EU did or does not always possess sufficient competence to adopt certain educational projects or legal instruments. All these factors, and probably also others, play their part in explaining why parallel to EU action in higher education, the Member States have often also pursued matters in an intergovernmental context, sometimes within the EU but outside its formal legal structures, and sometimes completely outside, such as in the case of the Bologna Process. Chapters 3 and 4 taken together constitute an analysis of EU Higher Education law. This chapter will be devoted to a discussion of the legal competence and the legislation and policy initiatives of the EU in higher education, whereas the next shall delve into the case law of the European Court.

2. THE DEVELOPMENT OF EU COMPETENCE IN HIGHER EDUCATION

In federal states, the division of competences between the federal level and the state level is a well-known phenomenon. The same goes for international organizations, where competences need to be demarcated between the organization and the participating states. Competence being equivalent to power, it is not surprising that tensions exist where they need to be divided. In general, one could say that the clearer the rules that determine the division of competences, the less power struggle one can expect. Furthermore, transparency of power allocation allows for control and accountability of the ones who exercise the power. At the same time, the division of competences is unavoidably difficult, not only because of the competing interests that are involved, but also because policy areas are by nature not easily divisible. Very much unlike 'watertight compartments', policy areas are intrinsically connected to each other. These difficulties appear to be in some way magnified in the context of the EU, which explains why the power division between the Union and its Member States is often far from clear. The tension and controversy surrounding potential yielding of state sovereignty has at times led to the obscure wording of Treaty provisions, reflecting a political compromise. Furthermore, apart from the normal complexity of dividing powers along policy field lines, the functional nature of some EU powers leads to even more potential spill-over.

The delimitation of the powers of the Union and the Member States has been characterized as 'determined rather fluidly, by a mixture of action and initiative on the part of the relevant Community institutions, which can be challenged during the political process or ultimately before the Court of Justice in the event of opposition'.[3] As the allocation of competences determines the scope of EU influence, it is the continuous subject of broad political and public debate, and constituted a contentious issue in all the Treaty reforms in the past decades. The field of education is a case study *par excellence* for these findings. It is a competence that has been subject

3. De Búrca & De Witte 2002, 1.

to litigation before the ECJ, a competence that has consistently (been) expanded and that has also been restricted during the course of the European integration process and which is, therefore, highly exemplary of the tensions between the Member States and the EU. It finds itself in the midst of the interplay of forces. To a certain extent, this is the result of the fact that the exact scope of EU powers in education seems indeed unclear and ambiguous, thereby leaving room for discussion and contestation. This also serves to explain why the European Court has played such a crucial role in its development. At the same time, these competing forces themselves contribute to the ambiguity of the educational powers of the EU. On the one hand, competences are transferred to the EU in the fields of mobility and diploma recognition, but at the same time a prohibition of harmonization has been called into existence. It is unclear how these potentially contradictory provisions (are intended to) relate to each other.

This is not to say, however, that there exist no fundamental rules on the division of competences in EU law. The nexus of EU power and Member State power is Article 5 TEU (ex Article 5 EC). Its second sentence provides that 'under the principle of conferral, the Union shall act only within the limits of the competences conferred upon it by the Member States in the Treaties to attain the objectives set out therein. Competences not conferred upon the Union in the Treaties remain with the Member States'. This is the expression of the principle of attributed competences, which embodies the position that everything belongs to the competence of the Member States, unless attributed to the EU by means of an explicit legal provision in the Treaty, or implicitly by the systematic and teleological interpretation of the Treaty.[4] This principle is not new, as it coincides with the general rule that an international organization possesses only those powers that have been attributed to it, either implicitly or explicitly, by its founding legal instrument. The third sentence of Article 5 TEU stipulates:

> Under the principle of subsidiarity, in areas which do not fall within its exclusive competence, the Union shall act only if and in so far as the objectives of the proposed action cannot be sufficiently achieved by the Member States, either at central level or at regional and local level, but can rather, by reason of the scale or effects of the proposed action, be better achieved at Union level.

Regulating the lawfulness of the exercise of EU competence, it expresses the idea that decisions have to be taken at a level as close to the citizen as possible.[5] This means that the Member State level takes precedence over EU involvement, unless good reasons justify the departure from this default position.

These general and fundamental principles of power division constitute the background against which the specific provisions attributive of competence in confined policy areas as scattered throughout the Treaty need to be interpreted. The detail with which these specific powers are defined actually outmatches the

4. Jacqué 2004, 123–130.
5. Craig & De Búrca 2003, 132.

precision of the constitutions of most federal states.[6] Article 165 TFEU (ex Article 128 of the EC Treaty/ Article 149 EC) lays down the competence of the EU in education by means of five extensive paragraphs which stipulate the national autonomy paradigm of educational action by the EU, list the possible aims of EU action, deal with the external dimension of the competence and specify the appropriate measures and procedures. Although now firmly established in the Treaty framework, Article 165 TFEU was not always there. The original Treaty of Rome of 1957 did not confer any specific powers to the European Community for the development of a common educational policy.[7] In fact, the EEC Treaty did not even mention the word 'education'.

This absence of explicit educational competence did not deter the ECJ to expand the influence of the EU in educational matters and to (help) establish a 'Community law of education'.[8] The ECJ stated in 1974:

> although educational and training policy is not as such included in the spheres which the Treaty has entrusted to the Community Institutions, it does not follow that the exercise of powers transferred to the Community is in some way limited if it is of such a nature as to affect the measures taken in the execution of a policy such as that of education and training.[9]

This approach of the Court is based on sound logic. After all, the EU is endowed with a number of functional powers to achieve certain policy objectives, such as the creation of the common market and therein the free movement of persons, which may require changes in all kinds of sectors, including education.[10] It is therefore nothing less than logical that many policy fields that were initially not intended to be EU business can be and have been affected in the slipstream of the implementation of these functional powers, even in the absence of explicit legal competence.[11]

Moreover, there was not a complete lack of explicit competence in educational matters in the Rome Treaty. The Founding Fathers were cognizant of the fact that a free movement of persons could not be achieved without adopting measures for the mutual recognition of diplomas when they conferred upon the Community legislative power for that purpose in the old Article 57 EEC (now Article 53 TFEU, ex Article 47 EC). Furthermore, the EEC Treaty also provided for competence in the education-related area of vocational training, to wit in Article 128 (now Article 166 TFEU, ex Article 150 EC). It is in fact on the basis of this provision that the European Court has initially developed general education rights. The ECJ interpreted vocational training so as to include an element of 'general education' in its consequential *Gravier* judgment,[12] which it further developed in the *Blaizot*

6. De Búrca & De Witte 2002, 2.
7. Van der Mei 2003, 333.
8. De Witte 1989.
9. Case 9/74, *Donato Casagrande v. Landeshauptstadt München* [1974] ECR 773.
10. De Witte 1989, 10.
11. De Witte 1987, 236.
12. Case 293/83, *Gravier* [1985] ECR 593.

case,[13] clarifying that also university education could qualify as vocational training, as long as the course was intended to prepare the student for an occupation. The same provision was furthermore interpreted so as to provide for sufficient legal competence to support a far-reaching student exchange programme in the landmark *ERASMUS* case.[14]

Shortly after the judgment in *Gravier*, the Commission presented the ambitious new European Community Action Scheme for the Mobility of University Students (ERASMUS) programme for student exchange solely under the vocational training heading of Article 128 of the EC Treaty.[15] As Pépin notes, the positive interpretation of the Treaty in Gravier 'marked a turning point in the development of education at Community level, enabling the Commission to propose the Comett and ERASMUS programmes using the new legal opportunities offered by Article 128'.[16] Despite the Commission's proposal, the Council modified the legal basis by unanimous vote, adding Article 235 of the EC Treaty (now Article 352 TFEU, ex Article 308 EC).[17] Although the final vote was unanimous, one should note that not all the Member States disagreed with using Article 128 EEC as the sole legal basis. Greece, Italy, Luxembourg, Spain and Portugal did not think that the addition of Article 235 EEC had been necessary.[18] Due to the strong views of some other Member States, however, the Programme had to be adopted on the basis of both Article 128 and Article 235. This resulted in Council Decision 87/327/EEC of 15 June 1987 adopting the ERASMUS.[19] In the minutes of the Council meeting, the Commission had already expressed its disagreement and discontent with the addition of Article 235, and subsequently it followed up on that criticism by bringing an action for annulment of the Decision before the ECJ.[20] Logically, the Commission was careful not to risk throwing its baby out with the bathwater. Therefore, it argued for the annulment as regards the inclusion of Article 235 only.[21] The Council defended its position, arguing that the additional reference to Article 235 was necessary, first, because the measures planned under the ERASMUS programme went beyond the powers conferred on the Council by Article 128 in the area of vocational training and, secondly, because the subject matter of the programme exceeded the scope of 'vocational training'.

This did not seem to be an unreasonable statement. As Lenaerts argued, it seemed unacceptable that not only all university education was to be included in the concept of vocational training, but also that all vocational training was to be regulated in all its aspects by the Community on the basis of Article 128 EEC,

13. Case 24/86, *Blaizot v. University of Liege* [1988] ECR 379.
14. Case 242/87, *Commission v. Council (Erasmus)* [1989] ECR 1425.
15. De Witte 1989, 16.
16. Pépin 2007, 124. The Comett programme supported university-industry partnerships providing high-level training in the area of new technology.
17. Lenaerts 1989, 115.
18. *Ibid.*, 116.
19. OJ 1987, L 166, 20.
20. Lenaerts 1989, 116.
21. Shaw 1992, 420.

which required a simple majority vote in the Council. As there had to be 'an inherent limit in the Community's power to deal with education matters', Lenaerts argued that the Decision with its important impact on the legislation in the field of university education went 'beyond the "general principles" assigned as a limit to Community measures in Article 128'.[22] Thus, he concluded, it was appropriate to include Article 235 in order 'to provide for a solid Community law basis to the whole of the Decision'.[23] As to the result, the Court agreed, finding for the Council and thus upholding the Decision as based on both Articles 128 and 235. But this was only because the Court found that elements of the ERASMUS programme dealt with scientific research, which could not be considered part of the concept of vocational training. The Court sided with the Commission on most of the other, more crucial points.

The Court held that the Council was entitled to adopt legal measures providing for Community action in the sphere of vocational training and imposing corresponding obligations of cooperation on the Member States. Such an interpretation was, according to the ECJ, in accordance with the wording of Article 128 and ensured the effectiveness of that provision. The Court stated that the measures envisaged under the ERASMUS programme did not exceed the limits of the powers conferred on the Council by Article 128 of the Treaty in the area of vocational training, although 'subject to examination of the question whether that measure exceeded the scope of vocational training'.[24] The fact that the ERASMUS programme applied to all university studies did not mean, according to the Court, that the measure exceeded that scope. The Court reasoned that in general the studies to which the ERASMUS programme applied fell within the sphere of vocational training, and that only in exceptional cases the action planned under the programme would be found to be applicable to university studies which, because of their particular character, were outside that sphere. 'The mere possibility of the latter' could not 'justify the conclusion that the contested programme goes beyond the scope of vocational training and that therefore the Council was not empowered to adopt it pursuant to Article 128 of the Treaty.'[25] The ECJ thus fobbed off the Council and the Member States, and opened the potential of Article 128 as an independent legal basis for far-reaching Community action in education.

Via Article 128 EEC, Article 57 EEC and the normal application of the Treaty provisions (e.g., Article 48 EEC) to situations located in the educational sphere, inroads were increasingly made into the heart of the national education systems. This growing impact of the EU in the area of education led to various concerns. The idea that education was not only to be approached from an economic perspective led to propositions to actually strengthen the EU's position, by attributing it with explicit powers in the field of general education, so as to ensure that also the socio-cultural value of education would be taken into account on the

22. *Ibid.*, 121–122.
23. *Ibid.*, 125.
24. Paragraph 21 of the judgment.
25. Paragraph 27 of the judgment.

European level.[26] Other concerns, however, prompted a more restrictive approach. The developments that took place in the absence of explicit competence alarmed the Member States who were hesitant to concede any national autonomy or sovereignty in this field, especially to the (then) relatively undemocratic EU.[27] Both concerns were accommodated in the eventual compromise: the adoption of a specific provision for education by the 1992 Treaty of Maastricht, entailing a limited transfer of educational powers to the EU. The brand new Article 126 of the EC Treaty (now Article 165 TFEU, ex Article 149 EC) in fact codified the existent practise, thereby providing the EU with explicit legitimacy for the de facto policy that had come into existence, and at the same time establishing clearly that that was as far as it should go.[28] Thus, with the inclusion of Article 126 of the EC Treaty, the Member States sought to 'clip the wings' of the EC by establishing clear limits for EU action in this sensitive policy field.[29]

At first sight, it seems that the Member States indeed succeeded at severely limiting the powers of the EU in educational affairs. The national autonomy paradigm as laid down in the first paragraph is not even the most restrictive aspect of Article 165 TFEU. The prohibition of harmonization or *Harmonisierungsverbot*, as enshrined in paragraph 4 was introduced by the Maastricht Treaty and constituted the first explicit negative limitation of competence in the history of EU law, together with the similar prohibitions in the fields of culture (now Article 167 TFEU) and health (now Article 168 TFEU). It also appears that Article 165 TFEU deals with Union powers in educational matters in a clear and exhaustive manner. Elaborate, specific and detailed, enumerating the tasks attributed to the EU and demarcating the limits of its educational powers, Article 165 TFEU is one very deceptive provision, as it does not tell one that there are several important complicating factors – other Treaty provisions to be precise – that need to be taken into account when determining the EU's competence in education. We have already mentioned these other provisions, predating Article 165 TFEU. For one, there are the two other policy areas that are closely related to education, if not a part of it, which have their own separate Treaty provision(s), namely vocational training and research. Secondly, diploma recognition has a specific legal basis in the form of Article 53 TFEU, giving the Union competence to legislate and even harmonize the content of certain specific studies, if such is necessary in the context of the free movement of professionals (e.g., doctors). To add to the complexity, it is not entirely clear whether the area of academic diploma recognition is excluded from the scope of Article 53 TFEU and thus only falls under Article 165 TFEU, or whether the situation is more nuanced.[30]

Most importantly, in addition to these specific legal bases, there exist also a several general legislative competences that allow for the adoption of measures

26. Van der Mei 2003, 344.
27. *Ibid.*
28. Verbruggen 2001, 15.
29. Lonbay 2004, 244. See on this point also: Dougan 2005, 949; Gori 2001; Shaw 1999.
30. See Ch. 6 for a discussion of this specific point.

harmonizing the laws of the Member States. These general competences, most notably Article 115, 116 and Article 352 TFEU (ex Articles 94, 95 and 308 EC), are broadly formulated – in function of the flexibility for which they intend to allow – which implies some uncertainty as to their reach. This flexibility is desirable from the point of view that the EU might be faced with unforeseen situations, which by their nature call for Union action but which are not defined as such in the Treaty. A too rigid approach to competence division would not allow the EU to fully attain the tasks that have been allocated to it, such as the creation of an internal market. The downside of such flexibility is the diminished control of power exercise, potentially leading to a covert increase of competence, sometimes referred to a 'competence creep'. It is not difficult to image the controversy that is inherent in the application of these general legislative provisions, which explains why they on several occasions have been the subjects of litigation before the ECJ. Although the Court has ruled that the regulatory competence on the basis of these two provisions is not unlimited, the provisions remain powerful under their current interpretation.[31]

It has sometimes been argued that inserting an exhaustive list of competences in the Treaty would be desirable to clarify the legal situation and to draw lines in the sand; in fact to exclude EU legislative action in certain policy fields. Such a list would not be in line with the reality of the current division of powers, however, where at most only a very small number of areas are exclusive Member State competence, or exclusive EU competence.[32] Nevertheless, elements of the rationale behind the proposal to establish such a *Kompetenzkatalog*, namely to exclude certain policy domains from EU legislation, can clearly be identified in the Treaty, namely in the *Harmonisierungsverbote*. Do these areas belong to the absolute no-go areas that fall within the exclusive competence of the Member States? Although the competence of the Union might not be very strong in these areas, it does exist. In education, Article 165 TFEU clearly lays down the complementary competence of the EU, which stipulates the right and the duty for the EU to support, coordinate and supplement national legislation where there is a clear European added value.[33] Moreover, to say that the Union has no right to adopt any legislative measure that would affect the area of education would neglect the reality of policy-making in general, and European policy-making in particular. The competence of the EU in the functioning and the establishment of the internal market constitutes a broad functional power which invariably covers many policy areas, including those in which the Member States have retained an autonomous or sometimes even primary

31. The two most important cases being the Tobacco Advertisement Case, Case C-376/98 *Germany v. European Parliament and Council* [2000] ECR I-8419, and *Opinion 2/94* [1996] ECR I-1759 where the European Court of Justice demarcated the boundary of the Arts 95 and 308 EC respectively.
32. The two areas that are generally considered to be within the exclusive competence of the Community are the competition rules that govern the functioning of the internal market and the common commercial policy vis-à-vis third countries and the WTO.
33. Davies*, 5.

capacity to legislate.[34] As will be argued in Chapter 6, this means that such areas as public health, culture and education can be affected by, or even constitute the subject of, a harmonization measure in the field of the internal market, even though a *Harmonisierungsverbot* applies.

The Lisbon Treaty that has recently come into force has not altered much in terms of the legal basis for action in education. Article 149 EC has been renumbered to Article 165 TFEU, under Title XII 'Education, Vocational Training, Youth and Sport'. Apart from the fact that sport as a policy field has been added to the education provision, nothing has changed. This could be taken to mean that the Member States are content with the provision as it stands, confirming a role for the Union in this area, but retaining the limits that have been put in place by the prohibition of harmonization and the national autonomy paradigm. The complementary character of the competence is further stressed in the new Article 6 TFEU, which lists education as one of the areas where the Union 'shall have competence to carry out actions to support, coordinate or supplement the actions of the Member States'. Article 2(5) TFEU states that such a complementary character is to mean that no harmonization is to be based on these provisions, which does not seem to add anything to the already existing prohibition of harmonization in the education provision itself. Education is mentioned one other time in the new Treaty, when Article 9 stipulates that 'in defining and implementing its policies and activities, the Union shall take into account requirements linked to the promotion of [. . .] a high level of education'. As an anecdotal final remark, it can be noted that at one point in the negotiations, Austria demanded a 'student mobility protocol' to be attached to the Treaty, exempting it from the obligation of equal treatment of students in terms of access to education. It was driving this hard bargain in the context of Commission proceedings against its legislation limiting the amount of foreign students in certain areas of study. This interesting case will be discussed in detail in the following chapter, and here it suffices to note that no such exception was made.

3. THE COMMUNITY METHOD, THE OMC AND INTERGOVERNMENTAL COOPERATION

Competence is there to be exercised, primarily by means of the adoption of measures. The EU has a multitude of tools at its disposal for making its law and policy, both formally binding and non-binding. Article 288 TFEU (ex Article 249 EC) lists five main instruments, to wit Regulations, Directives, Decisions, Recommendations and Opinions. The former three are binding whereas the latter two are not. Article 288 TFEU is far from exhaustive, and there is an indefinite number of other instruments in the toolbox of the EU, such as communications, deliberations, resolutions, declarations, action programmes, strategies and coordination

34. De Búrca & De Witte, 2002, 9.

processes.[35] These are sometimes referred to as atypical acts, 'legal instruments which do not feature in the nomenclature of Article 249 EC' (now Article 288 TFEU).[36] To a certain extent, the institutions are free to choose which instrument suits their intended policy goal best. Some areas require legislation accompanied by strong enforcement mechanisms. For other fields binding legal measures such as Directives or Regulations might not be appropriate. The Treaty guides the institutions to a certain degree, by means of general principles such as subsidiarity and the attribution of explicit legal competence that can be found in the specific provisions spread out through the Treaty, sometimes prescribing and occasionally prohibiting a certain type of measure. The ECJ has accepted atypical instruments not covered by the Treaty, on condition that they respect primary law.[37] In spite of the variety of titles, the Court has even accepted that some of them have legally binding force, and therefore qualify as a Decision.[38] The area of higher education has seen many different instruments over the years. There have been Directives and Regulations, but also Resolutions and Action plans sometimes stemming from the Council and sometimes the product of a more complex 'mixed formula' involving the Ministers for Education 'meeting within the Council' together with the Council, or even without the Council altogether.

In order to gain understanding of the complex landscape of European higher education policy, however, the subject matter shall be approached primarily by means of a classification not on the basis of the type of instrument used, but rather on the basis of the 'mode of governance' used. According to Treib, Bähr and Falkner, modes of governance denote different styles or instruments of political steering.[39] In recent years, the topic of governance has received an enormous amount of attention.[40] The discussion often focuses on the 'newer' flexible forms of policy-making, mostly 'soft law' mechanisms, and these are contrasted to and compared with 'traditional' hard law, mostly through the so-called Community Method. The purpose of the following discussion is not so much to analyse the measures in question so as to rigidly classify them in the light of the political science doctrines concerning modes of governance. Rather, the distinction between the following categories is intended to serve the reader in gaining some insight in the role of the EU and its various institutions in the adoption of the measures concerned on the one hand, and the role of the Member States on the other hand, and to see

35. See Craig & De Búrca, 2003, 144.
36. <http://europa.eu/legislation_summaries/institutional_affairs/decisionmaking_process/l14535_en.htm>.
37. Case 59/75, *Pubblico Ministero v. Flavia Manghera and Others* [1976] ECR 00091.
38. Case C-313/90, *Comité International de la Rayonne et des Fibres Synthétiques and Others v. Commission of the European Communities* [1993] ECR I-01125. The Court considers that if the decision-maker intended the instrument to have legal effects, the instrument in question is a decision. Thus, the Court considered that, given the circumstances, a Commission Communication actually constituted a Decision. See C-57/95, *Case French Republic v. Commission of the European Communities* [1997] ECR I-01627.
39. Treib, Bähr & Falkner 2005.
40. See, for instance, Eberlein & Kerwer 2004; Kilpatrick & Armstrong 2007, 649; Regent 2003; Scott 2002; Scott & Trubek 2002; Snyder 1993; Walker & De Búrca 2007, 519.

what institutional mechanisms (and, accordingly which constitutional safeguards) underlie the adoption of the measures. Of course it is relevant to be aware of the hard law – soft law distinction, but it is not distinguishing factor between the categories that will be distinguished: (1) the Community Method, which is used for all forms of EU law: legislation, incentive measures and recommendations; (2) the OMC; and (3) Intergovernmental Cooperation, within the EU framework, on its borders and outside.

3.1. The Community Method

As we have seen in section 2 of this chapter, the legal competence of the EU in the area of education appears limited. The case has already been made that the power of Article 165 TFEU should not be underestimated, and moreover that relevant legal competence also flows from the internal market provisions. This becomes clear if one examines the amount of legislative measures, in the form of Directives and Regulations, dealing with educational matters that have seen the light over the years. These legislative measures have come about by means of the 'classical' Community method. The Community Method is understood as the institutional operating mode for the first pillar of the EU. It proceeds from an integration-logic and features the exclusive right (monopoly) of legislative initiative of the European Commission, the general use of qualified majority voting in the Council, an active role for the European Parliament in co-legislating with the Council and uniformity in the interpretation of EU law and the respect for the rule of law ensured by the Court of Justice.[41] As Scott and Trubek point out, Article 294 TFEU (ex Article 251 EC), the 'ordinary legislative procedure', can be seen to constitute an embodiment of the Community Method.[42]

The Commission's White Paper on Governance defines the Community Method as 'a means to arbitrate between different interests by passing them through two successive filters: the general interest at the level of the Commission; and democratic representation, European and national, at the level of the Council and European Parliament, together the Union's legislature'.[43] In terms of legislative action, the Method has not often been used to regulate higher education as such, but rather to improve the functioning of the internal market, secondarily affecting higher education. Particularly the realization of the free movement of persons has affected higher education, both through legislation and case law. One of the most important bodies of legislation is formed by the measures dealing with the professional recognition of diplomas. In addition, many important higher education initiatives, such as the financial support programmes and the EQF, have been adopted by means of non-legislative measures such as Decisions and Recommendations. These are soft law measures, but with a firm legal foundation in the

41. European Commission, *European Governance – A White Paper*, COM (2001) 428, 8.
42. Scott & Trubek 2002, 1.
43. European Commission, *European Governance – A White Paper*, COM (2001) 428, 8.

Treaty and therefore in the overarching EU institutional framework. They are, in a way, a compromise between the interest in having a balanced procedure and a proper legal basis for action and the interest in non-binding action for reasons of flexibility and respect for national diversity in the sensitive area that education is.

3.1.1. Legislation

3.1.1.1. Migrant Workers and Their Children

The first, and probably most obvious category of individuals that have been granted educational rights by means of EU legislation is that of migrant workers and their children. The worker itself is the least disputed beneficiary of equal treatment in relation to education, for he or she is the embodiment of the free movement of persons in the internal market. Although nowadays it seems an uncontroversial notion that the achievement of this objective would be undermined if the worker were to be separated from his or her family, the fact that Community law provided for accommodation of the family members of the worker in the host state was a breakthrough development at the time. One of the most important pieces of legislation in this context is Regulation 1612/68. It fleshes out some of the substantive rights of EU workers, with the principle of equal treatment running through the Regulation as a red thread. Especially the right of children to equal access to education was recognized as a precondition for an effective mobile labour force. Article 7(3) provides that the worker shall 'by virtue of the same right and under the same conditions as national workers, have access to training in vocational schools and in retraining centres'. This Article has been held to confer equal rights of access to non-national workers to all the advantages grants and facilities made available to nationals.[44] With regard to the workers' children, Article 12 stipulates:

> The children of a national of a Member State who is or has been employed in the territory of another Member State shall be admitted to that State's general educational, apprenticeship and vocational training courses under the same conditions as the nationals of that State, if such children are residing in its territory.

In addition, the children of migrant workers have been the subject of a legal measure constituting a piece of veritable education policy, namely the Directive on language teaching for the children of migrant workers.[45] This Directive of 25 July 1977 contains an obligation to take positive action, namely to promote teaching of the mother tongue and culture of their country of origin (Article 3). There have been some difficulties in the transposition, implementation and monitoring of the Directive.[46] In a report of 1994, the Commission indicated that twelve

---

44. Craig & De Búrca 2003, 778.
45. Directive 77/486 (OJ 1977 L199/32).
46. European Commission, *Report on the Education of Migrants' Children in the European Union*, COM (94) 423.

years after the Directive came into force, implementation was still unequal.[47] Recently, the Commission has re-focused on this old piece of legislation. In its Green Paper 'Migration and mobility: challenges and opportunities for EU education systems' of July 2008, the Commission has returned to the Directive, addressing the fact that the Directive's implementation has still not been satisfactory:

> at least in part because the context of managed migration through bilateral agreements between Member States, in which the Directive was conceived, was not current anymore by the time of its adoption. Given the difficulty experienced in generating the bilateral cooperation needed for formal implementation within the then EC of nine member states, it is not clear how implementation can now be meaningfully improved within an EU of 27 Member States.[48]

The Commission put on the table whether the Directive could potentially play a constructive role in dealing with the increased volume of intra-EU mobility of workers from EU Member States since the enlargements and the shifting challenge in the context of migrant children and their (relatively lower) educational attainment, namely the education of children coming from third countries. The Commission expected a renewed interest in the promotion of heritage language learning among children of migrants in general, and posed the question whether this was 'best implemented via legislative instruments based on the Treaty's different legal regimes for EU and third-country nationals or via the promotion of voluntary arrangements – which might be within or outside the formal school system'.[49] Hence, the Green Paper proposed to undertake a consultation with interested parties about education policy for children from a migrant background. The interested parties have been specifically invited to make their views known about the future of Directive 77/486/EEC. In response, the Committee of the Regions has expressed its opinion that Directive 77/486/EEC should be repealed.[50]

3.1.1.2. Students

Students Directive 93/96 granted students the right of residence in the Member State of study, but under the conditions of sufficient health insurance and sufficient resources so as not to become a burden on the social assistance schemes of the host state. This Directive was repealed by Directive 2004/38/EC of 29 April 2004 on the right of citizens of the Union and their family members to move and reside freely within the territory of the Member States. The Directive constituted a consolidation

47. *Ibid.*, see also European Commission, *Report on the implementation in the Member States of Directive 77/486/EEC on the education of the children of migrant workers*, COM (88) 787.
48. European Commission, *Green Paper – Migration & mobility: challenges and opportunities for EU education systems*, COM (2008) 0423, para. 39.
49. *Ibid.*, para. 41.
50. Committee of the Regions, *Opinion on the Green Paper Migration and Mobility,* OJ 2009, C 120.

and clarification of all the legislation on the right of entry and residence for Union citizens, previously consisting of two Regulations and nine Directives. Students remain subject to the same conditions of sufficient health insurance and sufficient resources. Under Directive 2004/38/EC, Union citizens acquire the right of permanent residence in the host Member State after a five-year period of uninterrupted legal residence, without any further conditions. The Directive indicates specifically that host Member States are not required, prior to the acquisition of the permanent right of residence, to grant maintenance aid for studies, including for vocational training, in the form of grants or loans.

Directive 2004/114/EC deals with the position of students from third countries. The rationale behind the adoption of the Directive was, according to its preamble, to 'promote Europe as a whole as a world centre of excellence for studies and vocational training' by promoting the mobility of third-country nationals to the EU for the purpose of studies,[51] or, in the words of Fitchew 'to facilitate the admission and residence of groups of third-country nationals whose presence is welcome for economic reasons'.[52] This idea fits well with the Bologna aim to boost the international competitiveness and attractiveness of Europe's higher education, and the more general economic objectives set out in the EU's Lisbon Strategy. As the European Commission put forward in the explanatory memorandum to its proposal for the Directive: 'welcoming large numbers of third-country nationals to Europe's educational establishments, especially at master's and doctorate levels, can have a beneficial effect on the quality and dynamism of Europe's own training systems. Establishments will have an incentive to develop more and more high quality courses meeting the demand for internationalisation in education and for greater student mobility'.[53] The Directive distinguishes four categories of third-country nationals, to wit students, pupils, unpaid trainees and volunteers. The conditions for entry of students and pupils are that they have a valid travel document and, if minors, come with parental authorization, that they have sickness insurance and sufficient resources to cover their stay and that they have been accepted by a higher educational establishment or school. The Directive includes a provision whereby under certain conditions third-country students already admitted by a Member State may be granted right to mobility in the other Member States.[54] The Directive does not apply to the United Kingdom, Ireland and Denmark.

---

51. Preamble of *Council Directive 2004/114/EC of 13 December 2004 on the conditions of admission of third-country nationals for the purposes of studies, pupil exchange, unremunerated training or voluntary service*, OJ 2004 L 375, 12–18.
52. Fitchew 2009.
53. European Commission, *Proposal for a Council Directive on the conditions of entry and residence for third-country nationals for the purpose of studies, vocational training or voluntary service*, COM (2002) 548 final, 3. See Kuptsch 2006, 37.
54. See the website of the European Commission: <http://ec.europa.eu/justice_home/fsj/immigration/training/fsj_immigration_training_en.htm>.

3.1.1.3. *The Recognition of Diplomas for Professional Purposes*

The third, and arguably most important category of legislative measures adopted by the EU having a bearing on education, is that of the recognition of diplomas for professional purposes. Before we come to a brief discussion of this dense and complicated body of legislation,[55] a few distinctions should be made. In particular, one should be aware of the distinction between professional recognition and academic recognition of diplomas. Professional recognition deals with the rules of Member States that make access to or pursuit of a regulated profession in their territory contingent on possession of specific professional qualifications. Academic recognition, on the other hand, is concerned with the academic status of obtained degrees. An example of academic recognition would be if a graduate is granted a degree in another country on the basis of his or her studies in his or her home country, or if a student is admitted to further studies in another country without having to sit remedial or additional examinations.[56] Academic recognition is often regarded to lie outside the scope of formal EU powers. Although it could be argued that this distinction is ungrounded or outdated, the Commission has adopted and adhered to that restrictive view and therefore no legislation concerning the academic recognition of diplomas has been adopted.[57] It is professional recognition that is dealt with in the form of legislative measures, which could oblige Member States to recognize qualifications obtained in other Member States, allowing the holder of the qualifications to pursue the same profession there. Within the category of professional recognition, a further distinction should be made, namely 'between professions that are regulated from the standpoint of qualifications and non-regulated professions'.[58] A profession is 'regulated' when national legislation requires an individual seeking access to a certain profession to hold a diploma or some other occupational qualification. When there is no such legal obstacle to recognition, the 'rules of the labour market and the behaviour of that market' apply.[59] This distinction is thus relevant because it is only for the professional recognition of qualifications in the context of the regulated professions that the EU has enacted legislation.

Article 53 TFEU (ex Article 47 EC/ Article 57 of the EC Treaty) provides an explicit legal basis for such legislative action. Proceeding from the logic that the establishment of a common employment market would be fundamentally impaired if Member States were to leave in place their different statutory regimes for the

55. As the topic of diploma recognition has been extensively dealt within the academic literature, it will not be the aim of this project to elaborate on the historical developments and detailed content of the legislative measures. See for extensive discussions, Schneider 1995; Schneider & Claessens 2005; Lonbay 1999; Pertek 1998.
56. See <http://ec.europa.eu/education/programmes/socrates/agenar_en.html>.
57. The distinction between academic and professional recognition and the question whether this categorization is (still) valid will be discussed extensively in Ch. 6.
58. See <http://ec.europa.eu/education/policies/rec_qual/recognition/in_en.html>.
59. *Ibid.*

recognition of diplomas for professional purposes,[60] the drafters of the Rome Treaty included this provision authorizing potentially far-reaching legislative action, impacting education systems in more than an indirect way. Article 53 TFEU provides:

> 1. In order to make it easier for persons to take up and pursue activities as self-employed persons, the European Parliament and the Council shall, acting in accordance with the ordinary legislative procedure, issue directives for the mutual recognition of diplomas, certificates and other evidence of formal qualifications and for the coordination of the provisions laid down by law, regulation or administrative action in Member States concerning the taking-up and pursuit of activities as self-employed persons.
>
> 2. In the case of the medical and allied and pharmaceutical professions, the progressive abolition of restrictions shall be dependent upon coordination of the conditions for their exercise in the various Member States.

In the discussion on competence in educational matters, Article 53 TFEU is somewhat of a strange animal. Already present in the original Rome Treaty, this fully fledged legislative competence concerning professional diploma recognition has actually allowed for far-reaching measures in terms of the harmonization of the content of educational courses, without much controversy. As Craig and De Búrca state, in tandem with the developing case law of the ECJ, there has been an active legislative programme on recognition of professional qualifications for many years.[61] Perhaps the competence of the EU to legislate in this area has been perceived as a natural consequence of that fact that professional diploma recognition is particularly closely connected to the employment market, making its exercise so relatively uncontested.[62] But the impact of this legislation on the higher-education systems of the Member States is not to be underestimated. As Lonbay argues, the numerous directives on coordination of training and recognition of qualifications 'obviously have a direct impact on content of courses'.[63] For instance, Directive 78/687 has caused the entire dentistry curriculum of Italian universities to be recreated.[64]

As Schneider notes, over the years the EU has pursued various strategies with regard to the recognition of diplomas.[65] The vertical approach that was adopted in the 1970s aimed at tackling recognition problems profession-by-profession, and

---

60. Imagine that currently around 800 professions are regulated by one or more Member States in the EU. Without recognition, these professions would be 'carved out' of the common market.
61. Craig & De Búrca 2003, 834.
62. As the Commission notes on its website: 'Right of establishment, freedom to provide services and the free movement of workers are fundamental principles of the EC Treaty. In order to enable these freedoms to be exercised, several legal instruments concerning the recognition of diplomas, applicable solely to the regulated professions, were adopted at European level.' See <http://ec.europa.eu/education/policies/rec_qual/recognition/in_en.html>.
63. Lonbay 1989, 368.
64. Zilioli 1989, 51.
65. Schneider 1995; Schneider & Claessens 2005.

which entailed minimum harmonization of the education required for the respective profession, was eventually abandoned. The strategy changed to a mutual recognition approach, mainly for reasons of efficiency and effectiveness. Regulating diploma recognition per sector individually simply proved to be too arduous. The gradual move has resulted in the adoption of 'umbrella' Directive 2005/36/EC adopted on 7 September 2005.[66] This complex piece of legislation consolidated almost all the previous legislation, except for the specific directives on the provision of services and establishment of lawyers.[67] The Directive is applicable to all Member State nationals wishing to practise a regulated profession in a Member State other than that in which they obtained their professional qualifications, on either a self-employed or employed basis. In the context of temporary and occasional provision of cross-border services, the Directive lays down the general rule that all EU nationals that are legally established in a given Member State may provide such services in another Member State under their original professional title without having to apply for recognition of their qualifications. The host Member State may require the service provider to make a declaration, possibly to be accompanied by certain documents such as proof of nationality and professional qualifications, prior to providing any services on its territory and renew it annually including the details of any insurance cover or other means of personal or collective protection with regard to professional liability.[68] With regard to permanent establishment, the Directive incorporates and intends to improve the three previous systems of recognition:

(1) General system for the recognition of professional qualifications (Chapter I of the Directive). This system applies as a fallback to all the professions not covered by specific rules of recognition and to certain situations where the migrant professional does not meet the conditions set out in other recognition schemes. This general system is based on the principle of mutual recognition, without prejudice to the application of compensatory measures if there are substantial differences between the training acquired by the migrant and the training required in the host Member State. The compensatory measure may take the form of an adaptation period or an aptitude test. The choice between one or other of these tests is up to the migrant unless specific derogations exist.
(2) System of automatic recognition of qualifications attested by professional experience (Chapter II of the Directive). The industrial, craft and commercial activities listed in the Directive are subject, under the conditions stated, to the automatic recognition of qualifications attested by professional experience.
(3) System of automatic recognition of qualifications for specific professions (Chapter III of the Directive). The automatic recognition of training

66. Craig & De Búrca 2003, 834.
67. Directives 77/249/EEC and 98/5/EC.
68. See <http://europa.eu/scadplus/leg/en/cha/c11065.htm>.

qualifications on the basis of coordination of the minimum training conditions covers the following professions: doctors, nurses responsible for general care, dental practitioners, specialized dental practitioners, veterinary surgeons, midwives, pharmacists and architects.

The new directive does not substantially impact the higher-education systems of the Member States in a direct way. As it does not propose the harmonization of new professions, but simply applies a mutual recognition approach to the non-coordinated professions, it is less intrusive and less contested. Still, the mechanism of mutual recognition might have a profound effect on the national higher-education systems. One can theorize several potential consequences of the mutual recognition approach. It could put pressure on the national higher-education systems that are less competitive, attractive or 'efficient'. For instance, if in country A it takes one ten years to become qualified for a certain profession and in country B it takes six for that same profession, and if country A is to recognize country B's diplomas, it allows the students from the country B to undermine those of country A, and it encourages students from country A to go study in country B, which could lead to a brain drain in country A or it could undermine its education system entirely. It might bring country A to decrease the number of years it takes to qualify for the profession in question, perhaps even levelling it to country B's. A contrary development could however also be hypothesized. Perhaps country B is so unhappy being overflooded by country A's students, which it has to allow on an equal basis as nationals according to EU law, that it will lengthen its study programmes so as to cancel out the incentive for foreign students. Whichever way it might work out in reality, it shows that also a mutual recognition approach, although less intrusive by nature, can have a substantial influence on national higher education. Perhaps this partly explains why the implementation of the legislation has not been a model of faithfulness. In response to the Member States' failure to bring about the necessary changes in their national laws, the European Commission has been very active in enforcing the obligations arising from Directive 2005/36/EC. In recent years, it has brought several cases against Portugal,[69] Spain,[70] Luxembourg,[71] Belgium,[72] Greece,[73] the Czech Republic,[74]

69. Case C-307/07, *Commission v. Portugal* [2008] ECR I-nyr and Case C-43/06, *Commission v. Portugal* [2007] ECR I-73.
70. Case C-39/07, *Commission v. Spain* [2008] ECR I-nyr and Case C-286/06, *Commission v. Spain*, Action brought on 29 Jun. 2006.
71. Case C-51/08, *Commission v. Luxembourg*, Action brought on 12 Feb. 2008 and Case C-193/05, *Commission v. Luxembourg* [2005] ECR I-8673.
72. Case C-47/08, *Commission v. Belgium*, Action brought on 11 Feb. 2008.
73. Case C-61/08, *Commission v. Hellenic Republic*, Action brought on 18 Feb. 2008 and Case C-36/08, *Commission v. Hellenic Republic*, Action brought on 31 Jan. 2008 and Case C-84/07, *Commission v. Hellenic Republic*, Action brought on 15 Feb. 2008.
74. Case C-203/06, *Commission v. Czech Republic* [2007] ECR I-6 and Case C-204/06, *Commission v. Czech Republic* [2007] ECR I-7.

Austria,[75] Germany[76] and the United Kingdom[77] for failure to implement or meet the obligations arising out of the diploma recognition legislation.

3.1.2. Financial Support Programmes

Lonbay notes that in the area of education 'one can also see much progress in increased cross-border interaction, cooperation, and a growing mutual trust resulting from the significant influence brought to bear through the power of funding permitted under the EC Treaty'.[78] In general, this way of promoting mobility poses no real threat to the sovereignty of the Member States, as it does not imply binding legislation such as a Directive or Regulation, although a binding legal instrument, such as a decision, will often implement a specific programme for funding.[79] It has served as a very effective manner for the European Institutions to promote a European dimension in higher education and because it is considered to be without harm for Member State autonomy, it has managed to gather great importance. Large sums of money are involved for various action programmes. Without doubt, the most important and famous funding programme is the ERASMUS programme.[80] The programme, which was launched in 1987, established a European University Network, under which universities were encouraged by means of financial incentives to set up student and teacher exchange agreements.[81] It gives out grants to the participating students; covering the cost of linguistic preparation for the studies abroad, travel expenditure and compensation for the higher cost of living in the host state.[82] ERASMUS is very much a success story, both

75. Case C-262/05, *Commission v. Republic of Austria* [2006] ECR I-82 and Case C-437/03, *Commission v. Republic of Austria* [2005] ECR I-9373.
76. Case C-264/05, *Commission v. Germany* [2006] ECR I-83.
77. Case C-505/04, *Commission v. United Kingdom.*
78. Lonbay 2004, 249–250.
79. To give a recent example, the *Decision 791/2004 of the European Parliament and the Council of 21 April established the Community's action programme to promote bodies active at European level and support specific activities in the field of Education and Training by 2004 for the period up to the 31 December 2006.* The Decision established a legal basis allowing the Commission to continue to fund a range of bodies and activities which had previously been supported on the basis of budget lines in Part A of the EU Budget. The total budget allocation for the programme was EUR 77 million. See ECOTEC, *Final evaluation of the Community's action programme to promote bodies active at European level and support specific activities in the field of Education and Training Final Report.*
80. The Erasmus programme is a follow-up of the Joint Study Programme, which was also very successful. It involved recognition arrangements between higher education institutions. See Zilioli 1989, 65. See also Smith 1979.
81. See Van der Mei 2003, 390.
82. *Ibid.* See also Davies 1997. Do note that the second phase of the Socrates programme established a decentralization of the Erasmus mobility scheme. 'This implies that each of the participating countries manage the Erasmus mobility funds that has been allocated to them. The level of the grant thus depends on the national policy and the supplementary funding available at national level.' See Answer given by V. Reding on behalf of the Commission to Written Question E-0890/01 by Juan Naranjo Escobar (PPE-DE) relating to the Socrates programme for the years 2000 to 2006, OJ C 340 E, 1 Jun. 2001, 0117–0117.

in terms of numbers, outcomes and public perception.[83] It has served not only to create a favourable public image of the role of the EU in educational matters, but arguably also of the EU as a whole. The importance thereof, especially in this area where the Union has been often accused of crossing the boundaries of its mission and competence, cannot be overstated. At the same time this is slightly ironic, as the programme itself has been the subject of an important case before the ECJ, where the Commission and the Member States disagreed on the legal basis of its adoption.[84]

The Commission, in its publication 'The history of European cooperation in education and training,' states that the adoption of the ERASMUS Programme 'on the basis of a Council decision, a legal act which established stronger links between the Member States as part of a structured process of cooperation, was another step forward'.[85] As the Commission notes, the Decision made it possible to define the objectives of action, target groups and precise budgets:

> The budget bore no comparison to the levels of funding allocated previously for the implementation of the Resolution of February 1976. For the period 1990–94, the programmes implemented (Comett, Erasmus, PETRA, FORCE, Lingua, Tempus) represented more than ECU 1 billion, whereas the appropriations planned for the period 1980–85 for the implementation of the first action programme amounted to barely ECU 14 million.[86]

Nowadays, ERASMUS is one of the four pillars of the overarching Lifelong Learning Programme. The other three pillars consist of the Comenius (pre-school and primary to secondary schools) Grundtvig (adult education and alternative education streams) and Leonardo Da Vinci (vocational education and training) mobility schemes. The Lifelong Learning Programme covers the period 2007–2013, and is the successor to the Socrates I and II programmes. It has a EUR 7 billion budget to support projects and activities that foster interchange, cooperation and mobility between education and training systems within the EU. Although the ERASMUS programme might be considered as being limited in terms of its goals, for it only aims to promote short-term mobility and does not facilitate students who want to follow their entire studies abroad,[87] it has been so overwhelmingly

83. Naturally, the European Commission is eager to stress its success. In a 2007 publication, J. Figel stated: 'ERASMUS has been and remains a key factor in the internationalisation and "Europeanisation" of higher education in the EU. Those months spent abroad are also a turning point in the lives of thousands of individuals: 80% of participants are the first in their families to study abroad. Since the start of the programme in 1987, 1.500.000 students have benefited from an Erasmus fellowship, and the number of 3.000.000 should be reached before 2012.' European Commission, *Erasmus: Success Stories. Europe Creates Opportunities* (Luxembourg: Office for Official Publications of the European Communities, 2007).
84. Case 242/87, *Commission v. Council (Erasmus)* [1989] ECR 1425.
85. European Commission, *The History of European Cooperation in Education and Training. An Example of Europe in the Making* (Luxembourg: Office for Official Publications of the European Communities, 2006), 109.
86. *Ibid.*
87. Van der Mei 2003, 391.

successful within its own scope, and has reached out to so many young European citizens, having become a veritable part of student culture,[88] that it would not do justice to the programme to describe it in such terms. Zilioli predicted at the beginning of its implementation: 'the community institutions start exercising, through ERASMUS, a considerable influence on certain educational matters such as the promotion of exchanges, joint curricula and joint research projects'.[89] This has proven to be true.

In 2006, the Commission ordered a study to be undertaken, aimed to establish the impact of ERASMUS mobility on the mobile students' (and teachers') careers.[90] Almost all of the experts rated the competences of mobile students upon return as better or even much better than their non-mobile fellow students competences in the five areas addressed, namely: (1) foreign language proficiency (99%); (2) intercultural understanding and competences (97%); (3) knowledge of other countries (94%); (4) preparation for future employment and work (82%); (5) academic knowledge and skills (73%). In contrast, only between one quarter and none of the experts rated the mobile students as on even terms with the non-mobile students, and hardly any expert rated the mobile students as worse. Almost all experts considered the formerly mobile students upon graduation superior to non-mobile students with respect to socio-communicative competences.[91] The survey also found that internationally experienced students have an advantage in the transition process from higher education to employment. Participation in ERASMUS shortens the period during which the young graduate looks for a first job. Sixty per cent of the respondents to the survey considered language skills to be among the strong points that led to their first successful recruitment. Fifty per cent of respondents cited the element of international experience offered by ERASMUS, and almost 40% of the respondents felt that the ERASMUS period was directly responsible.[92] The survey showed that the percentage of students being able to work in a second language increased from 40% to 65% compared to those that did not participate in the ERASMUS mobility scheme and a large number of students declared that the period abroad allowed them to start or improve their skills in a third or even a fourth foreign language.[93] A period of ERASMUS mobility is

88. This is illustrated by the success of the film '*L'Auberge espagnole*' (2002) and its sequel '*Les poupées Russes*' (a third film is upcoming) which soon achieved cult-status. L'Auberge espagnole is a French film, about the protagonist Xavier, an Economics graduate student studying for a year in Barcelona, as part of the Erasmus programme, where he encounters and becomes part of a diverse group of students, coming from all over (Western) Europe. The film was released under many different titles: *Pot Luck* in the UK and Canada; *Euro Pudding* as an international title, and is also known as *The Spanish Apartment.* In Spain it came out as *Una casa de locos.* See Reed-Danahay 2007, 205. For a critical account of the films and their portrayal of Europe, see Erza & Sanchez 2002, 137–148.
89. Zilioli 1989, 67.
90. International Centre for Higher Education Research 2006.
91. *Ibid.*, 20.
92. European Commission, *Frequently Asked Questions: ERASMUS Programme, Facts and Figures*, MEMO/06/467, 2006, 1.
93. *Ibid.*, 2.

seen as one of the keys to facilitating a graduate's employability, and 50% of the representatives of the labour market confirm that the ERASMUS students are normally recruited into jobs with an international context. According to the ratings by employers, internationally experienced graduates possess a higher level not only of those competences which can be directly linked to international work tasks but also with respect to academic knowledge and skills, and general competences like adaptability, initiative, assertiveness, decisiveness, persistence, written communication skills, analytical competences, problem-solving ability, planning, coordinating and organizing. The survey also reveals that internationally experienced graduates work more often in positions with high responsibilities and that they generally have a higher salary than those without international experience.[94]

In addition to the positive impact on students, such as upgraded skills and enhanced employability, the institutional impact of Erasmus is also considered to be strong, particularly in larger institutions and in the new EU Member States, which became apparent following a 2008 study into the impact of ERASMUS on European higher education.[95] According to the study, ERASMUS has been a strong driving force in shaping the landscape of higher education in Europe by improving, opening up and modernizing both higher education institutions and education policies.[96] Most higher education institutions report that participation has led to innovation in 'areas such as teaching and learning methods, recognition of study periods, support services for students, research activities, business cooperation as well as institutional management'.[97] Almost 90% of the central Erasmus coordinators reported that regular progress was made on giving their institution a more international profile, and nearly 50% reported a high or very high impact of ERASMUS in making the management of higher education institutions more professional. Ninety-two per cent of higher management agreed that their institution's participation in ERASMUS supported institutional changes and modernization. Eighty-five per cent attested to the fact that student and staff mobility had stimulated the introduction of international offices and support services for both mobile and home students, that ERASMUS has had a positive impact on the quality of teaching and learning as the mobility of international students and teachers had led to the introduction of new teaching methods and exchange of good practices, and that it had triggered the modernization and internationalization of university curricula as well as the transparency and transferability of qualifications, such as the generalized use of the ECTS. Thirty per cent of the participating institutions

94. International Centre for Higher Education Research 2006, 105.
95. European Commission, *The Impact of ERASMUS on European Higher Education: Quality, Openness and Internationalisation*, Report by the consortium of CHEPS, INCHER & ESOTEC, 2008.
96. European Commission, *Where Would European Higher Education Be without the Erasmus Programme?* Press Release: IP/09/301, 20 Feb. 2009, available at: <http://europa.eu/rapid/pressReleasesAction.do?reference=IP/09/301&format=HTML&aged=0&language=EN&guiLanguage=en>.
97. *Ibid.*

reported that ERASMUS had achieved closer cooperation between universities and businesses. In response to the report, the Education Commissioner J. Figel stated:

> The Erasmus programme has been the grandfather of some of the biggest reform initiatives in higher education in Europe today. Erasmus paved the way for the European Credit Transfer and Accumulation System – ECTS – and the 'Bologna process', in which 46 European countries have agreed to establish a European Higher Education Area by 2010. This study reinforces my view that Erasmus, which celebrates its 22nd anniversary this year, should be further expanded in the future as a key vehicle for modernising higher education and promoting mobility opportunities for students.

3.1.3. Translation Devices to Enhance Credit and Degree Recognition

3.1.3.1. The ECTS

An important feature of the ERASMUS programme is the ECTS, which constituted Action 3 of the original Erasmus programme. It specified that a pilot scheme involving the transfer of credits would be promoted on a six-year experimental basis. Reportedly, it had been difficult to reach agreement between the Member States on the point that the universities participating in the pilot scheme would recognize a priori not only periods of study but also course units of all other participating universities. For some Member States this, without any harmonization, seemed incompatible with the traditional autonomy of those institutions.[98] The voluntary basis of the programme made this a surmountable obstacle. It turned out that the ECTS was the key in the efficient functioning of the ERASMUS/Socrates mobility programme, and it is now well established in EU framework. The existing ECTS for higher education and the emerging the ECTS for Vocational Education and Training (ECVET) facilitate individuals in combining education and training provisions from different countries. While the ECTS has been developed over a period of more than ten years and is already widely used in higher education, ECVET is currently being tested and a public consultation process will be launched. The ECTS will be discussed in more detail in Chapter 5.

3.1.3.2. Europass

The European Parliament and the Council established Europass by means of Decision 2241/2004/EC.[99] It was created as a portfolio of documents, aimed at helping citizens to make their competences and qualifications better understood throughout Europe and therefore facilitate their mobility. Europass brings together five documents developed at European level. Two Europass documents are to be

98. Zilioli 1989.
99. *Decision 2241/2004/EC of the European Parliament and of the Council of 15 December 2004.*

completed by European citizens themselves, namely through an assisted online tool made available in the Europass portal. This concerns the Europass CV, a competence-oriented document with which individuals present themselves, and the Europass language passport, where citizens self-assess their linguistic skills using the reference framework developed by the Council of Europe. The three other documents are issued to citizens when they have completed specific learning experiences: the Europass Mobility describes skills acquired in a mobility experience, the Europass Certificate Supplement explains vocational qualifications in terms of competences and the Europass Diploma Supplement, dealt with below, accompanies higher education diplomas, detailing the achievements of their holders. Participating countries include the Member States of the EU, Iceland, Liechtenstein and Norway. The Europass initiative is implemented through the network of National Europass Centres (NECs), coordinated by the Commission, and the Europass portal developed, hosted and managed by Cedefop[100] on behalf of the Commission.

3.1.3.3. European Qualifications Framework

The recent adoption of the EQF serves well to illustrate the increasing interaction and overlap between the intergovernmental non-EU Bologna Process and EU initiatives.[101] This latter aspect of the EQF will be dealt with in the next chapter, leaving us to focus on the creation of the EQF, which the Commission has described as 'an ambitious and far-reaching instrument which has implications for education and training systems, the labour market, industry and commerce and citizens'.[102] The EQF constitutes a European reference framework, which is intended to act as a translation device to make qualifications more readable across Europe. This way, it intends to promote the mobility of the European labour force as well as to facilitate the lifelong learning of the European citizens. The EQF consists of 8 levels, based on 'learning outcomes'. The process of adoption of the EQF commenced with Council Resolution of 27 June 2002 on lifelong learning, which invited the Commission, in close cooperation with the Member States and

100. The European Centre for the Development of Vocational Training (Cedefop) established in 1975, is a European agency that helps promote and develop vocational education and training in the EU. It is the EU's reference centre for vocational education and training. Originally based in Berlin, in 1995 Cedefop's head office was transferred to Thessaloniki. Cedefop has a liaison office in Brussels. Cedefop works to promote a European area of lifelong learning throughout an enlarged EU. It does this by providing information on and analyses of vocational education and training systems, policies, research and practice. Cedefop's tasks are to: compile selected documentation and analyses of data; contribute to developing and coordinating research; exploit and disseminate information; encourage joint approaches to vocational education and training problems; provide a forum for debate and exchanges of ideas.

101. *Recommendation of the European Parliament and of the Council of 23 April 2008 on the establishment of the European Qualifications Framework for lifelong learning*, OJ 2008 C 111, 1–7. See <www.cedefop.europa.eu/about/default.asp>.

102. European Commission, *The European Qualifications Framework for Lifelong Learning (EQF)*, Luxembourg: Office for Official Publications of the European Communities, 2008, 4.

the Council, to develop a framework for the recognition of qualifications for both education and training.[103] In July 2005, the European Commission launched a Europe-wide consultation process on the EQF.[104] One of the central questions, apart from the one whether the adoption of the EQF in whatever form was desirable, was the appropriate measure by which the EQF was to be implemented. The consultation process did confirm a broad support for the EQF, but 'the overwhelming consensus of stakeholders (Member States, social partners, sectors and others) was that an EQF should be entirely voluntary'.[105]

In 2006, the Commission proposed to establish the EQF via the legal instrument of a Recommendation of the European Parliament and of the Council, under Articles 149 and 150 EC (now Articles 165 and 166 TFEU). The instrument 'would recommend that the EQF be used by Member States on a voluntary basis as a translation device for comparing qualifications and facilitating their transparency and transfer throughout Europe'.[106] The reason why the Europass was based on a binding legal instrument and the EQF not might lie in the fact that the former is a very non-intrusive measure in which citizens are facilitated in making their own qualifications more transparent, whereas the EQF is a measure that deals with higher education courses in a more substantive manner, by establishing parameters and by qualifying them. On 28 April 2008 the European Parliament and the Council adopted the Recommendation on the establishment of an EQF for Lifelong Learning, following the procedure of Article 251 EC (now 294 TFEU) and on the basis of Articles 149(4) and 150(4) EC (now Articles 165(4) and 166(4)). The Member States are recommended to relate their national qualifications systems to the EQF by 2010, and to adopt measures so that by 2012 all qualifications certificates, diplomas and Europass documents[107] issued by the competent authorities from that date onwards contain a clear reference to the appropriate EQF level. This means that in principle, all European citizens obtaining some kind of qualification from that year onwards, will have on their diploma a reference to the EQF level of their particular education course, which will facilitate a foreign employer to rank this individuals' qualifications, initially by comparing it to the EQF levels of the employers' national education courses he or she is familiar with. The EQF project would however be truly successful if it would come to be the general framework of assessing the level of education courses, both nationally and

103. *Council Resolution of 27 June 2002 on lifelong learning*, OJ 2002 C 163, 1–3. Calls for the development of a European qualifications framework were further made in the 2004 Joint Interim Report of the Council and of the Commission on the implementation of the Education and Training 2010 work programme.

104. This was based on Commission Staff Working Document SEC(2005)957.

105. European Commission, *Proposal for a Recommendation of the European Parliament and of the Council on the establishment of the European Qualifications Framework for lifelong learning*, COM (2006) 479.

106. *Ibid.*

107. Decision No. 2241/2004/EC of the European Parliament and of the Council of 15 Dec. 2004 on a single Community framework for the transparency of qualifications and competences (Europass) introduced a set of European instruments to be used by individuals to describe their qualifications and competences.

internationally, in the same way that the ECTS has grown from a translation device into the standard credit system also for national purposes.

3.1.3.4. The Diploma Supplement

Much like the two translation devices mentioned above, the Diploma Supplement is relevant in the context of the Bologna Process, and it will therefore be discussed in Chapter 5. At this point, some general information should suffice. The Diploma Supplement is a European administrative annex to diplomas, which has been elaborated jointly by a working group of the European Commission, Council of Europe and UNESCO. In 1997–1998, this working group piloted and evaluated the Supplement. It was further tested as part of the Phare Multi-Country Project, *Recognition of Higher Education Diploma and Study Credit Points Across Borders*. The Supplement 'is designed to provide a description of the nature, level, context, content and status of the studies that were successfully completed by the individual named on the original qualification to which this supplement is appended'.[108] It is intended to be a purely descriptive, non-normative, translation device 'free from any value-judgments, equivalence statements or suggestions about recognition', 'designed to save time, money and workload'.[109] The Diploma Supplement describes the qualification in an easily understandable way, relating it to the higher-education system in which it was earned and to the overarching qualifications framework.[110]

The Supplement is divided into eight sections, providing information about:

(1) the holder of the qualification (name, place of birth);
(2) the identification of the qualification (name and title, field of study, name and status of the institution);
(3) the level of the qualification (level, length, access requirements);
(4) the contents and the results gained (mode of study, programme requirements, individual grades and credits, grading scheme, overall classification of the qualification);
(5) the function of the qualification (access to further study, professional status);
(6) additional information;
(7) certification of the supplement (date, signature); and
(8) the national higher-education system.

As to this latter, potentially laborious requirement, the explanatory notes to the Diploma Supplement specify that it should concern information on the higher educational system, its general access requirements, the types of institution and

108. European Commission, The Diploma Supplement, available at: <http://ec.europa.eu/education/lifelong-learning-policy/doc1239_en.htm>.
109. *Ibid.*
110. Bologna Process publication, *The European Higher Education Area*, available at: <www.ond.vlaanderen.be/hogeronderwijs/bologna/about/>, 7.

the qualifications structure. This description should provide a context for the qualification and refer to it. For efficiency's sake, in the explanatory report, it is suggested that a standard framework for these descriptions together with actual descriptions should be made available. At the moment, these standards are being created as a follow-up to the Diploma Supplement project and with the cooperation of the relevant National Academic Recognition Information Centres (NARIC), European National Information Centres on Academic Recognition and Mobility (ENIC), and the Ministries and Rectors' conferences.

3.1.4. The Creation of Education Institutions: The European Institute of Innovation and Technology

As we will see further below, there have been several attempts at the creation of common educational institutions through the Community method, such as schools for children of EU workers and a European University. The attempts have failed in the sense that the fierce controversy surrounding their creation has led them to be created outside the Union legal framework. The coming into being of the European Institute of Innovation and Technology, by contrast, has met much less resistance and has been adopted by means of a Regulation within the EU legal framework. The idea was proposed by Commission President Barroso, who put forward the idea of establishing a European Institute of Technology (EIT) as a contribution to the mid-term review of the Lisbon Strategy for Growth and Jobs in February 2005, inspired by the successful Massachusetts Institute of Technology (MIT) in the US. After a period of public consultation and relatively smooth negotiations between the Commission, the Parliament and the Council, a common position on a draft Regulation for the establishment of a European Institute of Innovation and Technology was adopted in the Council on 21 January 2008.[111] Two months later, Regulation 294/2008/EC of the European Parliament and of the Council was adopted, thereby formally establishing the EIT. To be based in Budapest, the Institute is to operate primarily 'through excellence-driven, autonomous partnerships of higher education institutions, research organizations, companies and other stakeholders in the form of sustainable and long-term self-supporting strategic networks in the innovation process'.[112] The Governing Board[113] of the EIT will select

---

111. See European Commission, *Implementing the Renewed Partnership for Growth and Jobs; Developing a Knowledge Flagship: The European Institute of Technology*, Brussels, COM (2006) 77, European Commission, *The European Institute of Technology: Further Steps towards Its Creation*, Brussels, COM (2006) 276, *Proposal for a Regulation of the European Parliament and the Council Establishing the European Institute of Technology*, Brussels, COM (2006) 6042. *European Parliament Legislative Resolution of 26 September 2007 on the Proposal for a Regulation of the European Parliament and of the Council establishing the European Institute of Technology, Council of Ministers' Common Position on a Draft Regulation for the Establishment of a European Institute of Innovation and Technology*, 15647/07.
112. Preamble of Regulation 294/2008/EC, para. 9.
113. According to the Statutes of the EIT, the Board shall consist both of appointed members providing a balance between those with experience in business, higher education and research

the institutions for these partnerships (which are called 'Knowledge and Innovation Communities', KIC's), and both the EIT and its KIC's should attract 'researchers and students from all over the world, including by encouraging their mobility'.[114] Operating through networks of already existing institutions, the EIT is much different from the MIT, as it does not constitute a university by itself.

The Regulation was adopted on the basis of Article 157(3) EC (now Article 173 TFEU), in the industry title, which allows action aimed at fostering better exploitation of the industrial potential of policies of innovation, research and technological development of the EU. Although it might be an appropriate legal basis, it does mean that there has been a deliberate choice not to base it on the research provision. It is not entirely clear why the research provision has been avoided in this context, but it might be because the European Commission was aware that such would make it instantly more controversial. The current political climate allows much more for initiatives directed at exploiting innovative potential for economic reasons, research for development so to say, than for the more educational and social aspects of research. Accordingly, the Institute has been created as a coordinating organ in the context of innovation, development and technological innovation rather than as an educational institution as such. Nevertheless, the EIT will be substantially involved in educational activities. The preamble of the Regulation states that:

> There is a need to support higher education as an integral, but often missing, component of a comprehensive innovation strategy. The agreement between the EIT and KICs should provide that the degrees and diplomas awarded through the KICs should be awarded by participating higher education institutions, which should be encouraged to label them also as EIT degrees and diplomas. Through its activities and work, the EIT should help promote mobility within the European Research Area and the Higher Education Area as well as encourage the transferability of grants awarded to researchers and students in the context of the KICs. All these activities should be carried out without prejudice to Directive 2005/36/EC of the European Parliament and of the Council of 7 September 2005 on the recognition of professional qualifications.[115]

This means that the EIT will offer educational services, like university degrees, albeit in an indirect way through its partner universities. As Article 6(1) of the Regulation provides, it is the KIC that undertakes the 'education and training activities at masters and doctoral level, in disciplines with the potential to meet future European socio-economic needs and which promote the development of

---

(appointed members) and members elected by and from among the higher education, research and innovation, technical and administrative staff, students and doctoral candidates of the European Institute of Innovation and Technology (EIT) and the Knowledge and Innovation Communities (KICs) (representative members).

114. *Ibid.*, para. 10.

115. *Ibid.*, para. 11.

innovation-related skills, the improvement of managerial and entrepreneurial skills and the mobility of researchers and students'. Nevertheless, the EIT will stimulate the development of 'innovative new curricula targeting in particular stronger entrepreneurial and multi-disciplinary skills'[116] and encourage the new ensuing degrees to be labelled 'EIT degrees and diploma's', which 'will be an important part of building the EIT brand'.[117] Following Article 8 of the Regulation, the participating higher education institutions shall award these degrees in accordance with national rules and accreditation procedures. That provision also provides that the EIT 'shall encourage participating higher education institutions to award joint or multiple degrees and diplomas, reflecting the integrated nature of the KICs'. In all this, Article 8(2) states that the EIT shall take into account '(i) Community action undertaken in accordance with Articles 149 and 150 of the Treaty; (ii) action undertaken in the context of the European Higher Education Area'.

3.2. The Open Method of Coordination

The OMC is a relatively new mode of governance that is rapidly winning ground in the EU. In defining the OMC, use is often made of terms as decentralization, best practice, mutual learning, qualitative and quantitative indicators, targets, benchmarking, periodic reporting, monitoring, peer review and multi-lateral surveillance.[118] These terms indicate that the OMC does not involve a 'traditional' legislative procedure. The OMC is indeed commonly perceived as a 'soft' or 'political' policy instrument, with a focus on cooperation rather than harmonization, thereby leaving considerable discretion to the Member States. This is why it is seen as a solution to the problem of nationally sensitive policy areas where coordination on the European level is nevertheless necessary. The supranational character of the traditional Community method makes it an unpopular policy method for the reluctant Member States when it concerns such culturally sensitive areas. The OMC, with its intergovernmental character, has therefore been considered as more appropriate. It has been described as flexible, respectful of national identity, in line with subsidiarity and is sometimes even seen to address some of the legitimacy problems of the EU.[119] Member States agree on certain objectives, but remain free to implement them in the way they see fit, taking into account their system differences, and they shall not be sanctioned for failures. Rather, the negative pressure to perform is seen to lie in the 'naming and shaming'-system. More positively, Member States are to be encouraged by the successes of other Member States.

---

116. European Institute of Innovation & Technology, *Draft Triennial Work Programme 2010–2012*, 2009, 2, available at: <http://eit.europa.eu>.
117. *Ibid.*
118. De La Porte 2002, 38.
119. See Hodson & Maher 2001.

The Lisbon summit of 2000 mentioned education as one of the sectors in which the OMC would find application.[120] The Lisbon Summit underlined education as a core labour market factor, as well as a factor in social cohesion, and asked for a focus on common concerns and priorities in the field of education.[121] According to Gomitzka, 'education received attention in Lisbon as part of a much larger agenda and political project. The whole knowledge and skills area was defined in Lisbon as a necessary component of an economic and social reform strategy'.[122] Up until now there has been little exercise of coordinative powers or social sanctions, but many actors have been busy, particularly with the determination of indicators and benchmarks.[123] Particularly the Commission's Education DG has played a central role in 'managing the process of indicator development'.[124] In 2001, the Council of Ministers agreed on three strategic goals for European education and training systems: (1) to improve quality and effectiveness of education and training systems; (2) to facilitate access of all to education and training systems; and (3) to open up education and training systems to the world. In 2002, these goals were refined in thirteen associated objectives adopted by the Education ministers.[125] Subsequently, in 2003, the Education Council strengthened the role of indicators and benchmarks by, on the basis of a Commission Communication,[126] setting five benchmarks for the improvement of education and training systems up to the year 2010.[127] The five benchmarks adopted covered: early school leavers; graduates in mathematics, science and technology; population having completed upper secondary education; key competencies; and lifelong learning.[128]

In January 2004, a first report was published; 'Progress towards the Common Objectives in Education and Training'.[129] A month later the Council and the Commission issued a Joint Interim Report, which 'underlined the need to improve the quality and comparability of existing indicators, particularly in the field of

120. As specified in the Lisbon Conclusions, para. 37, the OMC entails: '- fixing guidelines for the Union combined with specific timetables for achieving the goals which they set in the short, medium and long terms; – establishing, where appropriate, quantitative and qualitative indicators and benchmarks against the best in the world and tailored to the needs of different Member States and sectors as a means of comparing best practice; – translating these European guidelines into national and regional policies by setting specific targets and adopting measures, taking into account national and regional differences; – periodic monitoring, evaluation and peer review organised as mutual learning processes.'
121. Gomitzka 2005, 17.
122. Gomitzka 2006, 10.
123. Gomitzka 2005, 32.
124. *Ibid.*, 20.
125. *Ibid.*, 19.
126. European Commission, *European Benchmarks in Education and Training: Follow-Up to the Lisbon European Council* (COM (2002) 629).
127. European Commission, *Commission Staff Working Paper: New Indicators on Education and Training* SEC(2004)1524.
128. European Council, *Council Conclusions of 5 May 2003*, OJ 2003 C 134, 4.
129. Available at: <http://europa.eu.int/comm/education/policies/2010/doc/progress_towards_common_objectives_en.pdf>.

lifelong learning'.[130] It requested the so-called Standing Group on Indicators and Benchmarks and all existing Working Groups to propose by the end of that year a limited list of new indicators for development. In November 2004, as a preliminary response, the Commission published a Staff Working Paper with detailed suggestions on how to improve indicators and benchmarking, outlining possible short, medium and long-term strategies in nine indicator areas.[131] In May 2005, the Council followed up on this and emphasized in its Conclusions that 'it is desirable to develop a coherent framework of indicators and benchmarks to monitor performance and progress in the field of education and training'.[132] Subsequently, also in 2005, the Commission issued an extensive overview of the progress made towards the Lisbon objectives in education and training.[133] In the same year, the Council decided on new indicators, and the legal basis for Eurostat education statistics was strengthened.[134] In 2006, the European Institutions initiated a survey on foreign language competencies, by means of an OMC specific survey.[135]

In the same year, the Commission published a Communication on a 'modernization agenda for universities', through the OMC.[136] It exhibited an enterprising spirit and tone, strongly encouraging Member States to ensure 'real' autonomy and accountability for universities, to provide incentives for structured partnerships with the business community, to provide 'the right mix of skills' for the labour market, to make funding work more effectively in education and research, to enhance interdisciplinarity and transdisciplinarity, to increase knowledge in society and to make the European Research and Higher Education Areas more visible. The Commission itself would 'contribute through implementation of the Lisbon Programme, through policy dialogue and mutual learning, in particular under the Education and Training 2010 Work Programme, and through financial support to Member States and to universities in their modernisation activities',[137]

130. European Commission and European Council, '*Education and Training 2010*' – *The Success of the Lisbon Strategy Hinges on Urgent Reforms*, 26 Feb. 2004.

131. European Commission, *Commission Staff Working Paper: New Indicators on Education and Training* SEC(2004)1524.

132. European Council, *Council Conclusions of 24 May 2005 on New Indicators in Education and Training* OJ 2005 C 141, 04, para. 9.

133. European Commission, *Commission Staff Working Paper: Progress towards the Lisbon Objectives in Education and Training*, SEC (2005) 419.

134. Gornitzka 2006, 35.

135. *Ibid.* See The European Indicator of Language Competence. Commission Communication of August 2005 COM (2005) 356.

136. European Commission, Communication of 10 May 2006, 'Delivering on the modernisation agenda for universities: education, research and innovation', COM (2006) 208, available at: <http://europa.eu/scadplus/leg/en/cha/c11089.htm>.

137. The Commission offered to provide funding 'which will have a significant impact on universities' quality and performance. This includes incentives to help universities attain the objectives highlighted in the Commission communication. The mechanisms include the new programmes for 2007-13 (7th EU Framework Programme for R&D, Lifelong Learning Programme, Competitiveness and Innovation Programme), as well as the Structural Funds and European Investment Bank loans'. See also Commission communication of 20 Apr. 2005 'Mobilising the brainpower of Europe: enabling universities to make their full contribution to

providing 'fresh political impetus via coordinated interaction with Member States through the open coordination method, identifying and spreading best practice and supporting Member States in their search for more effective university systems'. The Commission called upon the Council and the European Parliament to demonstrate the EU's determination to implement the necessary restructuring and modernization of universities. In 2007, the Council issued a Resolution on education as the key driver of the Lisbon Strategy, inviting the Member States and the Commission to 'strengthen the Education Council's strategic role in the OMC in education and training, in particular by feeding the results into policy-making processes at both European and national levels, and by developing a solid knowledge base for education and training policy'.[138]

As statistics play an essential role in the operation of the OMC, the EU Institutions in April 2008 adopted Regulation 452/2008 concerning the production and development of statistics on education and lifelong learning.[139] The objective of the Regulation is the creation of common statistical standards that permit the production of harmonized data, based on the idea that comparable statistical information is essential for the development of education and lifelong learning strategies and for the monitoring of progress in their implementation. A recent example of the operation of the OMC in education, in the specific context of migrant children's school performance, can be found in the 2008 Commission Green Paper on that topic.[140] As the Commission stated: 'The Open Method of Coordination for Education and Training provides a forum for co-operation and exchange between Member States on common educational challenges.'[141] The Commission plans to make proposals for a new framework for this OMC process, to be expected in December 2008. The Commission suggested that this potential policy exchange could include the possible development of indicators or benchmarks related to the gaps in educational attainment and enrolment of migrant pupils.

The application of the OMC in the area of education is not uncontroversial. The OMC, which has no basis in primary law, could be regarded as a circumvention of the Treaties. This argument might be forwarded by critics of an increased role for the European Commission in education, who could see it as attempted power-grab on behalf of the European Institutions, pointing at the limited direct power base of Article 165 TFEU. To recall the concerns expressed by the House of Commons Education and Skills Committee in the context of their Bologna Process inquiry as discussed in Chapter 2, about the increased use of the OMC: 'the absence

the Lisbon Strategy', COM (2005) 152, available at: <http://europa.eu/scadplus/leg/en/cha/c11089.htm> and Commission Communication of 5 Feb. 2003 'The role of universities in the Europe of knowledge', COM (2003) 58, available at: <http://europa.eu/scadplus/leg/en/cha/c11089.htm>.

138. *Council Resolution of 15 November 2007 on education and training as a key driver of the Lisbon Strategy* OJ 2007 C 300, 1–2.

139. OJ 2008 L 145, 227–233.

140. European Commission, *Report on the Education of Migrants' Children in the European Union* COM (94) 423.

141. Paragraph 26.

of a Treaty base poses little constraint on what the European Commission and Member States may do voluntarily in the area of education, and more specifically higher education'.[142] Indeed, the European Commission, whose hands were tied by the resistant attitude of the Member States towards EU action in the field and who was sidelined by the Bologna Process, eagerly seized on the OMC to be able to play an effective role in higher education matters. As shall be discussed in Chapter 5, the OMC and the Lisbon Strategy, in general, have substantially broadened the Commission's basis for involvement in education. But also the Member States themselves seem to find the OMC way of working an attractive one when it comes to education. Supporters of the OMC often point at its voluntary character and flexible approach, arguably the most suitable way to undertake European-level action in this sensitive policy area. As a system of best-practice exchange and soft cooperation, it is believed that the OMC cannot do much harm.

However, this would deny the OMC's tangible effects in opening-up the national sectors. International standard setting and comparing are effective means to put pressure on 'underperforming' or 'deviating' states to conform to the European common standard. An example of this is Germany, where 'as a reaction to the country's unsatisfactory results in the Programme for International Student Assessment (PISA) study national attainment standards for compulsory schools are to be introduced'.[143] Not only does this amount to the creation of national standards in a country where such standards are uncommon, it might also impair the constitutional autonomy of the German *Länder*, which are normally in charge of educational matters. Moreover, the OMC might seem 'soft' and un-intrusive because of its non-binding character, but this only relates to its form and not necessarily to the content of the particular OMC in question. To clarify, imagine an OMC with the content of the Bologna Process. No one would deny that such a Bologna OMC would have a profound impact on national higher education. A question that should be asked is whether such an OMC, entailing a structural convergence of the Member States' higher-education systems, would in fact be compatible with the requirements of Article 165 TFEU, most specifically the prohibition of harmonization. The answer to that question relies on whether the Bologna Process amounts to harmonization in the sense of Article 165(4) TFEU. This particular question shall be addressed in Chapter 6, but it can be stated here that even though strictly speaking such an OMC would probably not be incompatible with Article 165 TFEU, for the absence of a binding, supranationally imposed European standard arguably saves it of the qualification as harmonization, it does show that the OMC is not so 'soft' as it might seem.

Somewhat ironically, the argument that the OMC might amount to a circumvention of the Treaty might also find favour with those who in fact support a strengthened EU in this area, for they could perceive the OMC as a watered-down version of real EU action, thereby undermining the potential application

142. United Kingdom Higher Education Europe Unit 2006, 32.
143. Ertl & Phillips 2006, 86.

of the Community Method.[144] This erosion does not only worry staunch integrationists, but also those who are worried about the decreased influence of the European Parliament in the OMC as compared to the Community Method. Although the OMC might seem to be respectful of national autonomy, it arguably lacks democratic legitimacy. In addition, the question could be raised whether the education sector is one that benefits from the target and performance-oriented approach of the OMC. This seems to be an important policy choice that should not be left un-discussed. The OMC was originally developed in an employment and social dialogue context, and its transposition to education is not necessarily appropriate. Although these policy areas share the characteristic of being politically sensitive and in need of a softer approach to accommodate diversity, they differ substantially in all other terms. Similarly, the specific common standards as defined in the OMC are not as neutral as they appear to be. They can often be found surrounded by figures and statistics, adding to their air of scientific neutrality, but it rather seems that also they are concrete expressions of policy choices. They have been qualified as 'frozen politics', which is a powerful image to describe this difficult concept of benchmarking. Arguably, this whole process should to a larger extent be subjected to debate and democratic scrutiny.

The Treaty on the Functioning of the European Union (TFEU) does not mention the OMC as such by name, but it does introduce its characteristic elements in specific Treaty provisions. Although the phrasing somewhat varies per article, it generally mentions coordination, the establishment of guidelines and indicators, the organization of exchange of best practice, and the preparation of the necessary elements for periodic monitoring and evaluation. The areas for which the OMC is now provided in the Treaty are: Article 149 TFEU (ex Article 129 EC) on employment, Article 153(2)(a) TFEU (ex Article 137 EC) and Article 156 TFEU (ex 140 EC) on social policy, Article 168(2) TFEU (ex Article 152 EC) on public health, Article 181(2) TFEU (ex Article 165 EC) on research and development, and Article 173(2) TFEU (ex Article 157 EC) on industry. This means that despite the fact that an education OMC was already in place, the TFEU omitted such a reference in the education provision. The reasons for this omission are entirely unclear. Although it seems unlikely that the signatories of the Lisbon Reform Treaty wanted to eradiate the OMC and prevent its further use from the field of education, their omission creates some legal ambiguity, which had better been avoided. In comparison with these other subject areas, where the use of the OMC methods is explicitly authorized, and sometimes the role of the European Parliament is specified, the education OMC has been deprived of an explicit legal basis.

3.3. Intergovernmental Cooperation: A Twilight Zone

As we have seen, the Bologna Process is a non-binding intergovernmental project. The Sorbonne and Bologna Declarations, which constitute the basis of the process,

144. European Commission, *European Governance, A White Paper*, COM (2001) 428, 22.

are political artefacts, constituting only declarations and not treaties, regulations or directives.[145] They may at best be regarded as 'public international soft law'.[146] The Bologna process takes place outside the institutional framework of the EU, although it deals with matters of diploma recognition and student mobility, which are – as we have seen – well-established policy fields of the Union. It could be said that the Bologna Process constitutes both a result and an illustration of the strong counter-forces on the educational battlefield. On the one hand, Bologna constitutes an important example of the *de*-nationalization of higher education policy, as it lifts the organization of higher-education systems to a European level. European governments felt it necessary to do so allegedly because they could not by themselves meet the challenges of worldwide competition and the transformation of their societies into a knowledge-economy. At the same time, from an EU perspective, Bologna constitutes a kind of *re*-nationalization of higher education. The Bologna Process withdraws the important areas of teacher and student mobility and diploma recognition from the supranational spheres of EU influence, and moves them safely to the intergovernmental realm where state autonomy still reigns as the paradigm. But although the Process takes place outside the EU framework, there is considerable material and institutional interaction. The European Commission, as a member of the Bologna Follow Up Working Group, is increasingly involved in the Process by means of funding and steering, and characterizes its contribution to the Bologna Process as part of the Lisbon Strategy.[147] The follow-up relies heavily on the EU presidency and the ECTS as was developed in the context of the EC's ERASMUS programme is being transposed into the Bologna Process' Bachelor-Master system. This makes the exact status of the Bologna Process somewhat obscure.[148]

3.3.1. The European University Institute

The Bologna Process is, although further-reaching than ever before, not the first European-level action in education to take place in the twilight zone between the EU framework and intergovernmental cooperation. One example is the Convention to set up the European University Institute in Florence.[149] The idea of a European University took shape at the Messina Conference of 1955. The foreign ministers of the original six met there, with a view to discuss projects which they hoped would wipe out of the failure of their previous attempts to enhance European integration, to wit a European Political Community and a European Defence Community.[150] It was Walter Hallstein who floated the idea

145. Amaral & Magalhaes 2004, 84.
146. Hackl 2001, 28.
147. European Commission, *Realising the European Higher Education Area*, Contribution of the European Commission to the Berlin Conference of European Higher Education Ministers on 18/19 Sep. 2003.
148. See on this specific topic Ch. 4.
149. See Palayret 1996. See also Corbett 2003, 315–330.
150. Corbett 2004, 6. See also Corbett 2003.

to create a European University, to 'provide Europeans with the appropriate skills as well as European minded citizens'.[151] The proposal was successful in that it received a Treaty base. Article 9, paragraph 2, of the Euratom Treaty stated that: 'an institution of university status shall be established; the way in which it will function shall be established by the Council acting by a qualified-majority on a proposal from the Commission'. The proposal was however unsuccessful in that the actual creation did not get off the ground. In spite of determined action on the part of the Italian government, the European Commission and the European Parliament, all attempts to realize a true European University failed, mainly due to opposition from General de Gaulle and national academic hierarchies.[152] The French government defended the so-called *Europe des Patries* and wished to avoid a university institution under EU law, in order to preserve state prerogatives in awarding degrees.[153] It was thus in an intergovernmental framework that heads of state and government met in Bonn in July 1961. The two conferences that followed, in 1970 and 1971 in Florence and Rome, led to a plan that was more modest than its initial ambitions in both size and content. The University in its watered-down form would no longer be a direct Community institution and would be reserved for postgraduate studies.

The first difficult negotiations eventually led to a Convention creating a 'European University Institute' signed by the six founding fathers of the EEC in 1972. Article 32 of the Convention indicates that it is a closed agreement, of which only EU Member States can become contracting parties.[154] According to the press release of the European Commission: 'After more than 15 years debate, Florence will finally have its "European University." [. . .] Strictly speaking, the Institute will not be a university but a post-graduate institute. But, after so many years of talk about a "European University," it would be difficult to deny it that title.'[155] The press release also stipulated:

> Although the apportionment of the cost of running the Institute is based on the principle of Article 200 of the Rome Treaty, the Community itself is not involved. Its role is limited to having one representative of the European Commission, without a vote, on the Superior Council. Although the Institute was born in a climate of cooperation among the six member states, it is not a Community organ.

The press release noted that the governments were not unanimous on that point. The press report defined the importance of the EUI as a 'first tangible accomplishment' in the field of educational cooperation between the Member States. According to the release, the Member States were still seeking common ground for further

151. *Ibid.*
152. See <www.iue.it/About/CreationOfEUI.shtml>.
153. *Ibid.*, see also in more detail Palayret 1996.
154. *Convention setting up a European University Institute*, OJ 1976 C 029, 1–10.
155. Commission of the European Communities, Press and Information DG, *European University Institute to be Set Up ('European University')* 19/72.

cooperation. 'Like the Institute, European Education can be either the product of intergovernmental cooperation or a function of the Community. The decision has yet to be made.' It seems that almost four decades later, the same still holds true. The European University Institute, whose mission is to foster the advancement of learning in fields that are of particular interest for the development of Europe, opened its doors to the first 250 researchers in November 1976.

3.3.2. The European Schools

A similar example of a project by the Member States of the EU, implemented outside the EU, is that of the 'European Schools'. In 1957, the six original Member States of the European Communities signed an international treaty on the creation of these European schools, designed for children of Community workers.[156] Finaldi-Baratieri notes that contrary to what one might expect, the European Schools were originally not founded in order to instil a European identity, but to ensure the preservation of national identity, by providing education for nursery, primary and secondary level pupils in their mother tongue.[157] Nowadays, they might in fact be the very embodiment of the EU's motto 'Unity in Diversity'. The teaching encompasses a blend of the different school curricula of the Member States, and the pupils are from a variety of nationalities with different languages and cultural traditions.[158] The school's mission is to accommodate these different backgrounds and accordingly to provide multilingual and multicultural education.[159] To date, there are fourteen European Schools[160] in seven countries[161] with a total of approximately 20,000 pupils on roll.[162] Obviously, there has always been a close relation between the EU and these schools, as they are its spin-off, providing education for the children of EU staff. Ever since the beginning, the EU has funded the schools by means of an annual subsidy and the ECJ has always had the sole jurisdiction in disputes between Contracting Parties relating to the interpretation and application of the Convention. But in the creation of the schools, the Member States were keen to keep the project out of the Community framework. Adopted on the basis of a traditional international Treaty, the schools were not part of the *acquis communautaire*. This found explicit confirmation by the ECJ in 1984, in the *Hurd* case. The ECJ stated that 'the mere fact that those agreements are

156. The Statute of the European School of 12 Apr. 1957, *United Nations Treaty Series*, vol. 443, 129. See also the subsequent Protocol of 13 Apr. 1962 on the setting up of European Schools with reference to the Statute of the European School, *United Nations Treaty Series*, vol. 752, 267.
157. Finaldi-Baratieri 2000, 5.
158. Verbruggen, 2001, 93–95.
159. See <www.eursc.eu/index.php?l=2>.
160. Alicante, Brussels I (Uccle), Brussels II (Woluwé), Brussels III (Ixelles), Brussels IV (Laeken, opened on the site of Berkendael in September 2007), Frankfurt am Main, Mol, Bergen, Karlsruhe, Munich, Varese, Culham, Luxembourg I & Luxembourg II).
161. Belgium, Netherlands, Germany, Italy, United Kingdom, Spain and Luxembourg.
162. See <www.eursc.eu/index.php?l=2>.

linked to the Community and to the functioning of its institutions does not mean that they must be regarded as an integral part of Community law' and that 'such cooperation between the Member States and the rules relating thereto do not have their legal basis in the Treaties establishing the European Communities and are not part of the law created by the Communities and derived from the Treaties'.[163]

This confirmed to the somewhat awkward situation that an institution so closely connected to the EU, in several ways, was yet not part of it. Some openly criticized this state of affairs. The European Parliament, for instance, expressed its disappointment in a resolution, opining that the European schools should have (had) a place within the Community framework.[164] According to the Parliament it was to be regretted that the project had been implemented by means of intergovernmental cooperation outside the EC.[165] Years later, however, an MEP rapporteur voiced quite a different opinion, in a report on the Proposal for a new Convention defining the statute of the European Schools. The rapporteur in question, A. Oostlander, pushed for the schools to either be closed down, or to be integrated into the education system of the respective host country.[166] He expressed criticism against the different treatment of the migrant group of children of EU workers, vis-à-vis other migrant groups. But it has been suggested that the real root of his opposition against the schools was his objection against the penetration of national education systems by the EU's educational principles as the way forward.[167] It actually resulted in the European Parliament blocking the budget for the European Schools, but eventually the Commission simply circumvented the Parliament, as the latter did not have budgetary powers in relation to the Schools anyway. The criticism of the Parliament, which stands in such stark contrast with the attitude expressed some thirty years before, was not very effective, in the sense that in the same year, the projected Convention Defining the Statute of the European Schools was adopted nevertheless.[168] The Convention was a response to the call for a new Convention by the Council and the Ministers of Education meeting within the Council, aiming to enhance the efficiency to the operation of the Schools and, remarkably, with a view to a 'greater recognition to the role played by the Community therein'. Although the preamble stressed that 'the European School system is "*sui generis*"; considering that it constitutes a form of cooperation between the Member States and between them and the European Communities', the Convention increased EU involvement to a considerable extent, with a Commission representative taking seat in the Board of Governors and the Administrative Board of each School. The Schools are now part of the European institutional framework in a remarkable fashion, as the

163. Case 44/84, *Derrick Guy Edmund Hurd v. Kenneth Jones (Her Majesty's Inspector of Taxes)* [1986] ECR 29, paras 20 and 37.
164. European Parliament, *Resolution of the European Schools*, OJ 1983 C 242, 81.
165. *Ibid.*
166. Oostlander Report 1993.
167. Finaldi-Baratieri, 2000, 12.
168. *Convention Defining the Statute of the European Schools*, OJ 1994 L 212, 3–14.

Convention became a 'mixed' agreement between all the Member States and the 'three Communities'.[169]

3.3.3. Intergovernmental Cooperation within the Council

In addition to these two projects outside, or on the borders, of the EU framework, there has been quite some intergovernmental cooperation within the institutional structures of the Union, but with a semi-EU status. In 1969, the European Parliament called for the Europeanization of universities as the foundation of a genuine cultural Community.[170] Two years later, on 16 November 1971, the Ministers for Education meeting within the Council spoke of the matter of educational cooperation for the first time within a (semi)-Community context.[171] The careful tone and careful method, adopting the Resolution not as the Council but as the ministers meeting within the Council, indicate that they felt they were not on firm ground. The word 'cooperation' was central to this first Resolution in educational matters, which furthermore set up a Working Party to explore whether there was room to create a European Centre for the Development of Education.[172] Almost three years later, the Ministers for Education returned to the subject, and the resulting resolution was in fact more resolute in tone and content, but still in this curious form of meeting within the Council, and not as the Council.[173] The Ministers confirmed 'the need to institute European cooperation in the field of education and their determination to achieve that cooperation by progressive stages' and established a few general principles for such cooperation:

(i) the programme of cooperation initiated in the field of education, whilst reflecting the progressive harmonization of the economic and social policies in the Community, must be adapted to the specific objectives and requirements of this field;
(ii) on no account must education be regarded merely as a component of economic life;
(iii) educational cooperation must make allowance for the traditions of each country and the diversity of their respective educational policies and systems.

169. De Witte 2001, 102.
170. See Pépin 2007, 123.
171. *Resolution of the Ministers for Education meeting within the Council of 16 November 1971 on cooperation in the field of education*, not published.
172. In 1975, the Council indeed set up the CEDEFOP, the European Centre for the Development of Vocational Training, by means of a Regulation, which it had contemplated in 1971, by means of *Council Regulation 1365/75*, OJ 1975 L 139, 1. The fact that the Centre was set up by means of a Regulation shows that the intergovernmental resolutions of the Ministers meeting within the Council can certainly lead to the adoption of binding legal acts within the Community framework. It is also noteworthy that the legal basis for the Regulation was Art. 235 of the EEC Treaty, rather than Art. 128 EEC. See Shaw 192, 420.
173. *Resolution of the Ministers for Education meeting within the Council of 6 June 1974 on cooperation in the field of education*, OJ 1974 C 98, 20.

Harmonization of these systems of policies cannot, therefore, be considered an end in itself.

The latter statement is important for several reasons. On the one hand, it shows that the Member States perceived education as an area where national diversity and state autonomy had to prevail and be accommodated. At the same time, it illustrates that the Member States were open to the idea of legal harmonization in the area of education, just not as an end in itself. This is logical if one realizes that on the very same day, the Council (proper) issued a Resolution on the mutual recognition of diplomas, certificates and other evidence of formal qualifications, in reference to the draft Directives on the mutual recognition of diplomas.[174] In February 1976, the Council decided on an Action Programme, this time adopted on the basis of a 'Resolution of the Council and of the Ministers for Education meeting within the Council'.[175] According to some, this was a formula 'unique in the machinery of the Community, for it combines the classical institutional machinery and procedures of the Council of the European Community with a voluntary commitment of the education ministers of the Nine to work together on a continuous basis outside the legal framework of the Council'.[176]

The mixed formula is one step closer to the EU compared to the 'Resolutions of the Ministers for Education Meeting within the Council', but still outside the official legal framework. This 'legal hybrid' could be considered as a reflection of the political controversy as to the proper allocation of powers in the field of education, or merely as a consequence of the absence of strong legislative competence in the area.[177] It had already been used in other areas, such as culture, public health and justice, which pose similar questions on legal competence.[178] The Action Programme declared the following goals:

(1) Better facilities for the education and training of nationals and the children of nationals of other Member States of the Communities and of non-member countries.
(2) Promotion of closer relations between educational systems in Europe.
(3) Compilation of the up-to-date documentation and statistics on education.
(4) Cooperation in the field of higher education.
(5) Teaching of foreign languages.

---

174. *Council Resolution of 6 June 1974 on the mutual recognition of diplomas, certificates and other evidence of formal qualifications*, OJ 1974 C 98, 20. The Council formulated a guideline for future work in the area: 'Given that, despite the differences existing between one Member State and another in training courses, the final qualifications giving access to similar fields of activity are in practice broadly comparable, directives on the mutual recognition of professional qualifications and on the coordination of the conditions of access to the professions should resort as little as possible to the prescription of detailed training requirements.'
175. *Resolution of the Council and of the Ministers for Education meeting within the Council of 9 February 1976 comprising an action programme in the field of education*, OJ 1976 C 38, 19.
176. Jones 1978, Pépin 2007, 123.
177. De Witte 1987, 274. See also Shaw 1992, 420.
178. Van Crayenest 1989, 127.

(6) Achievement of equal opportunity for free access to all forms of education.

The Resolution specified in relation to each aim what action/which measures were to be implemented 'at the Community level'. Over the years, the Resolution has remained a reliable asset for the Council in the formulation of educational policy goals. The mixed formula is still in use,[179] in tandem with the 'normal' Council Resolution.[180]

4. CONCLUSIONS

Seen in this light, the fact that the Bologna Process takes place outside the EU framework might not seem so surprising. Over the years, there have been several instances of large projects closely related to EU matters being implemented outside its legal framework. But did things not change since the time of the creation of the European Schools and the European University Institute? Back then, there was perhaps no solid ground for the adoption of such initiatives within the Community framework. EC competence in educational matters was indeed shaky and European integration generally much less advanced. And note that even back then the adoption of the Schools and the University Institute outside the Community framework was controversial. Now, more than thirty years later, the competence and influence of the EU in (higher) education has greatly increased and developed. As we have seen, in 1994 the position of the European Schools within the Union context was solidified by means of a new Convention. More recently the EU has created a European Institute of Innovation and Technology. The Institute was officially established by means of a Directive, without any real controversy surrounding its EU status. Additionally, student and teacher mobility and diploma recognition constitute well-established areas of European law, where extensive legislation and a firm body of case law constitute a dense and elaborate corpus legis. Thus it is remarkable that the Bologna Process, which deals with exactly these matters, was implemented outside the EU framework.

The competing forces in European higher education are strong. This helps to explain the continuous use of soft law and intergovernmental cooperation in this field, both within and outside EU structures. The Bologna Process is the most important and recent example of such cooperation outside the EU. Whether it

179. See, for example, the *Resolution of the Council and of the representatives of the Governments of the Member States, meeting within the Council regarding the framework of European cooperation in the youth field of 27 June 2002*, OJ 2002 C 168, 2. Interestingly, the mixed formula is – on occasion – also used in the context of Council Conclusions. The *Conclusions of the Council and of the Representatives of the Governments of the Member States, meeting within the Council of 22 May 2008 on promoting creativity and innovation through education and training*, OJ 2008 C 141, 17–20, constitute a recent example thereof.

180. See *Council Resolution of 25 November 2003 on making school an open learning environment to prevent and combat early school leaving and disaffection among young people and to encourage their social inclusion*, OJ 2003 C 295, 3–4.

was a strategic move or not, perhaps responding to the increasing influence of the Union in educational matters particularly through the case law of the ECJ, with the Bologna Process the Member States have certainly sidelined the EU in more than only a symbolic way. On top of keeping a final say in everything, even maintaining the possibility to – at any point they deem fit – disembark the whole project, the Member States also get some necessary European-level coordination done, and they get to pursue their own agenda. It is not difficult to see why, at least for the governments and governmental officials involved, this intergovernmental course of proceedings was more beneficial than operating within the EU framework, as they can now have their cake and eat it too. A valid question that can be posed is why the Member States do not do the same thing in other policy areas. The answer is most probably related to the fact that in education they can hide behind both the longstanding tradition of non-EU intergovernmental cooperation and the almost commonly accepted fallacy that the EU lacks sufficient competence in this area to run a Bologna-like project. Furthermore, it could be hypothesized that Member States cling more fervently to their sovereignty in education, because they feel it is one of the last bastions of Member State autonomy, with almost all other policy areas having been 'invaded' by the EU by now.

In any event, the tug of war between the EU and its Member States has led to the fact that the Process is now located in a grey zone, between the EU and the intergovernmental level. The following chapter delves into the overlap and interaction between the EU and the Bologna Process. This analysis will benefit the argument in Chapter 6 that the EU in fact possessed sufficient legislative competence to enact the content of Bologna as a binding measure. Apparently, the tug of war still continues, and with the Bologna Process the Member States appear to have won the most recent game. But whether they have played it by the rules is open for discussion.

Chapter 4

EU Higher Education Law II: The Case Law of the ECJ

1. INTRODUCTION

The role of the ECJ in the development of EU involvement in higher education can hardly be overestimated. Its dynamic and expansive interpretations of the Treaty, in terms of the competences that the latter attributes and the fundamental free movement rights it affords, have without a doubt contributed to a large extent to the substantial body of EU education law and policy that we have explored in the previous chapter. As a result of infringement proceedings brought by the European Commission as well as cases brought by individuals through the preliminary reference procedure, the ECJ has on countless occasions over the years been put in the difficult position to act as a referee in the power struggle between the EU and its Member States. Weighing the common EU interest against the national interests of the Member States in educational matters is not an easy task. On the one hand, Article 165 TFEU clearly lays down the principle of national educational autonomy, and reserves the power to organize and determine the content of educational courses for the Member States. On the other hand, the EU interest is often, at least in the long run, supposed to be also the interest of the Member States, and the cases do not always involve a simple balancing of an economic EU interest against a socio-cultural national interest. Another complicating factor is that many of the cases involve a 'sympathetic applicant': an individual European citizen who is denied access to education or financial support by a Member State for reason of not having the nationality of that state. Apart from the economic EU interest of a completed internal market, the personal interest of a European citizen is at stake in such a situation.

As we shall come to see, the Court has tried to strike a balance between these various competing interests by applying the formula that education, especially in its economically relevant capacity, is not an area excluded from the scope of application of EU law, whilst recognizing that certain educational objectives can trump the application of the internal market provisions. This means, for example, that the freedom of establishment is applicable to privately funded educational institutions when they provide educational services abroad, but that a Member State can subject these institutions to a quality review procedure before they enter the 'education market' for the purposes of maintaining a high level of quality in education. Although the theoretical merits of this approach can be defended, the Court has often been criticized for an overly expansive application of the first part of the formula, while being excessively restrictive in the context of the second part. Indeed, there is hardly a situation that has come before the Court that was not deemed to fall within the scope of the Treaty. And the two most notable exceptions, publicly funded education and maintenance grants, seem to have narrowed over the years. As to the application of the second 'justification' part of the formula, it seems that although the Court is relatively generous in recognizing in principle the possibility of a certain national educational interest as objective justifications for non-discriminatory measures that nonetheless hinder the exercise of the fundamental freedom in question, it will give preference to an EU educational objective in case of a conflict. Moreover, the thorough application of the proportionality test has on many occasions prevented the Member States from successfully invoking justification grounds in practice, although they were accepted in principle, because the measures in question were found to fail the proportionality test. This strengthens the impression that the Court operates with a fundamental pro-integration bias. Accordingly, several authors and politicians have qualified the Court's approach as overly intrusive and at odds with the educational autonomy paradigm of Article 165 TFEU.

In any event, the judgments of the Court show how closely related the internal market and higher education can be, and how the national education sectors can be deeply affected by EU law. Indeed, it is without question that the EU has a great impact on the educational systems of its Member States and the daily life of the individuals participating therein. Imagine your average classroom. There is a teacher, who, as we shall come to see, qualifies as a worker in the sense of EU law. There is a pupil or a student too. He or she benefits from the right to equal treatment on the basis of either his or her worker status, the fact that he or she is a child of a migrant worker, or simply as a European citizen. The teaching activity can constitute a service within the meaning of the Treaty. Accordingly, the school itself might be able to rely on the freedom to provide services or the freedom of establishment. This chapter shall explore the scope of this impact, focusing on the most recent developments in the area. Apart from the fact that the ECJ's case law and its underlying approach is a fascinatingly interesting issue by and of itself, it is also of specific importance in the context of some of the main underlying questions of this book. It is important in order to determine the extent of overlap between EU competence and involvement and the activities undertaken in the context of the Bologna Process. Furthermore, if it is found that the ECJ by means of its case law indeed increasingly erodes educational autonomy, this might help explain the

Member States' decision to create the Bologna Process outside the EU framework, beyond the reach of the activist judgments of the Court. Another question is then whether the European Court has good reasons to proceed in this manner, pushing (educational) integration, or whether it is overstepping the boundaries.

2. EDUCATION, THE INTERNAL MARKET AND EUROPEAN CITIZENSHIP

2.1. Teachers: Free Movement of Workers

A teacher, as he or she 'performs services of some economic value for and under the direction of another person in return for which he receives remuneration', qualifies as a 'worker' within the meaning of Article 45 TFEU (ex Article 39 EC) and therefore cannot be discriminated on grounds of nationality 'as regards employment, remuneration and other conditions of work and employment'.[1] The ECJ has confirmed in numerous cases that the teaching profession does not fall within the restrictively interpreted public service exception of Article 45(4) TFEU, even though teachers might have to take decisions as prescribed by national public law, such as awarding marks and deciding whether a pupil can move to a higher class. It does not matter whether it concerns a secondary school teacher,[2] a foreign language assistant at a university,[3] a university teacher[4] or even a trainee teacher,[5] for, in principle, they are all entitled to benefit from the rights attached to worker status. However, the ECJ has allowed an important and well-known justification in the *Groener* case,[6] where it let a Member State's cultural interest prevail over a teacher's fundamental right of free movement. A Dutch art teacher was refused a permanent post at a design school in Dublin because she did not possess sufficient knowledge of Gaelic. Such a language requirement obviously constituted indirect discrimination, caught by Article 39 EC (now Article 45 TFEU). Although Anita Groener did not need Gaelic for her job, as it was taught exclusively in English, the Irish government argued that the language requirement was justified 'by reason of the nature of the post to be fulfilled' within in the sense of Article 3 of Regulation 1612/68. According to the Irish government, it was justified to require teachers to have some level of knowledge of Gaelic as part of their function, as teachers had a special position in the implementation of such a culturally sensitive language policy. Somewhat surprisingly, the Court indeed

1. Case 66/85, *Lawrie-Blum v. Land Baden-Wuertemberg* [1986] ECR 2121. See on this topic in general Handoll 1989.
2. Case C-4/91, *Annegret Bleis v. Ministère de l'Education Nationale* [1991] ECR I-5627.
3. Case 33/88, *Pilar Allué and Carmel Mary Coonan v. Università degli studi di Venezia* [1989] ECR 1591.
4. Case C-290/94, *Commission v. Greece* [1996] ECR I-3285.
5. Case 66/85, *Lawrie-Blum v. Land Baden-Wuertemberg* [1986] ECR 2121.
6. Case C-379/87, *Anita Groener v. Minister for Education and the City of Dublin Vocational Educational Committee* [1989] ECR 3967.

recognized the arguments of the Irish government as an objective justification, stating:

> the importance of education for the implementation of such a policy must be recognized. Teachers have an essential role to play, not only through the teaching which they provide but also by their participation in the daily life of the school and the privileged relationship which they have with their pupils. In those circumstances, it is not unreasonable to require them to have some knowledge of the first national language.[7]

Although the case arguably also has to be seen in the light of the particularly sensitive issue of minority language, it does show that the ECJ is not wholly unresponsive to the sovereignty claims made by the Member States when it comes to the socio-cultural function of education. Nevertheless, as even also the *Groener* case illustrates, the general rule remains that teachers constitute workers in the same sense as anyone else engaged in economic activity, and that they dispose of free movement and benefits all the same.

2.2. Free Movement of Services and Freedom of Establishment

Also, educational institutions can derive rights from EU law.[8] Under certain conditions, the institution can qualify as a service provider within the meaning of Article 56 TFEU (ex Article 49 EC), and it also benefits from the freedom of establishment as provided by Article 49 TFEU (ex Article 43 EC). This allows foreign educational institutions to penetrate the 'education market' of other Member States, by offering courses, concluding cooperation agreements with national institutions, by opening subsidiaries and in many other ways. This might cause concerns of governmental control on the organization, content and quality of the higher education offered on their territory, and potentially stands in tense relation with Article 165(1) TFEU. The finding that education, albeit under conditions, can qualify as a service within the definition of Article 56 TFEU also has consequences for the legal qualification of pupils and students, as they become recipients of services and therefore potentially strengthen their rights under the Treaty, especially with regard to claims of equal (financial) treatment. This particular dimension of educational services will be discussed in the following section dealing with student mobility.

2.2.1. Freedom of Establishment: The *Neri* Case

The *Neri* case[9] is important and interesting for several reasons. It does not only show how educational institutions may benefit from the free movement of

7. Paragraph 20 of the judgment.
8. See on this topic in general: Skouris 1989.
9. Case C-153/02, *Valentina Neri v. European School of Economics* [2003] I-13555.

establishment provisions of the Treaty, but also how the non-recognition of diplomas – for academic purposes – can be construed as a restriction of the freedom of establishment. The latter is an important finding, and we will come back to it further below. Ms Neri, an Italian national, enrolled at Nottingham Trent University (NTU) with a view to acquiring a degree in International Political Studies. Apart from administering its courses of study at its establishment in the UK, NTU also made use of the option provided by Article 216 of the UK Education Reform Act 1988, which provided for another system by means of which universities could award degrees. Under this provision, the Secretary of State approved a list of bodies that could provide any course in preparation for a degree to be granted by a recognized body and approved by or on behalf of the recognized body. This list included the European School of Economics (ESE). ESE was a Higher Education College authorized according to the UK educational system to organize and provide the university courses of study approved by NTU. ESE did not award its own degrees but organized courses for the students enrolled with NTU, which then awarded a final degree of Bachelor of Arts with Honours. The quality of the courses of study provided by ESE was also subject to audit by the UK Quality Assurance Agency for Higher Education. ESE was established in the UK with a number of secondary establishments in other Member States, such as a branch in Genoa, Italy.

Ms Neri decided to stay in Italy and to attend university courses at ESE. Having enrolled for the first year and after paying the enrolment fee, she learned that ESE was not authorized to organize university-level courses and that recognition could not be granted to the university's degrees if they had been obtained on the basis of periods of study completed in Italy. Ms Neri claimed that she had made an undue payment. The national Court referred a preliminary question to the ECJ on the interpretation of Article 43 EC (now Article 49 TFEU). The ECJ ruled that the:

> organisation for remuneration of university courses is an economic activity falling within the chapter of the Treaty dealing with the right of establishment when that activity is carried on by a national of one Member State in another Member State on a stable and continuous basis from a principal or secondary establishment in the latter Member State.

The ECJ reiterated that Article 43 EC (now Article 49 TFEU) prohibited all measures that impeded or rendered less attractive the exercise of the freedom of establishment. The Court considered that for an institution like ESE, which organized courses intended to enable its students to obtain degrees capable of facilitating their access to the employment market, the recognition of those degrees by the authorities of a Member State was of considerable importance. It was clear that the administrative practice was likely to deter students from attending these courses, as was illustrated by Ms Neri herself, and thus seriously hindered the pursuit by ESE of its economic activity in Italy. The restriction of Article 43 EC (now Article 49 TFEU) was thereby established.

The Italian Government invoked the need to ensure high standards of university education. Italy maintained that the Italian legal order did not accept agreements such as the one at issue in the main proceedings since it remained attached to a view of such education as a matter of public interest, expressing the cultural and historical values of the State. According to the Italian Government, such an agreement on university education as in the underlying case prevented quality control. The Court considered that although the aim of ensuring high standards of university education was legitimate to justify restrictions on fundamental freedoms, the restrictions failed the proportionality test. Given that the Italian legal order did allow agreements between Italian universities and other Italian establishments of higher education which were comparable to the agreement entered into between NTU and ESE, and the non-recognition of degrees awarded in circumstances like those at issue in the main proceedings related solely to degrees awarded to Italian nationals, the European Court regarded the practice unsuitable for attaining the objective. The Court continued that in any event, it went further than necessary by precluding any examination by the national authorities and, consequently, any possibility of recognition.

The judgment goes to show how intrusive the 'normal' application of the internal market freedoms in the area of education can be. Although the Court recognized the need for quality control as a matter of principle, it was quite rigorous in application of the proportionality test. On the one hand, this is difficult to reconcile with the autonomy principle laid down in Article 165 TFEU. On the other hand, it could be argued that the judgment does not require the Italian government to recognize any diploma awarded by an educational institution recognized in another Member State when offering its courses on Italian territory, but rather that it requires a fair assessment of the diploma in question before either recognizing or rejecting it. This appears to be consistent with the Courts general approach in the area of diploma recognition, as we shall come to see further below, as well as with the requirements of the Lisbon Recognition Convention of the Council of Europe. In that sense, the Member States' autonomy is indeed restricted, in that it is called upon to account for its policy choices, but arguably for good reason. The EU interest requires an extensive interpretation and application of the fundamental freedoms. The Court does recognize the competing Member State interest in maintaining quality control and has this interest even triumph in the end by recognizing it as a legitimate interest that justifies a restriction of Article 49 TFEU, provided that the restriction is really about securing that interest and is part of a nuanced and well-reasoned policy. This is, one could say, the compromise between the internal market objectives and the educational autonomy paradigm of Article 165 TFEU at work.

2.2.2. Services: The *Schwarz* Case

In 1988, the ECJ was called upon to determine whether courses taught in a technical institute which formed part of the secondary education provided under the national education system were to be regarded as services for the purposes of

Article 59 of the EEC Treaty (now Article 56 TFEU), in the *Humbel and Edel* case.[10] The ECJ stated that the essential characteristic of remuneration was absent in the case of courses provided under the national education system, since the State, in establishing and maintaining such a system, was not seeking to engage in gainful activity but is fulfilling its duties towards its own population in the social, cultural and educational fields and because the system in question was, as a general rule, funded from the public purse and not by pupils or their parents. Five years later, however, the Court indicated that this would not necessarily be the case for all kinds of education. In the *Wirth* judgment, concerning a higher education institution primarily financed out of public funds, the Court maintained its previous *Humbel and Edel* reasoning, but qualified it to an important extent, by stating that the courses of higher education institutions financed essentially out of private funds, in particular by students or their parents, with a view to make an economic profit, would be considered to be services within the meaning of the Treaty.[11] This was subsequently confirmed in the *Schwarz* case.[12]

At issue in the latter case was the refusal by the German government to grant a tax relief to parents of school-going children on the ground that the private school attended was established in another Member State. According to the parents, Mr and Mrs Schwarz, such a refusal was contrary to the principle of the freedom to provide services, since, first, foreign private schools wishing to offer their services to the children of German taxpayers were hindered in their offer, and, secondly, German taxpayers who envisaged enrolling their children in a private school established in another Member State were deterred from doing so. In answering the question whether the circumstances of the case fell within the scope of Article 56 TFEU, the Court stressed that the essential characteristic of remuneration was that it constituted consideration for the service in question. Therefore, the Court had in previous judgments[13] 'excluded from the definition of services within the meaning of Article 50 EC courses offered by certain establishments forming part of a system of public education and financed, entirely or mainly, by public funds'.[14] However, the situation in the case at hand was different, according to the Court. The ECJ had already held before that courses given by educational establishments essentially financed by private funds, notably by students and their parents, could constitute services within the meaning of the Treaty, since the aim of those establishments was to offer a service for remuneration.[15] Therefore, the Court held Article 49 EC (now Article 56 TFEU) to be applicable in the situation at hand, where taxpayers of a given Member State sent their children to a private school established in another Member State which could be regarded 'as providing

10. Case 263/86, *Belgian State v. René Humbel and Marie-Thérèse Edel* [1988] ECR 05365.
11. Case C-109/92, *Stephan Max Wirth v. Landeshauptstadt Hannover* [1993] ECR I-06447.
12. Case C-76/05, *Schwarz and Gootjes-Schwarz v. Finanzamt Bergisch Gladbach* [2007] ECR I-6849.
13. Case 263/86, *Humbel and Edel* [1988] ECR 5365.
14. Paragraph 39 of the judgment.
15. Case C-109/92, *Wirth* [1993] ECR I-6447.

services for remuneration, that is to say which is essentially financed by private funds', which was for the national court to verify.[16]

It is clear that the decisive criteria for assuming that education services are provided for remuneration, triggering the application of Article 56 TFEU, are (1) the private financing of a school, to cover a large proportion of its costs; and (2) its intention to make an economic profit.[17] For now, it is clear that publicly funded education, which by its nature does not fulfil those conditions, remains excluded from the scope of application of Article 56 TFEU. The reason for that is, according to the ECJ, that:

> with the establishment and maintenance of a system of public education, normally financed from the public purse and not by pupils or their parents, the state does not intend to become involved in activities for remuneration, but carries out its task towards its population in the social, cultural and educational fields.[18]

It was in fact Advocate General Slynn in his opinion to *Gravier* who introduced the distinction between publicly funded and privately funded education.[19] He had argued that because privately funded education was usually provided by institutions with a view to making a profit, their educational services would normally fall within the scope of the Treaty. The situation, according to him, was different when it concerned public education as the fees had little or no relation to the actual cost of the education provided. State education, being funded by the general budget, did not meet the definition of a service. Indeed, the Court took this onboard in *Humbel* and *Wirth* and further endorsed it in *Schwarz*. Although the reasoning might hold in theory, it is somewhat more difficult to apply it in practice. The reality of the educational sector, often involving both private and public funding, is too complex to be simply subdivided into these two categories, and it is not exactly clear where the Court draws the line. At the same time the legal situation attached to the two categories differs enormously, for if the establishment (or part of its courses?) can be qualified as private, a whole set of EU law suddenly applies. If also applied to other kinds of financial benefits, such as study funding, this approach might, as Dougan puts it, 'have the effect of diverting Member State resources away from financial support for public sector education (within the domestic territory) towards private sector establishments (in other countries) – amounting in effect to a form of EU-led contracting out-cum-outsourcing'.[20]

A last recent case involving the service provisions of the Treaty being applied in an education context that deserves to be mentioned is the *Jundt* case.[21] The ECJ

16. See also Case C-281/06, *Jundt v. Finanzambt* [2007] ECR I-0000, as discussed in s. 2 of this chapter.
17. Paragraph 35 of the Opinion of Advocate General Stix-Hackl of 21 Sep. 2006 in Case C-76/05, *Schwarz and Gootjes-Schwarz v. Finanzamt Bergisch Gladbach* [2007] ECR I-6849.
18. Paragraph 30 of the ruling.
19. The ECJ did not deal with the service argument in Gravier.
20. Dougan 2005, 979.
21. Case C-281/06, *Jundt v. Finanzambt* [2007] ECR I-0000.

condemned another German law, this time denying a German national a tax concession for university teaching, because the teaching took place in another Member State. This means that the service in question was that of the teacher to a school rather than, as was the situation in the previous cases, by a school to a student and his or her parents. The German law was indeed held to be a restriction of the freedom to provide services as laid down in Article 49 EC (now Article 56 TFEU). Most interestingly, in answering the question whether this restriction could be justified, the Court used the objectives of Article 149(2) EC (now Article 165(2) TFEU), in particular the promotion of teacher and student mobility, to reject the argument of the German Government that the national legislation was justified by the promotion of teaching, research and development as an overriding reason in the public interest. Thereby the ECJ used Article 149 EC as an interpretation tool, somewhat broadening the scope of the service provisions. In weighing the interest of the German government in shaping its educational policy against the EU educational objectives (of teacher mobility), the Court gave full preference to the latter.

2.3. Students

Also, students as such are subjects of European education law, enjoying the right to freedom of movement and equal treatment, sometimes derived from their worker status, sometimes being children of migrant workers and sometimes simply by virtue of their studies, preparing them to be a worker, strengthened by their European citizenship. The fact that children of migrant workers qualify for equal treatment regarding education was a breakthrough development at the time, but seems rather uncontroversial now. Article 12 of Regulation 1612/68 provides that 'the children of a national of a Member State, who is or has been employed in the territory of another Member State, shall be admitted to courses of general education, apprenticeship and vocational training under the same conditions as the nationals of that State, if those children reside in its territory'. Being the least controversial beneficiaries of educational rights in the student category, the ECJ has, as Craig and De Búrca note, been very generous in its interpretation of this provision, in the kinds of education courses it covers, in terms of the broad meaning given to the phrase 'admitted to courses', including grants and other facilitative measures, in its reading of 'children' by including non-dependents over 21, and by extending the child's right to stay in education even after the migrant parent has returned to the home state.[22] More controversial nowadays is the non-economically active student who moves to another Member States solely

22. Craig & De Búrca, 2003, 744. See most notably, Case 76/72, *Michel S. v. Fonds national de reclassement social des handicapés* [1973] ECR 00457; Case 9/74, *Donato Casagrande v. Landeshauptstadt München* [1974] ECR 00773; Case C-7/94, *Landesamt für Ausbildungsförderung Nordrhein-Westfalen v. Lubor Gaal* [1995] I-01031, and Joined Cases 389/87 and 390/87, *G. B. C. Echternach and A. Moritz v. Minister van Onderwijs en Wetenschappen* [1989] ECR 00723.

for study purposes and claims equal treatment in that capacity. Member States are hesitant in accepting their full equal treatment, which is to a certain extent understandable. The equal treatment claims of students might vary from equal access to higher education, meaning that the student demands admission and/or the same financial support as nationals of the host state in terms of enrolment fees, to equal full support claims, implying that the student asks for the same general financial benefits that the host state offers to its nationals. It could be questioned whether foreign students should receive on an equal basis all the educational facilities, services and even grants made available by the host state to its nationals. One might argue it to be unfair, and financially untenable, that foreign students can enjoy all the efforts of the educational policy of the host state, without actually having contributed to the welfare system of that state. In this context, it is often pointed out that under Article 165 TFEU, the competence of the EU in education is complementary and that the Member States remain competent in the organization and content of their education systems. To require equal treatment of EC students might seem at odds with this national educational autonomy paradigm. Furthermore, there is no specific provision in the Treaty that explicitly lays down the equal treatment of non-economically active students.

The reasons why it is in the common interest of the Member States, and hence the EU, to support student mobility are eloquently set out by Advocate General Jacobs, in his Opinion to the *Austrian Education* case.[23] He firstly justifies the applicability of the Treaty to non-economically active students by pointing out that 'it is only to the extent that the chosen courses prepare the students to enter the employment market that they come within the scope of the Treaty'. Then he describes the students who move 'because of the excellence of the studies offered in other Member States and/or because those studies abroad are better adapted to their professional ambitions or talents'. These students have an improved potential for professional mobility within the EU, and they are more likely to act on that potential, 'spending a part or all of their professional lives in a country other than their country of origin, with all the economic, social and cultural consequences which that entails'. According to the Advocate General, 'they thus become crucial actors in disseminating and spreading their acquired knowledge throughout the EU, in contributing to the integration of the European employment market and, ultimately, when assessed in the light of the goals inspiring the EC Treaty, in promoting the 'ever closer union'. He argues that these students merit the public investment the host state has made in their education, in that 'they provide a return to the host State, either directly, because the students subsequently enter its employment market, or indirectly, because of the benefits arising to the EU as a whole'.[24] Note, however, that also the Advocate General recognizes that certain

23. Opinion of Advocate General Jacobs delivered on 20 Jan. 2005 in Case C-147/03, *Commission v. Austria* [2005] ECR I-5969.
24. The foregoing line of argument has been supported by other Advocates General at the ECJ, most notably by Advocate General Geelhoed in his Opinion to the Bidar case, and most recently by Advocate General Sharpston in the follow-up of the Belgian Education Case, Chaverot,

pitfalls do exist, in relation to a second category of mobile students, sometimes referred to as 'free-riders', which 'seek access to more liberal neighbouring education systems in order to escape restrictions in their Member State of origin'. The fact that these students often intend to return to their home state after their studies reduces the chance of direct payback to the host state. They, however, should still benefit from the rights provided by the Treaty in the same manner, according to the Advocate General.

2.3.1. Equal Access

The conclusion that could be drawn from the foregoing passage is that student mobility is generally beneficial for the entire EU, some free-riding concerns notwithstanding. Perhaps with that picture in mind, the ECJ has been active and forceful in developing rights of equal access to vocational/higher/university education for students.[25] In an interesting and judicially activist line of case law, the ECJ developed educational rights on the basis of Articles 7 and 128 of the EC Treaty (now Articles 18 and 166 TFEU, ex Articles 12 and 150 EC). It is important to keep in mind that most educational rights as developed by the Court find their origin in the provision on vocational training. The well-known line of case law commences in 1983, with the *Forcheri* case.[26] The non-discrimination principle as laid down in Article 18 TFEU (then Article 7 EC), read in conjunction with Article 166 TFEU (then Article 128 EC), allowed the Italian spouse of a migrant worker in Belgium access to a vocational training course on the same financial terms as nationals. The ECJ did recognize the fact that educational and vocational policies were not as such part of the areas of EU competence, but stated that nonetheless the opportunity for such kinds of instruction fell within the scope of the Treaty and thereby within the scope of Article 12 EC (now Article 18 TFEU). The ECJ built on this case law in the *Gravier* case,[27] where another discriminatory enrolment fee was found contrary to the Treaty. The fundamental difference with the *Forcheri* case was that the French student challenging the fee had no family members in Belgium and thus no right of residence there, apart from her claim as a student to such a right.[28] Stunningly, this did not deter the ECJ from ruling that the

Bressol & others. She stated: 'I likewise share the views expressed by Advocates General Jacobs and Geelhoed that whilst students may not contribute directly to the tax system of the State in which they pursue their university studies, they are a source of income for local economies where the university is located, and also, to a limited extent, for the national treasuries via indirect taxes. Taken to its logical conclusion, the argument that only those who have contributed through taxes should be allowed to benefit from State-financed benefits would bar a Member State's own nationals who have not so contributed, or who have done so only modestly, from claiming any such benefits.' See Opinion of Advocate General Sharpston, delivered on 25 Jun. 2009, in Case C-73/08, *Nicolas Bressol and Others and Céline Chaverot and Others v. Gouvernement de la Communauté française*, para. 96.

25. See Lonbay 2004, 257.
26. Case 152/82, *Forcheri* [1983] ECR 2323.
27. Case 293/83, *Gravier* [1985] ECR 593.
28. Craig & De Búrca, 2003, 746.

fee in question constituted discrimination. The Court held for the first time that a 'would-be student could claim a self-sufficient right of access to education which was not dependent on his first demonstrating that he could derive other rights from the Treaty'.[29]

The importance of the judgment can hardly be overestimated, as the Court laid down the legal foundations for a free movement of students within the EU.[30] In supporting its landmark decision that conditions of access to vocational training fell within the scope of the Treaty for the purposes of the principle of non-discrimination, the Court referred to a number of soft law instruments by the Council and the Ministers of Education meeting within the Council.[31] As Van der Mei notes, the fact that the Member States were adopting these soft law measures indicated that they did not intend to transfer to the EU the powers to grant or refuse non-nationals access to their education systems.[32] It was therefore remarkable that the Court took these measures as evidence that a vocational policy was being established and that it was suitable to deduct from this a general right of EU-wide access to education for all students. And if this was already far-reaching, the Court in addition stretched the interpretation of 'vocational training', stating it could also include an element of 'general education'. This latter point was subsequently further developed in the *Blaizot* case,[33] clarifying that also university education could qualify as vocational training, as long as the course was intended to prepare the student for an occupation. In the subsequent *Raulin* case,[34] the principle of non-discrimination deriving from Articles 7 and 128 EC was interpreted to mean that an EC national admitted to a vocational training course in another Member State must have a right of residence in that state for the duration of the course. The *Raulin* case anticipated the student's right of residence as laid down in Directive 90/366, which subsequently became Directive 93/96, and which has now been substituted by Directive 2004/38.[35] This is, in a nutshell, how the ECJ in quite a bold manner created a right for EU citizens to live and study in other Member States, under the same conditions of access as national students.

In this endeavour, the Court is not alone. The Court is dependent on, as well as bound to, the cases that come before it. Traditionally, higher education has been an

29. Flynn 1989, 95.
30. Van der Mei 2003, 398.
31. *Council Decision No 63/266/EEC of 2 April 1963*, OJ English Special Editon, 1963–1964, 25, *General Guidelines which the Council laid down in 1971 for drawing up a Community Programme on vocational training*, OJ English Special Ed, Second Series IX, 50, *Resolution of the Council and of the Ministers for Education meeting within the Council of 13 December 1976 concerning measures to be taken to improve the preparation of young people for work and to facilitate their transition from education to working life*, OJ 1976 C 308, 1, *Council Resolution of 11 July 1983 concerning Vocational Training Policies in the European Community in the 1980s,* OJ 1983 C 193, 2. See paras 21 and 22 of the judgment.
32. Van der Mei 2003, 373.
33. Case 24/86, *Blaizot v. University of Liege* [1988] ECR 379.
34. Case C-85/89, *Raulin* [1992] ECR I-1027.
35. OJ 1993 L 317, 59. See Craig & De Búrca 2003, 748.

area of private enforcement; that is, individuals bringing a case in their national court, invoking European law. As Shaw notes:

> the evolution of the interpretation of Article 128 EEC by the European Court was triggered not by the actions of the Commission in pursuing Member States for alleged treaty violations under its enforcement powers in Article 169 EEC, but by the actions of students moving to study and objecting to the unfairness of being charged fees which nationals were not charged.[36]

Certainly, the area of education still constitutes a prime example of the effectiveness of bottom-up enforcement of European law, by means of the preliminary reference mechanism. However, in recent years also the European Commission has taken up a very active enforcement-role in the context of higher/university education. For instance, over the past couple of years the Commission has lodged an overwhelming amount of actions against several Member States, to wit Portugal, Spain, Luxembourg, Belgium, Greece, the Czech Republic, Austria, Germany and the United Kingdom, for failure to implement or meet the obligations arising out of the European diploma recognition legislation.[37] The infringement proceedings brought against Belgium[38] and Austria[39] in 2003 are even more interesting examples of the Commission's increasing zeal in this area. Belgium and Austria are both small countries with large neighbouring countries that speak the same or a similar language, to wit France and Germany, and both had a very open and unrestricted higher education access policy in comparison with those neighbouring countries. This situation led to a high influx of French and German students into Belgium and Austria respectively, especially in the area of medical studies, which these countries sought to restrict in order to prevent the overburdening of their education systems and to prevent a shortage of medical professionals in the long run, as they expected the foreign students to return 'home' after their studies. The Commission decided to challenge the restrictive legislation, arguing it to be incompatible with European law. Instead of 'simple' enforcement in relation to non-implementation of European legislation, these actions constituted a more 'aggressive' prosecution of Member State educational policies deemed incompatible with EU educational objectives.

2.3.1.1. The Belgian/Austrian Education Saga[40]

In light of the concerns mentioned above, the French Community of Belgium had enacted legislation restricting the access of foreign EU students to its higher

36. Shaw 1992, 422.
37. Cases C-307/07, C-43/06, C-39/07, C-286/06, C-51/08, C-193/05, C-47/08, C-61/08, C-36/08, C-84/07, C-203/06, C-204/06, C-262/05, C-437/03, C-264/05, C-505/04, C-65/03 and C-147/03.
38. See Case C-65/03, *Commission v. Belgium* [2004] ECR I-6427. See Van der Mei 2003, 376.
39. Case C-147/03, *Commission of the European Communities v. Republic of Austria* [2005] ECR I-5969.
40. See Garben 2010a.

education institutions. In Article 1(b) of the Royal Decree of 20 July 1971, the conditions and procedure for granting equivalence to foreign diplomas and certificates of study were laid down, stipulating that granted equivalence was under no circumstances to have the effect 'of giving the recipient access to studies to which he does not have access in the country in which the diploma or certificate was awarded'. If the applicant in question could not prove that he or she qualified for admission in his or her country of origin, he or she had to take and pass an additional aptitude test that was not required of holders of secondary education diplomas obtained in Belgium. The Commission argued this to be an infringement of Articles 12 EC, 149 EC and 150 EC (now Articles 18, 165 and 166 TFEU). The ECJ first reiterated, as it had held in *Gravier*,[41] that access to vocational training fell within the scope of the Treaty. The Court went on to stress that Article 149(2) EC, second indent, expressly provided that Community action was to be aimed at encouraging mobility of students and teachers, *inter alia,* by encouraging the academic recognition of diplomas and periods of study. Further, Article 150(2) EC, third indent, provided that Community action aims to facilitate access to vocational training and encourage mobility of instructors and trainees and particularly young people. Thus, the Court reasoned, the first paragraph of Article 12 EC applied to the conditions set by the Member States for access to higher education. Seeing that the legislation in question placed holders of secondary education diplomas awarded in a Member State other than Belgium at a clear disadvantage (since they could not gain access to higher education organized by the French Community under the same conditions), the legislation was found to be discriminatory. Belgium did not bring forward any justification arguments and only argued that it had already remedied the infraction by the adoption of new legislation, which was true. But the application raised an important point that the Commission liked to see formally decided by the Court. The latter indeed decided the case favourably to the Commission.

One year and six days later, the Court handed down a similar judgment in relation to proceedings against Austria. Much like the Belgian legislation, Austrian law made holders of secondary education degrees acquired in other Member States, seeking access to higher education in Austria, subject to additional conditions apart from satisfying the general Austrian requirements for access to higher or university education. The additional requirement, applicable without distinction on grounds of nationality, was that these students were to prove that they met the entry conditions of the specific course they intended to follow as laid down by the Member State where the secondary education diploma was acquired. As the Austrian rules clearly put foreign EU students at a disadvantage, for a far higher percentage of nationals would have acquired their secondary education degree in Austria, it concerned a case of indirect discrimination, caught by Article 12 EC (now Article 18 TFEU). Different from the Belgian case, however, Austria did seek to justify its legislation. To that end, Austria invoked the interest in safeguarding of the homogeneity of the Austrian education system. According to the

41. Case 293/83, *Gravier v. City of Liege* [1985] ECR 593.

government, the legislation had been enacted to prevent the structural, staffing and financial problems that would result out of the excessively large number of holders of diplomas awarded in other Member States trying to attend university and higher education courses in Austria due to not being eligible for the same courses in their home state. The Advocate General pointed out that the excessive demand for access to specific courses could have been met by the adoption of specific non-discriminatory measures such as the establishment of an entry exam or the requirement of a minimum grade. The Court took this onboard, and added that Austria was not the only one to find itself in this situation, and referred to the Belgian restrictions, which had also been held incompatible with EU law. Moreover, Austria had failed to produce any real evidence that the legislation, preventive in character, was necessary and appropriate to maintain the balance of the education system. Therefore, the Austrian legislation was held incompatible with Article 12 EC (now Article 18 TFEU).

In rejecting the justification of the Austrian legislation, the judgment goes to show that the ECJ is willing to go far in enforcing the principle of equality in access to education, not afraid of the substantial impact the ruling might have on the organization of the domestic education system. The case caused considerable uproar in Austria and beyond. Chancellor Wolfgang Schüssel expressed fierce criticism directed at the Court. According to Schüssel, the Court should have borne in mind that education was a policy area reserved for the national government.[42] He told the German newspaper *Süddeutsche Zeitung*: 'In recent years [. . .] the ECJ has systematically expanded European competencies, even in areas where there is decidedly no Community law. Suddenly judgments emerge on the role of women in the German federal army, or on access of foreign students to Austrian colleges – that is, clearly national law.'[43] He was supported by other politicians, such as Danish Prime Minister Anders Fogh Rasmussen, who declared to Der Standard that: 'We all easily have the feeling that there [at the ECJ], decisions are being taken of which the basis of the judgments do not fully correspond with what we have agreed as the political basis of the development of the EU.'[44]

Contrary to the claims of the Austrian Chancellor, education is not completely shielded off from EU influence, and there certainly is EU law in the area. Article 9 TFEU requires the EU to make a contribution to education and training of quality. And not only does the EC Treaty provide for several EU competences dealing with education, such as the supportive or complementary competence of Article 165 TFEU, the legal basis of Article 53 TFEU for the adoption of legislation relating to the mutual recognition of diplomas and legal competence in the related fields of research and vocational training, the functional nature of the internal market

42. Parker 2006.
43. Interview mit dem künftigen Ratspräsidenten der EU, '300 Sprachen und 500 Dialekte – das ist mein Europa', *Süddeutsche Zeitung*, 13 Dec. 2005. See also Belien 2006.
44. The translation comes from the EUObserver.com at: <http://euobserver.com/9/20666> (by Mark Beunderman).

powers implies that education in its economically relevant capacity can and will be affected. But the question could indeed be raised whether the Court was right to declare Article 12 EC (now Article 18 TFEU) to be applicable in this situation, for although education might not in its entirety be outside the scope of the Treaty, it might be debatable whether the matter of university admissions lies within it.[45] It is submitted here that the position of the Court up to this point is defendable. It is in line with settled case law and, after all, Article 165 TFEU does explicitly mention student mobility as an area of EU competence, allowing it to judge that such matters fall within the scope of the Treaty for the purposes of Article 12 EC (now Article 18 TFEU).

However, the Court should have granted Austria more leeway. Unlike in its *Groener* judgment,[46] the Court ignored the sensitivity of the educational sector when assessing the potential justification. The Court considered that less intrusive means existed to meet the concern of excess in applications to university education, such as general entry requirements/restrictions. But the underlying aim of the Austrian government was not to restrict the overall access to higher education, which it indeed could have done by means of general entry requirements. Conversely, the Austrian policy aimed at free and unrestricted access to all levels of studies for Austrians (and other nationalities having acquired secondary school diplomas in Austria). That policy was meant to improve the percentage of Austrian citizens with a higher education qualification, which, according to the Austrian government, was amongst the lowest in the EU. Instituting general entry restrictions, equally applicable to all, would frustrate that aim. And if the conditions of access to higher education applicable in other Member States were not taken into consideration, there would be the risk of the more liberal and generous Austrian system being flooded by applications from students not admitted to higher education in more restrictive Member States. That influx would entail serious financial, structural and staffing problems and pose a risk to the financial equilibrium of the Austrian education system and, consequently, to its very existence.

The condemned Austrian law specifically intended to address the problem that a large part of the foreign students were German medical students, which would return to Germany once graduated. The Austrian government was worried that this would lead to a shortage of doctors in Austria. Perhaps these fears were ungrounded, but it could be argued that it is not for the ECJ to second-guess the national legislature in such a case. Furthermore, the law in question did not appear to be that unreasonable. German students were welcome to study medicine at Austrian universities (for free), as long as they met the conditions to be able to do so in Germany as well. That condition protected Austria from becoming the safety net for rejected German medical students. Although the general principle, it is submitted here, should be that a Member State cannot favour its nationals in

---

45. See for a strong critique of the *weak* exercise in *legal craftsmanship* of the ECJ, Hooghe 2007, 7–8.
46. Case C-379/87, *Anita Groener v. Minister for Education and the City of Dublin Vocational Educational Committee* [1989] ECR 3967.

access to education, even though they are residents of the country where the taxes are raised that finance higher education,[47] as a matter of justification, especially in the specific case where a small country with a liberal access policy is overflooded by nationals from a large neighbour with a similar language, the taxpayers argument as well as the free-rider argument should serve as a background. This would allow the Court to come to a more flexible approach to scrutinizing the justification of insufficient resources. The Court has been too insensitive and rigorous in the application of the proportionality test, thereby hollowing out the principle of Member State autonomy of Article 165(1) TFEU.

In 2006, both Austria and Belgium passed new legislation in response to the judgments. In what can be seen as a rebellion against the Court, both countries introduced quotas, Belgium for the enrolment of non-nationals and Austria for students that obtained their secondary education degree abroad. In response, the Commission contacted Austria and Belgium, 'asking them to submit their justifications for the introduction of these systems, which have discriminatory effects on other EU nationals'.[48] The Commission opined that the directly discriminatory measures in both cases appeared not to be justifiable. In January 2007, the European Commission sent Austria and Belgium letters of formal notice 'regarding restrictions of access to their higher-education systems by holders of secondary education diplomas from other Member States'.[49] The letter addressed to Austria was based on Article 228 EC (now Article 260 TFEU), relating the non-application of an ECJ ruling. Belgium on the other hand had abolished the old system that had been deemed discriminatory by the ECJ and had put in place a new one. Therefore, the infringement was deemed to be new and hence the letter of formal notice was based on Article 226 EC (now Article 258 TFEU).

Suddenly, however, ten months later the Commission officially decided to suspend the infringement cases against Austria and Belgium. On the record, it came to that conclusion on the basis of the information provided by both Member States in reaction to the formal notice. The Commission considered that there was 'prima facie evidence that without these restrictive measures, a problem could arise in the future for the Austrian health system, as a result of a potential shortage of health professionals practising in Austria' and similarly that the data provided by Belgium allowed 'the assumption of a risk that, without an appropriate safeguard measure, the French Community would be unable to maintain sufficient levels of territorial coverage and of quality in its public health system'.[50] Both countries were given five years to submit supplementary data to justify that the measures imposed are necessary and proportionate. Off the record, what actually made the

47. See Hooghe 2007, 8.
48. European Commission, Staff working document, *Annex to the 24th annual report from the Commission on monitoring the application of community law (2006) – Situation in the different sectors*, COM (2007) 398.
49. RAPID Press Release, *Free movement of students: the Commission sends letters of formal notice to Austria and Belgium*, 24 Jan. 2007, Reference: IP/07/76.
50. RAPID Press Release, *Access to higher education: the Commission suspends its infringement cases against Austria and Belgium*, 28 Nov. 2007, Reference: IP/07/1788.

Commission alter its stance was that Austria was driving a hard bargain in the context of the negotiations of the Lisbon Treaty. Austria demanded a special Treaty protocol, which would allow it to set a cap on the number of foreign university students it would take in.[51] A few days before the Lisbon summit, this was still one of the most important outstanding issues.[52]

The Commission made use of the discretion afforded to it by the Treaty and its interpretation by the ECJ, entailing that it is free to abandon the prosecution of a Member State at each moment during the course of the infringement proceedings, by making a concession to Austria at the summit of 18 and 19 October, although not in the form of an official protocol. The EU Observer reported: 'for the sake of an overall agreement, the EU's executive body itself has raised the white flag in the face of Austria's newly-introduced demand concerning an influx of medical students from neighbouring Germany'.[53] It was reported that Commission president Barroso had stated that the Commission was 'ready to work within the limits of Community law' adding that Austria would be given more time to provide Brussels with additional data.[54] An Austrian Federal Chancellery press release of 22 October 2007 stated:

> an interim solution seems likely in the conflict about the quota system governing access to Austrian medical faculties. In a letter to Federal Chancellor Alfred Gusenbauer European Commission President José Manuel Durão Barroso announced that the proceedings before the European Court of Justice (ECJ) against Austria would be suspended for five years.[55]

As could have been expected, the political truce between the Commission and Austria did not stand in the way of matters ending up before the ECJ once more. Only a few months after the Commission's decision, a reference for a preliminary ruling was made by the Belgian *Cour Constitutionnelle*, in relation to proceedings brought by Nicolas Bressol and Céline Chaverot and Others, a total of almost sixty students, against the *Gouvernement de la Communauté française.*[56] The Belgian Court in its referring judgment extensively dealt with the legislation under scrutiny and its legitimate justification, and provided many arguments why it felt that the ECJ should come to the conclusion that the legislation was indeed justified. The Belgian Court stated that the public funds were 'certainly not designed to deal with the consequences of the policy choices made by a large

51. Goldirova 2007.
52. Miller & Taylor 2008.
53. Goldirova 2007.
54. *Ibid.*
55. Federal Chancellery Austria, 22 Oct. 2007, available at: <www.austria.gv.at/site/infodate__22.10.2007/5396/default.aspx#id25402>.
56. Cour Constitutionelle, l'Arrêt n° 12/2008 du 14 février 2008, Numéros du rôle : 4034 et 4093. Reference for a preliminary ruling from the Cour constitutionnelle (formerly Cour d'arbitrage) Belgium, lodged on 22 Feb. 2008 – *Nicolas Bressol and Others and Céline Chaverot and Others v. Gouvernement de la Communauté française* in Case C-73/08. OJ 2008 C 116, 10.

neighbouring country'.[57] In addition, the Belgian Court pointed out that the specific requirements of the medical educational courses in question implied a reliance on human and material resources that were only present in limited supply within a close range to the educational facilities. After all, it was 'not easy to provide for more childbirths and live animals to be tended to', nor to provide for additional stage possibilities in the medical professions, the Constitutional Court added.[58] In the area of some courses, the percentage of holders of foreign secondary education diplomas – mostly of French nationality – was as high as between 78% and 86%.

Furthermore, the French Community had actually tried a system with a general entry-exam, in response to the ECJ judgment. However, it turned out that the non-discriminatory system had results detrimental to nationals. For instance, the general entry-exam for veterinary science in 2005 had attracted 795 participants, of which 192 possessed a secondary education diploma obtained in the French Community. Even more worrying, only 34 of the 250 successful participants belonged to that category. This could be explained by the small size of the French Community, as well as by the fact that many of the French applicants had already followed several post-secondary courses before entering the exam. In France, access to national veterinary courses was made dependent on following two years of post-secondary education. If the French students, after these two extra years of courses and subsequent exclusion from studying veterinary science due to the *numerus clausus* lottery, would compete with Belgian students, the latter would logically loose out. The Belgian Court concluded that if the French Community was to avoid the disproportionate exclusion of its own nationals, it was to establish a very restrictive *numerus clausus* regime, going along with the French regime, which would rob it from its autonomy and competence to organize higher education. And even then, due to the high number of French students applying, the chances were high that they would still be over-represented at the cost of nationals. Recalling the paradigm as laid down in Article 165(1) TFEU and referring to the agreement made between Austria and the Commission, the *Cour Constitutionelle* rolled the ball into the European Court.

Belgium saw all its justifications resolutely rejected by the Advocate General. She denied the danger of an excessive burden on public finance as an available justification in respect of access to education, and with regard to the problems that arose with the entrance examination, Advocate General Sharpston argued that 'appropriate remedies had to lie elsewhere'. She was very hesitant to accept even the theoretical possibility that indirectly discriminatory measures to counter a real, serious and imminent threat to the quality of university education could in

57. '*L'enseignement organisé en Communauté française est, pour l'essentiel, financé par les deniers publics qui sont limités et requièrent une discipline budgétaire stricte. Ces moyens ne sont à l'évidence pas destinés à remédier aux conséquences des choix politiques d'un grand pays voisin.*' Para. B.12.1 of the judgment.

58. *Ibid.*

principle be capable of objective justification, and the Advocate General remained unconvinced that this was the case in the present proceedings. Nor had it been proven that too few resident students would obtain diplomas for there to be, over a long period, a sufficient number of qualified medical personnel to ensure the quality of the public health system. Moreover, she concluded that the measures in question were directly discriminatory, which limited their scope for any possible justification even further. The Opinion did contain a final remark stating that 'the EU must not ignore the very real problems that may arise for Member States that host many students from other Member States'. But that proved to be a rather meagre consolation, as harmonization was presented as the solution, inviting 'the Community legislator and the Member States to reflect upon the application of these criteria [of subsidiarity] to the movement of students between Member States'. As a final thought the Advocate General added that Article 10 EC (now Article 4 TEU) was particularly pertinent in this situation, requiring 'both the host Member State and the home Member State actively to seek a negotiated solution that complies with the Treaty'.

In its judgment, the ECJ avoided the issue of direct discrimination, probably so as to be able to come to its desired conclusion, namely to allow the Belgian measures to be justified, albeit under limited conditions. The Belgian government had put forward three justifications. The first, relating to the excessive burden on the higher education budget, was rejected because it appeared that the financing of education in the French Community was organized through a 'closed envelope' system in which the overall allocation did not vary depending on the total number of students.[59] As to the protection of the homogeneity of the higher-education system, put in jeopardy because of the inherent limits in the capacity of the educational establishments and their staff, the Court felt that this argument needed to be examined only in the light of the third justification, relating to the safeguarding of public health. According to the Belgian government, the excessive number of non-resident students led to a potential threat to the public health system for two reasons. Firstly, the practical training – an indispensable part of quality medical education – could not be provided when a certain number of students was exceeded. For instance, with reference to the quality standards for veterinary education that require clinical practice by each student on a sufficient number of animals, it was not possible to train more than 200 veterinarians a year, while due to the influx of non-resident students the total number of students rose to 2,343 in 2002.[60] Secondly, the large number of non-resident students would

59. The ECJ did however not consider that when a closed envelope bears no relationship to the number of students, an excessive influx would be all the more damaging for the quality of education, seeing that the higher education institutions would have to make do with less financial resources per capita.

60. Reportedly, this led to absurd situations. There were examples of groups of forty students standing around one cow to observe a caesarean operation. Eventually the operation had to be filmed and broadcasted in the room next to the stable to allow all the students to properly study the operation.

cause a shortage in health professionals operating in the French Community in the long run, as they would go back to their home country after their studies.

The Court responded that the protection of health, and for that purpose the maintaining of a balanced high-quality medical service open to all, could indeed constitute a legitimate objective, capable of justifying an indirectly discriminatory measure. Enter the proportionality assessment. The Court first stressed that the national court had the sole jurisdiction to determine whether the conditions of the proportionality test were fulfilled. Then it went on to provide a long list of detailed indicators that should be used by the national court. Firstly, it had to be verified whether the invoked risks to public health were genuine, taking account of the fact that the link between medical training and maintaining a balanced high-quality medical service open to all, was 'only indirect and the causal relationship less well established than in the case of the link between the objective of public health and the activity of health professionals who are already present on the market'. This required a prospective analysis which had to 'extrapolate on the basis of a number of contingent and uncertain factors and take into account the future development of the health sector concerned, but also depend on an analysis of the situation at the outset'.

Although Member States were allowed to act before the shortage of health professionals or a deteriorated education quality materialized, they had to show that such risks actually existed, by means of 'an analysis of the appropriateness and proportionality of the measure' and 'by specific evidence substantiating its arguments'. 'Such an objective, detailed analysis, supported by figures' had to demonstrate 'with solid and consistent data' that there were genuine risks to public health. In concrete terms, the data needed to assess the maximum amount of students that could be trained, to show how many graduates were needed to maintain the health system, and in what sense the current figures would differ from these benchmarks. The Court issued the warning that it could not simply be assumed that all non-resident students would leave the country after their studies, nor that all resident students would stay. With regard to the appropriateness of the measure to achieve its purported aim, the national court had to scrutinize what the Court felt was a counter-intuitive argument that a limitation of the number of students could bring about an increase in the number of graduates ready to ensure the future availability of public health services within the French Community. Lastly, in relation to the matter of necessity, the Court urged the national court to consider whether the objectives could also be attained by a policy to encourage students who undertake their studies in the French Community to establish themselves there at the end of their studies, or by attracting professionals educated abroad. Around these directions, the Court wrapped some additional cautions, such as the consideration that the opportunity to gain access to higher education in other Member States constituted the very essence of the principle of free movement of students, which meant that a sufficiently wide access for mobile students needed to be guaranteed, and that the method of drawing lots was difficult to reconcile with the objective to pursue high-quality education and health care.

Understating it, the Court was rather reluctant to allow the Belgian measures. But, although the judgment might not feel like it, it did. Belgium will be content. It is very likely that the Constitutional Court will uphold the law, considering the way in which the preliminary questions were formulated. Also Austria will be relieved. Although in a case against Austria the Court would perhaps be less 'lenient', in light of the blatant disobedience of its judgment, for now it seems that both countries can congratulate themselves on a happy ending to an almost never-ending story. It probably is a good thing that the Court did not follow the Opinion of the Advocate General. Although the previous two judgments should not be considered as outright mistakes, for they have to be seen in their own context where the Belgian government did not attempt to justify the measures and where Austria provided only very limited proof for the justifications that it knew would be difficult to get accepted by the Court due to their hypothetical and preventive nature, the judgments were too insensitive to the exceptional circumstances of these two cases. Belgium and Austria did find themselves in unique situations, and although the German and French students should not be blamed for making use of the rights available to them, the cases did demonstrate a 'hole in the system', disproportionately affecting the tax payers of one country to the benefit of another. For the beneficiaries, France and Germany, there was no incentive to agree on a bilateral solution, for they could get their future doctors and veterinarians trained for free. Indeed, Belgium tried to negotiate with France on the issue, but the latter was not interested. This opportunism might border on the disloyal, but it would be unrealistic to require Austria and Belgium to lodge proceedings against their neighbours. Belgium's problems should not be brushed away by presenting harmonization as the solution. What kind of measure would deal with this problem in a satisfactory manner; a harmonization of entry requirements for certain studies all over Europe? What would be their content? A European-level imposed *numerus clausus*? A European-level imposed 'free access without charge' regime? Although it is perhaps not impossible to find some kind of arrangement, the fact that Member States would be forced to accept it as the only solution severely impinges on their freedom to organize higher education in the way they see fit. In a way, this is turning the harmonization rationale on its head. Harmonization should focus on removing the obstacles in the internal market that are left in place because even though they impede free movement they are legitimate and justified. It should not be used as a reason why national measures limiting free movement in order to protect legitimate interests are not justified.

Apart from it being the right thing to do, it was also politically wise for the Court to reject the hard-line approach, for the outcry would have been enormous and the situation could have escalated. The issue had already proved to be of an explosive sensitivity. But the Court, by means of its proportionality assessment, did not let the Member States of the hook that easily. In fact, many will still regard the judgment as overly intrusive and disrespectful of national autonomy. It is true that the proportionality assessment is extraordinarily detailed and elaborate, and demands extraordinarily high standards of (statistical) proof. The Court really seems to be interfering with national policy-making. Dougan identifies a similar tendency of the Court to reject justifications if not accompanied by hard evidence in the area of health care services,[61] and predicted it to apply also in the area of student mobility:

> assuming the Court found territorial restrictions on student finance to amount to an obstacle to free movement, the real danger for Member States when it comes to objective justification is perhaps not so much the matter of principle as the matter of practice. By this stage in the free movement analysis, the burden of proof lies on the national authorities, and the Court can sometimes seem surprisingly unreceptive to Member State arguments about the possible detrimental effects of liberalizing national funding for the cross-border enjoyment of public services, where such concerns are not supported by hard empirical evidence.[62]

Of course, one can argue that all this second-guessing is not the task of the judge, let alone the European judge. But Member States all too often want to have their cake and eat it too. They say one thing; then do another. It is the ECJ that has to navigate the cross-currents of Member States' often contradictory desires and interests. It seems that there is a consensus among the Member States, both within and outside an EU context, that student mobility is an indispensable part of a twenty-first century Europe, where it plays an important role in constructing a European knowledge economy. The ECJ helps the Member States to live up to their own expectations, agreements and promises. Sometimes the circumstances may require an exception to the general rule of free movement and equal treatment. But such exceptions should be very carefully circumscribed, particularly because Member States should not think too lightly of such a justification possibility. It is desirable that the Court challenges and destabilizes all too easy made assumptions about the dangers and costs of student mobility. When Member States determine their education budget in times of economic hardship, foreign students are easy victims. These 'free-riders, that come to take national places without ever having paid taxes', are the ones to blame. The ECJ should rationalize the debate, addressing factors that the Member States tend to overlook. It should point out that it is not certain that foreign students will go back home and nationals will stay, and that there is no reason to assume that, if the demand for health professional increases, professionals will not be prepared to settle in Belgium. It should bring to their attention that foreign students contribute to their host country's economy while living there, that there are economic, social and cultural benefits to student mobility that play on a larger scale, and that highly qualified foreign students boost the quality of education of national students.

Of course, all these effects are very difficult to measure. It is especially the costs that lend to simple calculation, while the benefits are less clear-cut. It is not the ECJ that should make the final call, and it didn't. Albeit with some difficulty,

61. Dougan mentions Case C-368/98, Vanbraekel [2001] ECR I-5363 and Case C-385/99, Müller-Fauré [2003] ECR I-4509. See Dougan 2005, 983.
62. *Ibid.*

the ECJ practised the necessary bit of deference in letting the national court eventually apply the indicators to the case at hand. In *Bressol*, the Court was stuck between a rock and a hard place. It needed to accommodate highly charged national concerns while maintaining its principles on student mobility and remaining consistent with previous case law. The Court chose the middle way, exploiting the proportionality test to the fullest. Convenient balancing tool that it is, the proportionality assessment enabled the Court to accommodate all sides and forge a compromise. It avoided more general questions and took a casuistic approach. This way, it could allow the necessary exception for Belgium's particularly difficult situation, while upholding the importance of student access to higher education across the EU.

2.3.2. Equal Full Support

Although it could be argued that, conceptually, the matter of student maintenance grants and loans is a part of equal access to education just as much as tuition fees are, the Court has been careful to distinguish them as a separate category. Probably conscious of the fact that it would politically constitute a bridge too far to require Member States to offer foreign students the full package of financial benefits made available to national students on the basis of the, in itself already thin, *Gravier* construction, this is where the Court initially drew a line in the sand.[63] But as time went by and the Treaty underwent changes, most notably the introduction of a separate Treaty article dealing with general education and the creation of European citizenship, these lines faded. A few years ago, the Court revised its initial restrictive stand and included student maintenance for the purposes of the application of the prohibition of discrimination as a matter of principle. The European Court has, however, allowed for such extensive derogation of this principle that under the current state of affairs only those students of foreign EU nationality are eligible that have spent about five years in the host state before applying. If one estimates the average age for commencing higher education at 18, this means that the person in question should have lived there since he or she was 13. It can hardly be called controversial that these young people that have spent such a large percentage and important part of their entire life span in another EU country should not be discriminated against in terms of study funding when seeking access to higher education in that latter 'host' country. In practice, therefore, not much has changed for the EU student, moving from one Member State to another for the sole purpose of studying there, seeking a maintenance grant. Nevertheless, the line of

63. See on this point De Witte 1993, 190–191. De Witte argues that the European Court by distinguishing the matter of maintenance grants from tuition fees contradicted its own reasoning in the *Casagrande* case, where it held that in the case of migrant children, there was an intimate connection between formal rights of access and a study grant. De Witte also offers as an explanation for this move by the Court that it acted out of considerations of judicial policy. Lonbay concurs that the European Court made this distinction for pragmatic reasons rather than on the basis of sound logic. Lonbay 1989, 370.

case law leading up to this point is interesting and controversial and merits a discussion.

2.3.2.1. *The Lair and Brown Cases*

The issue of equal full support, including maintenance grants and student loans, was first dealt with by the Court in *Lair*[64] and *Brown*.[65] In *Lair*, a French woman moved to Germany where she worked on a series of part-time contracts. Upon having decided to study for a language degree at the University of Hannover, she applied for a maintenance grant from the German government. The ECJ held that persons who had previously pursued an effective and genuine activity in the host state could still be considered workers, and so were entitled to a maintenance grant under Article 7(2) of Regulation 1612/68, which stipulates the principle of equal treatment in the context of social advantages, for workers and their family members. Taking the (financial) interest of the Member State into account, the ECJ did add the proviso that a link between the previous occupational activities and the studies needed to exist for the Member State to be required to offer the maintenance grant on the same conditions as for nationals. This proviso was mitigated by the Court, when it added that when a migrant worker became involuntarily unemployed, the link did not need to exist.[66] The *Lair* judgment indicated that the Court would decide a case where a non-worker would apply for a maintenance grant differently. That was confirmed in *Brown* case, concerning a French student applying for a maintenance grant for his engineering studies at Cambridge University. Brown did not qualify as a 'worker' and therefore based his claim on the general prohibition of discrimination as laid down in Article 12 EC (now Article 18 TFEU). This indeed constituted a bridge too far for the ECJ, who considered that at that stage of development of European law the assistance given to students for maintenance and training fell outside the scope of the Treaty for the purpose of Article 12 EC. This position was subsequently strengthened by Directive 93/96, which explicitly excluded maintenance grants from its scope.

2.3.2.2. *Via Citizenship towards Social Security Entitlements*

The introduction of European Citizenship altered the Court's stance on the matter. The distinction introduced by the Court between assistance in registration and other fees on the one hand and assistance for maintenance on the other was abandoned in the landmark *Grzelczyk* case.[67] After acknowledging that it had held in

64. Case 39/86, *Lair v. Universitat Hannover* [1988] ECR 3161.
65. Case 97/86, *Brown v. Secretary of State for Scotland* [1988] ECR 3205.
66. See Barnard 2004, 282.
67. Case C-184/99, *Rudy Grzelczyk v. Centre public d'aide sociale d'Ottignies-Louvain-la-Neuve* [2001] ECR I-6193.

that case that assistance given to students for maintenance and training fell in principle outside the scope of the Treaty, the ECJ observed that:

> however, since Brown, the Treaty on European Union has introduced citizenship of the European Union into the EC Treaty and added to Title VIII of Part Three a new Chapter 3 devoted to education and vocational training. There is nothing in the amended text of the Treaty to suggest that students who are citizens of the Union, when they move to another Member State to study there, lose the rights which the Treaty confers on citizens of the Union. Furthermore, since Brown, the Council has also adopted Directive 93/96, which provides that the Member States must grant right of residence to student nationals of a Member State who satisfy certain requirements. The fact that a Union citizen pursues university studies in a Member State other than the State of which he is a national cannot, of itself, deprive him of the possibility of relying on the prohibition of all discrimination on grounds of nationality laid down in Article 6 of the Treaty.

Although maintenance remained excluded, other social security benefits were not. Subsequently, in the *D'Hoop* case,[68] this new line of case law was further developed. Ms D'Hoop, a Belgian national, completed her secondary education in France. Ms D'Hoop proceeded to study at a university in Belgium. In 1996, Ms D'Hoop claimed a tideover allowance, which was refused because she had not completed her secondary education in an establishment subsidized or approved by the Belgian State. In relation to her rights on the basis of the citizenship provisions, the Court held that 'it would be incompatible with the right of freedom of movement were a citizen, in the Member State of which he is a national, to receive treatment less favourable than he would enjoy if he had not availed himself of the opportunities offered by the Treaty in relation to freedom of movement'. The Court continued to say that that consideration was particularly important in the field of education. After all, the objectives set for the activities of the EU included, in Article 3(p) of the EC Treaty, a contribution to education and training of quality. That contribution needed, according to the second indent of Article 126(2) of the EC Treaty (now Article 165(2) TFEU), to be aimed at encouraging mobility of students and teachers. By linking the grant of the allowance to the condition of having obtained the required diploma in Belgium, the national legislation placed at a disadvantage certain of its nationals simply because they had exercised their freedom to move in order to pursue education in another Member State, which was precluded by EU law.

2.3.2.3. *The Bidar Case*

The day that maintenance grants were included for the purposes of Article 12 EC (now Article 18 TFEU) finally came on the 11 March 2005, almost seventeen years

68. Case C-224/98, *Marie-Nathalie D'Hoop v. Office national de l'emploi* [2002] ECR I-6191.

after the Court's judgment in *Brown*, in the case of Dany Bidar.[69] Mr Bidar was what one could call a sympathetic applicant. His story was 'not a happy or an ordinary one'.[70] He came to the UK forced by his mother's illness. Due to her passing away, he had to stay with his only remaining family member, his grandmother, who took care of him. Although he managed to get through his secondary education in the UK without having to rely on social assistance, he struggled financially when studying economics at the University College in London due to having to combine studying with work and looking after his grandmother. He applied for the student loan to help him cover his maintenance costs, having no other resources to turn to. Being refused this student loan by the UK government, he brought a case. The ECJ acknowledged the fact it had ruled out maintenance grants for students in *Lair* and *Brown*, but considered that the legal situation in the field of education had changed since then. The adoption of Directive 2004/38, repealing Directive 93/96, obliging Member States to grant a right of residence under certain conditions, and the new provision on education and vocational training as introduced by the Maastricht Treaty led the ECJ to conclude that:

> the situation of a citizen of the Union who is lawfully resident in another Member State falls within the scope of application of the Treaty within the meaning of the first paragraph of Article 12 EC for the purposes of obtaining assistance for students, whether in the form of a subsidised loan or a grant, intended to cover his maintenance costs.[71]

It was remarkable that the Court used Directive 2004/38 as an argument why maintenance grants would in principle be included for the purposes of the non-discrimination principle, for Article 24(2) of that very Directive stipulated that in the case of persons other than workers, self-employed persons, persons who retain such status and members of their families, the host Member State was *not* obliged to grant maintenance assistance for studies, including vocational training, consisting in student grants or student loans, to students who had not acquired the right of permanent residence. The Court tempered this activism with the statement that the right to equal treatment regarding maintenance grants was not unconditional. The Court acknowledged that:

> although the Member States must, in the organisation and application of their social assistance systems, show a certain degree of financial solidarity with nationals of other Member States, it is permissible for a Member State to ensure that the grant of assistance to cover the maintenance costs of students from other Member States does not become an unreasonable burden which could have consequences for the overall level of assistance which may be granted by that State.[72]

69. Case C-209/03, *The Queen, on the Application of Dany Bidar v. London Borough of Ealing and Secretary of State for Education and Skills* [2005] ECR I-2119.
70. Golynker 2006, 391.
71. See para. 42 of the judgment. See also Dougan 2005, 961.
72. Paragraph 56 of the ruling.

It was thus legitimate for a Member State to grant assistance only to students who could demonstrate a 'certain degree of integration' into the host society. According to the Court, the existence of a certain degree of integration could be regarded as established by a finding that the student in question has resided in the host Member State for a certain length of time, such as three years. Eligible students were those who, by virtue of Article 18 EC (now Article 21 TFEU) and Directive 90/364, were lawfully resident in the territory of another Member State where they intended to start or pursue higher education. These students could claim, after proving the 'certain degree of integration', maintenance grants on equal basis as national students, by virtue of Article 12 EC (now Article 18 TFEU). This right could however not be derived from Directive 93/96, as Article 3 excluded the right to payment of maintenance grants when the right of residence is based on that Directive.

Then the judgment took another turn, and the Court seemed to take away what it had just given. Since the UK legislation precluded any possibility of a national of another Member State obtaining settled status as a student, the legislation made it impossible for such a national, 'whatever his actual degree of integration into the society of the host Member State', to satisfy that condition and hence to enjoy the right to assistance to cover his maintenance costs. The Court therefore held that the legislation was not proportionate to the legitimate aim it intended to secure. After all, it prevented a lawfully resident student who was an EU national and who received a substantial part of his secondary education in the host Member State, thus having established a genuine link with that society, from being able to pursue his studies under the same conditions as nationals. Although some uncertainty existed about the exact scope of the judgment, it certainly seemed that in *Bidar* the Court established a right for students to a maintenance grant. Indeed, clearly some strings were attached to this right, but as long as the student could prove some degree of integration in the host society and was legally resident, he or she had a strong case. Furthermore, knowing the ECJ, it was not unreasonable to expect this right to be further strengthened in the following cases.

2.3.2.4. The Förster Case

In the *Förster* case, the ECJ was invited to further refine the concept.[73] Ms Förster was a German national who had moved to the Netherlands to pursue a course of higher education at the Hogeschool van Amsterdam and who initially also performed paid work there during her studies. Ms Förster applied for the Dutch *studiefinanciering*, financial assistance to cover her study and maintenance costs, in relation to a period during which she was no longer economically active. Her application was refused on the grounds that she neither retained the status of an EU worker nor fulfilled the requirement of lawful residence in the Netherlands for a continuous period of at least five years. Ms Förster challenged the refusal, arguing it to be contrary to EU law. The case essentially raised the question whether and

73. Case C-158/07, *Jaqueline Förster v. IB-Groep* [2008] ECR I-8507.

under what conditions the eligibility for a student grant could be made dependent on the requirement that the student concerned be lawfully resident in the host Member State for a period of five years before applying for financial support. The fact that seven countries intervened reflects that the stakes of the case were high.[74] The majority of these Member States in their submissions stressed that they enjoyed wide discretion in terms of the criteria used to assess the degree of connection to society in respect of a social benefit as the student finance. However, as Advocate General Mazák pointed out, the Member States still had to 'abide by the limits imposed by Community law, in particular the principle of proportionality'.[75]

In the opinion of the Advocate General, the five-year criterion as laid down in the Dutch legislation was too general and 'systematically excluded students, regardless of their actual degree of integration into society, from being able to pursue their studies under the same conditions as nationals of the host Member State'. Although the Advocate General acknowledged that the Member States were to some extent allowed to apply 'general conditions which did not require further individual assessment', in his view the criterion still had to be indicative of the degree of integration into society. He considered the five-year residence requirement as being too general, because it was likely that there existed a substantial number of students that would have the necessary degree of integration into society well before the expiry of that period. He concluded that a residence requirement of five years prevented students who made use of their right to move and study in another Member State from benefiting from their right to equal treatment in respect of study allowances, regardless of the actual link they might have established with the host Member State's society. As to the relationship with Article 24 of Directive 2004/38, the Advocate General pointed out that that directive was not applicable to the facts of the present case and that it could not detract from the requirements flowing from Article 12 EC (now Article 18 TFEU) and the general principle of proportionality.

Somewhat surprisingly, the Court disagreed and rejected Ms Förster's claim. The Court held that the legislation was justified by the objective of ensuring that students who are nationals of other Member States have to a certain degree integrated into the host society. A condition of five years' uninterrupted residence was appropriate to achieve that aim, and was not excessive. The Court, in *Bidar* so unconcerned with Directive 2004/38, now faithfully relied on Article 24(2), even though it held it was not as such applicable to the situation. Although the Court confirmed, or maybe even strengthened the *principle* of equal treatment in the area of maintenance grants, by holding that 'that a student who is a national of a Member State and travels to another Member State to study there can rely on the first paragraph of Article 12 EC (now Article 18 TFEU) in order to obtain a maintenance grant where he or she has resided for a certain duration in the host

---

74. The German, Austrian, Belgian, Swedish, Finnish and United Kingdom Governments submitted written observations, and apart from Austria and Finland those parties were also represented at the hearing on 23 Apr. 2008, at which, additionally, the Danish Government was represented.
75. Opinion of Advocate General Mazák delivered on 10 Jul. 2008.

Member State', the five-year criterion was held to be justified. And despite the Court's statement that the judgment was to be 'without prejudice to the option for Member States to award maintenance grants to students from other Member States who do not fulfil the five-year residence requirement should they wish to do so', the effect of the judgment will most likely be that all Member States adopt the five-year rule. This means that with the Förster judgment, the Court has brought the situation in line with Directive 2004/38. It can certainly be considered a partial reversal of *Bidar*, at least in emphasis, tone and spirit. The reason for this partial reversal is not entirely clear. It could be that the Court wanted to be careful not to further upset the Member States, also in light of the aftermath of the *Belgian and Austrian Education* cases. Although the restraint in *Förster* goes further than in *Bressol*, both judgments could be interpreted as signs of increasing caution on the part of the ECJ.

2.3.3. Exportability of Maintenance Grants

Up to now, we have discussed the obligations of the host state when it comes to access and funding of the education of foreign students. Taking a reverse angle, the matter of study grants has another important side, namely that of 'exportability'. Does a national of a Member State have the right to take his or her study grant with him or her when he or she goes to another Member State to pursue studies there? Although European law entails that Member States are obliged not to impose any restrictions on their nationals wishing to move to another Member State, they have generally not been required to give them 'a bonus for leaving'.[76] Member States could argue that it would upset the financial equilibrium of the national education budget to allow for exportation. However, this argument is not very convincing, as the amount of financial support for studies abroad can certainly be levelled to the amount for studies in the home state. In that situation, 'the exportation of student support would be financially neutral to the treasury, to the extent that the latter need not subsidize the more expensive tuition and subsistence costs potentially incurred in other Member States'.[77] This approach would mimic that adopted in the area of health care, where the State is only obliged to compensate for treatment abroad up to the level of expenses that would be reimbursed for the same treatment at home.

Furthermore, it might very well be financially beneficial for Member States to have nationals export their grants for studies in other EU countries. Study finance often does not measure up to the actual cost of education and it is mostly the State that bears the additional expenses. So it could in fact prove to be a good budget deal for the State to send its nationals abroad with a study allowance, thereby saving the otherwise additional costs of providing the student with the actual education and furthermore 'relieving pressure on university resources of both staff and

76. Opinion of Advocate General Geelhoed delivered on 28 Sep. 2006 in Case C-212/05, *Gertraud Hartmann v. Freistaat Bayern* [2007] ECR I-6303, para. 86.
77. Dougan 2005, 982.

infrastructure'.[78] In addition, as Van der Mei argues, it might be preferable to impose the burden of providing students with financial aid on the home state instead of the host state.[79] The current situation where the cost of educating non-nationally resident schoolchildren is borne by their host Member State is only tenable while the number of migrants is small, concurs Davies.[80] Until their graduation, students should arguably still be seen as members of the State where they lived prior to studying and to which they will often return upon completion of their studies. Van der Mei points out that it is in that Home State that students or their parents have paid taxes, thereby contributing to the financing of education and grant schemes, and it is that State which will benefit from the acquired skills and knowledge of the students. Thus, it could be argued that it makes most sense to promote student mobility by means of exportability of maintenance grants. The ECJ dealt with this matter in the cases *Di Leo*, *Bernini*, *Meeusen* and *Morgan and Bucher.*[81]

2.3.3.1. The Morgan and Bucher Case

The legislation at issue provided that the award of an education grant for studies in another Member State was conditional on having attended a German education or training establishment for a period of at least one year previous to the study abroad (the first-stage studies condition). Having completed her secondary education in Germany, Ms Morgan, a German national, spent one year working as an au pair in the United Kingdom. In 2004, she began studies in applied genetics at the University of the West of England in Bristol. She applied to the German authorities for a grant for her studies in the UK, claiming that courses in genetics were not offered in Germany. This application was rejected since she did not satisfy the first-stage studies condition. Ms Bucher, also a German national, experienced similar difficulties when she began studies in ergotherapy at the Hogeschool Zuyd in Heerlen in the Netherlands. Also her application for an education grant was rejected. The appeals lodged by Ms Bucher and Ms Morgan both ended up before the Administrative Court in Aachen, which decided to refer preliminary questions to the ECJ because it was uncertain whether the German legislation was compatible with the Treaty, in particular Articles 17 and 18 EC (now Articles 20 and 21 TFEU). Interestingly, the six intervening governments had different opinions about what the answer to that question should be. The Netherlands, Austrian and United Kingdom governments concurred with the German government, maintaining that the first-stage studies condition was not a restriction of the free movement of persons, a view that was quite remarkably supported by the Commission.

78. *Ibid.*
79. Van Der Mei 2005, 172–176.
80. Davies 2006, 24–25. See also Davies 2005a, 227, Davies 2005b, 43.
81. Case C-308/89, *Carmina di Leo v. Land Berlin* [1990] ECR I-4185; Case C-3/90, *M. J. E. Bernini v. Minister van Onderwijs en Wetenschappen* [1992] ECR I-1071; Case C-337/97, *Commission of the European Communities v. Grand Duchy of Luxembourg* [1999] ECR I-3289; Joined Cases C-11/06 and C-12/06, *Morgan and Bucher* [2007] ECR I-9161.

The Italian, Finnish and Swedish Governments expressed the opposite view, maintaining that the first-stage studies condition amounted to a restriction of freedom of movement for citizens of the Union. However, almost all of the intervening parties agreed that if this was a restriction, it was at least justified. Only Italy argued that it was not, and the Finnish government took the view that it was for the referring court to assess whether the restriction was justified.

In response to the submissions of many of the governments and the Commission, maintaining that under Article 149(1) EC (now Article 165(1) TFEU) the Member States were primarily competent as regards the content and the organization of their education systems, the ECJ stated that it was 'nonetheless the case that that competence must be exercised in compliance with Community law, and, in particular, in compliance with the Treaty provisions on the freedom to move and reside within the territory of the Member States as conferred by Article 18(1) EC'. Considering that national legislation placing certain nationals at a disadvantage simply because they exercised their freedom to move and to reside in another Member State constituted a restriction on the freedoms conferred by Article 18(1) EC (now Article 21(1) TFEU), the Court repeated its *Grzelczyk* and *D'Hoop* findings that the Treaty opportunities of free movement for Union citizens could not be fully effective if a citizen could be deterred by obstacles placed in the way of his or her stay in another Member State by legislation of his or her home state, penalizing the mere fact that he or she has used those opportunities, a consideration of particular importance in the field of education. Thus, the first-stage studies condition, which on account of the personal inconvenience, additional costs and possible delays that it entailed was liable to discourage students to move, was a restriction of the right of free movement as provided in Article 18(1) EC.

The Court proceeded to scrutinize the justifications brought forward by the German government. First, Germany had argued that the purpose of the condition was to enable students to show their willingness to pursue and complete their studies successfully and without delay. The Court however pointed out that although this objective could constitute a legitimate aim, the first-stage studies condition seemed rather to imply an increase in the overall duration of studies. Also the second justification, entailing that the condition enabled students to determine whether they made 'the right choice' in respect of their studies, was rejected by the ECJ, which held that the legislation in fact discouraged change of study courses. Thirdly, the German Government had claimed as a justification that the legislation, taken as a whole, was in fact very generous, by making available grants for studies abroad, including certain travel costs, registration fees and medical insurance. The merit of this argument lied in the fact that Germany's legislation was more generous than it actually needed to be, considering that Member States were under no obligation to offer grants for studies abroad. This did not convince the Court, which responded that such admittedly useful facilities did not serve to justify the restriction. The ECJ opined that *if* such a grant was made available, *then* it needed to be done in accordance with the relevant provisions of EU law.

The fourth argument was a financial one, claiming that maintenance grants for studies abroad would constitute an unreasonable burden 'which could lead to a general reduction in study allowances granted in the Member State of origin'. The Court acknowledged that such considerations could constitute a justification, but rejected it in the underlying situation, because 'the degree of integration into its society which a Member State could legitimately require must, in any event, be regarded as satisfied by the fact that the applicants in the main proceedings were raised in Germany and completed their schooling there'. The fifth and last argument, submitted by Austria, Sweden, the UK and the Commission, was perhaps the most interesting one from a doctrinal point of view. Referring to the absence of coordinating provisions between the Member States so far in relation to education or training grants, the four parties pointed out that there was a risk of duplication of entitlements if a condition such as the first-stage studies condition were to be abolished. Indeed, it turned out that Ms Morgan received from the United Kingdom authorities financial support in the form of an allowance for tuition fees and maintenance costs, as well as a loan. But the Court pointed out that the first-stage studies condition was in no way intended or designed to prevent or take account of duplication of grants, and could hence not be justified as such.

Although the Court might seem insensitive to the (financial and other) concerns of the Member States in regulating exportability of grants, at the current state of development of EU law Member States do remain free to determine their educational policy on the matter of exportability of grants. Under the current interpretation of the law, there is no right for students to export their grants. Member States decide whether to exclude or allow 'export', and when they allow it they can formulate and attach conditions to such a possibility. If they decide to make grants available for 'exportation', however, the conditions need be in accordance with the requirements of EU law. One of the problems with this construction is that it incentivizes Member States to deny exportability. If they cannot easily attach conditions, for fear of incompatibility with European law, they might prefer to negate the right altogether. Another interesting aspect of the case is the point that was raised regarding the risk of duplication of entitlements, in the absence of common measures coordinating study grants. Advocate General Ruiz-Jarabo Colomer argued that this risk does not only occur in situations of grants awarded by home and host Member State, but also on different levels.[82] Due to the variety of financial sources for study aid, to be distinguished in private, national and European sources, there are plenty of possibilities for overlapping entitlements. His point was that appropriate legal mechanisms existed, and were already in place, to regulate such risks. Be that as it may, it is submitted here that coordinating measures on the European level would greatly facilitate a transparent system with just arrangements, aligning the matters of exportability of entitlements from the home state and equal entitlements in the host state.

82. Opinion of Advocate General D. Ruiz-Jarabo Colomer of 20 Mar. 2007 in Joined Cases C-11/06 and C-12/06 *Morgan and Bucher* [2007] ECR I-9161, fn. 78.

2.3.4. Students as Recipients of Services

A potentially powerful recently proposed approach to students and their rights under EU law is to classify them as the recipients of services. We have seen that under the conditions of being privately funded and operating with a view to profit, educational establishments can rely on the service provisions of the EC Treaty to demand equal treatment. In that line of reasoning, the students attending these establishments would qualify as service recipients, potentially allowing a stronger legal basis for their claim than the current construction that is mostly based on their European citizenship. Recently, Advocate General Ruiz-Jarabo Colomer in his Opinion in the *Morgan and Bucher* case, argued in favour of this interpretation of the service provisions. He argued that 'obstacles to attending classes outside the country of origin, as well as limiting the range of options available to the students, have an effect on the educational establishment, by reducing their opportunities for attracting foreign students'. He went on to draw the expectable analogy with health care, arguing that the Court had already held that 'the freedom to provide services includes the freedom for the recipients of services, including persons in need of medical treatment, to go to another Member State in order to receive those services there, and also paid medical care' and that this reasoning had to be extended to the realm of higher education. He stated that universities normally offer education in exchange for remuneration, in terms of registration charges or monthly instalments, so any obstacle to attending their classes had to be regarded as a restriction on the freedom to provide services.

The Opinion of the Advocate General was delivered in March 2007, and although the Court in its *Morgan* judgment did not touch the issue, it implicitly gave a tentative answer in the *Schwarz* judgment of September 2007. The Schwarz case concerned the refusal to grant tax relief on the ground that the private school in question was established in another Member State. The Court held that the German legislation impeded the possibility of taking advantage of offers of education emanating from such a school, meaning that its freedom to provide services was impaired. It was, according to the ECJ, settled case law that 'the freedom to provide services includes the freedom of the persons for whom the services are intended to go to another Member State, where the provider is, in order to enjoy the services there'.[83] With the *Schwarz* judgment, the Court has already begun to transpose its approach to medical services to the area of education, and the Court might very well hold this reasoning to be applicable in the case of migrant students. In that case, Article 56 TFEU would become the default basis upon which student claims should be primarily dealt with, since it takes precedence over Article 21 TFEU.[84] If the Court decides to go this way, it will probably have

83. Joined Cases 286/82 and 26/83, *Luisi and Carbone* [1984] ECR 377, paras 10 and 16, as cited by the ECJ in Case C-76/05, *Schwarz and Gootjes-Schwarz v. Finanzamt Bergisch Gladbach* [2007] ECR I-6849, para. 36.
84. Case C-92/01, *Stylianakis* [2003] ECR I-1291, para. 18, and Case C-208/05, ITC [2007] ECR I-0000, para. 64.

the effect of strengthening student claims to equal treatment, including maintenance grants, should the establishment in question operate as a private school.[85] Dougan has pointed out that this would 'have the effect of diverting Member State resources away from financial support for public sector education (within the domestic territory) towards private sector establishments (in other countries) – amounting in effect to a form of Community-led contracting out-cum-outsourcing'.[86]

2.3.5. Academic Recognition

An important dimension of the education rights of students is that of the recognition of degrees and periods of study. If course credits obtained abroad or entire diplomas are not recognized in other Member States, this obviously impairs the free movement of persons within the EU. At this point it is relevant to reiterate that doctrinally, a distinction is made between academic and professional recognition of diplomas. Traditionally, academic recognition has been perceived as outside the legislative competences of the EU.[87] Professional recognition, on the other hand, is perceived to have more direct consequences for the labour market. For several professions, such as the legal and medical professions, the entry into that profession is regulated. One way to remedy these obstacles is to establish rules guaranteeing the mutual recognition of professional qualifications between States. As Verbruggen points out, there still appears to be a 'quasi-consensus' that matters of academic recognition lie outside the realm of EU law.[88] EU law under its current interpretation does indeed not seem to require Member States to recognize diplomas issued in other EU countries for academic purposes. Such obligations do exist, but are formulated rather in the context of Council of Europe conventions and to a certain extent in the framework of the Bologna Process.

Nevertheless, it is submitted here that recent EC case law provides indications that a change in that situation might be impending. As we have already seen, matters of academic recognition can play an important role in the context and application of the internal market freedoms of workers, services and establishment. The *Neri* case constitutes a prime example thereof. In that case, the refusal to recognize the degree in question without any fair comparative assessment by the national authorities was construed as a restriction of the freedom to provide services by the educational institution granting the degree. This can be seen as an important move into the direction of requiring an objective comparative assessment of academic qualifications, similar to what is required of the Member States in the context of professional recognition. According to settled law, the applicant for professional recognition has the right to be subjected to a comparative

85. See on this point, and on the application of the service provisions to education in general Jørgensen 2009.
86. Dougan 2005, 979.
87. Schneider & Claessens 2005, 160.
88. Verbruggen 2001, 283.

examination, taking into account all relevant qualifications and experience, before the decision on recognition is taken. Although the *Neri* case did not provide the applicant with the right to such an assessment, for the case was dealt with from the perspective of ESE, the judgment does go into that direction. Recognition of academic qualifications can also play a role for the purposes of professional recognition, and a failure to take account of academic qualifications in such a context might indirectly lead to a breach of the fundamental freedoms. The academic qualifications of an applicant have to be assessed if this is important for his or her professional recognition, and if the governmental authorities fail to do so, this might constitute a restriction of the free movement of workers or establishment. The *Morgenbesser* case[89] is the most important case, dealing with these complex issues of indirect academic recognition.

2.3.5.1. The Morgenbesser Case

Ms Morgenbesser was a French national who resided in Italy. In France, she had studied law and obtained the academic qualification of *maîtrise en droit*. Thereafter she had practised as a lawyer in Paris chambers for eight months, before commencing practice in chambers in Genoa. Ms Morgenbesser applied to the *Consiglio dell'Ordine degli Avvocati di Genova* (Genoa Bar Council) for enrolment in the register of trainee lawyers. The Council rejected the application because Italian law required possession of a law diploma either issued or confirmed by an Italian university. Ms Morgenbesser lodged an appeal, alleging infringement of the Treaty rules on fundamental freedoms. The *Consiglio Nazionale Forense* (National Bar Council) rejected the appeal on the ground that Ms Morgenbesser had not been entitled to pursue the profession of lawyer in France, and that she did not have the professional title necessary to entitle her to enrolment as a trainee lawyer. Ms Morgenbesser's request for recognition in Italy of her academic qualification was rejected by the Ministry of Justice, which declared itself not competent on the ground that it was an academic qualification in issue and not recognition of the exercise of the profession of lawyer. The University of Genoa made confirmation of her French qualification dependent on Ms Morgenbesser following a two-year course, passing thirteen examinations and submitting a thesis. This implied she had to re-engage in extensive law studies, as she was exempted from only six mandatory subjects and seven optional ones. On appeal, Ms Morgenbesser requested to be enrolled in the register of trainee lawyers, notwithstanding that her academic qualification has not been approved in Italy, on the ground that the academic qualification she obtained in France ought to be recognized in Italy automatically.

In answering the preliminary question of the Italian Supreme Court, the ECJ made it first clear that the application for recognition of the *maîtrise en droit* diploma constituted the subject matter of another dispute, which was pending

89. Case C-313/01, *Morgenbesser v. Consiglio dell'Ordine degli avvocati di Genova* [2003] ECR I-13467.

before the *Consiglio di Stato* and was therefore not part of the preliminary question. Since *in casu* the provisions of Directive 98/5 (profession of lawyer) and Directive 89/48 (mutual recognition of diplomas) did not apply, it had to be examined whether Ms Morgenbesser could rely on Articles 39 EC and 43 EC (now Articles 45 and 49 TFEU), particularly in light of the ECJ's judgment in *Vlassopoulou.*[90] The Bar Council of Genoa had argued that the provisions of Articles 39 and 43 EC did not apply to training activities, but the ECJ rejected this view. The activities comprised the pursuit of activities, normally remunerated by the client or by the firm, and therefore triggered the application of – depending on the factual circumstances – either Article 39 or 43 EC. Since the exercise of these fundamental rights was hindered if national rules failed 'to take account of learning, skills and qualifications already acquired by the person concerned in another Member State', the competent national authorities were obliged to measure whether such factors sufficiently demonstrated that missing learning and skills had been acquired. The Court reiterated that settled case law thus required:

> the authorities of a Member State, when considering a request by a national of another Member State for authorisation to exercise a regulated profession, ... [to] take into consideration the professional qualification of the person concerned by making a comparison between the qualifications certified by his diplomas, certificates and other formal qualifications and by his relevant professional experience and the professional qualifications required by the national rules for the exercise of the profession in question.[91]

Referring to earlier judgment in the *Hocsman* case,[92] the Court held that that obligation extended to all diplomas, certificates and other evidence of formal qualifications as well as to the relevant experience of the person concerned. It was in that context that the *maîtrise en droit* as well Ms Morgenbesser's other qualifications, both practical and academic, had to be examined. It therefore did not concern, according to the Court, 'a simple question of recognising academic qualifications'.[93] This is a relevant statement, because it implies that the Court did not consider there to be a duty of academic recognition as such. The ECJ stated that it was 'true that the recognition, for academic and civil purposes, of the equivalence of a diploma obtained in one Member State may be relevant, and even decisive, for enrolment with the bar of another Member State'. But it did not follow that the comparative examination required 'to examine the academic equivalence of the diploma relied upon by the person concerned in relation to the diploma normally required of nationals of that State'. In the opinion of the Court, the taking into account of the *maîtrise en droit* in question had to be 'carried out in the context of

90. Case C-340/89, *Irene Vlassopoulou v. Ministerium Für Justiz, Bundes-und Europaangelegendheiten Baden Württemberg* [1991] ECR I-02357.
91. See para. 57 of the *Morgenbesser* judgment.
92. Case C-238/98, *Hugo Fernando Hocsman v. Ministre de l'Emploi et de la Solidarité* [2000] ECR I-6623.
93. Paragraph 63 of the ruling.

the assessment of the whole of the training, academic and professional, which that person is able to demonstrate'. The Court did make it clear that if the comparative examination resulted in the finding that the knowledge and qualifications certified by the foreign diploma corresponded to those required by the national provisions, 'the Member State had to recognise that diploma as fulfilling the requirements laid down by its national provisions'. Apparently, the Court considers this recognition to be a case of professional recognition, for the purpose of which assessment of academic qualifications are necessary.

Most commentators agree that this judgment is potentially very important, as it extends the right of mobility to those still in training and not yet lawyers.[94] Schneider and Claessens concur that the 'revolutionary potential' of the Morgenbesser judgment lies in that for the first time the *Vlassopoulou* doctrine was applied 'to a person who could not be considered to be a fully qualified professional.[95] It is not clear whether the obligation of comparison will also apply outside the context of the regulated professions, in matters of pure academic recognition. Schneider and Claessens do state that *Morgenbesser* implies that 'the *Vlassopoulou* test has to be used when a purely academic qualification is at stake',[96] although they seem to confine this obligation to the earlier stages of professional recognition and don't extend it to academic qualifications in general, outside the scope of the regulated professions. They do see potential for the judgment in the context of the EHEA, a prediction that can also be found with Terry. She argues that the *Morgenbesser* case is of importance in the context of general academic recognition, and specifically in the context of the Bologna Process, because it 'places additional pressure on EU countries to have a process that will provide information about higher education systems and promote greater recognition of degrees'.[97] It is submitted here that the *Morgenbesser* judgment seems to somewhat blur the distinction between professional and academic recognition. It could be another step towards an obligation to a comparative procedure for academic recognition. This is to be encouraged, as the lack of academic recognition clearly affects the professional careers of those involved, making it a matter of EU importance. Arguably, this could also justify the adoption of more general EU measures relating to academic recognition.[98] This strengthens the argument put forward in Chapter 6, that there would have been sufficient legal competence for the EU to adopt the Bologna Declaration as a binding measure, such as a directive.

3. CONCLUSIONS

At this moment, the ECJ finds itself at a crossroads. Criticism of its judicially activist approach to educational integration is mounting. Both its friends and foes have expressed concerns about the erosion of the paradigm of national educational

94. Horspool & Humphreys 2008, 434.
95. Schneider & Claessens 2005, 151.
96. *Ibid.*
97. Terry 2008, 130.
98. See on this point De Witte 1993, 192.

autonomy. Politicians cry out that legitimate national socio-cultural interests are not taken seriously. Although it fits well within the overall scheme of European law not to allow education as a policy area to be carved out of the internal market, a barely limited application of the fundamental freedoms to all educational actors and their acts is at odds not only with state autonomy, but also potentially forces a neo-liberal approach on education. At the same time, as is often the case when European integration finds itself politically in an impasse, individual citizens look to the Court in order to help make educational mobility, promised to them in political rhetoric, a reality. Hidden behind the national claims to socio-cultural interests sometimes lies a protectionist attitude or a mere lack of (financial) solidarity. In such situations, the Court is confronted with a classical situation of contradictory Member State interests. On the one hand, Member States have pledged to a mobile labour force, have created the concept of the 'European citizen' which can move and reside freely within EU territory, and they have ordered the EU specifically to promote student and teacher mobility, as provided in Article 165 TFEU. In addition, the Member States are striving to create an exceedingly ambitious European Area of Higher Education, in which educational mobility is the top priority. On the other hand, in concrete situations they are hesitant to extend financial benefits to foreign EU students, or to national students going abroad, and they are mistrustful of (the quality of) other Member States' educational institutions and their diplomas.

What is the European Court to do? The ECJ would be well advised to exercise some restraint. Especially in the area of student mobility, the Court at this moment in time has the possibility to make a crucial difference. The first signs that the Court might indeed be considering to (temporarily) tone down its progressive approach has already been identified in the *Förster* and *Bressol* cases. In addition, a decisive moment is drawing near in the services area. The Court has already qualified privately funded education provided for a profit as a service within the meaning of the Treaty. It now has to decide whether it will take the logical, but potentially precarious, next step of qualifying the students of such higher education institutions as recipients of services, and accordingly to base their right to equal treatment on Article 56 TFEU in conjunction with Article 18 TFEU (ex Article 12 EC). This would have consequences from a practical as well as a more ideological point of view. It would most probably strengthen student rights, but it would also contribute to the commercialization of higher education, by fostering the trend that can already be identified in the UK that students are treated as 'customers' and higher education institutions are qualified as businesses operating in the higher education 'market'. Furthermore, as was pointed out above, it might 'have the effect of diverting Member State resources away from financial support for public sector education (within the domestic territory) towards private sector establishments (in other countries) – amounting in effect to a form of Community-led contracting out-cum-outsourcing'.[99]

A strong enforcement of the free movement of teachers and students is certainly desirable, and the foregoing is in no way intended to convey the message that

99. Dougan 2005, 979.

the Court should leave the individuals seeking access to (jobs in) education on an equal basis as nationals in the cold. But there is no reason to argue for absolutely uncurbed free movement and equal treatment rights for students, and the Court should not be afraid to enforce some exceptions here and there. European law, as interpreted by the European Court, affords these citizens affluent rights, and a few constraints to accommodate certain specific concerns, do not undermine their generally privileged position. To realize this, one only has to point out that the mobility of students in the United States is more difficult than it has become in the EU.[100] For example, according to settled case law of the US Supreme Court, 'a distinction between residents and non-residents for tuition purposes does not violate equal protection, nor chills the right to travel'.[101] Such distinctions (in European law jargon qualified as discrimination) are deemed to pursue legitimate state goals, 'such as the one of making sure that state resources are primarily reserved for those who made a contribution to state wealth'.[102] As Strumia points out, this unexpected contrast could be attributed to different logics and needs of integration. In the US, unconstrained travel within union territory has always been a general right, 'and judges use notions of citizenship to guard this general entitlement against threats raised by state particularism'. In the EU, instead, the ECJ tends to apply citizenship as an expansive tool 'making it the core of a judicial effort to shift the doctrine of free movement from a model of economically active entitles categories to one of generalized entitlement'. However, as Strumia also notes, the ECJ should not overstretch the concept, for although it represents great promise, 'the European Court of Justice is bestowing upon European citizenship a task it is not equipped to handle'.[103]

100. Strumia 2005, 715.
101. Strumia 2005, 741.
102. *Ibid.* As Strumia points out, limits to the permissible differentiation between in-state and out-of-state students has been established in *Vlandis v. Kline*, where it was held that while durational residency for instate tuition is admissible, non-rebuttable presumptions of out-of-state residence are illegitimate and quotas of admission based on residence cannot be established.
103. Strumia 2005, 714.

Chapter 5

The EU, the Council of Europe and the Bologna Process: Common Objectives?

1. INTRODUCTION

The previous four chapters have been devoted to an in-depth discussion of the genesis, content and implementation of the Bologna Process, and an overview and analysis of the EU's case law and policy in the area of higher education respectively. It is now time to weave these discussions together, delving into the complex matter of the interaction between the Bologna Process and the EU. As has been noted before, the Bologna Process is not an EU project but there is a large extent of overlap with various EU initiatives. In addition, the European Commission has become increasingly involved in the follow-up. In that sense, the Bologna Process takes place in a twilight zone: just outside the borders of the EU framework while having a substantial relationship with it. The aim of this chapter is to elaborate on this relationship between the EU and the Bologna Process, focusing on the material and institutional interaction between them. Such a discussion would, however, not be complete without taking the role of the Council of Europe into consideration. The Council of Europe is the other protagonist of European Higher Education, and its relation with both the EU and the Bologna Process should not be neglected. It is important to realize that the current plenitude of EU measures dealing with education has been preceded by a phase in which even the soft law approach within the EU framework was deemed inappropriate for the sensitive policy area of education. In that very beginning educational cooperation was 'left in the hands of the strictly intergovernmental Council of Europe'.[1] Only when the European integration project was well underway, some twenty years after its genesis, the European

1. See Pépin 2007, 122 and Lonbay 2004, 243.

Institutions carefully started to touch on the topic of education, in parallel with the Council of Europe.

Founded in 1949, the Council of Europe seeks to develop throughout Europe common and democratic principles based on the European Convention on Human Rights and other reference texts on the protection of individuals.[2] Its *raison d'être* is laid down in Article 1c of its Statute: 'the aim of the Council of Europe is to achieve greater unity between its members for the purpose of safeguarding and realizing the ideals and principles which are their common heritage and facilitating their economic and social progress'.[3] With its forty-seven member countries, the Council of Europe has a genuine pan-European dimension.[4] Within its intergovernmental framework, Member States adopt conventions or agreements. These documents are legally binding for the states that ratify them. Over the years, more than 200 conventions have been adopted by the Council of Europe, all of them international treaties in the sense of the Vienna Convention on the Law of Treaties.[5] In addition, the Member States issue recommendations, which intend to be 'standard setting', but are not legally binding. One of the most important achievements of the Council of Europe is without doubt the European Convention of Human Rights, which enjoys high authority all over Europe and has its own influential Court. In the field of higher education, the most important measure is the joint Council of Europe and UNESCO Convention on the Recognition of Qualifications concerning Higher Education in the European region that was adopted and opened for signatures in Lisbon on the 11 April 1997.

In general, it can be said that the coexistence between the Council of Europe and the EU is peaceful and complementary, and that cooperation takes place whenever necessary. The EC Treaty provides in Article 303 that 'the Community shall establish all appropriate forms of cooperation with the Council of Europe'. The Statute of the Council of Europe contains a general non-interference clause, stipulating that 'participation in the Council of Europe shall not affect the collaboration of its members in the work of the United Nations and of other international organisations or unions to which they are parties'.[6] This has been taken to mean that the Council of Europe either steers clear of questions on which other organizations are already working, or – if this is impossible or undesirable – cooperates with these organizations, putting its expertise at their disposal.[7] There are indeed several areas of overlap between the Council of Europe and the EU that therefore

2. See Council of Europe Official Website: <www.coe.int/T/e/Com/about_coe/>.
3. See Benoit-Rohmer & Klebes 2005, 19.
4. Albania, Andorra, Armenia, Austria, Azerbaijan, Belgium, Bosnia and Herzegovina, Bulgaria, Croatia, Cyprus, Czech Republic, Denmark, Estonia, Finland, France, Georgia, Germany, Greece, Hungary, Iceland, Ireland, Italy, Latvia, Liechtenstein, Lithuania, Luxembourg, Malta, Moldova, Monaco, Montenegro, Netherlands, Norway, Poland, Portugal, Romania, Russian Federation, San Marino, Serbia, Slovak Republic, Slovenia, Spain, Sweden, Switzerland, 'the former Yugoslav Republic of Macedonia', Turkey, Ukraine, United Kingdom.
5. Benoit-Rohmer & Klebes 2005, 13.
6. Article 1 c of the Statute of the Council of Europe.
7. Benoit-Rohmer & Klebes 2005, 22.

necessitate cooperation and coordination, most notably human rights. The overlap between the activities of the European Organizations in the human rights sphere, such as the establishment of a human rights agency by the EU, has received critical attention in academic writing.[8] The major concern relates to the Union's recent active involvement in this area, which is feared to lead to *double emploi*, thereby potentially upsetting or undermining the already existing, coherent and well-functioning Council of Europe system of human rights protection. Following the influential Juncker report on the future of the EU's relationship with the Council of Europe,[9] the Memorandum of Understanding between the EU and the Council of Europe that was adopted in May 2007, seeks to overcome the tension by specifying that the EU will refer to the relevant Council of Europe norms and will take into account the decisions and conclusions of the monitoring bodies, when developing its standards in the field of human rights.[10]

With regard to education, the Treaty contains a specific provision, recognizing the necessity of cooperation with the Council of Europe. Article 165(3) TFEU (ex Article 149(3) EC) states: 'The Union and the Member States shall foster cooperation with third countries and the competent international organisations in the field of education, in particular the Council of Europe.' Both the Council of Europe and the EU are now well-established actors in European higher education. The respective missions of the Council of Europe and the EU are substantially different, which means that most of the specific areas and aspects of education they cover are related but separate. The Council of Europe is concerned with protecting human rights, democracy and the rule of law. The EU on the other hand, has a more economic slant to it, and can therefore be expected to approach education primarily in its economically relevant capacity. Indeed, the EU's legislation on topics of higher education has often been linked to the free movement of (future) labour factors in the internal market. And indeed, the Council of Europe often deals with educational matters from the socio-cultural perspective. It has been responsible for the adoption of numerous initiatives dealing with a range of issues connected to education, democratic culture and diversity, such as history teaching,[11] intercultural education and access of minorities to education,[12] education for democratic citizenship[13] and academic freedom and university autonomy.[14] But the distinction

8. Benoit-Rohmer & Klebes, 2005, 128 and 132–134. De Schutter 2007.
9. Juncker 2006.
10. *Memorandum of Understanding between the Council of Europe and the European Union, adopted at the 117th Session of the Committee of Ministers held in Strasbourg on May 10–11, 2007*, CM (2007) 74 (10 May 2007). De Schutter 2007, 511.
11. Council of Europe Official Website: <www.coe.int/t/dg4/education/historyteaching/default_EN.asp?>.
12. Council of Europe, Parliamentary Assembly, *Access of Minorities to Education*, Recommendation (1998)1353 and <www.coe.int/t/e/cultural_co-operation/education/Intercultural_education/_Intro.asp#TopOfPage>.
13. Council of Europe, Committee of Ministers, *Education for Democratic Citizenship*, Recommendation (2002)12.
14. Council of Europe, Parliamentary Assembly, *Academic Freedom and University Autonomy*, Recommendation (2006)1762.

is certainly not absolute. Working within the EU framework and cooperating within the Council of Europe are not two mutually exclusive alternatives. Many education matters have received attention in both forums over the years.

The most important area of overlap when it comes to education is that of student and teacher mobility and the closely related matter of diploma recognition. The Treaty establishes a firm role for the Union in this field, providing in Article 165(2) TFEU that the Union is to encourage 'mobility of students and teachers, by encouraging *inter alia*, the academic recognition of diplomas and periods of study'. Furthermore, mobility is intrinsically connected to the free movement of persons in the internal market, such as teachers in their capacity as workers, and the Treaty's principle of equal treatment has been held to apply to students. At the same time, as General Rapporteur Deloz of the Council of Europe pointed out: 'the mobility of teachers, researchers and students has always been and remains a central concern of the Council of Europe'.[15] As we have already come to see, the issue of diploma recognition is often divided in two categories, that of professional and academic recognition. Generally, the task division between the Council of Europe and the EC has been modelled around this distinction. Professional recognition has been subject to extensive legislation by the EC, whereas academic recognition has been primarily dealt with in the context of the Council of Europe. But the distinction is far from watertight. As we have seen in Chapter 3, academic recognition can constitute an important factor in professional recognition and a failure to recognize a diploma obtained in another EU Member State for academic purposes might constitute an infringement of one of the fundamental freedoms. And of course, academic recognition is one of the most important pre-conditions for student mobility, the latter being an explicit EU competence and established area of action. It is at this very interface of diploma recognition and mobility where both the Council of Europe and the EU operate that also the Bologna Process comes into play.

2. COMMON OBJECTIVES?

Indeed, as it happens, diploma recognition is also a key objective, if not *the* key objective, of the Bologna Process. The Sorbonne Declaration, albeit implicitly, acknowledges this correspondence:

> A convention, recognising higher education qualifications in the academic field within Europe, was agreed on last year in Lisbon. The convention set a number of basic requirements and acknowledged that individual countries could engage in an even more constructive scheme. Standing by these conclusions, one can build on them and go further. There is already much common ground for the mutual recognition of higher education degrees for professional purposes through the respective directives of the European Union.

15. Report of the General Rapporteur, *Academic Mobility in Europe*, Report of the Conference, Strasbourg: Council of Europe Publishing, 1983, 4.

In previous paragraphs, the Sorbonne Declaration had already stipulated that 'the fast growing support of the EU, for the mobility of students and teachers should be employed to the full' in order to achieve the objectives set out in the Declaration. The work undertaken in the framework of the Bologna Process apparently was not intended to double the legislation and programmes of the European Organizations, but to build on them and to deploy them fruitfully, in order to take matters a step further. The 2001 Trends Report states that 'a major strength of the process is its complementarity with other developments in progress. It reinforces and it is being reinforced by other tools/factors which point in the same direction: Lisbon Convention, Diploma Supplement, European Network for Quality Assurance (ENQA), EU Directives, EU mobility programmes including the ECTS, ENIC/NARIC network'.[16] As we shall come to see in this section, a beneficial interaction between the Bologna Process and several initiatives of the European Organizations can indeed be detected. But at the same time, even a brief glance at the ten Bologna objectives as developed over the years reveals such a great amount of overlap with the spheres of activity and specific initiatives of the European Organizations, that it does raise the question whether the Bologna Process is not in reality taking over the activities that it purports to build on.

The most obvious reference point for EU action in education, Article 165 TFEU, expressly contains all but one of the six original Bologna objectives. Indeed, except for the introduction of a two-cycle system, none of the initial Bologna goals were new or had not been addressed by the European Commission, and to a lesser extent also the Council of Europe, in previous years.[17] The one Bologna objective not mentioned in Article 165 TFEU is different in character from the others, in that it calls for a specific measure to implement the other objectives. This is in fact the means to all the other ends, rather than a goal in itself. To recall, the six initial common objectives adopted by the signatories of the Bologna Declaration were:

(1) the adoption of a system of readable and comparable degrees;
(2) the adoption of a system based on two main cycles, undergraduate and graduate;
(3) the establishment of a credits system, like the ECTS;
(4) the promotion of mobility;
(5) the promotion of European cooperation in quality assurance; and
(6) the promotion of a European dimension of higher education.

The first, third and fourth Bologna aims, dealing with mobility and diploma/credit recognition, can be found in Article 165(2) TFEU, second indent, which states that Union action shall be aimed at 'encouraging mobility of students and teachers, by encouraging *inter alia*, the academic recognition of diplomas and periods of study'. In addition, the third Bologna aim explicitly mentions the ECTS, the Community study credit transfer mechanism developed in the context of the ERASMUS student

16. Haug & Tauch 2000, 2.
17. Balzer & Martens 2004, 12.

exchange programme. These aims also link in to the Council of Europe's long-standing work on the recognition of qualifications, most notably the Lisbon Recognition Convention, and the Diploma Supplement.[18] As for the fifth Bologna objective, European cooperation in quality assurance is also specifically mentioned in Article 165(1) TFEU, which states that 'the Union shall contribute to the development of quality education'. The sixth action line, aimed at promoting a European dimension in higher education, finds its mirror image in Article 165(2) TFEU, stipulating that EU action shall be aimed at 'developing a European dimension in education'. In addition, the Council of Europe's activities such as the Legislative Reform Programme and the European Studies for Democratic Citizenship 'have provided valuable results necessary for [the] implementation [of] some of the action lines of the Bologna Declaration', such as the European dimension of higher education.[19]

The overall resemblance between the original Bologna action lines, Article 165 TFEU and the activities of the Council of Europe is striking. This also holds true for the objectives that added to the list in the follow-up. In 2001, the Prague Communiqué included:

(7) lifelong learning;
(8) the partnership of higher education institutions and students;
(9) promoting the attractiveness of the EHEA.

Again, there is some correspondence between these objectives and those mentioned in Article 165 TFEU, in that the eighth objective is very similar to the provision's second paragraph, third and fourth indent, stipulating that Union action shall be aimed at 'promoting cooperation between educational establishments' and at 'developing exchanges of information and experience on issues common to the education systems of the Member States'. The concept of lifelong learning does not appear in Article 165 TFEU. The concept was however first given priority in a Union context, most specifically by the European Council's launch of the Lisbon Strategy in 2000. The Council Conclusions stated that 'a European Framework should define the new basic skills to be provided through lifelong learning'.[20] But already before that, the EU was active in this domain. For example, the European Parliament and the Council, by means of Decision 95/2493/EC, established 1996 as the 'European Year of Lifelong Learning'. In 1998, also, the Council of Europe started a project on lifelong learning, in line with the priorities defined by the Second Summit of Heads of State and Government of the Council of Europe in

18. Article IX.3 of the Convention stipulates: 'The Parties shall promote, through the national information centres or otherwise, the use of the UNESCO/Council of Europe Diploma Supplement or any other comparable document by the higher education institutions of the Parties.' Note that the Diploma Supplement is a joint product of the Commission, the Council of Europe and UNESCO/CEPES.
19. Council of Europe official website: <www.coe.int/t/dg4/highereducation/EHEA2010/CoE1999-2001_EN.asp#TopOfPage>.
20. Lisbon Presidency Conclusions 2000, 7.

1997, which called for a new strategy of social cohesion.[21] The third novelty of the Prague Communiqué, the attractiveness of the EHEA, is also not explicitly mentioned in Article 165 TFEU, although – as we shall see further below – the rationale behind it, namely boosting the international competitiveness of Europe through its higher-education systems, resonates with the EU's strategic objectives as set out in the Lisbon Strategy.

It has been argued that the insertion of these three new objectives heralded an increased involvement of the European Commission in the Bologna Process and illustrates an even further increased convergence of the Process with EU higher education policy, in particular the Lisbon Strategy. The tenth and last action line, added by the Ministers in 2003 at the Conference in Berlin, fits that picture perfectly:

(10) doctoral studies and the synergy between the EHEA and the European Research Area.

Research has its own Treaty provisions, namely Articles 163 to 173 EC, and has been a longstanding policy objective of the EU, and thus used to be pursued in 'a pure EU context'.[22] In Balzer's view, the fact that the European research area was included in the communiqué of Berlin was another step towards giving the Commission a more important role in the Bologna.[23] Although this is true, it should be noted that at the same time it was yet another established area of EU educational activity that was taken over in the framework of the Bologna Process. The consequences of this development will also be addressed further below.

2.1. Specific Areas of Overlap

The foregoing first-glance comparison of Bologna's objectives catalogue with Article 165 TFEU and the main areas of Council of Europe activity in education shows remarkable similarities. At this point, we should take a closer look at the most important specific areas of overlap, to see whether and what kind of interaction is taking place.

21. Note that the preamble of the ensuing *Recommendation on Higher Education Policies in Lifelong Learning* referred to the Bologna Process: 'Having regard to the Joint Declaration on harmonization of the architecture of the European higher education system (Sorbonne Declaration) adopted in Paris on 25 May 1998, to the Joint Declaration of the European Ministers for Education signed in Bologna on 19 June 1999 and to the communiqué adopted at their meeting in Prague on 19 May 2001.' Council of Europe Committee of Ministers, *Recommendation of the Committee of Ministers to Member States on Higher Education Policies in Lifelong Learning*, Rec(2002)6.
22. Balzer & Martens 2004, 14.
23. *Ibid.*

2.1.1. Student Mobility and Academic Recognition

By far the most important area of overlap between the Bologna Process and the activities of the European Organizations is that of student mobility and the closely related matter of academic recognition of degrees. The fact that both European Organizations were involved in these matters, and that this was something that could pose difficulties, was noted by the European Parliament some time before the birth of the Bologna Process, when it called for 'harmonization of the actions' of the 'several international organizations working in the field of recognition of diplomas' and called for the 'reinforcement of their collaboration'.[24] With the Bologna Process, another policy forum dealing with diploma recognition was added.

2.1.1.1. The Council of Europe and Mobility/Academic Recognition

The activity of the Council of Europe in the area of academic recognition dates back to the 1950s. In those early years of European cooperation and integration, the Council of Europe adopted a number of conventions on the recognition of qualifications.[25] Further conventions were adopted in the late 1970s. The impracticality of having a patchwork of several different conventions, in addition to the fact that they had become somewhat outdated, led to the initiative in the mid-1990s to create one comprehensive convention, replacing all the existing ones.[26] So it happened that in 1997, the Lisbon Recognition Convention was adopted. The fundamental principle of the Convention is that all applicants have 'the right to a fair assessment of their qualifications within a reasonable time limit and according to transparent, coherent and reliable procedures, without discrimination'.[27] It is the only joint Convention of the Council of Europe and UNESCO, and constitutes the 'main international legal text that aims to further the fair recognition of qualifications'[28] dealing with procedures of recognition of degrees and parts of study in the European countries. In a certain sense, the Lisbon Recognition Convention foreshadowed the Bologna Process, in that it deals with exactly the issues that the Bologna signatories are concerned with. Therefore, it is perhaps not so surprising that the Lisbon Convention has become an important part of the Bologna Process.

The Sorbonne Declaration refers to the Convention, when it states that 'a convention, recognising higher education qualifications in the academic field within Europe, was agreed on last year in Lisbon'. It continues by stating that 'the convention set a number of basic requirements and acknowledged that individual countries could engage in an even more constructive scheme'. However,

24. European Parliament, *Resolution on the Commission' s communication on recognition of qualifications for academic and professional purposes* (COM (94) 0596 – C4-0123/95) OJ 1995 C 323, 48.
25. European Conventions ETS Nos 15, 21, 32 and 49. See Bergan & Rauhvargers 2005, 8.
26. *Ibid.*
27. Rugaas 2003, 9.
28. *Ibid.*

contrary to what the text of the Declaration suggests here, the Lisbon Convention does not contain a provision explicitly encouraging or acknowledging that the individual countries or a group of countries engage in a more constructive scheme. The Convention's preamble does state that it is to provide 'a framework for the *further* development of recognition practices in the European region',[29] which indicates that such further action would not be incompatible with its aims. Furthermore, Article II.3 of the Convention stipulates that nothing in the Convention is 'to derogate from any more favourable provisions concerning the recognition of qualifications issued in one of the Parties contained in or stemming from an existing or a *future* treaty to which a Party to this Convention may be or may become a party'.[30] Of course, it can safely be said that a project of enhanced cooperation in recognition matters would very much be in line with the objectives of the Lisbon Convention. What is curious is that the drafters of the Sorbonne Declaration chose to directly refer to the Lisbon Convention as authorizing them the power to do so, while a specific provision is absent. Perhaps the authors felt the need to justify their enhanced cooperation outside the Council of Europe/Lisbon Recognition scheme, or they wanted to base themselves on a document of legal value, in order to provide more solid legal ground for their endeavour.

The Lisbon Recognition Convention has been qualified as the 'only legally binding text in the Bologna Process'.[31] The meaning and legal value of this qualification is not entirely clear; there is nothing about the Bologna Process that is binding and the Lisbon Convention, that obviously is binding, dates from before the birth of the Process and remains independent from it, in terms of legal structure. The statement might serve as further evidence that the actors in the Bologna Process were for some reason eager to have a certain kind of legal document as a basis or point of departure. In addition to the Lisbon Convention, the signatories have involved another binding Council of Europe measure in the Bologna Process, to wit the European Cultural Convention. Initially, the conditions for participation in the Bologna Process were connected to EU membership, or participation in the EU education programmes Socrates, Leonardo da Vinci and Tempus.[32] In 2003, at the Berlin Ministerial Conference, the conditions were disconnected from the EU and linked to the Council of Europe instead, by deciding that all countries party to the European Cultural Convention were eligible to take part in the Bologna Process provided they apply for accession and submit a satisfactory plan for implementation of the Bologna goals in their higher-education system. Thus, two legal instruments of the Council of Europe now serve to support the Bologna Process.

Certainly, it is not only the Bologna Process to profit from the Lisbon Convention, but even more so the other way around. The Convention, which did come

---

29. Emphasis added.
30. Emphasis added.
31. Rauhvargers & Bergan 2008, 8. Also the Council of Europe agrees with this view, which implies that the Convention has now been subsumed in the Bologna Process: 'The Council of Europe is fully committed to the Bologna Process [...] by providing, with UNESCO, the only binding text of the Process: the Lisbon Recognition Convention.' See Bergan 2007.
32. Corbett 2006, 9.

into force in 1999 with the first five ratifications, actually had some trouble with gathering the signatures and ratification of the other countries. It can be argued that it was the Bologna Process that provided the new and necessary impetus, by making its ratification an integral part of the Bologna objectives. In the Berlin Communiqué of 2003, it was stated that: 'Ministers underline the importance of the Lisbon Recognition Convention, which should be ratified by all countries participating in the Bologna Process.' Two years later, the Bergen Communiqué provided another push:

> We note that 36 of the 45 participating countries have now ratified the Lisbon Recognition Convention. We urge those that have not already done so to ratify the Convention without delay. We commit ourselves to ensuring the full implementation of its principles, and to incorporating them in national legislation as appropriate.

By means of the 'commitments' made in the Communiqué's, the Convention was firmly put on the Bologna agenda. Obviously, this was a very positive development for the Lisbon Convention, which found itself stuck in the ratification morass before. The results are tangible. Of the EU Member States, four had initially not signed the Convention, to wit Belgium, the Netherlands, Ireland and Spain. They all proceeded to do so after the Berlin and/or Bergen Communiqué's.[33] And of the EU Member States among the original signatories, a large group consisting of Denmark, Finland, Germany, Malta, Poland and the United Kingdom ratified the Convention only until after the Berlin push.[34] Today, of all the EU Member States only Greece has not signed the Convention, and only Italy still has to ratify it. Maybe it was not so much the Communiqués in themselves, which are non-binding documents after all, as the renewed interest and Bologna momentum behind the Communiqués that triggered the Member States to join the Convention or pick up their delayed ratification. Either way, the importance of the Bologna Process for the success of the Lisbon Convention is quite clear.

The fact that the Lisbon Recognition Convention and the Bologna Process have become closely intertwined should not distract one from the fact that the Convention operates separately and independently from the Bologna Process. By means of Articles X.1 and X.2, the Convention provides for its own implementation measures, most notably through the setting up of a Committee of the Convention on the Recognition of Qualifications concerning Higher Education in the European Region. Also the ENIC network, mentioned further below, is appointed as a body charged with overseeing, facilitating and promoting the implementation of the Convention. The Committee may adopt recommendations, declarations, protocols and models of good practice to guide the signatories in their implementation of the Convention and in their consideration of applications for the recognition of

33. The Netherlands ratified before, on the 14 May 2002, but it could be argued that this was inspired by the developments in the context of the Bologna Process all the same.
34. See <http://conventions.coe.int/Treaty/Commun/ChercheSig.asp?NT=165&CM=1&DF=2/24/2009&CL=ENG>.

higher education qualifications. While they are not bound by such texts, 'the Parties shall use their best endeavours to apply them, to bring the texts to the attention of the competent authorities and to encourage their application'. The Committee has adopted four recommendations so far.[35] Although the Bologna Process has pushed the ratification of the Convention, the Committee and ENIC have been responsible for most of the work with regard to its implementation. As the Council of Europe website notes: 'only one official Bologna event was organised on the topic of recognition of degrees. This was the seminar organised by the Council of Europe and Portuguese Ministry of Education, on the 5th anniversary of the Lisbon Recognition Convention, in April 2002 in Lisbon'.

2.1.1.2. The EU and Mobility/Academic Recognition

Although perhaps not very generously, the Sorbonne Declaration does at some point recognize the role of the EU in matters of mobility by stating that: 'the fast growing support of the European Union, for the mobility of students and teachers should be employed to the full'. The activities of the EU in this area have already been set out and discussed in the previous chapter, which means that at this point we are only interested in how these interact and overlap with the Bologna Process. The most obvious subject of interaction is the ECTS, for it is explicitly referred to in the Declarations. Without the European Commission's knowledge, it thus turns out, a few Member States decided to copy this successful Commission policy tool into the Sorbonne/Bologna framework. The Commission in turn, after the launch of the Bologna Process with its introduction of a two-tier bachelor-master structure, came up with its own EQF, thereby – at least at first face value – doubling some work done in the context of Bologna. The place that the even more recent Europass initiative, adopted by the Council and Parliament, takes in this picture will also be discussed.

2.1.1.2.1. The ECTS System

As also the European Commission notes, the main area of overlap of Union higher education policy with the Bologna Process is the SOCRATES/ERASMUS programme, most specifically the ECTS.[36] The ECTS was developed by the Commission in the context of the ERASMUS exchange programme, to enable student to take the credits obtained during their period of study abroad and use them within their home curriculum, and finds explicit mentioning by the Sorbonne and Bologna Declarations. In a 2008 report on the impact of ERASMUS on European higher education,

35. *Recommendation on International Access Qualifications*, adopted by the Intergovernmental Committee of the Lisbon Recognition Convention in Vilnius on 16 Jun. 1999, *Recommendation on Criteria and Procedures for the Assessment of Foreign Qualifications*, adopted by the Lisbon Recognition Convention Committee at its second meeting, Rīga, 6 Jun. 2001, *Code of Good Practice in the Provision of Transnational Education*, adopted by the Lisbon Recognition Convention Committee at its second meeting, Rīga, 6 Jun. 2001, *Recommendation on the Recognition of Joint Degrees*, adopted by the Committee of the Convention on the Recognition of Qualifications concerning Higher Education in the European Region on 9 Jun. 2004.
36. European Commission, *Contribution to the Berlin Ministerial Conference*, 2003, 2.

the Bologna Process was mentioned as the most visible example of the ERASMUS impact on policy-making. According to the study, ERASMUS' 'impact on Bologna is visible in terms of agenda setting, infrastructure and content (action lines)'.[37] It was pointed out that 'the Bologna reform agenda builds to a large extent on the ERASMUS acquis' and that 'five out of six of the action lines of the Bologna declaration are directly drawn from the ERASMUS programme'.[38] Furthermore, the report finds that 'the ERASMUS programme provides many of the building blocks for the Bologna process' by supporting the Bologna Stocktaking exercises, the biennial Ministerial Conference, the EUA conventions, EUA Trends reports, the ESU student survey 'Bologna with Student Eyes', and a series of other seminars and projects.[39]

Initially, the Bologna signatories seemed to have the intention to create a credit system similar to the ECTS for the purposes of the Bologna Process. The reason to create a new system was the desire to have a system of accumulation of credits rather than just of transfer, but the introduction of a new system would most likely have led to serious difficulties. It would have been detrimental for an efficient and transparent administration of periods of study abroad by universities if there were two similar but separate credit systems in place. Soon enough, the Bologna participants recognized this, and the European Commission itself took the lead in exploring what the possibilities for an extension of the ECTS for the purposes of the Bologna Process were. In February 1999, the European Commission established a steering group to undertake a study on the possible development of the ECTS into a system allowing for transfer and accumulation within a Long Life Learning perspective, under the heading of the ECTS Extension Feasibility Project. Justly labelling credit systems as 'powerful enabling devices, which aid mobility between various forms of education and training', the report established that the current state of the ECTS was 'relatively healthy and buoyant'.[40] As one of the most successful projects of the European Commission, the ECTS had been accepted and used by over 1,000 higher education institutions in Europe.

It thus provided the Bologna participants with the luxury of a tried and tested tool, which had been shown to be effective. But up until then, the ECTS had only been used as a transfer mechanism, not as an accumulation system. The latter system would mean that the students' entire educational programme was expressed in terms of European credits. The study noted that there existed some scepticism about the introduction of credit accumulation, as some feared that it would create 'an *à la carte* framework in which the student has complete freedom to mix credits/units (different types and levels of education) at will, and then demand a recognised qualification'.[41] The study comfortingly emphasized that this was not possible, nor

37. European Commission, *The Impact of ERASMUS on European Higher Education: Quality, Openness and Internationalisation*, Report by the consortium of CHEPS, INCHER & ESOTEC, 2008, 4.
38. *Ibid.*
39. *Ibid.*, 5.
40. Committee on Prague 2001 Newsletter, October, 2000, available at: <www.esib.org/prague/documents/ects_feasability.htm>.
41. Adam & Gemlich 2000.

envisaged, it being left to each relevant national structure to determine how educational programmes are validated and constructed, for universities to take the ultimate decision. The report found that with the appropriate support and guidance, the ECTS could easily be employed as an accumulation system. In addition, the study mentioned that the application of a credits-based approach to lifelong learning aid the harmonization of the architecture of education systems in Europe. The study constituted the basis of the discussions in the first of the international seminars held in the context of the Bologna Follow Up, on the specific issue of credit accumulation and transfer systems.[42]

2.1.1.2.2. Europass

As was discussed in the Chapter 3, the European Parliament and the Council created Europass as a portfolio of documents, aimed at helping citizens to make their competences and qualifications better understood throughout Europe. Apart from a standardized *curriculum vitae* and a few other documents to be filled out by the individual himself or herself, in order to make the individual's academic and practical attainments readable in an international context, the Europass portfolio includes the Diploma supplement, or in the case of a vocational student a Certificate Supplement, issued by the higher education institution where the education in question was obtained. As we have seen, the Diploma Supplement, developed jointly by the Council of Europe, the European Commission and UNESCO, has become an important Bologna Process action line. As such, all these projects have become interrelated. This finds illustration in the fact that a 2008 report by the Commission included in its methodology surveys completed by Bologna experts. The report, which argued that the implementation of Europass in the first years of operation was broadly successful, cost-effective and focused on the right priorities, explicitly encouraged cooperation with the relevant Bologna actors at the European level, such as the Bologna Process secretariat, and at the national level, such as Bologna experts.[43] Europass, although adopted on the basis of a Decision and therefore classified as adopted following the Community Method in Chapter 3, constitutes an ideal soft tool for the promotion of mobility, in line with the philosophy of the Bologna Process.

2.1.1.2.3. The European Qualifications Framework

Also the recent adoption of the EQF serves well to illustrate the increasing interaction and overlap between the Bologna Process and EU initiatives.[44] As was discussed in Chapter 3, the EQF constitutes a European reference framework, which is intended to act as a translation device to make qualifications more readable across Europe. This way, it intends to promote the mobility of the European

42. Lourtie 2001.
43. European Commission, *Report to the European Parliament and the Council on the First Evaluation of the Europass Initiative*, COM (2008) 427.
44. *Recommendation of the European Parliament and of the Council of 23 April 2008 on the establishment of the European Qualifications Framework for lifelong learning*, OJ 2008 C 111, 1–7.

labour force as well as to facilitate the lifelong learning of the European citizens. As was mentioned in Chapter 3, the process of adoption of the EQF commenced with Council Resolution of 27 June 2002 on lifelong learning.[45] In July 2005, the European Commission launched a Europe-wide consultation process on the EQF,[46] confirming broad support for a voluntary EQF measure.[47] In the meantime, the Bergen Conference of the European Ministers Responsible for Higher Education of 2005 adopted an 'overarching framework for qualifications in the EHEA'. This framework comprises three cycles (and within national context the possibility to include intermediate qualifications) and generic descriptors for each cycle based on learning outcomes, competences and credit ranges in the first two cycles. At the Bergen Conference, the Ministers 'committed themselves' to elaborating national frameworks compatible with the qualifications framework of the EHEA by 2010. As to the potential overlap with the EQF, the Bergen Communiqué notes:

> we underline the importance of ensuring complementarity between the overarching framework for the EHEA and the proposed broader framework for qualifications for lifelong learning encompassing general education as well as vocational education and training as now being developed within the European Union as well as among participating countries. We ask the European Commission fully to consult all parties to the Bologna Process as work progresses.

In 2006, the Commission proposed to establish the EQF as a Recommendation of the European Parliament and of the Council, under Articles 149 and 150 of the Treaty (now Articles 165 and 166 TFEU). In the European Commission's explanatory memorandum to the EQF proposal, it takes notice of this call by the Bergen Communiqué. The Proposal reports that a series of studies launched by the BFUG has contributed directly to the formulation of the EQF proposal. The Report of the BFUG on a Framework for qualifications in the EHEA had 'helped to clarify functions of the EQF, in particular as to the relationship between the national and European level'. On 28 April 2008, the European Parliament and the Council adopted the Recommendation on the establishment of an EQF for Lifelong Learning, recommending the Member States to relate their national qualifications systems to the EQF by 2010, and to adopt measures so that by 2012 all new qualifications certificates, diplomas and Europass documents[48] issued by the

45. *Council Resolution of 27 June 2002 on lifelong learning*, OJ 2002 C 163, 1–3. Calls for the development of a European qualifications framework were further made in the 2004 Joint Interim Report of the Council and of the Commission on the implementation of the Education and Training 2010 work programme.
46. This was based on Commission Staff Working Document SEC(2005) 957.
47. European Commission, *Proposal for a Recommendation of the European Parliament and of the Council on the establishment of the European Qualifications Framework for lifelong learning*, COM (2006) 479 final.
48. *Decision No 2241/2004/EC of the European Parliament and of the Council of 15 December 2004 on a single Community framework for the transparency of qualifications and competences (Europass)* introduced a set of European instruments to be used by individuals to describe their qualifications and competences.

competent authorities contain a clear reference to the appropriate EQF level. The Commission has done its best to ensure the compatibility between the two qualifications frameworks. The broader EQF integrates the framework of the EHEA in a rather comprehensive and clear way, which means that there is no real danger of contradictions or harmful overlap. Although the story of the EQF shows that it is possible to combine and coordinate overlapping initiatives in the context of the Bologna Process and the EU, it does not entirely relieve the fact that it is confusing to have different qualification frameworks in place (see Table 5.1).

Table 5.1 The European Qualifications Framework

	Knowledge	*Skills*	*Competence*
Level 1	Basic general knowledge	Basic skills required to carry out simple tasks	Work or study under direct supervision in a structured context
Level 2	Basic factual knowledge of a field of work or study	Basic cognitive and practical skills required to use relevant information in order to carry out tasks and to solve routine problems using simple rules and tools	Work or study under supervision with some autonomy
Level 3	Knowledge of facts, principles, processes and general concepts, in a field of work or study.	A range of cognitive and practical skills required to accomplish tasks and solve problems by selecting and applying basic methods, tools, materials and information	Take responsibility for completion of tasks in work or study; adapt own behaviour to circumstances in solving problems
Level 4	Factual and theoretical knowledge in broad contexts within a field of work or study	A range of cognitive and practical skills required to generate solutions to specific problems in a field of work or study exercise self-management within the guidelines of work or study contexts that are usually predictable, but are subject to change	Supervise the routine work of others, taking some responsibility for the evaluation and improvement of work or study activities

Table 5.1 Cont'd

	Knowledge	*Skills*	*Competence*
Level 5[a]	Comprehensive, specialized, factual and theoretical knowledge within a field of work or study and an awareness of the boundaries of that knowledge	A comprehensive range of cognitive and practical skills required to develop creative solutions to abstract problems	Exercise management and supervision in contexts of work or study activities where there is unpredictable change; review and develop performance of self and others
Level 6[b]	Advanced knowledge of a field of work or study, involving a critical understanding of theories and principles	Advanced skills, demonstrating mastery and innovation, required to solve complex and unpredictable problems in a specialized field of work or study	Manage complex technical or professional activities or projects, taking responsibility for decision-making in unpredictable work or study contexts; take responsibility for managing professional development of individuals and groups
Level 7[c]	Highly specialized knowledge, some of which is at the forefront of knowledge in a field of work or study, as the basis for original thinking; Critical awareness of knowledge issues in a field and at the interface between different fields	Specialized problem-solving skills required in research and/ or innovation in order to develop new knowledge and procedures and to integrate knowledge from different fields	Manage and transform work or study contexts that are complex, unpredictable and require new strategic approaches take responsibility for contributing to professional knowledge and practice and/or for reviewing the strategic performance of teams
Level 8[d]	Knowledge at the most advanced	The most advanced and specialized skills and	Demonstrate substantial authority,

Table 5.1 Cont'd

	Knowledge	*Skills*	*Competence*
	frontier of a field of work or study and at the interface between fields	techniques, including synthesis and evaluation, required to solve critical problems in research and/or innovation and to extend and redefine existing knowledge or professional practice	innovation, autonomy, scholarly and professional integrity and sustained commitment to the development of new ideas or processes at the forefront of work or study contexts including research.

[a] The descriptor for the higher education short cycle (within or linked to the first cycle), developed by the Joint Quality Initiative as part of the Bologna Process, corresponds to the learning outcomes for EQF level 5.
[b] The descriptor for the first Bachelor cycle in the Framework for Qualifications of the EHEA corresponds to the learning outcomes for EQF level 6.
[c] The descriptor for the second Master cycle in the Framework for Qualifications of the EHEA corresponds to the learning outcomes for EQF level 7.
[d] The descriptor for the third Doctoral cycle in the Framework for Qualifications of the EHEA corresponds to the learning outcomes for EQF level 8.

2.1.1.3. Common Initiatives

2.1.1.3.1. The Diploma Supplement

The Supplement is a European administrative annex to diplomas, which has been elaborated jointly by the European Commission, Council of Europe and UNESCO. It is intended to facilitate the implementation of the Lisbon Recognition Convention. Its pilot project was launched in September 1997 and two years later the Ministers of Education picked it up in the Bologna Declaration. This has provided the launching pad for its widespread use in higher education institutions throughout Europe. In several countries, the use of the Diploma Supplement is now supported by legislative measures.[49] Its use has also been recommended in an EU context, for example, by the 2001 Council and European Parliament Recommendation on mobility,[50] but it could be argued that the Bologna Process has propelled it to its current success. Especially the Berlin Conference has stimulated and defined its use, setting the objective that every student graduating as from 2005 should receive the Diploma Supplement automatically and free of charge, issued in a

49. See *Proposal for a Decision of the European Parliament and of the Council on a single framework for the transparency of qualifications and competences (Europass)*, COM (2003) 0796 – COD 2003/0307.
50. *Recommendation of the European Parliament and of the Council of 10 July 2001 on mobility within the Community for students, persons undergoing training, volunteers, teachers and trainers*, OJ 2001 L 215, 30.

widely spoken European language.[51] The Commission in turn has introduced a Diploma Supplement label for higher education institutions fulfilling these requirements.[52]

2.1.1.3.2. The European Recognition Networks

In practical terms, much of the actual work of facilitating mobility takes place 'on the ground'; at the level of the Recognition Networks, or rather the individual recognition information centres located in the various European countries of which the networks are composed. It is here where one can detect the existence of a cooperative triangle between the Council of Europe, the EU and the Bologna Process, and where their initiatives and legislation proves of value for the European citizen. The Bologna Process actively involves the two European Recognition Networks, to wit the ENIC on the one hand, and the NARIC on the other. The Council of Europe operates the former while the latter falls under the responsibility of the EU. The two recognition networks 'serve as the main agents for the implementation of the Lisbon Convention and, more generally, for better recognition within Europe'.[53] As Terry notes, the networks have submitted documents jointly to the Bologna Process and they are generally important contributors to Bologna Process discussions and developments.[54] For example, in 2001 NARIC published a report entitled 'Recognition Issues in the Bologna Process', that serves as a guideline for further improvement of the recognition system.[55]

The NARIC network belongs to the EU and is formed by a group of national centres of the EU/EEA, covering the specific tasks within the EU, including contact points in the framework of professional recognition.[56] It aims at improving academic and professional recognition of diplomas and periods of study in the Member States of the EU, the EEA countries and also the associated countries in Central and Eastern Europe and Cyprus.[57] It was created in 1984, as an initiative of the European Commission. It is part of the SOCRATES/ERASMUS programme. ENIC, on the other hand, is part of the joint programme of implementation of the Lisbon Recognition Convention, run by the Council of Europe and UNESCO. In light of 'the

51. The Ministers set 'the objective that every student graduating as from 2005 should receive the Diploma Supplement automatically and free of charge. It should be issued in a widely spoken European language. They appeal to institutions and employers to make full use of the Diploma Supplement, so as to take advantage of the improved transparency and flexibility of the higher education degree systems, for fostering employability and facilitating academic recognition for further studies'. Berlin Communiqué of Ministers responsible for Higher Education, September 2003.
52. *Proposal for a Decision of the European Parliament and of the Council on a single framework for the transparency of qualifications and competences (Europass)*, COM (2003) 0796 – COD 2003/0307.
53. See Reichert & Tauch 2003 and Rauhvargers 2004, 336.
54. Terry 2008, 137.
55. Rauhvargers 2004, 336.
56. Bergan 2003, 31.
57. See the ENIC-NARIC official website at: <www.enic-naric.net/index.aspx?s=n&r=g&d=about#ENIC>.

need for relevant, accurate and up-to-date information', the Lisbon Recognition Convention in Article IX.2 stipulated that each State party to the convention was to establish or maintain an information centre for academic recognition. The national centre provides information on:

(1) the recognition of foreign diplomas, degrees and other qualifications;
(2) education systems in both foreign countries and the centre's own country; and
(3) opportunities for studying abroad, including information on loans and scholarships, as well as advice on practical questions related to mobility and equivalence.[58]

By virtue of Article X.3 of the Convention, the national information centre established or maintained under Article IX.2 was to be appointed as a member of the ENIC network. This network itself was, as Article X.1 sub b pointed out, established by decision of the Committee of Ministers of the Council of Europe on 9 June 1994 and the UNESCO Regional Committee for Europe on 18 June 1994. Most of the European countries already had the national information centre established under the Commission's NARIC network, and therefore did not need to create a new one. The same national centres that were part of the NARIC network became part of ENIC, which meant that the national centres of the EU countries simultaneously participated in both European networks and had to coordinate their activities accordingly.

This had potential advantages as well as disadvantages. By providing information on both matters of academic and professional recognition, stemming from instruments of the Council of Europe and the EU, the ENIC/NARIC centres could greatly facilitate recognition and mobility for European citizens, constituting a kind of one-stop shop for the necessary information on diploma recognition. In practice, this means that the European citizen does not have to distinguish between whether his or her problem constitutes one of academic or professional recognition, and between whether he or she needs to address Council of Europe or EU measures. But the existence of these two networks operated by different European Organizations, in addition to the existence of other information networks such as EURYDICE and CEDEFOP, also bore the risk of confusion and *double emploi.* In the early nineties, EU institutions called for closer links between the various networks, clearer demarcation of their respective tasks and better involvement of the Council of Europe.[59] The two networks are nowadays known to cooperate very closely, supplying each other with information on a particular qualification or status of a higher education institution/programme through the so-called listserver,

58. *Ibid.*
59. European Parliament, *Resolution on the Commission's communication on recognition of qualifications for academic and professional purposes*, OJ 1995 C 323, 48. The preamble of the resolution provides: 'whereas there is a wide number of information networks concerned with education, vocational training and recognition of diplomas, already established by the European Community, such as EURYDICE, CEDEFOP, NARIC, etc., and whereas it is necessary to reinforce their efficiency and coordinate their action'.

holding joint annual meetings and sharing a common website portal.[60] Furthermore, in 2004, under the auspices of the Lisbon Convention, ENIC and NARIC memorialized their cooperation agreement in a fourteen-page Charter.[61] The Charter contains, among many other things, a note in the preamble that expresses the awareness of the fact that 'the ENIC Network encompasses members of the European Union as well as other countries party to the European Region, and that the specific provisions and legislation of the EU apply only to national centres of countries of the European Union, the European Economic Area and EU candidate countries'. The networks have established ad hoc working groups for the amelioration of diploma recognition in Europe, for example, the working group that developed the format of the joint European Diploma supplement. The ENIC and NARIC networks have also drafted two important legal documents to supplement the Lisbon Convention: (1) the Recommendation on Criteria and Procedures for the Assessment of Foreign Qualifications; and (2) the Code of Good Practice in the Provision of Transnational Education.[62]

Rauhvargers offers an interesting insight in the national situation of the ENIC/NARIC centres. In most countries the centres are the hubs of expertise, where all the knowledge of foreign educational systems is concentrated and therefore the substantial evaluation of credentials is provided.[63] Sometimes, every holder of a foreign qualification must receive a statement from an ENIC/NARIC centre in order for it to be recognized. In many European countries the centres are well equipped and staffed, which means they can veritably constitute the one stop shop for diploma recognition, but there are exceptions where the national centre may in fact only be a single ministry employee, combining several other duties. As Rauhvargers points out, in these latter instances the centre is still in a position to offer advice, but cannot deal with the recognition of individual qualifications or individual information requests, 'which would also mean that the assessment of foreign qualifications by numerous individual higher education institutions takes place in an uncoordinated way'.[64] In 2002, the European Parliament asked the Commission for information on the effectiveness of the NARIC centres and the results achieved by them, and since the Commission could at that point not produce reliable statistics, 'which would only be available from individual NARIC's', the Commission vowed to examine 'whether such statistics could be elaborated'.[65]

---

60. Rauhvargers 2004, 336.
61. The Committee of the Convention on the Recognition of Qualifications concerning Higher Education in the European Region, *Joint ENIC/NARIC Charter of Activities and Services*, adopted on 9 Jun. 2004. See Terry 2008, 137.
62. Rauhvargers 2004, 335.
63. Rauhvargers 2004, 337.
64. *Ibid.*, 336.
65. Answer given by Mrs Reding on behalf of the European Commission, 15 Nov. 2002, to Written Question P-2950/02 by Juan Ojeda Sanz of 14 Oct. 2002, on information network on education in Europe.

2.1.2. Quality Assurance

The mutual recognition of diplomas is based on a principle of mutual trust, something that can only exist in combination with, or on the basis of, a certain kind of quality assurance. The more serious parties will take their commitment to the full recognition of diplomas obtained abroad, the more likely they will be to set up some kind of mechanism to control the quality of the foreign education they are asked to recognize. The slow but steady development of the importance attached to quality assurance can therefore be seen as reflecting a growing commitment to diploma recognition. At the same time, it should be kept in mind that quality assurance is controversial, for States will be reluctant to open up their education systems for assessment, evaluation and criticism by other European countries. The acknowledgement of the necessity of quality assurance was developed in the context of ERASMUS programme and started to take real form by the end of the 1990s. Some years before, the European Commission had organized ERASMUS pilot projects to test external quality review of university education. The insights acquired through these projects were presented to the Education Ministers, which led to the Council Recommendation on European cooperation in quality assurance in 1998.[66] The Recommendation,[67] which called upon Member States to support or establish quality assurance systems and to encourage higher education institutions and competent authorities to cooperate and exchange experience, laid the foundation for the creation of the ENQA Network.[68] The ENQA in Higher Education was established in 2000 to promote European cooperation in the field of quality assurance. In November 2004, the General Assembly transformed the Network into the European Association for Quality Assurance in Higher Education (ENQA).[69] The European Commission has, through grant support, financed the activities of ENQA since the very beginning. Most Member States have by now created one or more quality assurance agencies, aiming at quality improvement through external evaluation. At the same time, higher education institutions have been encouraged to set up their own internal quality assurance mechanisms.[70]

---

66. European Commission, *The Impact of ERASMUS on European Higher Education: Quality, Openness and Internationalisation*, Report by the consortium of CHEPS, INCHER & ESOTEC, 2008, 5.
67. *Council Recommendation of 24 September 1998 on European cooperation in quality assurance in higher education (98/561/EC)*, OJ 1998 L 270, 56.
68. See *Report from the Commission on the implementation of Council Recommendation 98/561/ EC of 24 September 1998 on European cooperation in quality assurance in higher education*, COM (2004) 620.
69. <www.enqa.eu/history.lasso>. For an overview of the national member organizations see <www.enqa.eu/agencies.lasso>.
70. 'The internal quality assurance activities are supported through a pilot scheme organised by the European University Association EUA. Six groups of universities and other higher education institutions have worked together for one year on themes such as "research management", "teaching and learning" and "implementing Bologna reforms". The pilot scheme helped the institutions to introduce internal quality assurance mechanisms, improve their quality levels and being better prepared for external evaluations. The pilot demonstrated the need for strong

The Commission credits the Bologna Process, as well as the Lisbon Strategy, to have added new momentum to the quality agenda.[71] Indeed, the Prague Communiqué asserted the important connection between quality assurance and recognition in May 2001, followed by a strong commitment to quality assurance in Berlin in 2003. The Ministers recommended ENQA to contribute even more directly to the European quality assurance process. In the Berlin Communiqué ENQA received a double mandate from the Ministers to explore ways of ensuring an adequate peer review system for quality assurance agencies and to develop an agreed set of standards, procedures and guidelines on quality assurance.[72] In the Bergen meeting of May 2005, the European Ministers of Education adopted the Standards and Guidelines for Quality Assurance in the EHEA drafted by ENQA. The Ministers committed themselves to introducing the proposed model for peer review of quality assurance agencies on a national basis. They also welcomed the principle of a European register of quality assurance agencies based on national review and asked that the practicalities of its implementation would be further developed by ENQA, which was also on this occasion accepted as a new consultative member in the Process. In 2007, in London, the ministers agreed to set up the European Register for Quality Assurance Agencies (EQAR), emphasizing its voluntary and independent nature.

In addition, the ERASMUS programme continues to play a central role in this area. The Commission supports many activities in this prominent Bologna action line though ERASMUS and Tempus. Furthermore, ERASMUS was 'instrumental in supporting the establishment of the EQAR launched in March 2008, based upon the Standards and Guidelines for Quality Assurance in the EHEA' and it 'supported Qrossroads database that provides information on quality assured and accredited higher education in Europe'.[73] Another important stimulus for quality assurance, not mentioned by the Commission, is the Lisbon Recognition Convention, adopted in the same year as the Council of Ministers Recommendation. The Lisbon Convention in section XIII on information on the assessment of higher education institutions and programmes, in which parties commit to stating which institutions and programmes they consider as part of their own higher-education systems, did foreshadow 'the current concern with quality assurance and institutional recognition'.[74] As Rauhvargers reports, since the spring of 2002 common issues of recognition and quality assurance have been analysed by a joint ENIC/NARIC working group, in cooperation with the European Network of National

university leadership and university autonomy in developing a quality culture. The Commission intends to continue the pilot with a second group of universities, thus spreading this experience across a variety of institutions in Europe.' See European Commission, *Contribution to the Berlin Ministerial Conference*, 2003.

71. *Ibid.*, 2.
72. <www.enqa.eu/bologna_overview.lasso>.
73. European Commission, *The Impact of ERASMUS on European Higher Education: Quality, Openness and Internationalisation*, Report by the consortium of CHEPS, INCHER & ESOTEC, 2008, 5.
74. Rugaas 2003, 10.

Quality Assurance Agency (ENQAA).[75] 'In their statement on the European Higher Education Area (Vaduz statement) adopted at their joint meeting May 18-2003, the ENIC and NARIC networks fully supported the principle that the recognition of qualifications be made contingent on the provider of education having been subjected to transparent quality assessment.' In a few years, states have come to accept that quality assurance is a necessary precondition for recognition, so that now the discussion is not about whether a formal quality control system is necessary, but merely 'about how the system should operate'.[76]

2.1.3. Research

The tenth and last action line added to the Bologna wish list was research. The European Commission, traditionally active in this field of longstanding Union competence, welcomed the proposed extension of the Bologna reforms to the doctoral level. In the framework of Bologna, the Signatory States were called upon to adjust the legislative framework so that joint doctorates could be implemented more easily and obstacles to recognition removed. On 18 July 2003, the Commission adopted the Communication *Researchers in the European Research Area, One Profession, Multiple Careers*,[77] recommending that doctoral programmes take into account broader needs of the labour market and integrate structured mentoring as an integral part.[78] In 2003–2004, the Commission supported a pilot project examining the status of doctoral candidates, the functioning of doctoral programmes in Europe, ways to improve them and to promote pooling of resources in cross-border activities and programmes, possibly leading to a 'European Doctorate'. Subsequently, in March 2005, the Commission adopted the European Charter for Researchers, defining the roles and responsibilities of researchers, including of doctoral candidates.[79]

---

75. Rauhvargers 2004, 339.
76. Rugaas 2003, 10. The agency ENQA (European Network for Quality Insurance) was created by the Commission in 1999 to accomplish the recommendation of 24 Sep. 1998 (agenda L270 1998). The objectives assigned to this agency are to encourage the institutions to adopt check procedures of quality and to stimulate the exchange of information on the quality and the cooperation between institutions in this field. Its publications indicate its will to contribute to establish a European common framework and the diffusion of the good practices (Lindeberg & Kristoffersen 2002; Danish Evaluation Institute 2003). The members of the ENQA are national agencies working on the question of the quality and EURASHE, ESIB, EUA. See Charlier & Croché 2004, 13.
77. European Commission, *Communication to the Council and the European Parliament – Researchers in the European Research Area: one profession, multiple careers*, COM (2003) 0436.
78. European Commission, Contribution to the Berlin Ministerial Conference, 2003, 6.
79. European Commission, *Recommendation of 11 March 2005 on the European Charter for Researchers and on a Code of Conduct for the Recruitment of Researchers*, OJ 2005 L 075, 67–77.

2.2. Avoiding the Frameworks of the Council of Europe and the EU

In the light of the discussion in the previous section, the question that raises itself is whether it would not have made more sense to create, adopt and implement the Sorbonne and Bologna Declarations within one of the formal institutional frameworks of the European Organizations. What better way to build on the 'achievements' the Declarations mention, and to avoid overlap and confusion, than by intensive cooperation with the European Organizations that have been responsible for them? However, the Sorbonne and Bologna Declarations have, as we know, been created as independent declarations, sidestepping both the EU and the Council of Europe. One paragraph of the Sorbonne Declaration, following the one addressing the Lisbon Recognition Convention of the Council of Europe and the legislation on the mutual recognition of diplomas for professional purposes of the EU, is very telling in that context: 'Our governments, nevertheless, continue to have a significant role to play to these ends, by encouraging ways in which acquired knowledge can be validated and respective degrees can be better recognised.' Here the signatories explicitly contrast themselves with, and distance themselves from, the European Organizations, by affirming that their governments *nevertheless*, that is regardless of the actions and achievements of the two European Organizations and their competence, continue to have a significant role. This role they decide to take (or retake) upon themselves at the very occasion of this Declaration. It thus purports to build on the initiatives of the European Organizations, but is very different from them in that it belongs to the governments and only the governments,[80] and thereby arguably disowns the European Organizations from their tasks and competences in this matter. In this sense, the Bologna Process is as much a *re-nationalization* of higher education as it can be qualified as *de-nationalization.*

It appears that the question of adopting the Sorbonne and Bologna Declarations within the framework of the Council of Europe was not explicitly considered or addressed at all, not at the occasion of the Sorbonne Declaration, not at the Bologna Conference, and not during the run-up to the Bologna meeting in the period between the adoption of the two Declarations. In contrast, the question of the relationship between the Sorbonne/Bologna Declarations and the EU was perceived as more problematic and did receive extensive attention in the early phase of what would later become known as the Bologna Process. The Sorbonne Declaration was deliberately signed in an intergovernmental fashion, at an occasion where no EU representative was present, which reflects the clear determination of the original initiators to have this initiative created and implemented independently from the EU and its institutions. Muller & Ravinet have identified various reasons on behalf of the initiators for resisting Commission involvement: the French minister wanted to demonstrate that the national governments did not need the Commission to create a Europe of universities, the German

80. Or, in fact, rather to governmental officials than to the governments.

minister needed to circumvent the Länder level, and the UK minister wanted to avoid the chance of increasing EU competences.[81] But this in itself was not sufficient to resolve the question of EU involvement. First of all, looking back, the Sorbonne Declaration was rather the informal starting point of the Bologna Process than the *produit fini*. The content, form and method of the Declaration were renegotiated among the full number of EU Member States and some other associated European countries in the months following Sorbonne, leading to the final result in the Bologna Declaration. This means that also the matter of whether or not to cooperate within an EU framework was on the table. Secondly, since the initiative involved mostly the Member States of the EU, it was logical that they would take up the matter in an EU context, at Council meetings or other events.

Indeed, under the auspices of the Austrian Presidency in the second half of 1998, the Sorbonne initiative was taken up within an EU framework, at an informal Education Council meeting in Baden on 24 October. This was the first opportunity for the EU education ministers to discuss the Sorbonne Declaration after its signing in May that year.[82] It thus provided the occasion for the 'other' countries to air their discontent with the exclusionary behaviour of the 'big four' of Sorbonne. Ravinet notes that the Austrian presidency played a crucial role here, by 'washing away the original sin' of Sorbonne by publicly condemning the Sorbonne method, thereby providing the political room for a way forward.[83] Supported by the European Commission, the need to include all EU Member States was stressed, and subsequently recognized at this event. With that out of the way, it was at this meeting of the Council in Baden, and thus within an EC context, that the major set-up of the Bologna Forum was prepared.[84] Together with the Italians, who were in charge of hosting the upcoming conference, the Austrians invested a lot of energy in advancing the Sorbonne project, and they were keen to do things differently, departing from *style Allègre* which was characterized by its strong resistance towards the Commission, by letting the Commission back in the game.[85] The Austrians proposed the creation of a working group, charged with presenting the Bologna Process to the Higher Education Committee – the informal meeting of the Directors General for Higher Education of the EU – a few days later.[86] The European Commission, with one representative, was invited to take place in the group.

This working group became known as the Sorbonne Follow-Up Group. Its set-up had remarkably close links with the EC, in that it consisted of:

(1) the Troika[87] for the first six months of 1999, to wit Austria, Germany and Finland;

81. Muller & Ravinet 2008, 656.
82. See Racké 2006, 9 and Hackl 2001, 22.
83. Ravinet 2008a, 358.
84. Knudsen 1999, 2.
85. Muller & Ravinet 2008, 657.
86. Ravinet 2008a, 358.
87. The Troika constitutes a threesome of EU Member States, consisting of the previous, current and future EU Presidencies.

(2) a representative from Italy, the host of the upcoming Conference in Bologna;
(3) a representative of the European Commission;
(4) representatives of the European Rector's Organisations.

Austria was to take the chair. Ravinet argues that this institutional arrangement closely resembles existing arrangements within the EU framework and that it imitates the way in which the Member States are used to working at the European level.[88] Ravinet provides us with some valuable insights on this matter, having interviewed an official from the Direction for Higher Education of the Austrian Ministry. In the interview, the official labelled the Sorbonne Follow Up Group as 'the regular scheme', which he clarified as 'the Troika and so on'.[89] The official confirmed the connection between EU structures and the way the Sorbonne Follow Up Group was organized, explaining that 'the easiest way to function among the EU countries is always the EU scheme, so it was actually quite obvious to agree on that, because nobody had an alternative proposal. It was just how people were used to working'.[90]

The Process thus seemed to be heading in the direction of cooperation within the EU framework. Among the options discussed in the run-up to the Bologna Conference was to continue using informal Council meetings for the follow-up on the Bologna Declaration, and it was suggested to take up elements of the Sorbonne initiative as part of EU cooperation where possible.[91] At the EU Council meeting of the education ministers in Luxembourg, the 7 June 1999, the upcoming Bologna Conference was referred to as a 'conference of EU education ministers'.[92] In this spirit, the draft text of the Bologna Declaration initially contained a reference to cooperation within the framework of the EU:

> We will pursue the ways of intergovernmental co-operation, together with those in the framework of the European Union (where applicable, on the basis of the subsidiarity principle and availing ourselves of the Strengthened Co-operation instrument) and of the other governmental and non-governmental European organisations with competence on higher education.[93]

88. Ravinet 2008a, 359.
89. *Ibid.*
90. *Ibid.*
91. Racké 2006, 9.
92. 'The Council took note of the information given by the Italian delegation on the Conference of EU- Ministers of Higher Education in Bologna. This conference, on the theme of "the European space for higher education", can be considered as a follow-up to the conference in the Sorbonne (Paris) of 25 May 1998, which resulted in a "Joint declaration on harmonization of the architecture of the European Higher Education system" by the responsible Ministers from France, Germany, Italy and the United Kingdom. The Conference in Bologna will involve all the EU Member States.' See minutes 2187th Council meeting Luxembourg, 7 Jun. 1999, 8875/99 (Presse 184).
93. Zgaga 2004, 185.

Although quite ambiguous and certainly open for various interpretations, the inclusion of this phrase would certainly have made much difference. Indeed, the 'ways of intergovernmental cooperation' are mentioned, but together with those ways of cooperation 'in the framework of the EU'. This would have provided the Commission with the political possibility to take on a more coordinative function. Possibly, the Commission could have proposed an OMC or it could have launched a public consultation, and perhaps it could have steered the Process in the direction of firmer legal EU ground. However, probably for exactly these reasons,[94] the United Kingdom strongly objected to this phrase and the change of character it would introduce in the Process that, with the Sorbonne Declaration, had been initiated outside the EU. The UK managed to round up the necessary support of all the other signatories (except Luxembourg), and so the reference was eventually removed.[95] This way, the UK managed to halt the dynamic after the Sorbonne Declaration that was carrying the Member States and their project into the direction of the EU framework. The UK's success becomes apparent upon reading the final text of the Bologna Declaration, where reference to cooperation in the EU framework is completely absent and even cooperation *with* the EU is omitted, and is in fact rejected by the statement: 'we will pursue the ways of intergovernmental co-operation, together with those of *non* governmental European organisations with competence on higher education'.[96] This is hardly anything short of saying that cooperation with governmental European organizations with competence on higher education, that is the EU and the Council of Europe, is *not* pursued.

2.3. The Difficult Position of the European Commission

In addition to the fact that the states decided to operate *outside* the EU, they also decided to proceed *without* the Union, which meant the exclusion of the European Commission as a participating partner. This exclusion already characterized the launch of the Process with the Sorbonne Declaration, where the resistance vis-à-vis the Commission was quite explicit.[97] Especially the French minister Claude Allègre opposed to the Commission being associated in any way. This was reflected in the fact that no Commission representative was invited to the Sorbonne Conference, and that the Sorbonne Declaration did not credit or even mention the Commission for its achievements in the domain since the 1980s. But as noted, the Sorbonne Declaration only constituted the very early starting point of the Bologna

94. Verburggen notes that the official explanation for the removal of the reference to cooperation within the Community framework was that there were not only EU Member States present at the signing of the Bologna Declaration, but also third countries. This is, as Verbruggen rightly points out, unconvincing considering the fact that all of the original Bologna signatories were either EU Member States, candidate Member States or were closely associated with the EC and its education programmes. Verbruggen 2001, 504.
95. *Ibid.*
96. Bologna Declaration. Emphasis added.
97. Ravinet 2008b, 19.

Process. Most of the other European countries, which had been at the Sorbonne event but were not at that occasion invited to draft and sign the Declaration, had condemned Sorbonne's political ways. For them, the involvement of the European Commission would constitute a safeguard that they would not be left out again.[98] Indeed, at the Bologna Conference, the Italian organizers as well as some smaller countries supported the idea to have the European Commission fully involved as a partner. This position also made sense from an objective point of view, as there was a large overlap of the Bologna Action Lines with Union activities. Moreover, it should be recalled that the European Commission had in the meantime become an official member of Sorbonne Follow Up Group. It had been actively involved in the preparations of the Bologna Conference and Declaration, providing its expertise and resources in the area of European higher education that it had gathered over the years mainly through the administration of the mobility programmes.[99] There existed considerable disagreement on the issue and Racké reports that it constituted one of the biggest bones of contention at the Conference.[100] Nevertheless, Allègre and the UK junior minister Tessa Blackstone stuck to their original positions and vehemently opposed any Commission involvement, and the discussion ended in their favour.[101]

Although this could arguably be seen as maintaining or returning to the initial Sorbonne stance on Commission involvement, the exclusion was in fact quite sudden and politically very sensitive in light of the Commission's participation in the preparatory phase of Bologna. In fact, the entire discussion took place in the presence of a Commission representative, who now was a participant in (and head sponsor of) the Conference. Not involving the Commission in the Sorbonne initiative was still something quite different from expelling it after it had become involved in the run-up to Bologna. Furthermore, while the Sorbonne initiative could perhaps still be seen as a 'blip', a one-time act of recalcitrance by four Member States, the Bologna Declaration carried much more weight. All the EU Member States signed the Bologna Declaration. This did not only make the involvement of the Commission even more logical, and hence its exclusion even more curious, it also made the exclusion more painful because all the Member States endorsed it, instead of only a handful. It is not entirely clear why Allègre and Blackstone were so vehemently opposed to continued Commission involvement, and how they managed to convince the other Member States. In the preparatory discussions, the Commission had explicitly supported the idea that the Sorbonne initiative did not aim at harmonization, and it had emphasized that in its view the Union did not have any competences in the field of higher education structures and that the restructuring of the higher-education systems therefore was a matter left to the Member States.[102] But the Commission had also made efforts to represent

98. Racké 2007, 42.
99. Hackl 2001, 26.
100. Racké 2007, 38.
101. *Ibid.*
102. Racké 2006, 7–8.

the interest of the Union, in that it had stressed on several occasions in the run-up to the Bologna Conference that it was necessary to ensure the compatibility of the Bologna initiative with the EU framework. The Commission representative had underlined the fact that mobility fell within EU competence, and that only matters that could not be dealt with within EU framework should be the subject of the intergovernmental Bologna Conference.[103] The representative had also proposed the idea of the Bologna Declaration to be a mixed document, thus including EU responsibilities. Perhaps it was because of this that the ministers Blackstone and Allègre insisted on banning the Commission.

Seen in the light of their exclusion, it is somewhat remarkable that the rhetoric and actions of both the Council of Europe and especially the European Commission have been and remained almost exclusively supportive, positive and encouraging of the Bologna Process.[104] In their own words:

> the Council of Europe and the European Union will co-operate in building a knowledge-based society and a democratic culture in Europe, in particular through promoting democratic citizenship and human rights education. They will support the Bologna process aimed at establishing a higher education area by 2010, as well as education networks and student exchanges at all levels.[105]

The Council of Europe has sponsored conferences, published books and reports, and has engaged in other activities that support the Bologna Process.[106] The European Commission has done the same, to an even greater extent. Of course, the fact that the Member States suddenly proved themselves to be prepared and committed to objectives that had been the subject of several decades of arduous pursuit by these two European Organizations, might very well have enthused them. The Bologna Process mainstreams many of the activities 'the European Commission had been trying to do for the last fifteen years'.[107] And should there be a slightly bitter aftertaste, in terms of 'why suddenly now, and why suddenly without us', it would politically be very unwise to express such objections indeed, and one would do better to try and seize on it to advance one's own agenda along the way. We have seen that the Council of Europe has managed to benefit substantially from the Bologna Process, in that its Lisbon Recognition Convention has been lifted to a higher level of priority. For the Council of Europe, which operates in a more intergovernmental manner and which has more modest ambitions in terms of

103. Hackl 2001, 23.
104. The only reports of the Community or Commission's disapproval of the Bologna Process are found in the press. See, for example, D. Jobbins, 'It's Now or Never to Bring on Bologna', *Times Higher Education*, 28 Mar. 2003: 'Bologna originated in the Sorbonne declaration signed by ministers of France, Germany, Italy and Britain in Paris. As a political initiative, it deliberately excluded the European Commission (much to Brussels' annoyance).'
105. *Draft Memorandum of Understanding between the Council of Europe and the European Union on Education, youth and the promotion of human contacts*, Text of the Chair sent to delegations on 31 Jan. 2007.
106. Terry 2008, 133.
107. Balzer & Rusconi 2007, 57–75.

integration, the course of proceedings of the Bologna Process was probably not at all difficult to accept. But this must have been different for the EU and especially the Commission. Not only were its major areas of activity in education somehow purloined, it was suddenly also deprived from having a say.[108]

The European Commission had since long been aware that attempts to meddle deeply in the sensitive area of education would be counter-productive.[109] Therefore, it has been careful not to step on too many toes.[110] In a 1989 Communication, the Commission stated explicitly that it was not the objective of the Commission to harmonize the higher educations sector. It stated that 'blanket harmonization or standardization of the educational systems' was 'entirely undesirable'.[111] This it did, because it knew that Member States perceived such to be entirely undesirable, certainly when coming from the Commission in an EC context. Nevertheless, it seems that the suspicion of the Commission among certain Member States, perhaps triggered or fuelled by the Commission's successful strategy with the ERASMUS case,[112] lingered.[113] This might explain why the Member States felt the need to create an explicit prohibition of harmonization in the field of education in the Maastricht Treaty. It might also explain why the Commission's effort to steer clear of harmonization rhetoric and to support the Bologna project, even though it was created outside the EC framework, could not prevent its exclusion. But this longstanding awareness of the sensitivity of education as a policy field and the knowledge of the Member States' hostility towards Union-level involvement in this area must have helped the Commission to swallow its defeat and remain supportive and positive about the Bologna enterprise, knowing this to be for its own good. And so, it continued to fully endorse the Bologna Action Lines, to fund and facilitate the Process, even after it was excluded.

After the Bologna Conference, the Commission has not in the same way tried to emphasize the need for compatibility and the prevention of overlap between Union initiatives and competences, and the actions in the Bologna framework. It seems to have completely departed from its position of EU preference, entailing that the Process should only deal with matters that could not be dealt with within the EU framework. On the contrary, it has generally modestly positioned its own initiatives *in function* of the Bologna Process, stating that its 'actions ranging from the Diploma Supplement label, promoting transparency of qualifications, to the launch of *Erasmus Mundus*, fostering the attractiveness of European higher education on a global scale' were all there to support the fulfilment of the Bologna

---

108. Ravinet concurs, arguing that 'The project of a EHEA is [. . .] explicitly challenging the EU actors, especially the European Commission.' Ravinet 2008b, 11.
109. Lonbay 1989, 374.
110. Furlong 2005, 56.
111. European Commission, *Education and Training in the European Community, Guidelines for the Medium Term: 1989–1992*, COM (89) 236, 4.
112. See Ch. 4 for an in-depth discussion of the case.
113. See on this point Balzer & Martens 2004, 8.

objectives.[114] Furthermore, the Commission has taken the view that the two different frameworks do each other no harm, and rather only serve to reinforce each other:

> all these measures, which are part of the overall EU approach to educational matters, and the – geographically wider – Bologna process are reinforcing each other, improving the chances of the genuine implementation of declared objectives across the various higher education systems. Such synergies are illustrated, for instance, by the impact of EU mobility actions on the call for more transparency and recognition of qualifications in Europe. The latter, in its turn, supports the EU's broader reform agenda under the Lisbon strategy.[115]

Although it can be regretted that the Commission has given up on these valid points of concern from an EU perspective, and thereby has left the EU in a certain sense defenceless, it was strategically speaking the wisest position to take. It was left somewhat powerless and empty-handed after the Bologna Conference. Arguably, there was nothing left for it to do than to face the reality that, apparently, it was not in a position to beat the big drum. If with the Bologna Process the governments intended to stage some kind of coup against the Commission, they were successful. The now dethroned Commission had to make the best out of a bad bargain. And, as a matter of fact, the Commission did well out of it. By faithfully taking the back seat when directed to do so, it has managed to steadily increase its influence since the nadir of its exclusion. It has seen some of its projects, such as the ECTS been raised in profile and it has expanded its own platform for action, as we shall come to see. It can however be expected that the Commission still harbours the same ambiguous feeling towards the Process and its (in)compatibility with EU law and EU initiatives as in the beginning, albeit in silence. The only time that the Commission has shown a crack in its 'façade of supportiveness' was in a 2003 Communication, where it stated that:

> for the 31 countries involved in 'Education and Training 2010', there should also be closer coordination with the Bologna process. Generally speaking, the case for unintegrated parallel action will be increasingly weaker in the future, be it in higher education or in vocational training, unless it is manifestly more ambitious and more effective.[116]

At this point it should be noted that although the exclusion of the European Commission was of paramount political significance, its practical consequences should not be overestimated. The Commission still took part in the Sorbonne Follow-Up Group, which met one last time after the Bologna Conference, in order to terminate

114. European Commission, *Realising the European Higher Education Area. Achieving the Goals*, Contribution to the Bergen Ministerial Conference 2005, 2. See also European Commission, *From Berlin to Bergen. The EU Contribution*, 2003.
115. *Ibid.*
116. European Commission, '*Education & Training 2010*': *The Success of the Lisbon Strategy Hinges on Urgent Reforms*, COM (2003) 685.

its work and to develop some plans for the future.[117] On this occasion, the importance of the Commission's role in the Process was stressed and recognized, and the Commission was included as a participant in the proposed future Bologna working group.[118] This proposal was accepted by the EU's Ministers, assembled in Tampere in September 1999. They decided to establish two different follow-up groups, one smaller steering group and an enlarged group.[119] The enlarged group consisted of the representatives of the twenty-nine signatory countries, the Confederation of EU Rectors' Conferences and the Association of European Universities (CRE), and indeed the European Commission. The enlarged group met for the first time in Helsinki, on the 16 November 1999, under Finnish EU Presidency. Much like the Sorbonne Follow Up Group, the smaller steering group was composed of the representatives of the EU Troika, the Czech Republic as the host for the coming Ministerial Conference, the CRE, and the European Commission. This group met for the first time in Lisbon, on the 31 January 2000, under the Portuguese EU Presidency. Probably because of the fact that BFUG's activities were only formally set-up/recognized in the Prague Communiqué,[120] most commentators regard the 2001 Prague meeting as the moment of the Commission's inclusion. Furthermore, it was not until Prague that the Commission received the special status of 'full additional member'. Also the Commission sees Prague as the moment of its official inclusion:

> The Bologna process coincides with Commission policy in higher education over the years through the European co-operation programmes and notably Socrates-Erasmus. In Prague, this fact was acknowledged and the Commission was invited to become a full member of the Bologna follow-up structure, alongside the Signatory States.[121]

But it is important to be aware that already in the two years before Prague, the Commission had kept its seat at the table, by participating in both the smaller and the enlarged Bologna follow-up groups.[122]

The fact that the Commission was included in the follow-up provided it with the opportunity to prove itself of value. The Commission, keen on playing a facilitative role, provided the necessary funding for required studies and for the organization of the meetings. As we have seen, it also proved willing to adapt its

---

117. Hackl 2001, 29.
118. *Ibid.*
119. Lourtie 2001, 6.
120. Ravinet 2008b, 12.
121. European Commission, *Realising the European Higher Education Area*, Contribution to the Berlin Ministerial Conference, 2003.
122. Subsequently, in 2003, the Berlin Communiqué stated that a Board was to be created to oversee the work between the meetings of the Follow-up Group. Again, the Commission was awarded full participation and membership. The Board is composed by: (1) the EU Troika; (2) the country hosting the next Ministerial Conference; (3) the European Commission; (4) the four consultative Members, including the Council of Europe; and (5) three participating countries elected by the BFUG for one year.

the ECTS for the purposes of the Bologna Process, commissioning a study entitled the 'The ECTS Extension Feasibility Project'.[123] Balzer reports that at the intermediary meetings – in which the Commission took part – between the official ministerial conferences in Bologna and Prague it was still explicitly not meant to include the Commission in the Process as a full partner.[124] But notice was taken of the 'the strong support which several constituent aspects of the convergence process were enjoying from the European Commission'.[125] And at the Prague Conference itself, the Commission was invited as full member. It appears that this decision was very much pushed by the Swedish presidency.[126] Balzer also mentions that it constituted an acknowledgement by the states that the activities of the Commission were very much concordant with the goals of the Bologna Process.[127] Obviously, the Member States were already well aware of this before the Prague Conference. It is doubtful that in 2001 they suddenly realized that the Commission had also been involved in educational mobility matters, touching upon Bologna issues, and that for the past twenty years. It appears that it was pure necessity combined with an appeased impression of the Commission that led the UK and France to agree to the Commission's inclusion. This would probably not have happened if the Commission had detracted its support and had stopped funding the Bologna Process after the precarious situation at the Bologna Conference. It would certainly not have happened if it had publicly expressed itself in a critical way about its exclusion, or about the Process in general. The Prague Communiqué not for nothing reads that the ministers 'took note of the constructive assistance of the European Commission'.

Compared to the Council of Europe, the EU has had a more substantial influence on the Bologna Process ever since the beginning. It was only in 2000 that the Council of Europe was first included. The Council of Europe itself had approached the Portuguese Presidency of the EU on the occasion of the Education Committee in Rovaniemi,[128] and had requested a meeting to discuss the possibility of participating. This was taken up in the steering group meeting of 31 January 2000, in Lisbon. After some discussion the steering group agreed that it was for the Ministers in Prague to decide whether, how and when new countries could join. They did conclude, however, that already before the Prague meeting, the Secretariat of the Council of Europe could be invited as an observer, if accepted by the enlarged follow-up group, meaning with the permission of the signatory

123. The ensuing report provided the basis for the discussions of an international seminar held in February 2000 in Leiria, under the Portuguese Presidency. The report found that a credit accumulation system used in the framework of the Bologna Process, indeed important for improving mobility, should be built upon the ECTS given that it was already widely known and used.
124. Balzer & Martens 2004, 10.
125. Haug & Tauch 2000.
126. Balzer & Martens 2004, 10.
127. *Ibid.*
128. The meeting of the Directors General of vocational education in Rovaniemi, 24–28 Sep. 1999.

countries.[129] Indeed, in 2000, the Council of Europe, as well as a Student Platform and EURASHE, were added as observers to the enlarged group. Subsequently, the observers were appointed as consultative members in the Prague Communiqué. Remarkably, it took an initiative from the Council of Europe itself to become involved, whereas the Commission had been drawn into the Process more or less naturally, mostly because the governmental representatives and education ministers of the EU Member States seized on every available moment as an opportunity to discuss the Sorbonne Declaration, therefore mostly at EU events where the Commission was also present. The Council of Europe, one of the longstanding authorities in European higher education, was apparently not 'in the loop', and therefore had to actively seek involvement. It was an example of the lack of political etiquette that characterized the initial phase of the Bologna Process.

The role of the Commission in the Bologna Process is varied, ranging from funding to undertaking studies,[130] setting benchmarks[131] and adapting its own programmes to achieve the Bologna aims.[132] Ever since its Prague inclusion the Commission has been using its membership to the fullest, actively influencing the targets and goals of the Bologna undertaking.[133] It is reported that the Commission has been making use of its mandate to occupy the floor for a great amount of time during conferences, and has been frontrunner in spreading ideas about how to proceed with activities and proposals on 'what to do next'.[134] Unlike the Council of Europe, the Commission has voting rights.[135] The Commission acquired this right a few years after its Prague membership, in 2005. In addition, the importance of the Commission's participation in the preparatory working groups should not be underestimated, as this is where many of the ideas are developed and where the content of the Bologna Process takes actual shape. Here the Commission has the opportunity to get certain issues taken up in the draft outline, which constitutes the point of departure of the discussions at the actual Ministerial Conference. It has been argued that this way, the Bologna Process has slowly become included in the work of the European Commission and that the 'Commission influenced and has been able to change the character of Bologna without intervention by the Member States'.[136] Illustrative of this increased influence of the Commission in the

129. Portuguese presidency, notes of the meeting of the Bologna Follow Up Group in Lisbon, 31 Jan. 2000.
130. European Commission, *Investing Efficiently in Education and Training: An Imperative for Europe*, COM (97) 563.
131. European Commission, *European Benchmarks in Education and Training: Follow-Up to the Lisbon European Council*, COM (2002) 629.
132. The Socrates programme has been adapted so as to financially support the introduction of the Diploma Supplement. See European Commission, *From Berlin to Bergen: The EU Contribution.* See also Lonbay 2004, 254.
133. Balzer & Martens 2004, 13.
134. *Ibid.*
135. Terry 2008, 118.
136. Balzer & Martens 2004, 4.

Bologna Process is that the Action Lines added since Bologna, most specifically lifelong learning and doctoral research, have been inspired by the Commission's higher education policy priorities. Although it is true that the original source of the lifelong learning and research policies is the European Council, and thus the Member States, which launched the overarching framework of a European knowledge economy encompassing these specific objectives, it does signal the impact of the Commission's contributions in the follow-up groups. There are diverse communications by the Commission underlining that the thematic interest of the Commission has been included in the later Bologna Process.[137]

This development illustrates that with Bologna, the Commission is pursuing its education objectives in two different forums, both within the EU framework and outside. Perhaps the Commission does so with the intent to optimize its overall output. It is natural that the Commission sees golden opportunities in the Bologna Process to promote its own policies, such as increased mobility through the increased use of the ECTS. In the words of a Commission representative: 'the Bologna process should ultimately lead to making measures such as the ECTS and Diploma supplement more widespread'.[138] The Commission respectfully phrases its own initiatives as facilitative tools in service of the Bologna Process, but it could be speculated that its intentions are the other way around. Keeling argues that the Bologna Process has in fact served to significantly broaden the European Commission's basis for involvement in the higher education sector.[139] In her opinion, 'the Commission's dynamic association of the Bologna university reforms with its Lisbon research agenda and its successful appropriation of these as European-level issues have placed its perspectives firmly at the heart of higher education policy debates in Europe'.[140] Furlong goes one step further and argued that 'the increasing involvement of the European Commission may suggest that the Commission is seeking to integrate the Bologna process into EU business and to drive it in its desired direction'.[141]

Indeed, with its increased influence the Commission might aim for greater convergence between the two forums. Such convergence is already taking place, and several authors concur that this way the Bologna Process is slowly being subsumed in the EU framework. According to Furlong, 'the momentum behind the Bologna process has been followed by renewed activism on the part of the

---

137. Here one can mention the communication 'The role of the University in a Europe of Knowledge' (2003), which was highly acknowledged by all sides in the Bologna process. In July 2003, the Commission also published a communication on 'Researchers in the European Research area, one profession, multiple careers.' In addition, another communication on 'Making lifelong learning a reality' (2001) is closely linked to the discussion around Bologna. Balzer & Martens 2004, 14.
138. Answer given by Mrs Reding on behalf of the Commission to Written Question E-0890/01 by Juan Naranjo Escobar (PPE-DE) to the Commission, on the Socrates programme for the years 2000 to 2006, OJ C 340 E, 1 Jun. 2001, 0117–0117.
139. Keeling 2006, 203.
140. *Ibid.*
141. Furlong 2005, 55.

European Commission' which 'might presage the future incorporation of Bologna commitments into the *acquis communautaire*'. Accordingly, he argues that:

> it is not fanciful to envisage that current non-binding intergovernmental commitments may acquire legal status in the EU. The public international soft law of Bologna could foreseeably become EU hard law, subject to its usual policy procedures. It would be hard politically for Member States who have already signed up to Bologna to resist this process.[142]

He rightly points out that if this would happen, it 'would have major implications both for the content of the reform process and for the eventual legal status of the decisions'.[143] There are several things to say about this development.[144] If the Commission aspires to draw the Bologna Process into the EU framework, with the view to eventually give a firm legal foundation to the project, its course of action should, it is submitted here, be encouraged. It could serve to enhance the legitimacy of the Bologna project, which up to now lacks a legal foundation. It could create more certainty about the source and nature of the obligations and the relationship with other EU initiatives, which is to be applauded from a transparency perspective. But there are some specific concerns to point out. Until the moment that the Bologna Process becomes officially part of the EU, this strategy implies that the Commission pursues EU objectives *outside* the EU. In addition to the Member States' move to 're-nationalize' higher education policy by embarking on the Bologna Process via intergovernmental cooperation outside the EU, this marks a certain kind of *de-communitarization* of the Commission's higher education policy, which can be regarded as worrying.

Bologna objectives such as research are firmly established areas of activity of the EU, and the EC Treaty provides explicit description of the tasks and competences in that field.[145] It is true that the research and development provisions see to 'only' a complementary role of the EU,[146] giving priority to the Member States, and that the position of the European Commission is quite strong in this field vis-à-vis the European Parliament.[147] But it is still questionable whether the

142. *Ibid.*, 57.
143. *Ibid.*, 55.
144. For one, the legal competence of the EU to adopt the Bologna Process as a binding measure needs to be addressed. Indeed, as Ch. 6 extensively discusses, the present author concurs that the Bologna Process could become hard law, but a thorough legal analysis of the competence of the EU in higher education needs to precede that conclusion. Note however at this point already that if one agrees on the possibility of the Bologna Process being incorporated in the *acquis*, logically one should also support the argument that the Bologna Declaration could have been adopted as a binding Community measure in the first place, such as a Bologna Directive.
145. Title XVIII of the EC Treaty.
146. Article 164 EC stipulates: 'In pursuing these objectives, the Community shall carry out the following activities, complementing the activities carried out in the Member States.'
147. Article 165 EC provides that for the purposes of coordinating the 'research and technological development activities of the Community and the Member States', 'so as to ensure that national policies and Community policy are mutually consistent', 'the Commission may take any useful initiative' 'in close cooperation with the Member State'.

Commission should be able to move its higher education policies to an arena completely separated from the official EU framework. This matter becomes even more pressing upon realizing that the Commission and its policy do not only influence the Bologna Process, but that the same applies vice versa. By shifting research, student and teacher mobility, recognition, the ECTS and other well-established fields of EU activity into the intergovernmental Bologna arena, the content of these policies is altered. It means that suddenly the Commission is only a 'voting member' on these issues (which it *nota bene* has only been since 2005, meaning that before that it could not even vote on these core issues of its legal competence in higher education) and that non-EU countries that participate in the Bologna Process co-determine their content and development.[148] The Commission is only one of the many voices that have a say in the Process, and it cannot veto unwanted developments. In sum, the content of the EU's higher education policies is altered in a non-EU, non-binding, intergovernmental context completely detracted from the scrutiny of the European Parliament and the European Court.

An example of this projected development is the matter of exportability of maintenance grants. In 2005, at the Bergen Conference, the Bologna ministers 'confirmed their commitment to facilitate the portability of loans and grants'.[149] As we have seen in Chapter 4 when discussing the case law of the ECJ in the area of higher education, maintenance grants have become included in the scope of EU law for the purposes of the application of the non-discrimination principle of Article 12 EC (now Article 18 TFEU). In that sense, they can be a subject of equal treatment claims under European law in two ways; either a foreign student applies to a grant in the host Member State where he or she pursues his or her studies, or a national of a Member State applies to his or her own authorities for a maintenance grant, to be used in relation to studies in another EU country. The Court of Justice has ruled that the right of a student to a grant in the first situation can be subjected to an integration requirement, and has held that a student cannot derive from European law a direct right to export his or her grant, but then when a Member State decides to make this possible, the conditions should be in conformity with European law. Apart from the fact that this position might very well develop further, watering down the justifiable conditions for the first situation and developing a right to exportability in the second, the fact that this is a matter falling within the realms of EU law means that it is worrying that Ministers are trying to solve the matter outside the EU framework.

The fact that rights of foreign students to receive maintenance grants in their host state can overlap with exportability possibilities in their home state, thereby potentially leading to double entitlements, implies that coordination on the European level is needed. It is an example of the phenomenon that negative integration leads to (a need for) positive integration. Although therefore European-level coordination is desirable, it should arguably be done within an EU context

148. Although, it should be pointed out that in the context of the legislative procedure of the Community, the Commission has not voting rights – 'only' the right of initiative.
149. Bologna with Student Eyes Report, 31.

considering its close relation to the fundamental freedoms granted by the Treaty. One might be tempted to think that tackling these issues is of greater importance than the way in which that happens, but such a conclusion would neglect the fact that these two elements are intertwined. Within an EU framework, the coordinative measures could have direct effect, meaning that an individual could derive rights from it, enforceable in court. Within the Bologna Arena, however, no such possibility exists, unless the voluntary character of the process is abandoned and Bologna objectives would be made into international treaty law instead. The Guardian of the Treaty has however done nothing to stop the Member States from exporting the matter to the intergovernmental Bologna Arena, and has in fact stated in its contribution to the Berlin Conference that it 'welcomed proposals to make student loans and grants portable in order to enable students to carry out short periods of study or full cycles in other European countries'.[150]

Most of the concern with the increased involvement of the European Commission in the literature is not so much concerned with this aspect, but rather the other way around, and is critical about the prospect of the Bologna Process being integrated into the *acquis communautaire.* A recent report from the UK House of Commons provides a good example of this opinion. It states that 'worries have been expressed in written and oral evidence the role played by the European Commission might be contrary to the principles that inspire Bologna in that it may increase bureaucracy, centralize control and encourage conformity, whilst diminishing flexibility, responsiveness and creativity'.[151] Apparently, there is nothing the Commission can do to disprove the suspicion that it will show its real face as a 'harmonizer' as soon as provided with the opportunity.[152] Although the Commission has always respected the non-harmonization paradigm, the Member States suspect it to do so only *nolens volens.*[153] Obviously, it would be rather difficult for the Commission to go and 'harmonize' the education sector on its own, without the Member States onboard. The Commission does not pass legislation by itself. But the concern is that it has only taken a restrictive stance in these matters because it was forced to do so, and in order to be able to gain influence later on. Although the point that the Commission politely swallowed its exclusion from the Bologna Process only or mainly because it needed to regain a seat at the table is endorsed here, but that is not to say that the increased influence of the Commission is not to be supported. The value of having a coordinator with resources at the table should not be underestimated, let alone the importance of having someone try and maintain compatibility with the EU.[154] Perhaps controversially, it is submitted here that it is this latter task that the Commission should be taking more seriously.

150. European Commission, *Contribution to the Berlin Ministerial Conference*, 2003, 7.
151. House of Commons, Education and Skills Committee 2007a, 32.
152. Garben 2009.
153. Wächter 2004, 271.
154. This point will be discussed at length in Ch. 6.

2.4. Increasing Convergence with the Lisbon Strategy

The above discussion has shown that the Commission has managed to gain influence in the Bologna Process, thus increasingly pursuing its objectives *outside* the Union framework. According to most commentators, Bologna has also allowed the Commission to gain influence *within* a Union context, mainly by – in reaction to the Bologna Process – developing 'its higher education discourse as a key for the Europe of knowledge'.[155] The Commission has been able to do this because many of the ideas of the Bologna Process have found clear correspondence with European Council documents, most importantly the Lisbon Council Conclusions, and therefore it has seen its political mandate in the higher education sector expanded. The Lisbon European Council was not a one-time event, and the goal to become a European knowledge economy has been firmly positioned on the European agenda ever since. Two years after the Lisbon Council, in Barcelona, the European Council made even cleared reference to the emerging common area of higher education, calling for further action to 'introduce instruments to ensure the transparency of diplomas and qualifications (the ECTS, diploma and certificate supplements, European CV) and closer cooperation with regard to university degrees'.[156]

The most obvious example of this increased mandate of the Commission to act within the Union framework is the introduction of the OMC in education by the Lisbon Strategy. The Commission plays a central role in the OMC, and is now in a position to set overarching goals for the European higher education sector. These are not legally binding, but it does boost the Commission's political power in this field. Nevertheless, although it is true that the Commission has thus been able to affirm its role in higher education matters within the EU context as a consequence of the Lisbon Strategy, and has used the increased interest in achieving a knowledge economy to advocate its aims and programmes in higher education, it seems that at least initially this was more a natural consequence of the momentum behind both the Bologna Process and the Lisbon Strategy than deliberate tactics of the Commission. It was the European Council that shortly after the Bologna Declaration lifted the latter's overarching philosophy to a higher level, in making it part of Europe's most important strategic objective. As Kahn put it: 'two years before the European Council of Lisbon, the Sorbonne and Bologna Declarations foreshadowed the EU's well known "strategic goal for the next decade: to become the most competitive and dynamic knowledge-based economy in the world" '.[157] This is, of course, not to say that the Commission was not pleased with this development, and that it is not making the most out of it while it can, because it is.

This momentum, of which the Lisbon Strategy within the EU and the ever-developing Bologna Process outside are part, causes them to increasingly converge. Considering the fact that many of the goals and ideas expressed in the

155. Ravinet 2008a, 357; Muller & Ravinet 2008; Keeling, 2006.
156. See Zgaga 2003.
157. Kahn 2002, 2

context of the Lisbon Strategy concur with the overarching philosophy as well as concrete aims of the Bologna Process, this convergence is not surprising. The OMC plays a key role in this merging 'into one policy framework'.[158] Most of the elements or characteristics of the OMC, for example, setting timetables, establishing indicators and benchmarks and operating accordingly, setting specific targets and periodic monitoring, evaluation and peer review, can now also be found in the activities around the Bologna Process. Some even claim that the Bologna Process is now considered to be part of the OMC.[159] Since Berlin 2003 the Commission coordinates monthly 'Bologna seminars,' which seek to push forward the spread of best practice through the OMC.[160] The ENQAAs plays an important role in the implementation of the Bologna Declaration. As Furlong notes, the ENQAA is a typical OMC institution in its structure and operations, set-up and supported by the European Commission. In Berlin, this institution was mandated to develop standards, procedures and guidelines on quality assurance. Bologna has however, up until now, not been formally incorporated in the EU framework. Therefore it cannot be called a part of the OMC, or the Lisbon Process, as such. Rather it is seen that the activities of the Commission in the framework of Bologna are considered to be part of the OMC, or the Lisbon Process. The Commission itself formulates it as follows:

> The Lisbon Strategy encompasses the Commission's contribution to the intergovernmental Bologna Process, aiming to establish a European Higher Education Area by 2010, mainly in the areas of curricular reform and quality assurance. The Bologna process coincides with Commission policy in higher education supported through European programmes and notably Socrates-Erasmus, Tempus and Erasmus Mundus. The Commission stimulates Bologna initiatives at European level and participates as a full member in the Bologna Follow-up Group and the Bologna Board.

The focus of much of the research in this area is on the European Commission as a policy actor in the higher education sector, which is understandable because of its importance as well as fascinatingly difficult position. But it should not be forgotten that the EU Member States are the main driving forces behind the reform movement sweeping European higher education, in their capacity as the Council and in Bologna's intergovernmental arena. The States seem keen to pursue the related objectives in several political contexts, both inside and outside the EU. It is not entirely clear why, and whether, they would be in favour of increased convergence. It is most likely that the states, if provided with the choice, would prefer to keep Bologna separate from the EU framework. But at the same time, they do benefit from an increased convergence, or perhaps rather profusion of Bologna and the Lisbon Strategy. Apart from the objective aims to achieve in European higher education, the national political actors are suspected to have embarked on the

158. See most notably Huisman & Van de Wende 2004, 34–35.
159. Lonbay 2004, 253.
160. Furlong, 55.

Bologna Process for more subjective reasons, as we have seen in Chapter 2. Many political scientists have reported on the 'two-level game' that was played by the main political actors of Bologna.[161] The Bologna Process has been described as a 'red herring', which the national governments use for their own domestic purposes.[162] As Kahn notes:

> it is a highly convenient pretext for nations to evade the responsibility for structural reforms, always necessary and suddenly indispensable because of an abstract and disembodied European constraint. If they cannot lay the blame for the constraint on some little 'bureau' in Brussels or elsewhere – there isn't one – they can always plead the fulfilment of undertakings to their partners: they must follow their partners' example or will lose ground.

Perhaps the Member States even created, or conveniently did not resolve, the mistake that the Bologna Process was imposed by 'Europe', taken to mean the EU. Here it is relevant to repeat some of the observations of Chapter 2. Ravinet has argued in this context that the governmental players 'manipulate the objectives and use them as leverage and justification for reforms, even though they are not unilaterally obliged to implement these objectives':

> The Bologna Process seems to have an element of juridicity (Pitseys, 2004), in that it appears to be legally binding in nature, especially when participating countries misinterpret their commitments as requiring conformity to superior and legally binding European policies. This lack of clarity can be used as a means to legitimise national reforms. This misconception is reinforced when Bologna declarations and communiqués are presented as texts of quasi-legal value, even though initially the Bologna Process did not have any official legal status.[163]

In addition, several authors also argue that the use of the knowledge-economy rhetoric has contributed to the increasing sense of 'being bound' to the Bologna objectives by the signatories themselves. Ravinet argues convincingly that the overlap between the Bologna objectives and those of the EC is, to a certain extent, 'where they derive their authority and importance from, at least partly explaining why their use contributes so much to a sense of bindingness'.[164] Fejes concurs, stating that 'planetspeak rhetoric such as the ideas of the knowledge society, employability, lifelong learning, quality assurance and mobility . . . constitute a way of thinking that makes participation in the Bologna process and the implementation of its objectives a rational way to act'.[165] In that sense, one can say that the Process has begun to lead its own life, once the 'soft' and flexible product of informal intergovernmental cooperation, now turning into something that 'needs to

161. Racké 2007; Ravinet 2008a.
162. Kahn 2002, 4.
163. Ravinet 2008a, 353.
164. *Ibid.*, 357.
165. Fejes, 2005, 219.

be done' without anyone knowing exactly why, or having different reasons to think so. This partly explains the surprising force of this voluntary project of policy convergence. All the actors appear to have their own objectives, which can be located in some common rhetoric and therewith a powerful platform for action is created. As Corbett puts it, 'governments want to use Europe to introduce domestic reform. The Commission wishes to extend its competence in higher education. University presidents want recognition. They each bring elements of the solution, as embodied in Bologna'.[166]

3. CONCLUDING REMARKS

As Halvorsen & Nyhagen point out 'we still have a long way to go before we fully understand how the Sorbonne declaration, the Bologna Process and the now 35-year old EU initiatives within higher education have mixed, and will mix in the future'.[167] It is difficult to see what has exactly led to what, what came first and what has come as a consequence of something else. One could say that the Bologna Process originates in the Lisbon Recognition Convention of the Council of Europe, while another could argue that it rather stems from the initiatives of the European Commission in higher education, most notably its mobility programmes, dating back to the 1980s. Someone else could link the Bologna Process in its entirety to the emergence of a new thinking in Europe about education and the economy, making the Lisbon Strategy and the Bologna Process parts of the same overall political philosophy sweeping the European continent. This philosophy is often qualified as one of the commercialization and economization of higher education, as part of a neo-liberal approach to education. Although this fits well within the stereotype of the EU as an economically driven organization, and although there is more than a grain of truth in that, it should have become clear by now that it is really the Member States – the national governments – that are behind the wheel here. As is often the case, most probably all these factors do their part in explaining the Bologna Process and its relation to the European Organizations and their activities.

What we have seen in this chapter is the enormous amount of overlap of interaction between the Institutions and the Bologna Process. This has had some beneficial effects, in mainstreaming them, making their actual fulfilment more likely. In that sense, the alignment of objectives has led to a kind of cross-fertilization between the Bologna Process and the work of the European Organizations. As Karlsen points out the Process 'can be perceived as a national implementation of central elements in EU's policy' and similarly the Council of Europe's higher education policy.[168] But the overlaps also bear the danger of an overall loss of transparency and the risk of undermining the policy and general

166. Corbett 2004.
167. Halvorsen & Nyhagen 2005, 6.
168. Karlsen 2005, 4.

authority of the European Organizations, especially the EU. The Bologna Process takes the matter of diploma recognition out of the hands of the European Organizations, taking over some initiatives and pre-empting others by occupying the entire space of academic recognition and – even broader – student/teacher mobility. Although the European Commission is playing an increasingly influential role in the Process, the compatibility with the EU framework is far from secure. From an EU perspective, the increased involvement of the European Commission might in fact be worrisome, for this way established fields of EU competence and action are transferred to a non-transparent, non-EU arena: that of public international soft law making.

The fact that the Bologna Process and the EU are becoming increasingly intertwined was only to be expected. All the Member States of the EU are signatory to the Bologna Declaration. The follow-up is structured around EU presidency. The coordination and cooperation within the Process are heavily dependent on the financial support and expertise of the European Commission. Most importantly, the Bologna Process deals with well-established EU policies in education, incorporates by reference several EU initiatives and is supported in many direct and indirect ways by various EU projects.[169] In fact, this convergence seems more logical than the decision to implement the Process outside the EU in the first place. In the literature, the mounting convergence has often been described with a somewhat critical or worried undertone, for the influence of the European Commission in the Bologna Process is far from uncontroversial. If one takes the perspective that higher education should fall within the reign of national sovereignty, excluding any competence of the EU apart from some facilitating role in financing and information gathering through the commissioning of studies, then the increasing influence of the European Commission in the Bologna Process might indeed be perceived as worrying. At the same time, the entire Bologna Process with its far-reaching reforms and increasing sense of bindingness might then be worrying. If one, on the other hand, adheres to the view that the EU should have a substantial role to play in higher education matters, especially in light of the apparent consensus among the European countries that a mobile highly educated labour force of European citizens is the key to a prosperous Europe in the future and that structural harmonization of the higher-education systems is the way to get there, the only discontentment with this increased convergence would be that it could be even better if the Bologna Process was instantly subsumed into EU hard law.

169. Terry 2008, 120.

Chapter 6

The Bologna Process from a European Law Perspective*

1. INTRODUCTION

The foregoing chapters have paved the way for the final, critical analysis of the topic of inquiry of this book, the Bologna Process. The preceding chapter has been devoted to fleshing out the strained relationship between the Bologna Process and the EU, in terms of institutional relations as well as material interaction. Having explored the complexities and the curiosities of the relationship between the Bologna Process and the EU and the Council of Europe in terms of policy overlap and institutional interaction, it is now time to consider the alternative scenarios that existed to adopt the Bologna Declaration, particularly within the EU framework, but also addressing the possibility of a Council of Europe Convention. Setting out the available alternatives to adopt a Bologna measure will not only give a good insight in the – often underestimated – competence of the EU in higher education matters, but will also provide us with the appropriate background information to proceed with our end game, to wit the normative assessment of the Bologna Process, from an EU law perspective.[1] After all, the competence question is intrinsically connected with both the extent of the peculiarity and the legitimacy of the Bologna Process as it is currently operated. Should we come to conclude that there existed one or more possibilities to adopt the Bologna Declaration within the EU framework, the question why this was not pursued becomes all the more pressing, and the absence of a sound rationale even more curious. Moreover, it adds a new dimension to scrutinizing the legitimacy of the Bologna enterprise. As shall be

* A previous version of this chapter has been published in the European Law Journal, see Garben 2010.

1. Although strictly speaking we are diverging somewhat from a pure EU law perspective, by also taking into account the possibility of adopting the Bologna Declaration as a Council of Europe Convention.

seen, the fact that legal competence existed to enact a 'Bologna Directive' has severe consequences for the lawfulness of the Bologna Process in the way it has actually been adopted and implemented. But even if the Bologna Process strictly speaking holds up to the standard of lawfulness, it might fail the test when applying other important, constitutional norms such as democracy, transparency and accountability, as well as the standards of efficiency and individual protection.

2. ALTERNATIVE SCENARIOS

The first part of this last chapter is devoted to the question whether the content of the Bologna Declaration and Process could have been forged into an EU measure. Four different scenarios of a Bologna measure integrated into the EU legal framework will be discussed, namely a Bologna Directive, a Bologna mixed agreement, a Bologna OMC and Bologna through intergovernmental cooperation within the Council. A fifth scenario is the Bologna Declaration as a Convention in the institutional framework of the Council of Europe.

2.1. A Bologna Directive

Would there have been legal competence to adopt the content of the Bologna Declaration as an EU measure? In trying to answer this question, Article 165 TFEU (ex Article 149 EC), which sets out the formal powers of the Union in educational matters, constitutes the obvious starting point. Although the provision contains the promising statement that one of the aims of EU action is 'encouraging mobility of students and teachers, by encouraging *inter alia*, the academic recognition of diplomas and periods of study', the general impression is that EU powers are severely restricted in this field. The first paragraph defines the role of the EU as supportive and supplementary to Member State action, basically restricted to encouraging cooperation between Member States. It stresses that the Member States remain responsible for the organization of their education systems. Moreover, paragraph four stipulates that the Union may only adopt so-called 'incentive measures', excluding any harmonization of the laws and regulations of the Member States. The *ratio legis* of Article 165 TFEU is quite clear, and the prohibition of harmonization seems to put all discussion on legislative competence instantly to an end. However, such a conclusion would be premature. First, it should be assessed whether the Bologna Process actually entails harmonization. Secondly, the Treaty also provides other potential legal bases for EU action in the field of education. Is there such an alternative legal basis that could have supported Bologna as an EU measure? Does Article 165(4) TFEU (ex Article 149(4) EC) stand in the way of the use of another Treaty provision to adopt a harmonizing measure in the field of higher education?

The question whether the Bologna Process constitutes or amounts to a harmonization of the laws and regulations of the Member States obviously depends on one's definition of the term harmonization. In the context of European law, harmonization is generally taken to mean the approximation of national laws in order to create one European standard, by means of legislation.[2] The strongest argument to support the view that the Bologna Process implies such harmonization is that Bologna standardizes the structure of the higher-education systems of the participating states by constructing a system of undergraduate studies followed by graduate studies, and comparable degrees. The Declaration states that 'access to the second cycle shall require successful completion of first cycle studies, lasting a minimum of three years. The degree awarded after the first cycle shall also be relevant to the European labour market as an appropriate level of qualification. The second cycle should lead to the master and/or doctorate degree as in many European countries'. The introduction of the two-cycle Bachelor-Master system clearly constitutes a uniform standard. Furthermore, the Sorbonne Declaration, which is seen as the basis for the Bologna Declaration and Process, carries the term 'harmonization' in its very title.

However, in contrast with the Sorbonne Declaration, the Bologna Declaration carefully avoids the use of the word. In fact, the question whether the envisaged Bologna project constituted 'harmonization' is reported to have been a highly contentious issue that had to be resolved before the Declaration could be signed.[3] There had already been discussion about the use of the term in the run-up to the conference. Most of the participating countries deemed the type of standardization entailed by harmonization to be undesirable in the field of higher education. Although the French minister Claude Allègre tried to convince his colleagues that 'harmonization' as used in the text of the Declaration was not to mean 'standardization' in its unwanted sense, the majority of participants preferred to stay on the safe side and leave out the term. Hence, it appears that the participants have agreed that the Bologna Process does not constitute harmonization. Moreover, the Process does not entail substantive harmonization, seeing that the content of each course is still determined by the individual countries and their universities. The Bologna Declaration aims for 'structural comparability but content diversity'.[4] The Process resembles a voluntary cooperation project towards policy convergence, unfit for the label 'harmonization'. However, the relevant question to answer is whether the Bologna Declaration *if adopted as a binding EU measure*

2. With the exception of Art. 99 EEC, regarding indirect taxes, the term harmonization was introduced by the Single Act, most notably in what was then Art. 100a EEC (now Art. 95 EC). The wording of this provision indicates that harmonization refers to Community law measures for the approximation of the provisions laid down by law, regulation of administrative action in Member States, which have as their object the establishment or functioning of the internal market. See Van Gerven 2005, 227–254. The concept of harmonization has been broadly interpreted by the ECJ, for example, also the creation of a coordinating agency can constitute harmonization in the sense of Art. 95 EC.
3. Kirkwood-Tucker 2004.
4. Vogel 2007, 131–133. The Bologna Declaration claims to take full respect of 'the diversity of cultures, languages, national education systems and of University autonomy'. It states that to that end, 'the ways of intergovernmental co-operation' will be pursued, 'together with those of non governmental European organisations with competence on higher education'.

would qualify as harmonization. Indeed, the imposition by an EU legislative measure of the Bachelor-Master system as the uniform standard meets the definition, even if the content of the courses and the duration of the cycles are left to the Member States. Hence, a directive or regulation with the content of the Bologna Declaration could not have been based on Article 165 TFEU.

2.1.1. Articles 46, 53 and 62 TFEU (Ex Articles 40, 47 and 55 EC)

Nonetheless, the Treaty provides for other provisions attributive of competence in higher education. Because of the fact that the EU is endowed with a number of functional powers, such as the creation of the common market and therein the free movement of persons, many policy fields that were initially not intended to be 'Union business' can be and have been affected in the slipstream of the implementation of these functional powers.[5] Higher education constitutes such a policy field. As the ECJ stated in 1974, in its landmark *Casagrande* judgment: 'although educational and training policy is not as such included in the spheres which the Treaty has entrusted to the EU Institutions, it does not follow that the exercise of powers transferred to the EU is in some way limited if it is of such a nature as to affect the measures taken in the execution of a policy such as that of education and training'.[6] Considering the close ties between higher education and the labour market, it is not surprising that internal market legislation can indeed also deal with educational matters. Especially the free movement of persons, which is one of the fundamental pillars underpinning the internal market, is interrelated with educational matters. In the recent *Schwarz* case, the ECJ confirmed that privately funded education constituted a service within the meaning of the Treaty, and that restrictions on cross-border movement to receive these services would have to be justified.[7] And we have seen in the *Neri* case that failing to offer an objective academic recognition procedure could be to constitute a restriction of the freedom of establishment.[8]

Furthermore, the objective to abolish obstacles to the free movement of persons and services includes the right to pursue a profession, in a self-employed or employed capacity, in a Member State other than the one where a European citizen has obtained his or her professional qualifications.[9] Articles 46, 53 and 62 TFEU (ex Articles 40, 47 and 55 EC) grant the EU competence to adopt measures to bring about the free movement of workers, make it easier for persons to take up and pursue activities as self-employed persons, and to facilitate the provision of services. It is common ground that the mutual recognition of diplomas as a part of the free

5. De Witte 1987, 236.
6. Case 9/74, *Donato Casagrande v. Landeshauptstadt München* [1974] ECR 773.
7. Case C-76/05, *Schwarz v. Finanzambt Bergisch Gladbach,* judgment of 11 Sep. 2007, not yet reported.
8. Case C-153/02, *Valentina Neri v. European School of Economics* [2003] I-13555.
9. See para. 1 of the Preamble of *Directive 2005/36/EC of the European Parliament and of the Council of 7 September 2005 on the recognition of professional qualifications*, OJ 2005 L255/22.

movement of persons is a well-established policy field of the EU. After all, diploma requirements 'can as much constitute obstacles to the completion of the internal market as, for example, the use of different safety standards for technical goods'.[10] Ever since the Treaty of Rome, the EU has been competent to enact legislation in this area, including harmonizing measures, even dealing with the content of certain studies.[11] Access to the medical profession, for example, has been almost completely harmonized by European legislation. As the Bologna Process aims to enhance the readability and compatibility of degrees to facilitate mutual recognition thereof, one could argue that the Bologna Declaration could have been adopted in the form of an EU measure making use of (one of) these legal bases.

The standard counterargument is that Union competence under Article 53 TFEU is limited to the *professional* recognition of diplomas. *Academic* recognition, on the other hand, allegedly lies outside the realm of the EC's legislative powers, as this is where Article 165(4) TFEU applies. This situation leads to the curious result that Member States have attributed the EU with full competence to legislate in the sensitive area of education/diploma recognition for the regulated and liberal professions, such as medicine, law and architecture, which are the professions where public interest plays an important role and hence legal standards are deemed necessary, whereas the Union is not competent to deal with the much less politically sensitive matter of academic recognition of all other higher education. The reason for that would be that such professional recognition is more closely connected to the labour market, and hence an EU affair. But it could be argued that the doctrinal distinction made between academic and professional recognition is artificial and should be abolished, which would allow for a fully fledged Union competence in diploma recognition. This is supported by the fact that the text of Article 53 TFEU does not explicitly exclude the academic recognition of diplomas. Its first paragraph stipulates that: 'in order to make it easier for persons to take up and pursue activities as self-employed persons, the Council shall, acting in accordance with the ordinary legislative procedure, issue directives for the mutual recognition of diplomas, certificates and other evidence of formal qualifications'. Indeed, Davies argues that the assumption that the EU's jurisdiction over qualifications is confined to the professional is mistaken, and that Article 53 TFEU (ex Article 47 EC):

> enables broader legislation covering the mutual recognition of diplomas, certificates and other evidence of formal qualifications. It extends the recognition

---

10. Schneider & Claessens 2005, 123.
11. For sake of clarity and transparency, Directive 2005/36/EC of the European Parliament and of the Council of 7 Sep. 2005 on the recognition of professional qualifications, OJ 2005 L 255, has rationalized the system by replacing Council Directives 89/48/EEC and 92/51/EEC, as well as Directive 1999/42/EC of the European Parliament and of the Council on the general system for the recognition of professional qualifications, and Council Directives 77/452/EEC, 77/453/EEC, 78/686/EEC, 78/687/EEC, 78/1026/EEC, 78/1027/EEC, 80/154/EEC, 80/155/EEC, 85/384/EEC, 85/432/EEC, 85/433/EEC and 93/16/EEC concerning the professions of nurse responsible for general care, dental practitioner, veterinary surgeon, midwife, architect, pharmacist and doctor, and combining them in a single text.

> of qualifications beyond the professional and into the 'purely' academic. In doing so, it does more than merely impinge on the Bologna Process, it actually offers an instrument for instituting its over-arching qualifications framework.[12]

Furthermore, as the case law of the ECJ shows, the two areas are very much interconnected. We recall the *Neri* case, where failure to offer an objective academic recognition procedure was construed as a restriction of the freedom of establishment, if it concerned a foreign provider of higher education. Even more strikingly, in the *Kraus* judgment the ECJ held that Articles 48 and 52 EEC (now Articles 45 and 49 TFEU) precluded national measure governing the conditions under which an academic title obtained in another Member State may be used, where such measures were liable to hamper or to render less attractive the exercise by EU nationals of fundamental freedoms guaranteed by the Treaty.[13] In 1995, the European Parliament in a Resolution on the Commission's communication on recognition of qualifications for academic and professional purposes stated that it expected the Commission to 'introduce coherent rules on the mutual recognition at European level of qualifications (professional *and* academic diplomas) so that employees with professional qualifications can exercise the right of freedom of movement'.[14] In that context, the Parliament even went so far as to express the belief that 'in the longer term consideration should be given to comparable requirements in final examinations and that the aim should be to approximate training periods and certificates', adding that the Member States or individual universities should be responsible for the content of courses.

On the other hand, with the insertion of Article 126 of the EC Treaty (now Article 165 TFEU), dealing with general education and explicitly mentioning academic recognition, the position that academic recognition falls outside the scope of Article 53 TFEU has gained ground. The ECJ had never ruled on the question, but one could read some clues in the ERASMUS case that academic recognition was regarded to be included, or at least not clearly excluded, from Article 53 TFEU.[15] Nevertheless, the subsequent Maastricht Treaty placed academic

12. Davies*, 8.
13. Case C-19/92, *Dieter Kraus v. Land Baden-Württemberg* [1993] ECR I-01663.
14. European Parliament, Comm. Culture, Youth, Education and the Media, *Resolution on the Commission' s communication on recognition of qualifications for academic and professional purposes* (COM (94) 0596 – C4-0123/95) OJ 1995 C 323, 0048. Emphasis added.
15. Case 242/87, *Commission v. Council (Erasmus)* [1989] ECR 1425. In assessing what provision of the Treaty would have been the appropriate legal basis for the adoption of the ERASMUS Programme, the Commission arguing that Art. 128 of the EEC Treaty would have sufficed whereas the Council contended that the addition of Art. 235 of the EEC Treaty was necessary, the Court also dealt with the question whether Art. 57 of the EEC Treaty (now Art. 47 EC) would have been a possibility. After establishing that Art. 128 of the EEC Treaty could (without support of Art. 234) carry the ERASMUS Programme, the Court stated: 'although it is true that Action 3 of the program concerns "measures to promote mobility though the academic recognition of diplomas and periods of study," examination of the various measures provided for in this part of the programme shows that they are designed merely to prepare for and encourage the

recognition explicitly, and probably not coincidentally, within the limited ambit of Article 126 of the EC Treaty (now Article 165 TFEU). Thus, one could say, academic recognition has been implicitly carved out of the material scope of Article 53 TFEU, and is exclusively dealt with in Article 165 TFEU, where it operates under the direct application of the prohibition of harmonization instead. Then again, in the same paragraph that deals with academic recognition, Article 165 TFEU also mentions the encouragement of teacher and student mobility as an aim for EU action. It seems that if the Union would want to regulate the free movement of teachers, for instance, it would be competent to do so within the context of the free movement of workers, to wit Article 46 TFEU. It would not be held back by the prohibition of harmonization as laid down in Article 165(4) TFEU, nor would it be a convincing argument to say that Article 165 TFEU has carved the area of teacher mobility out of the scope of Articles 45 and 46 TFEU. The legal situation on this matter is not altogether clear and one would need a judgment of the ECJ on the matter to be certain of the correct interpretation of Articles 53 and 165 TFEU. The wording of the provision, which speaks of 'recognition' without qualifying it as only professional recognition or excluding academic recognition points into one direction, but a conjoined reading with Article 165 TFEU into another. The majority opinion is that Article 53 TFEU does not offer legislative competence to regulate the matter of academic recognition. Still, even if that were the correct understanding, Articles 46 and 62 TFEU could carry the Directive by themselves.

It is quite possible to argue that establishing a uniform structure of higher education requiring a two-tier system, guaranteeing a smoother student exchange and an improved mutual recognition of degrees, directly affects and benefits the functioning of the internal market by substantially facilitating the free movement of persons. Disparities in the higher-education systems leading to a hampered recognition of degrees or credits due to incompatibilities and obscurities constitute an important obstacle to free movement, not only for students but also for the labour force in general. The existence of structural disparities between the education systems of the Member States hampers seeking access to a foreign labour market. Not only is it more difficult to temporarily study in the foreign country where one would like to ameliorate employment opportunities, seeing that differences in term, credit and degree structures will obstruct a trouble-free exchange, but the differences between the Member States will also deter employers from hiring a person with whose study programme and credentials he cannot identify. The Bologna Declaration itself stresses this point, by stating that it proposes to adopt 'a system of easily readable and comparable degrees [...] in order to

---

recognition envisaged; that recognition itself is not the subject-matter of the action. The nature of the action is thus sufficient to show that it does not fall under the exclusive scope of application of Article 57 of the Treaty'. Careful reading suggests that if the subject matter of the ERASMUS Programme were the academic recognition of diplomas and periods of study, it would have fallen under the (exclusive) scope of application of Art. 57 of the EEC Treaty. This could lead one to believe that at that time, Art. 57 EEC did encompass academic recognition.

promote European citizens employability'. The ECJ has gone a long way in providing students with the right to study in other Member States. The case could be made that students need to be facilitated in making use of this right, and that when they become workers they need to be able to reap the rewards of their (domestic and/or foreign) study in the entire territory of the EU, which is something that a Bologna Directive would help them to do.[16]

2.1.2. Article 21 TFEU (Ex Article 18 EC)

In addition to the viable possibilities outlined above, an arguably even more appropriate legal basis for the Bologna Directive, or at least a provision that could be used in conjunction with the aforementioned legal bases, can be found in Article 21(2) TFEU (ex Article 18(2) EC). This provision, added by the Maastricht Treaty, is well known for introducing the concept of European citizenship, and for the role it has played in the case law of the ECJ in strengthening the rights of the non-economically active individuals under the Treaty. In addition, it provides legal competence to enact measures to facilitate the free movement of Union citizens, stating that if action by the Union should prove necessary to attain the objective that every citizen of the Union shall have the right to move and reside freely within the territory of the Member States, and if the Treaties have not provided the necessary powers, the European Parliament and the Council, acting in accordance with the ordinary legislative procedure, may adopt provisions with a view to facilitating the exercise of these rights. The most important measure adopted on the basis of this provision is Directive 2004/38/EC on the right of citizens of the Union and their family members to move and reside freely within the territory of the Member States.[17] The fact that this general umbrella Directive already deals with some very specific student issues, such as their rights to grants and loans,

16. As O'Leary points out, in addition to the specific legal provisions on free movement, the Union may sometimes also revert to a number of general legislative provisions designed to permit legislation that facilitates the achievement of the internal market. Art. 114 TFEU (ex 95 EC), which is the most commonly used general internal market competence, is not applicable in the field of persons. Its less powerful twin provision, Art. 115 TFEU (ex Art. 94 EC), does apply. This provision grants competence to the EU to approximate the laws of the Member States in the context of the functioning of the internal market by means of directives. The fact that the provision requires unanimity in the Council explains and counterbalances its rather flexible wording. Relying on Art. 115 TFEU, one would have to argue that the Bologna Directive would directly affect the functioning of the internal market. However, adopting the measure on the basis of these specific internal market provisions would exclude the possibility of adopting the measure under the general internal market competences. The specific provisions take priority over the general ones, which means that if it is accepted that the Bologna Directive is adopted in order to facilitate the free movement of persons in the internal market, there is no room to draw in Art. 115 TFEU. O'Leary 1996, 152.
17. *Directive 2004/38/EC of the European Parliament and of the Council of 29 April 2004 on the right of citizens of the Union and their family members to move and reside freely within the territory of the Member States amending Regulation (EEC) No 1612/68 and repealing Directives 64/221/EEC, 68/360/EEC, 72/194/EEC, 73/148/EEC, 75/34/EEC, 75/35/EEC, 90/364/EEC, 90/365/EEC and 93/96/EEC*, OJ 2004 L 158, 77–123.

could be taken as an illustration that the provision would be appropriate for dealing with student mobility in a more comprehensive manner in the form of a Bologna Directive as well. As the Commission notes, the mobility of people involved in training, education or voluntary work is becoming an increasingly important aspect of the assertion of European citizenship.[18]

Article 21(2) TFEU is not a particularly strong legal basis all by itself, especially considering its wording as a subsidiary legal basis, only applicable when the Treaties have not provided the necessary powers. In its Second Report on Citizenship of the Union of 27 May 1997 the Commission recommended revising Article 18(2) EC (now Article 21(2) TFEU), upgrading it from a supplementary legal basis to a specific legal basis for the free movement and right of residence.[19] Although this has not been done, the provision as it now stands would constitute an appropriate and valuable supportive basis for a Bologna Directive, and it could help counterbalance the preponderantly economic rationale of the other provisions. After all, also the ECJ in its cases relating to mobile students takes Article 21(1) TFEU (ex Article 18(1) EC) as the basis for the formulation of their rights. By adding Article 21(2) TFEU as a legal basis, the rationale behind student mobility and the Bologna Directive is altered from a purely economic to a dual one, adding an important more social dimension. It would mitigate the fear of relentless commercialization of higher education, by approaching the matter of student mobility as one flowing from the rights of the European citizen to move and study anywhere in the European territory on the same conditions as all other EU citizens. As we have seen in Chapter 4, the ECJ has not yet decided whether it will characterize students of private higher education institutions as recipients of services and will judge their claims accordingly. Although it would be a logical second step in the development of the case law as it now stands, it has been submitted that European citizenship is a more appropriate basis for student mobility rights. In that same line of argument, Article 21(2) TFEU should not be omitted in the hypothetical adoption of a Bologna Directive.

2.1.3. The Prohibition of Harmonization

The foregoing shows that with enough political will, it would not have been impossible to find an appropriate legal basis to adopt a Bologna-like measure. But does Article 165(4) TFEU have a role to play in this matter? Does it not prevent any legislative measure, no matter what legal base, that entails the harmonization of national laws in higher education? Hablitzl has argued for such a far-reaching interpretation, maintaining that the creation of a specific and narrowly formulated competence in the field of education, in the form of Article 165 TFEU, has prevented any further action in the field of education on the basis of the internal

18. European Commission, *Third Report on Citizenship of the Union*, COM (2001) 0506.
19. Bulvinaite 2005. See European Commission, *Second report on Citizenship of the Union*, COM (97) 0230.

market competences.[20] In his view, the *Harmonisierungsverbot* of Article 149(4) EC (now Article 165(4) TFEU) is of general application, thereby prohibiting any harmonization on any legal basis, including the internal market competences, in the field of education. This might remind one of a similar argument, raised by the German government in the *Tobacco Advertisement* case[21] in the context of public health. In this case, Germany challenged a directive that imposed a general ban on the advertising or sponsorship of tobacco products in the EU, maintaining that it had been adopted ultra vires. As the Community did not have a general power to legislate in the area of public health, the measure had been adopted on the basis of Articles 100a, 57 and 66 of the EC Treaty (now Articles 114, 53(2) and 62 TFEU). The relevant provision dealing with public health, Article 168 TFEU (ex Article 129(4) of the EC Treaty/Article 152(4) EC), has a structure very similar to Article 165 TFEU. In particular, Article 168(5) TFEU also expressly excludes harmonization of national law. The German government argued that this *Harmonisierungsverbot* led to the invalidity of the directive. It is relevant to quote Advocate General Fennelly, who disagreed with the German government:[22]

> Although it is not contested that the Directive could not have been adopted on the basis of Article 129(4), it would be surprising (and inimical to legal certainty) if the authors of the Treaty on European Union had, when providing new Treaty powers in respect of public health, so severely restricted existing competence in a different field simply because it sometimes has a bearing on health. Articles 100A and 129 are not, in any respect, inconsistent. As we have seen, Articles 100A(3) and 129(1), third indent, combine to show that Article 100A may be used to adopt measures which aim at the better protection of health. The limitation expressed in Article 129(4) is not in conflict with these provisions. It affects, in its own terms, only the incentive measures for which it provides.[23]

In essence, the Court agreed with the view expressed by the Advocate General. It stated that the prohibition of harmonization as laid down in Article 129(4) EC (now Article 168(5) TFEU) did not mean that harmonizing measures adopted on the basis of other provisions of the Treaty were prohibited to have any impact on the protection of human health. Although other articles of the Treaty were not to be used as a legal basis in order to circumvent the express exclusion of harmonization laid down in Article 129(4) of the EC Treaty, this was not to mean that the Community legislature was prevented from relying on the legal basis of Articles 100a, 57(2) and 66 of the EC Treaty on the ground that public health protection was a decisive factor in the choices to be made. Although the Court ultimately annulled the directive, as the internal market rationale could not justify a general ban on

20. Hablitzel 2002, 407–414.
21. Case C-376/98, *Germany v. European Parliament and Council* [2000] ECR I-8419.
22. Note that Art. 100A is now Art. 95 EC and that Art. 126 is now Art. 154 EC.
23. Opinion of Advocate General Fennely, delivered on 15 Jun. 2000 in Case C-376/98, *Germany v. European Parliament and Council* [2000] ECR I-8419.

advertisement, this was not because Article 129(4) of the EC Treaty prohibited all harmonization per se. Applying the same reasoning here, Article 165(4) TFEU does not prevent the adoption of a harmonizing measure affecting the field of higher education, if fulfilling the conditions of, for example, Articles 21, 46, 53 and 62 TFEU. To interpret Article 165(4) EC as excluding any effect on education by internal market measures would be contrary to the *Tobacco Advertisement* ruling as well as the spirit of the Treaty, especially in the way the Treaty has been interpreted by the Court of Justice.[24] Hablitzel argues that the *Harmonisierungsverbot* as introduced by the Treaty of Maastricht has broken through this Treaty system of functional powers, at least in the sense that these negative limitations of competence are absolute. It is submitted here that this is an overly extensive interpretation of Article 165(4) TFEU, and an incorrect reading of the *Tobacco Advertisement* judgment. It does not follow from the ruling that Article 168(5) TFEU prevents all harmonization related to public health. The ECJ merely signalled that precaution is necessary and that it should not be deprived of all meaning by reverting to internal market competences at will. The judgment implies that it remains possible to enact internal market legislation that has a bearing on public health, which is explicitly confirmed by the Treaty in Article 114(3) TFEU, as long as it does not constitute 'circumvention' that is a legislative measure that has health policy as its centre of gravity and only marginal internal market side-effects. The same reasoning should hold for the field of education.

Admittedly, the impact of the hypothetical Bologna Directive on the higher education sectors of the Member States would be greater, or more fundamental, than the impact that the Tobacco Directive had on the public health sector. The measure in the *Tobacco Advertisement* case was not concerned with partial harmonization of the structure of the national healthcare systems, while the Bologna Process fundamentally reorganizes the higher-education systems of the Member States, which is normally considered to be a national prerogative. Still, nothing in the case law of the ECJ suggests that the extent of the impact of a legislative measure on the respective policy field constitutes a criterion to determine competence. The decisive point in the *Tobacco Advertisement* case, causing the directive in question to fall, was that the measure was in fact really aimed at public health protection rather than internal market functioning, because it hardly contributed to free trade. As it contained a full prohibition of tobacco advertisement, it actually dealt with substantive health policy, arguably even restrictive of trade.[25] The directive did not contain a provision guaranteeing the free movement in the EU of the products satisfying the relevant requirements (magazines), and the

24. To repeat once more what was explicitly stated by the ECJ in the *Casagrande* judgment: 'although educational and training policy is not as such included in the spheres which the Treaty has entrusted to the Community Institutions, it does not follow that the exercise of powers transferred to the Community is in some way limited if it is of such a nature as to affect the measures taken in the execution of a policy such as that of education and training'.
25. Although the restricted tobacco market was different from the markets intended to benefit from the measure, the overall restrictive effect on trade of the directive was arguably larger than its trade-facilitating effect.

prohibition arguably did not facilitate trade for other banned advertisement material (ashtrays and parasols). The Bologna Directive, on the other hand, would be truly aimed at increasing the mobility of students, teachers and the general labour force, in the same line of reasoning as the existing legislation on the mutual recognition of diplomas. Indeed, 'many of the concerns expressed in the Declaration [. . .] are intended to increase the immediate value of higher education in relation to the labour market or as a service to students and employers'.[26] Therefore, the Bologna Directive or Regulation could qualify as a real internal market measure, not circumventing the prohibition of Article 165(4) TFEU. Such an interpretation would not deprive the prohibition of harmonization of its meaning. There are plenty of types of actions or measures in the field of education that are firmly excluded, due to paragraph four. For instance, the EU has to steer clear of elementary school, both in terms of content and organizational structures. Also secondary school would most probably be deemed off-limits. Common sense implies that internal market measures are not likely to intrude in these areas of education. It is only at the crossroads of higher education and the market, where education links in with labour market entry, that the internal market competences really become relevant for this policy field.

The view expressed above finds further confirmation in the recent Commission Proposal for a directive on the application of patient's rights in cross-border healthcare.[27] The Commission proposes the establishment of a Community framework for cross-border healthcare, structured around three main areas:

(1) common principles in all EU health systems, dividing between Member States the responsibilities for setting and monitoring healthcare standards;
(2) a framework for cross-border healthcare, dealing with the extent of entitlements of patients;
(3) European cooperation on healthcare, establishing cooperation in border regions, mutual recognition of prescriptions and data collection.

The proposal for the directive is based on Article 114 TFEU (ex Article 95 EC). According to the Commission, this legal base is justified by both the objective and the content of the proposal, as the aim is to establish 'a general framework for provision of safe, high quality and efficient cross-border healthcare in the European Union and to ensure free movement of health services and a high level of health protection, whilst fully respecting the responsibilities of the Member States for the organization and delivery of health services and medical care'. The need for such a framework was catalysed or induced by the case law of the ECJ, which over the years developed a strong right for patients to be treated in other Member States and to be reimbursed for such treatment. The Court has based this right on Article 56 TFEU (ex Article 49 EC), holding it to include the freedom for the recipients of services, such as persons in need of medical treatment, to go to another Member Sate in order

26. Bergan 2003, 32–33.
27. European Commission, *Proposal for a Directive of the European Parliament and of the Council on the application of patients' rights in cross-border healthcare*, COM (2008) 414.

to receive those services there. The proposed framework serves to ensure 'a more general and effective application of these internal market rights in practice, and to ensure that they can be exercised in a way which is compatible with overall health system objectives of accessibility, quality and financial sustainability'. This shows that a far-reaching framework for patient mobility is considered to be compatible with the objectives of Articles 114 and 168 TFEU, including the prohibition of harmonization, confirming the argument presented in the foregoing paragraphs. Furthermore, it illustrates the logic behind the need for such a framework, and how that could equally be applied to the area of education. The case law of the Court, both on education qualifying as a service as well as on the topic of student mobility, could be argued to trigger a similar need for an EU framework – such as a Bologna-like Directive. Important issues of student mobility arising from the case law, such as uneven mobility burdening some Member States disproportionately and potential double entitlements to maintenance grants, could then have been addressed and dealt with in a comprehensive way, together with matters of degree-cycles, credit transfer, diploma recognition and quality assurance.

In line with Davies, therefore, it is submitted here that subsuming the Bologna Process into internal market regulation would have been (and perhaps still is) a realistic option.[28] The foregoing analysis shows that it is possible, if not probable, that the Court would uphold a measure like the hypothetical Bologna Directive as legitimately adopted on a basis of an internal market competence.[29] Having said that, the question of competence also has an external dimension that should not be neglected. As was stated before, the Bologna Process is not an exclusive Member State happening; on the contrary, it involves many non-EU countries. Although the four initiators of the Sorbonne Declaration are all Member States, currently also nineteen non-Member States take part. Yet, this does not exclude the possibility of the Bologna Declaration as an EU instrument. The Union is endowed with external competence, also in the field of education. Article 165(3) TFEU provides that 'the Union and the Member States shall foster cooperation with third countries and the competent international organizations in the field of education, in particular the Council of Europe'. The Member States could have arranged matters as an EU measure internally, without having to exclude other countries from participation in general. Agreements could have been concluded with the third countries. This kind of cooperation in educational matters that concern the EU, involving binding legal instruments, the EU institutions and (resulting in) agreements with third countries is not at all uncommon.[30] An argument that could be made is that in such a scenario

28. Davies*, 8.
29. Practically speaking, the fact that Art. 94 EC requires unanimity in the Council implies that there is less chance that a measure adopted on that basis would find itself challenged as having been adopted ultra vires. All the Member States need to agree on the measure, so challenging it after adoption would be illogical. Also the Commission as initiator of the measure and the consulted Parliament are unlikely to bring a claim, which means that the only probable source of challenge would then be an illegality plea before the national court.
30. See Decision 2006/910/EC of 4 Dec. 2006 concerning the conclusion of the Agreement between the European Community and the United States of America renewing the cooperation

the other countries would not feel equal members of the project, because it would be primarily 'known' or 'felt' as an EU project. Not having any formal position in the internal decision-making process of the EU, the other countries would only have the possibility to 'opt-in' on a 'take it or leave it' basis. However, depending on the mode of proceedings, the non-EU countries could have negotiated on an equal footing, before putting the international agreement down in an internal EU measure. Moreover, we can see that even now, in the intergovernmental non-EU Bologna Process, the EU Member States play a dominant role. The follow-up relies heavily on the EU presidency. Member States are in a better position to influence the Process, in ways that non-EU states do not have at their disposal. In sum, the argument that also non-EU states take part is not convincing in terms of negating competence, nor does it take into account the current reality of the Bologna Process.

2.2. The Bologna Declaration As an EU Agreement

At this point it should be examined whether it would have been possible to adopt the Bologna Declaration as a mixed agreement in order to take these last-mentioned considerations onboard nevertheless. This would mean that both the EU Member States and the EU would be party to the international agreement, on an equal footing with third countries, excluding the necessity of an internal measure. This method is often used in areas where the EU and the Member States share competence.[31] The mixed agreement is an expression of the obligation that in fields where competence is shared the EU and the Member States must cooperate closely together in the negotiation and the conclusion of agreements.[32] The representative of the European Commission that was involved in the follow-up of the Sorbonne Declaration leading to the eventual Bologna initiative had in fact proposed this possibility. It was, however, not taken on board, and might even have contributed to an increased suspicion of the Commission by the UK and France and thereby might have led to the temporary exclusion of the Commission from the Bologna Process.[33] In order to be able to adopt a Bologna EU agreement, the Union would have had to prove the existence of implied external competence in

---

programme in higher education and vocational education and training, OJ L 346; Council Directive 2004/114/EC of 13 Dec. 2004 on the conditions of admission of third-country nationals for the purposes of studies, pupil exchange, unremunerated training or voluntary OJ L 375; Decision No. 1720/2006/EC of the European Parliament and of the Council of 15 Nov. 2006 establishing an action programme in the field of lifelong learning OJ L 327; Decision No. 2317/2003/EC of the European Parliament and of the Council of 5 Dec. 2003 establishing a programme for the enhancement of quality in higher education and the promotion of intercultural understanding through cooperation with non-EU Member Countries (Erasmus Mundus) (2004 to 2008) OJ L 345.

31. See Cremona 1982, 393.
32. See Craig & De Búrca 2003, 131. See also *Opinion 1/78* [1979] ECR 2871.
33. See Ch. 5 on this topic.

accordance with the conditions formulated by the Court in *Opinion 1/76*.[34] In this ruling, the ECJ built on and clarified its landmark *AETR* case,[35] dissociating the existence of implied competence from the exercise of the internal competence, meaning that it was not necessary for there to be internal legislation on the issue that was the subject of the external measure, as long as the external measure was necessary to achieve the aim of the provision granting the internal competence.[36] Thus if third-country participation was indeed integral to the agreement, which would also be one of the reasons not to adopt Bologna as an internal legal measure combined with external agreements, this could have constituted a possibility. The problem is, however, that Article 165(3) TFEU is the most appropriate legal basis for external cooperation in educational matters. As we have discussed above, the prohibition of harmonization, as contained in the fourth paragraph of the very same provision, stands in the way of a Bologna measure being adopted on that basis. The other legal bases we have found, to wit the free movement of persons in the internal market and European citizenship, are appropriate to carry an internal measure, but it might be a stretch to argue that third-party involvement is necessary for the achievement of the aims set out in Articles 21, 46, 53 and 62 TFEU. Due to these constraints, this scenario is not the most viable alternative.

2.3. The Bologna Process via the OMC

As we have seen in Chapter 3 and Chapter 5, the relatively new mode of governance that is rapidly winning ground in the EU, dubbed the OMC, is also relevant for the field of education. The Lisbon summit of 2000 explicitly mentioned education as one of the sectors in which the OMC would find application.[37] Having the goals of the Bologna Declaration be achieved in a such a framework of voluntary policy convergence seems to concur with the needs and desires expressed by the participating states in the Bologna Process, to wit their wish to remain fully in charge so as to respect diversity and national autonomy, while at the same time allowing for better coordination with other EU mobility and degree recognition policies. In fact, the Bologna Process so strongly resembles the entire set-up of the

---

34. Opinion 1/76, *re: Draft Agreement establishing a European laying-up fund for inland waterway vessels* [1977] ECR 741.
35. Case 22/70, *Commission v. Council* (re: European Road Transport Agreement) [1971] ECR 263.
36. Koutrakos 2006, 93.
37. As specified in the Lisbon Conclusions, para. 37, the OMC entails: '- fixing guidelines for the Union combined with specific timetables for achieving the goals which they set in the short, medium and long terms; – establishing, where appropriate, quantitative and qualitative indicators and benchmarks against the best in the world and tailored to the needs of different Member States and sectors as a means of comparing best practice; – translating these European guidelines into national and regional policies by setting specific targets and adopting measures, taking into account national and regional differences; – periodic monitoring, evaluation and peer review organised as mutual learning processes.'

OMC, that some authors mention the Bologna Process as part of the OMC.[38] This confusion might also be because the European Commission, as a member of the Bologna Follow Up Working Group, is increasingly involved in the Process, and even characterizes its own contribution as part of the Lisbon Strategy.[39] As we have seen in Chapter 5, there has been considerable institutional and material interaction between the Bologna Process and the EU. The developments in the arena of the Bologna Process have influenced the course of the OMC in education to a large extent. In the beginning of the OMC in education the Bologna Process was responsible for the fact that only little attention was devoted to higher education, even though the link between the goals of the Lisbon strategy and higher education is more obvious than that with lower education. This is explained by the fact that the higher education reform agenda was 'captured' by the Bologna Process.[40] Subsequently, however, the Bologna Process turned out to be a stimulus for the OMC. In 2004, the Bologna Process was linked to the 'Education and Training 2010' OMC process, as the 'EU's integrated policy framework for education and training.'[41] The Bologna Process raised the awareness and broke the taboo of European coordination in the area of education. Nevertheless, despite the interaction with the EU institutions and the OMC, the Bologna Process is not an OMC process. The confusion on this matter is not only illustrative of the lack of transparency, caused by the double action at the 'European level', but also shows how peculiar it actually is that the Bologna Process was not adopted in the EU framework. Admittedly, at the time of the Bologna Declaration in 1999, the OMC had not yet officially been introduced in the field of education, as the Lisbon Council took place in 2000. Nevertheless, it seems that the governments involved could have anticipated it, or could have decided to transform Bologna into an OMC process, after 2000.[42]

2.4. Bologna through Intergovernmental Cooperation within the Council

Another, non-legislative, means of action that is provided for by the EU framework that could have served to adopt or implement Bologna is intergovernmental cooperation within the Council. As has been discussed in Chapter 3, this form of cooperation has been popular in the educational sector. Indeed, in the 1970s, when ministers responsible for education in their respective Member States first met, they did not meet as an 'Education Council' but 'within the Council' and later

38. Lonbay 2004, 253.
39. European Commission, *Realising the European Higher Education Area*, Contribution of the European Commission to the Berlin Conference of European Higher Education Ministers on 18/19 Sep. 2003.
40. Gomitzka 2006, 27.
41. *Ibid.*
42. However, as will be discussed in the next section, the use of the OMC is not desirable and perhaps even illegitimate if competence for a Directive exists.

as a 'Council and Ministers of Education meeting within the Council'.[43] This so-called mixed formula leaves room for Member State autonomy as it allows for educational cooperation without having respecting the formal decision-making procedures. It enables the states to issue non-binding resolutions, on the basis of intergovernmental cooperation.[44] It therefore aligns with the objectives of the states in the Bologna Process, namely to remain fully in charge. The practical advantage of being together in the framework of the Council obviously facilitates cooperation, whereas the choice to qualify it as something different than the Council provides the ministers with the desired flexibility. It seems that the Bologna Declaration could just as well have been adopted on this basis. However, since the insertion of Article 128 of the EC Treaty (now Article 165 TFEU) this formula has become outdated. This makes sense because the Treaty itself now provided for a specific legal basis for the adoption of non-binding incentive measures. Article 165 TFEU provides the Council with the opportunity to adopt incentive measures, declarations and recommendations to be taken in the educational sphere. It stipulates that the Council should do so following a Commission proposal, and in consultation with the Economic and Social Committee and the Committee of the Regions. Actually, it could be argued that after the introduction of this specific provision, intergovernmental cooperation in the Council has become inappropriate. If the Council itself is explicitly competent to adopt (non-binding) measures in the respective field, there is no reason to adopt it not as the Council but within the Council. It is a valid point that the Commission's right of initiative and the consultative role of the Committees should not be undermined by resorting to intergovernmental cooperation in that case.

That point touches upon one of the core issues of the following section. To what extent are Member States free to choose the procedure in the adoption of a certain measure or action programme? Although this question will be addressed in more detail in the following section, it is necessary to pose the question here whether the supposition that intergovernmental cooperation cannot not be used if the Treaty provides for a legal basis itself means that the Bologna Declaration could/should have been adopted as a non-binding incentive measure on the basis of Article 165 TFEU rather than via intergovernmental cooperation in the Council. This is a complex question to answer. The incentive measures authorized by Article 165 TFEU explicitly exclude any harmonization of the laws of the Member States. Now, it might seem contradictory to prohibit 'incentive measures' to be harmonization, as the definition of harmonization is usually taken to imply 'hard-core' legislation. This brings us back to the discussion whether the Bologna Declaration/Process constitutes harmonization. The conclusion was drawn that especially the binding nature of a Bologna Directive would make it qualify as harmonization. But the *ratio legis* of Article 165 TFEU implies that also a plan to harmonize educational structures through non-binding measures would not be appropriately based on Article 165 TFEU. If one reasons from there, it means that

43. Racké 2007, 40.
44. De Witte 1993, 194.

perhaps intergovernmental cooperation within the Council was a possibility after all.[45]

2.5. The Bologna Declaration as a Council of Europe Convention

In addition to the four scenarios of adopting the Bologna Process within an EU framework, also the Council of Europe could have provided the Bologna signatories with an alternative for their project. The Member States could indeed have adopted a Convention, legally binding for the states that ratify it, with the content of the Bologna Declaration. A part of the Bologna aims is already laid down by means of such a Council of Europe Convention, to wit in the Lisbon Recognition Convention of 1997, which as we have seen has come to play an important part in the Bologna Process. The Convention pre-dates the Bologna Process, but it deals with one of the most important preconditions for a well-functioning EHEA: (academic) recognition of credits and diplomas. It is therefore not surprising that the Bologna signatories have – to a certain extent – incorporated the Lisbon Convention into the Process. But what is surprising is that they did not create the Sorbonne-Bologna project in the Council of Europe context in the first place. They had already been working on these issues of student mobility and diploma recognition with the Lisbon Convention. They wanted to 'build on it and take it further', as stated in the Sorbonne Declaration. It therefore would have been a logical choice to continue their cooperation on these matters within the Council of Europe framework. It would have provided them with the luxury of existing structures and procedures, the expertise present within the Council of Europe, the benefits of intergovernmental cooperation while having a more legitimate basis for their cooperation at the same time, and the possibility for non-EU states to participate on an equal basis. In addition, the EU could have been invited as a participant, in order to guarantee coherence with EU law and policy in the field. It seems that in many ways, this was really a very attractive option for the Member States to take, both politically and legally.

Although the answer to the question why they have chosen to avoid the Council of Europe framework is even more abstruse than the one to the question why the EU was avoided, one can imagine a few factors that might have played a role in this decision. One factor might be that many of the participants initially simply did not think of this. Although this might seem peculiar, especially in the light of the Lisbon Convention that had just been adopted, it would explain why the Council was at no point consulted or invited to participate in the Process, and only became involved because of its own efforts. As we have seen in Chapter 5, it was

45. Do note, however, that conclusion is rendered wrong by the considerations as discussed in the following section, that boil down to the point that if competence existed to adopt a binding measure such as a Directive, intergovernmental cooperation – either within or outside the Community institutional structures – is illegitimate.

only in 2000 that the Council of Europe was first included after the Council of Europe itself had approached the Portuguese Presidency of the EU on the occasion of the Education Committee in Rovaniemi,[46] and had requested a meeting to discuss the possibility of participating. The Council of Europe was apparently not 'in the loop', and therefore had to actively seek involvement. Furthermore, it should not be forgotten that the Bologna Process, for all the structured organization and Follow-Up it has now, was a very unprofessional undertaking in its very beginning. It came into existence through a spur-of-the-moment agreement of four individuals, and its redefinition took only one year. It was in that in-between year that the character of the Bologna Process was determined, and once the Process got on track in its own sui generis way, it was too late to start reconsidering the fundamentals. In that sense, it might not have been such a conscious decision not to cooperate within the Council of Europe framework, but rather a consequence of the dynamic that the Sorbonne-Bologna enterprise happened to have at that moment. Another factor that might have deterred the politicians from opting for Council of Europe cooperation, should they have thought of it during the initial phase of Bologna, might be that even though working within the context of the Council of Europe is intergovernmental, a Convention would still have constituted a binding legal measure. Even though the enforcement mechanisms are not as strong as within an EU context, there would be the political pressure of a legal obligation to comply nonetheless. The non-binding nature of the Bologna Process has been identified as one of its most popular features among politicians. It appears that the Member States found the Council of Europe context still not soft and flexible enough.

2.6. Intermediate Conclusions

The foregoing scenarios are not by any means exhaustive. There exist several combinations between the described measures and methods that could have been used to create the Bologna Process within the framework(s) of the European Organizations. For instance, the states could have decided to adopt a Council of Europe Convention, in combination with a subsequent internal EU measure such as a Directive, giving stronger effects to the commitments of the Convention. This would have allowed the participation of both European Organizations, and therefore arguably a better coordination. Another possibility would have been to separate the core objective, namely the establishment of a common tiered system, from the secondary objectives, such as quality assurance and a European dimension in education. The former could then have been adopted by means of hard law, for example, a Directive or a Convention, laying down the specific details of that system, whereas the latter could have been implemented through soft law, for instance absorbed in an OMC using benchmarks and indicators. A disadvantage of separating the objectives is that it might make the already complex picture even

46. The meeting of the Directors General of vocational education in Rovaniemi, 24–28 Sep. 1999.

more confusing, and it would give up the idea of a package deal, in which all various aspects of educational mobility are dealt with in the same framework. That could, on the other hand, also constitute the main advantage. It would allow separate attention for the objectives, thereby almost automatically raising the profile of the somewhat neglected secondary aims. Furthermore, such tailor-made governance would allow one to apply the most effective and appropriate governance method to each part of the Bologna Process.

The previous discussion goes to show how much uncertainty surrounds the legal competence of the EU in the field of education. In a way, this is remarkable, considering that it has existed for almost twenty years and that it is one of the most contested policy areas. The discussion has also shown that much of the uncertainty is caused by the prohibition of harmonization. Partly, this is caused by the fact that this *Harmonisierungsverbot* is somewhat of an oddity within the structure of the Treaty. The fact that hardly any case law exists on the interpretation of this phenomenon does not help to clarify the legal situation. It has become clear, in any event, that the legal competence of the EU in the area of higher education is broader than generally assumed. The EU disposes of several modes of governance to develop policy and even legislate in the field of higher education. As we have seen, the adoption of the Bologna Declaration as a Directive would have been a viable option. This begs the question whether Member States can avoid the EU framework by resorting to international cooperation at will. In other words, was it a legitimate option for the Member States to embark on the Bologna Process the way they did, outside and without the EU, its institutions and procedures? But also within the EU framework itself, are Member States free to shop around for the procedure they like best? In other words, would all the procedural modes as enumerated above have been a legitimate option? These are the questions that will be addressed in the following section, where we come to judge the Bologna Process from a constitutional perspective.

3. THE LEGITIMACY OF BOLOGNA FROM A EUROPEAN LAW PERSPECTIVE

As Senden notes, 'legitimacy is often understood solely in the sense of democratic legitimacy, referring then in particular to the influence of representatives of the people in the decision-making process, but it seems appropriate to give it a broader meaning so as to encompass rule of law requirements'.[47] In several respects, the notions of effectiveness, accountability, transparency and the option of legal review are related to democracy and the rule of law. These are the yardsticks against which the Bologna Process shall be tested in this section. Although these questions about the Bologna Process taken alone already constitute a relevant analysis, a comparison with the other option, namely to create the project as a Bologna Directive, allows us to draw some even more interesting conclusions and

47. Senden 2004, 62.

to embed them in a more general discussion about the EU and about hard law versus soft law.

3.1. Lawfulness

Was it lawful for the Member States of the EU to embark on the Bologna Process in the intergovernmental way they did? In the previous section it has been argued that the EU possessed sufficient legal competence to adopt a 'Bologna Directive'. If this argument is accepted, it means that the Member States had the option to act within the EU legislative framework. This is an important realization from a political perspective, as the exclusion of the EU can therefore be qualified as deliberate, and hence can be seen as an important indicator of the tense political relationship between the EU and its Member States. In the tug of war between the Union and its Member States in the area of competence in education, the Member States have won the most recent game by keeping the Bologna Process intergovernmental and out of the hands of the EU. But whether the Member States have played the game by the rules is yet another question. Assuming there was sufficient competence for the adoption of a Bologna Directive, was this really merely an option or was it in fact a legal obligation? At this point, the proposition that once the conditions of a provision attributive of legislative competence in the Treaty are satisfied, Member States are forced to make use of this competence *when they desire to legislate jointly*, should be examined. It would mean that Member States have forfeited their right to intergovernmental cooperation among themselves in the field of mobility in the higher education sector, and that therefore they have gone out of bounds with the Bologna Process.

Admittedly, this is a far-reaching statement; especially if one realizes the specific sensitivities of the education sector where state sovereignty and national educational autonomy have always reigned as the main paradigms, which finds reflection in the restricted nature of the competence attributed to the EU in the field of education. EU competence in the area of educational qualifications and mobility in the educational sector is not exclusive but shared, which means that Member States remain free[48] to act unilaterally, cooperate bilaterally and – in principle – multilaterally in this field. But it is worth examining the proposition on its merits. For it is not a matter of distinguishing the competence of the EU from that of an

48. Their actions need to be in accordance with Community law nonetheless. In the *Matteucci* case the ECJ held with regard to a bilateral educational exchange agreement between Italy and Germany that: 'Article 5 of the Treaty provides that the Member States must take all appropriate measures, whether general or particular, to ensure fulfillment of the obligations arising out of the Treaty. If, therefore, the application of a provision of Community law is liable to be impeded by a measure adopted pursuant to the implementation of a bilateral agreement, even where the agreement falls outside the field of application of the Treaty, every Member State is under a duty to facilitate the application of the provision and, to that end, to assist every other Member State which is under an obligation under Community law.' (Art. 5 of the EC Treaty is now Art. 4(3) TFEU). See Case 235/87, *Matteucci v. Communauté Francais de Belgique* [1988] ECR 5589.

individual Member State to act autonomously, but of defining the competence of the Member States to conclude an agreement collectively, *that is* all Member States together, outside the EU framework.[49] This question refers to agreements entered into by all the Member States of the EU on a topic where the EU is also, but not exclusively,[50] competent, outside the EU legal framework. Although the best known advocate of the theory that such subsidiary conventions are not compatible with EU law has expressed this opinion a long time ago, many elements of the logic still stand, and it has also been authoritatively argued, in qualified terms, more recently.[51]

Schwarz argues that resort to subsidiary conventions is excluded whenever the EU could itself have attained the objective by means of legislation.[52] In his opinion, once the conditions contained in the Treaty conferring legislative power upon the EU institutions are satisfied, the governments of the Member States no longer have the power to regulate the subject between themselves by means of an agreement under international law (treaty, convention, protocol, act, declaration, etc.).[53] This means that there is no freedom to choose between the international and the EU procedure, even if the institutions have not yet exercised their legislative powers. One of the main arguments brought forward in favour of this proposition is that the law-making powers of the EU are framed in 'the legal imperative', requiring the institutions to act if necessary. According to Schwarz, the provisions do not contain any reservation in favour of any law-making powers on the part of the Member States acting jointly. Moreover, the very logic of the EC Treaty requires such a precedence of the EU system. To allow Member States to jointly legislate on the same matters as the EU undermines its *raison d'être*. Furthermore, it is liable to deprive the Treaty of its *effet utile* and undermines and frustrates the activities of the EU institutions. As the establishment and functioning of the internal market, including educational mobility as a part of the free movement of persons, is a key Union objective, it is a valid argument that this objective should be attained by making use of Union structures.

Schwarz expressed this point of view before the insertion of the subsidiarity principle. Does this principle alter the claim that Member States are excluded from acting jointly outside the EU framework if the Union is in fact competent? Article 5 TEU (ex Article 5 EC) provides that in areas which do not fall within its exclusive competence, the EU shall take action only if and insofar as the objectives of the proposed action cannot be sufficiently achieved by the Member States and can therefore, by reason of the scale or effects of the proposed action, be better achieved by the Union. It is not clear from this wording whether 'achieved by the Member States' is meant to include collective action by the Member States in

49. See Schwartz 1978, 615–616.
50. If the competence of the EC were exclusive, the Member States would per definition have lost their power to act.
51. De Witte 2001.
52. Schwartz 1978, 614.
53. *Ibid.*, 615.

the form of intergovernmental cooperation. That interpretation would undermine Union action in all but the fields in which it has exclusive competence. The subsidiarity principle deals with the relation between the EU vis-à-vis the Member States unilaterally. It is not likely that it entails that Member States, should they consider collective action at the European level necessary, should first try to achieve these objectives by means of intergovernmental conventions before taking Union action. It appears that if Member States cannot sufficiently deal with a certain matter alone, for example, because of the cross-boundary characteristics of the matter, it is pre-eminently a case for the EU to take up. That is exactly what the EU is for and any other interpretation would deprive the EU of its very meaning. Indeed, this interpretation finds itself supported by various authoritative authors.[54] In fact, the subsidiarity principle works both ways. Apart from containing a prohibition, it also constitutes an authorization for EU action if Member State level action does not provide satisfactory solutions for a certain (cross-border) problem. Therefore, the most logical interpretation of the term 'Member State level' in Article 5 TEU is that it refers to the action of a Member State alone. It means action *by* the Member States themselves, not *between* themselves.

Having said that, it is important to consider the relevant case law of the ECJ, which ruled on the question of collective Member State action in areas of shared competence in the *Bangladesh* case.[55] The European Parliament brought actions for the annulment of an act adopted at the 1487th session of the Council with a view to the grant of special aid to Bangladesh and of the means adopted by the Commission for the implementation of that act. As the contested act was not an act of the Council but an act taken by the Member States collectively, the application brought by Parliament against the Council was declared inadmissible.[56] The importance of the judgment for our purposes lies in the statement of the Court that 'the Community does not have exclusive competence in the field of humanitarian aid, and that consequently the Member States are not precluded from exercising their competence in that regard collectively in the Council or outside it'.[57] Although at first glance, this statement seems to mean that in cases of shared competence Member States are free to embark on collective action, it is also possible that the statement is less general than it seems. If the statement of the Court is seen in the particular context of humanitarian aid, where action by the Member States in addition to action by the EU cannot do much harm – and is actually never enough, it becomes less obvious to extend the ruling to all situations of shared competence. In other

54. Lenaerts & Van Ypersele 1994, 46; Toth 1992, 1098–1099; Verbruggen 2001, 64–65. However, as Verbruggen notes, this point of view is not uncontested. Especially German writers have challenged this view, arguing that 'by the Member States' does refer to the possibility for Member States to solve matters in an intergovernmental way. See Hochbaum 1993, 236.
55. Joined Cases C-181/91 and 248/91, *European Parliament v. Council of the European Communities and Commission of the European Communities*, [1993] ECR I-3685.
56. This illustrates one of the problems that occur with such inter-governmental policy making in the Council: it is not subject to legal review and the European Parliament can be sidestepped easily.
57. Paragraph 16 of the judgment.

instances of shared competence it might be that the exercising of a competence by one actor (either the EU or Member States collectively) will imply that the other actor can no longer act, by nature of the subject matter, in that two measures regulating the same issue could not coexist. The principle of primacy, entailing that all national law needs to be in accordance with EU law, and Article 4(3) TEU (ex Article 10 EC),[58] which requires the Member States to cooperate loyally with the EU and to refrain from action that would obstruct the EU in the attainment of its tasks, imply that if the subject matter excludes simultaneous acting it is for the Union to act, excluding joint Member State action.

Despite the fact that this interpretation of the judgment seems most reasonable, it is at odds with its literal wording. The Court states that Member States are not precluded from collective action *as a consequence* of the fact that the EU does not have exclusive competence. There is no reference to compatibility or the special nature of development assistance. If the Court did not mean to give carte blanche to Member States to act collectively whenever they see fit, the wording of the judgment is somewhat careless, to say the least. If the ECJ did mean to give such a blank check, it is submitted here that a revision of this case law is desired, as it leads to objectionable results. The distinction between shared and exclusive competence is more aptly applied in cases where a Member State desires to legislate something individually while acting in a policy field where the EU is also competent, and the doctrine designed for those purposes should arguably not be applied by simple analogy to the present question of division of competence between the EU and the Member States collectively. As De Witte notes, the possibility for Member States to jointly conclude international agreements in areas of EU competence is problematic for reasons of democracy, legal protection and efficiency.[59] It threatens the effectiveness of European law and the EU as a whole. As Schwarz notes, allowing the Member States to jointly create law on the same subjects as the EU impairs the capacity of the Union to carry out its tasks, destroys the unitary nature of its legal system and substantially limits the scope of EU law.[60] This is an expression of the same logic that supports the aforementioned views of the numerous authors that argue that the subsidiarity principle does not lay down a preference for intergovernmental action among the Member States to the detriment of EU action.[61] It is commonly accepted that subsidiary agreements may, in any event, not detract from EU law.[62] It is submitted here that the subsidiary

58. Article 4(3) TEU provides: 'Pursuant to the principle of sincere cooperation, the Union and the Member States shall, in full mutual respect, assist each other in carrying out tasks which f low from the Treaties. The Member States shall take any appropriate measure, general or particular, to ensure fulfilment of the obligations arising out of the Treaties or resulting from the acts of the institutions of the Union. The Member States shall facilitate the achievement of the Union's tasks and refrain from any measure which could jeopardise the attainment of the Union's objectives.'
59. De Witte 2001, 104.
60. Schwartz 1978, 625.
61. Lenaerts & van Ypersele 1994; Toth 1992; Verbruggen 2001.
62. Kapteyn & VerLoren van Themaat 1995, 212. See also Senden, 58.

agreements in question *by definition* detract from EU law, and for that reason are unlawful. In line with De Witte I therefore argue that autonomous parallel agreements in areas of concurrent EU competence are unnecessary and damaging, and therefore might very well be contrary to Article 4(3) TEU (ex Article 10 EC).

The Bologna Process serves well to exemplify these dangers of subsidiary action by Member States. Although the Bologna Process in terms of its aims could be argued to be consistent with EU objectives (such as convergence in higher education for the purpose of facilitating mobility of students and the labour force in general), the way in which it takes place is less laudable. Note that the EU interest as protected by Article 4(3) TEU is 'not simply an expression of the collective interest of the Member States, but represents an aspect of the autonomy of the Community system'.[63] Although the Bologna Declaration might pursue objectives of the EU, the Declaration can still be contrary to the Union interest for the simple reason that it takes place outside the EU's framework and sphere of control, thereby disowning the European Institutions of their tasks in the field. Not only are certain aspects of EU policy, such as student mobility and diploma recognition, being doubled in Bologna, which impedes their proper functioning on both levels, the fact that Member States are doing 'it' collectively prevents the EU from doing 'it', and from doing 'it' better. The Bologna Process is plagued with coordination problems and divergent implementation. As will also be discussed in the following section, the Declaration grants no rights to individuals. There is no authority to appeal to in case of an uncertainty of the content of one of the obligations, let alone an enforcement mechanism to guarantee that *pacta sunt servanda.*[64] Thus, the actual attainment of the objectives set by Bologna, which are also the objectives of the EU, is severely threatened. And because the adoption of the Bologna Declaration impedes such an initiative from the Union, it has become difficult to successfully attain these objectives. This could lead to the conclusion that with the Bologna Declaration and Process, the Member States have obstructed the EU institutions in the exercise of their tasks, and have thereby failed to meet their obligations under EU law, in particular Article 4(3) TEU, especially if one realizes that according to settled case law this latter provision 'is the expression of the more general rule imposing on Member States and the Community mutual duties of genuine cooperation and assistance'.[65]

63. Cremona 2008, 127.
64. In fact, there is not even a real 'pact', because participation in the process is merely voluntary. States can decide to deviate from the set norms, and can decide to disembark the whole project altogether, at any point they see fit.
65. See in particular, Case 230/81, *Luxemburg v. European Parliament* [1983] ECR 255. If Member States fail to cooperate loyally with the Community an infringement action can be brought against them by the European Commission (Art. 226 EC). It is highly unlikely that the Commission will ever start such infringement proceedings against the Member States on the basis of the Bologna Process. In the current political situation, where also the Commission is strongly involved in the Bologna Process as a full participating member, the Commission's hopes lie with trying to steer the Process from the inside towards better compatibility with the Community. See Ch. 5.

If it is accepted that Member States cannot act jointly in matters of EU competence, the question is whether cooperation such as in Bologna qualifies as 'joint action'. As has already been discussed in relation to legal competence, the Bologna Process does not only involve the Member States of the EU, but also third European countries. This did not seem to make a difference as to the existence of competence to enact a Bologna Directive, as it could have been adopted as an internal measure, combined with external agreements. But the fact that also third countries are involved might alter the legal obligation of the Member States to follow the EU procedures. Could the Bologna Declaration still be classified as a 'subsidiary convention' or an 'autonomous parallel agreement' for which the Member States were not free to opt for intergovernmental cooperation and which hence cannot be reconciled with EU law? The argument that the situation is one of classic international cooperation, stretching beyond what is the EU, for which international law-making is most suited, especially within the framework of the Council of Europe, is convincing. The most plausible interpretation of the current legal situation would therefore be that strictly speaking, it was not contrary to European law to embark on the Bologna Process by means of a parallel agreement, for it also includes third countries and thereby stretches beyond the EU.

The foregoing notwithstanding, the mere fact that there are additional participants does not relieve the concerns and objections as outlined above. It would be easy for the Member States to circumvent their EU obligations simply by inviting a third country to participate in a certain project. As Martens and Wolf note, 'the strategic inclusion of non-EU members in the Bologna process served as a protection against too much Commission leverage'.[66] In order to avoid such frustration of EU interests, but at the same time taking into account the need for some flexibility in the realm of international relations, it would be desirable to come to a legal situation where a 'mitigated obligation' would lie on the Member States when, in an area where the EU is also competent, they decide to act jointly but together with third countries. The default position would then be that Member States enact an EU measure internally whenever possible, also when third countries are involved, and that the 'burden of proof' rests with the Member States to show why it was necessary to avoid the EU framework whenever they decide to deviate from that default position. Once the threshold of participation by all the Member States is reached, this presumption of precedence of the EU procedure should kick in. The decision to adopt and implement a certain legal instrument outside the EU might well be justified, especially when it is done in the context of the Council of Europe, but it should be for the Member States to show why the course of proceedings in question did not obstruct the Union in the attainment of its tasks. This interpretation of the law would however need to be endorsed by the Court first, for it does not reflect the current situation.

A last theoretical point of interest that deserves some exploration is what the possibilities of the Member States are in terms of 'soft law' within the Union framework, now – for exploration's sake – imagining that the Bologna Process

66. Martens & Wolf 2005, 12.

would only have involved EU Member States. The Bologna Declaration is a declaration of intention, and hence a classic example of soft law. The participating states have at several occasions expressed the opinion that the voluntary character of the Bologna Process constitutes one of its most important advantages. Is it possible for the Member States to embark on non-binding cooperation in accordance with EU obligations? The EU framework does provide for non-legislative means of action. For one, there exists the possibility of intergovernmental cooperation in the Council. In the 1970s, when ministers responsible for education in their respective Member States first met, they did not meet as an 'Education Council' but 'within the Council' and later as a 'Council and Ministers of Education meeting within the Council'.[67] This mixed formula leaves room for Member State autonomy as it allows for educational cooperation without having to respect the formal decision-making procedures. It enables the states to issue non-binding resolutions, on the basis of intergovernmental cooperation.[68] However, it is doubtful whether this mode of governance would have constituted a legitimate method to enact the Bologna Declaration and Process. After all, it would qualify as an 'autonomous parallel agreement' and would constitute a circumvention of the EU procedures all the same. If it is held that Member States were not free to adopt the Bologna Declaration outside the EU framework, then they were not free to adopt it as a Resolution of the Council and of the Representatives of the Governments of the Member States, meeting within the Council, either.

Perhaps the OMC could then have provided for a possibility for the Member States to cooperate on a voluntary basis, whilst respecting European law. The Lisbon summit of 2000 mentioned education as one of the sectors in which the OMC would find application. Setting the goals of the Bologna Declaration to be achieved in a such a framework of voluntary policy convergence seems to concur with the needs and desires expressed by the participating states in the Bologna Process, to wit their wish to remain fully in charge so as to respect diversity and national autonomy, while at the same time allowing for better coordination with other EU mobility and degree recognition policies. In fact, the Bologna Process so strongly resembles the entire set-up of the OMC, that some authors mention the Bologna Process as part of the OMC.[69] This might also be because the European Commission, as a member of the Bologna Follow Up Working Group, is increasingly involved in the Process, and even characterizes its own contribution as part of the Lisbon Strategy.[70] At the time of the Bologna Declaration in 1999, the OMC

67. Racké 2007, 40. See Ch. 4.
68. De Witte 1993, 194.
69. Lonbay 2004, 253.
70. 'The Lisbon Strategy encompasses the Commission's contribution to the intergovernmental Bologna Process, aiming to establish a European Higher Education Area by 2010, mainly in the areas of curricular reform and quality assurance. The Bologna process coincides with Commission policy in higher education supported through European programmes and notably Socrates-Erasmus, Tempus and Erasmus Mundus. The Commission stimulates Bologna initiatives at European level and participates as a full member in the Bologna Follow-up Group and the Bologna Board.' European Commission, *Realising the European Higher Education Area*,

had not yet been introduced in the field of education, as the Lisbon Council took place in 2000. Nevertheless, it seems that the governments could have decided to transform the Bologna Declaration into an OMC process, after 2000, making it an official part of the EU institutional framework. Still, it can also be questioned whether the OMC would have been a legitimate way to implement the Bologna Process within the EU framework. As the European Commission has stated, 'the use of the open method of co-ordination must not dilute the achievement of common objectives in the Treaty or the political responsibility of the Institutions'.[71] According to the Commission, the OMC should not be used when legislative action under the Community method is possible. Although this position has not (yet) been confirmed by the ECJ, it is supported here, and it does go to show how tense the relationship is between intergovernmental cooperation and the Union interest. Moreover, it fits perfectly in the reasoning as outlined above against the conclusion of subsidiary conventions, for the same concerns apply.

To summarize the foregoing analysis, it could be said that the Member States have straddled the border of loyal cooperation. The fact that also a substantial amount of third countries participates in the Bologna Process makes the difference in that it cannot be maintained that the Member States have actually breached their obligations under the Treaty by adopting their subsidiary convention. Nevertheless, the numerous concerns and drawbacks clinging to their course of action still stand. Even if one holds that the scrutiny applied above has been too severe, in light of the sensitivity of the education sector, the complementary nature of the EU's powers in this context and the paradigm of national educational autonomy, as laid down in Article 165(1) TFEU, it should still provide some food for thought. It is submitted that the extent of the powers of the EU in education should not be underestimated. Nor should the choice between the EU and the international framework, and between hard law and soft law, be left entirely to the discretion of the Member States. This indeed means that the freedom of the Member States in European policy-making is circumscribed, but arguably that is for good reasons. The justness of this outcome is confirmed by findings in the following paragraphs, where several concerns inherent in international soft law making are considered.

3.2. Transparency and Democratic Legitimacy

For years, the EU has been criticized for lacking transparency, openness and a closely related phenomenon: democratic legitimacy. In the field of education, this criticism is mainly directed at the way in which the EU institutions have somehow managed to gain influence in the sector even in the absence of real competence. According to Murphy, 'the fuzzy, blurred, and covert history of education policy in Europe does not contribute much to a sense of optimism regarding the

Contribution of the European Commission to the Berlin Conference of European Higher Education Ministers on 18/19 Sep. 2003. See also Ch. 4.

71. European Commission, *European Governance – A White Paper*, COM (2001) 428 final, 22.

strengthening of European democratic legitimacy, a key and indispensable component of any effective post-national form of citizenship'.[72] It is true that, as we have seen in Chapters 3 and 4, especially the ECJ's extensive interpretations of the Treaty have served as a basis to expand EU influence in higher education affairs to an extent unforeseen, un-provided and unsupported by the Member States. But ironically, similar concerns of democratic legitimacy and covert and confused policy-making can be held against the Bologna Process. The Sorbonne Declaration, where the essential ideas were born and introduced, came into being at the birthday-party of a prestigious university by a select group of ministers among themselves. Also the subsequent Bologna Declaration was signed at an elite party, as an intergovernmental piece of soft law but with far-reaching ambitions, without any recourse to the institutional framework of the EU, thereby avoiding its built-in safeguards, checks and balances. There was no parliamentary involvement, barely any public consultation, and many reforms were rushed through in only a few years. This becomes all the more worrying upon considering the enormous consequences of both Declarations, which are responsible for the most far-reaching reform process European higher education had ever seen.

With regard to the higher education actors involved in the Process, it should be recalled that apart from the governmental representatives, the two organizations representing universities at the European level, the Confederation of European Union Rectors' Conferences and the Association of European Universities, became included shortly after the Sorbonne Declaration. They were both kept informed about the preparation of the Bologna conference and have also been involved in drafting the final declaration.[73] And indeed, an increasing amount of stakeholders is participating in the Process. Still, although the governments proudly speak of the bottom-up approach of the Bologna Process, meaning that the state is in full control as opposed to supranational rule-making, many opine that the changes of the Bologna Process were imposed on the actors in the field in a top-down manner with little or no opportunity of debate, which finds illustration in the short amount of time in which most of the legislation was pushed through.[74] It appears that many of the higher education sectors were in some kind of shock, being suddenly overwhelmed by intrusive reforms, where it normally takes years of negotiations to even agree on the smallest kind of governmentally imposed change. When the governments praise the lack of 'top-down' enforcement in the Bologna Process, they mean that they are happy with the absence of a coordinator such as the Commission telling them what to do. Contrary to what they would perhaps like to convey, the Member States do not mean that they in their turn won't impose the Bologna changes in a top-down manner on the national higher education sector.

Furthermore, the activities undertaken in the framework of the Bologna Process substantially overlap with already well-established EU and Council of

72. Murphy 2003, 560.
73. Racké 2007, 37.
74. Lonbay 2004, 253.

Europe policies, such as the Diploma Supplement, the ECTS, and the promotion of teacher and student mobility in general.[75] The fact that activities in these areas are now pursued on several different planes is not transparent, not efficient. In a field where European action is on the one hand necessary to meet the needs of contemporary societies but which is on the other hand so culturally sensitive and hard to sell to the general public, one should proceed with caution. This caution requires transparency more than anything. Having various actors acting in various capacities on various European levels does not foster intelligibility and might lead to *double emploi*. Indeed, since the Bologna reforms are often accompanied by broader, national 'rider' reforms, and because they seem to converge with parallel processes such as the Lisbon Strategy and a broader international development of the globalization and commercialization of higher education, there exists a lot of confusion among the higher education institutions, the students and the public at large, about what the Bologna Process does and does not entail. The extent of this confusion becomes apparent in the massive crowds of protesters, especially in Southern Europe, that have taken the streets to protest against the higher education reforms in their countries. The protests, which shall be discussed in more detail further below, are mostly formulated as opposition to the Bologna Process, but often actually concern the cutbacks and commercialization-measures that national governments have instituted as part of the Bologna reforms on their own motion. In that sense, the strategy to pass unpopular measures by reference to European level 'imposed' Bologna requirements seems to be backfiring, but it can be stated that it is exactly this level of in-transparency that has allowed the governments to pass all the reforms, Bologna related or not, in the first place. Planting more trees so as to prevent anyone from seeing the forest, sowing opaqueness and confusion, has arguably proved key to the 'success' of the Bologna enterprise.

A certain loss of democratic control seems to be inherent in international policy-making. By definition, international negotiations take place between country representatives, not entire parliaments or governments. These representatives, sometimes ministers but often non-elected high functionaries, might be under the control of their national government, but are (often quite literally) far away from the control of their national parliament, the public and stakeholders. Ratification requirements for binding international measures are intended to ensure that the national parliaments get something of a say in the matter, but this control limited in practical terms. Since the entire text has already been agreed upon and the representative has already signed before the international agreement is to be ratified, the members of parliament can do little more than to assent or dissent. The fact that amendments cannot be made, and the agreement thus becomes a 'take-it-or-leave-it package', means that minor but also serious objections will not often lead to a no-vote, if not worth to obstruct the entire agreement. Moreover, in the case of non-binding international agreements or declarations, there is not even a ratification procedure. The international measures, non-binding but still very influential, are *fait accomplis*. For interest groups and the public at large, it

75. Hackl 2001, 26.

is difficult to hold their representative accountable. If negotiations took place behind closed doors, it cannot be known whether the official in question argued for or against a certain matter and what compromises he or she has made.

This is how, as argued by Moravcsik, 'international cooperation redistributes domestic power in favour of national executives by permitting them to loosen domestic constraints imposed by legislatures, interest groups, and other societal actors'.[76] The international level can constitute an efficient smokescreen for governments to agree on unpopular reforms, as the conferences and conventions where the deals done between governmental officials are largely distracted from parliamentary scrutiny. When the country representative returns, the international agreement already stands, and reforms can be passed as if there was no choice, referring to the international political obligations. These concerns apply especially when it concerns international soft law such as the Bologna Declaration. The Bologna Process only involves governmental officials and a limited number of higher education actors. Indeed, many universities have complained about the fact that the far-reaching changes have been imposed on them in a short period of time, without any real consultation. Since the Bologna Declaration is not a Treaty, but merely an intergovernmental proclamation, it does not require ratification. Although the participating states are not bound by international or European law, there is political pressure to legally implement the Declaration nonetheless. The governments can push the Declaration's implementation, arguing that the 'international obligations' need to be met. Perhaps some of the governmental actors even created, or conveniently did not resolve, the mistake that the Bologna Process was 'imposed' by 'Europe', taken to mean the EU. Once more, we should come back to Ravinet, who argues that the governmental players 'manipulate the objectives and use them as leverage and justification for reforms, even though they are not unilaterally obliged to implement these objectives':

> The Bologna Process seems to have an element of juridicity (Pitseys, 2004), in that it appears to be legally binding in nature, especially when participating countries misinterpret their commitments as requiring conformity to superior and legally binding European policies. This lack of clarity can be used as a means to legitimise national reforms. This misconception is reinforced when Bologna declarations and communiqués are presented as texts of quasi-legal value, even though initially the Bologna Process did not have any official legal status.[77]

The Bologna Process has enabled the national governments to implement national reforms that were at least to a certain extent already contemplated before the ministers for education met in Paris. As Davies puts it: 'Bologna owes its origins in the Sorbonne Declaration of 1998 – to the fact that the French and Italian education ministers Allègre and Berlinguer resorted to inter-governmental action

76. Moravcsik 1994, 1.
77. Ravinet 2008a, 353.

in order to deploy the weight of Europe for domestic purposes.'[78] Indeed, most Bologna commentators, both in academia and in public debate,[79] agree that apart from certain possibly genuine European reasons, at least an important part of most national politicians' participation in the Process was to push national reforms under the pretext of European obligations. As Papatsiba states, through the Bologna Process national governments were able to 'advocate the "Bologna" context to introduce long-standing unwelcome national reforms'. As she mentions, the latter phenomenon has been referred to as 'externalization'.[80] The same mechanism has been described as 'a two-level game', following Racké's application of Moravcsik's theory to the Bologna Process.[81] In the context of our research, concerned with the relationship between the Bologna Process and the EU, these considerations are relevant because they might provide us with a reason why the EU framework was deliberately avoided.

The above findings of international policy-making are, after all, more suitable to describe 'traditional' intergovernmental policy-making outside the EU context than to describe the way of governing within the EU system. Within the context of the EU, these concerns have been responded to by the creation of a complex system of checks and balances. True, the EU has since long suffered from allegations concerning its democratic deficit and to a certain extent, the concerns are real and well-grounded. But the EU, in all its complexity, does provide for a relatively transparent and democratic legislative process. The co-decision procedure illustrates the power-balance between the various institutions, representing various interests. The European Parliament, with ever-increasing powers, has become the expression of a European concept of democracy, where the will of the majority of the European population prevails. The Commission has in recent years shown its commitment to good governance by frequently openly consulting the sector in issue, the specialists as well as the public at large. The interest of the governments is still firmly represented in the Council, the most powerful legislative organ in the EC. And the ECJ is there to ensure respect for the rule of law, and safeguards the interests of the individual.

One could put forward that in the case of the EU, with far-reaching legislative powers, such mechanisms are also more necessary than in other international contexts, where there are no supranational elements present and where enforcement mechanisms are weak. But intergovernmental policy-making outside the EU can also be very powerful, of which Bologna constitutes an example *par excellence.* And when contrasted with the EU's constitutional framework, the intergovernmental modus operandi is bleach in comparison. Some have argued that the fact that in intergovernmental policy-making the governments remain fully in charge is actually more democratic than the EU method, as the governments can – at least in

78. Davies, 6. Emphasis added.
79. See, for example, *The Economist*, May 2009, 'Another reason why some governments embraced Bologna was to give cover for reforms they wanted anyway.'
80. Papatsiba 2006, 96.
81. Moravcsik 1994, 1.

theory – count on the majority support of their national parliaments. In this view, the European Parliament is not much to treasure as a source of democratic legitimacy, especially since it suffers from low turnouts. However, national elections generally suffer identical problems and, more importantly, as we have already seen, the control of the national parliaments over the international negotiations and the end product is minimal. The fact that they theoretically could impeach their government if not satisfied with the situation obviously does not amount to a large democratic control in practice. If it is accepted that European-level policy-making suffers from democratic legitimacy in the sense put forward by Moravcsik, it should be admitted that the EU's institutional framework is the lesser of two evils.

3.3. Efficiency and Effectiveness

Not only can the way in which the Bologna Declaration was adopted and implemented be said to be less democratic than if it would have been a measure adopted via the Community method,[82] it can also be argued that it is less effective. Because the EU is supranational, because it diminishes national sovereignty to a certain extent, because it has the power to impose obligations on the Member States and because it can actually enforce these obligations, it has been able to effectively implement many policies. Concessions in terms of sovereignty are often necessary to reach the goals that the Member States set themselves. According to Barnier and Vitorino, it is clearly shown that cooperation based on an independent regulatory system with independent bodies ensuring sound operation on a permanent basis is much more effective than traditional international cooperation.[83] International treaties, whose implementation has been left to the goodwill of the contracting states, have generated less effect than the EC Treaty.[84] The Bologna Declaration does not even qualify as an international treaty, but rather as 'public international soft law', and is thereby completely devoid of any system of legal enforcement.[85] Admittedly, this might paint a picture too rosy, as there are problems with the timely and correct implementation of Directives and Regulations. Furthermore, it can be argued that the more flexible and lenient modes of policy-making are more respectful of diversity and Member States' interests, and can therefore rely on more support and compliance. Perhaps, in certain fields, soft steering can achieve more

82. In a 2002 contribution from Mr Barnier and Mr Vitorino, members of the Convention, to the European Convention on the Future of the Union, the Community method is defined as: 'the decision-making process in areas coming under the EC Treaty and, in particular, the interaction of the institutions as part of this process'. The so-called *pure* Community method is the system whereby the Commission enjoys the monopoly of legislative initiative, and whereby the Council and the European Parliament adopt acts proposed by the Commission in co-decision. In particular, the Council votes by qualified majority. Barnier & Vitorino 2002.
83. *Ibid.*, 6.
84. Barnier and Vitorino mention the area of cross-border television broadcasting services where both an international convention and a Community directive have been issued, and where the latter has been much more successful. Barnier & Vitorino 2002, 6.
85. Hackl 2001, 28.

than a hard approach. Regarding the Bologna Process, it is indeed true that already halfway the deadline most of the signatories had adapted their national legislation so as to meet the requirements of the Declaration. And it could be assumed that the Bologna Process would not have been embarked upon at all, if not for its soft law character. It is also true that a certain amount of flexibility and discretion is desirable, as it concerns a far-reaching reform project in a politically sensitive area. Member States should be granted the freedom to adapt their systems so as to bring them in line with the Bologna commitments in the way they see fit. They are in the best position to judge their educational structures, and are the ones ultimately responsible for it.

Nevertheless, a Bologna Directive, drafted in similar style and spirit as the Commission Proposal for a directive on the application of patient's rights in cross-border healthcare,[86] would also have been able to provide this flexibility, without sacrificing effectiveness and transparency. It cannot be denied that because the Bologna Process lacks a binding character there might be problems in effective enforcement. This is disturbing as its real success does depend on coherent and consistent implementation and application in the participating countries. It is safe to say that nothing would be worse in promoting mobility than a hodgepodge of national legislation. Furthermore, as the 2007 'Bologna with Student Eyes' study reports, 'despite the fact that mobility is considered to be one of the core goals of the Bologna Process it is still far from being reached. Too often politicians and stakeholders bring discussions only to a declarative level while consensus on concrete action is rarely made and action is taken even more rarely'.[87] The fact that Bologna is a Declaration, and not a binding instrument, is illustrative of that finding. This risk of inconsistent transposition is further aggravated by the lack of 'top-down' coordination. Although many participants perceive this lack of centralized coordination and enforcement one of the most attractive features of Bologna, it shall be clear that it impedes the creation of the standardized and consistent framework of degree-cycles, thereby standing in the way of the very recognition that they aim to achieve. Regardless of good or bad faith, implementation will differ in the various countries in the absence of unambiguous standards, uniform interpretation of these standards and some extent of supranational coordination of their implementation.

Indeed, although at first face value it appears as if the Bologna requirements are quite diligently followed by the signatories, as many have adopted the necessary legal provisions and many students are already currently enrolled in Bachelor/Master-programmes, various inconsistencies can be detected. To name a few, while some countries have opted for 4 + 1 structures, others have decided to go with 3 + 2, and a few have even settled for 3 + 1.[88] Moreover, the 2007

86. *Proposal for a Directive of the European Parliament and of the Council on the application of patients' rights in cross-border healthcare*, COM (2008) 414.
87. Bologna with student eyes.
88. These figures indicate the length of the Bachelor and Master cycle, which means that countries with, for example, a 4 + 1 structure have implemented a four years Bachelor programme followed by a one-year Master.

'Bologna with Student Eyes' study reports that 'there is a substantial lack of real curricular reform throughout the EHEA'. The report states that 'an alarming number of national unions of students report that the old, long programmes in their country have been simply "cut" into two, with the new first cycle qualification having an unclear value to students and to the labour market'.[89] Furthermore, in some countries vocational schools are included in the Bachelor-Master system, while in others they are not. Also, the application of the two-tier system is not equally applicable to all higher education in all countries. For example, in most countries medical education has been excluded from the Bachelor-Master system, whereas some others have included it. Furthermore, the practical value of the Bachelor degree is uncertain in many countries with regard to legal education, where a Master degree is needed to be admitted to the legal profession. In addition, although the ECTS is formally in place in the vast majority of Bologna signatory countries, an achievement to be credited rather to the European Commission's ERASMUS programme than the Bologna Process, no country uses the ECTS for accumulation and transfer, the new application of the ECTS as proposed by Bologna. In this context, the dominant majority of countries still have significant problems that need to be addressed.[90] Moreover, only a small percentage of universities issue the Diploma Supplement with their degrees, although this is explicitly required under the Bologna Process.

In addition, many higher education actors have complained about the lack of true government support, in financial and other terms, to make the reforms bearable and doable. As Trends 2007 found:

> Institutions were often critical of governments with regard to support for reform. This was most often mentioned in relation to lack of financial support to reform, reinforcing the finding of the Trends V questionnaire where two thirds of respondents stated that they had not received any additional financing to implement reforms. However, comments were not limited to financial matters. In many instances, institutions reported that dialogue with government over the policy objectives for higher education was insufficient, and that legislative changes had not been made with adequate involvement of the key stakeholders in society. This was not a feature limited to the Bologna process – more a reflection of 'normal' societal practices. Yet as many legislative measures have been explained by governments in terms of necessary system adjustments to meet Bologna objectives, the Bologna process has sometimes become a focus of tension, with institutions perceiving their government as being more interested in the rhetoric of reform than in providing genuine support to institutions. Many academics questioned how they could be expected to make a radical change to their thinking about curriculum, at the same time as adapting to more rigorous quality demands, while receiving

89. ESIB 2007, 7.
90. ESIB 2007, 8.

> no incentives for additional work, and while the overall level of financial support from government was decreasing.

Schrieber reports that the national implementation measures in relation to Bologna have had counter-productive and perverse effects. For example, 'experience accumulated so far with the newly defined courses of study give grounds for believing that student mobility throughout Europe in not increasing but rather decreasing, as a result of the shorter time available and the increase in mandatory requirements to complete a degree course'.[91] This means that due to the Bologna reforms, fewer students will be able to make use of exchange programmes such as ERASMUS, another example of how Bologna can get in the EU's way. Of course, all the concerns mentioned above, including this last one, can be addressed by the governments, which can decide to amend their laws accordingly. The Process has been described as 'gigantic field experiment'.[92] On the one hand, this flexibility, illustrative of the fact that the participants are involved in a process rather than implementing a static piece of legislation, allows Bologna to respond to inconsistencies in a better way than perhaps a formal legal enforcement mechanism would. But the continuous episodes of reform, partly due to this 'trial-and-error'-approach, are arguably not only inefficient; they increasingly burden the individuals that are subjected to the reforms. The position of these individuals, which shall be addressed in more detail in the following section, is indeed quite weak under the Bologna Process. As a point relevant to the foregoing argument of Bologna's ineffectiveness and inefficiency, it needs to be noted that because the Sorbonne and Bologna Declarations do not grant any rights to individuals, there can be no so-called 'bottom-up enforcement' of the agreements. Since there is, for example, no guarantee for students that have concluded a Bachelor programme to have it recognized at another university in order to be admitted to a Master programme, they cannot invoke the Declaration, to be applied in a national court. It is generally accepted that litigation by private parties, through the preliminary reference procedure of Article 234 EC and the concepts of supremacy and direct effect as developed by the ECJ, constitutes a key to the success of EU legislation. This bottom-up enforcement is completely absent in the context of the Bologna Process.

3.4. The Position of the Individual Student

Although the students of Europe are the central subjects of the entire Bologna enterprise, it is doubtful whether they actually benefit from the reforms in the way the Declarations promise. First, the ten-year implementation process is long and the reforms are patchy; in some countries hasty and sloppy and in other countries slow and uncertain. This means that several generations of students will have received their entire higher or university education in the midst of this

91. Schriewer 2009, 47.
92. Krücken 2007, 1.

enormous reform process that is by no means smooth and well coordinated. Furthermore, there are reasons to believe that some of the governments will employ the Bologna Process to introduce cutbacks, for example, by limiting the grant of subsidies or study finance to Bachelor diplomas and leaving Master courses to be paid for by the students themselves. This links in to a more general problem with the Bologna Process, namely the fact that signatory states are using the Bologna reforms as an opportunity to introduce other so-called rider-reforms, mostly unpopular with students and/or staff as they include the commercialization of higher education, general cutbacks,[93] the introduction of tuition fees,[94] overhauling departments and reorganizations. Perhaps it is especially the feeling of detrimental reforms being introduced through the backdoor that had lead to fierce protests against the Bologna Process in several European countries.[95] According to the EU Observer, 'students argue that while it may be popular

93. As John MacDonald, the European Commission's education, training and culture spokesman stated: 'some governments have chosen to use the impetus of the Bologna Process to institute other changes over funding and governance at the same time'. See Phillips 2008. 16 November: 10,000 people took to the streets of Rome in protest at proposed cuts in education funding. Demonstrators fear the cuts will result in the loss of 86,000 teaching jobs. Another 44,000 administration posts could also be lost, amounting to a 17% reduction in the number of jobs in education across the country. See also Bompard 2006.

94. On the 3 Aug. 2008, addressing a gathering of about 100 students outside the Department of Education in Dublin Mr Kenny (president of the Union of Students in Ireland) said third level education must be funded through taxation and not fees. The protest was called in response to suggestions by Minister for Education Batt O'Keefe that fees for third level might be reintroduced. See IrishTimes.Com, *Students protest against reintroduction of fees,* Wednesday 8 Aug. 2008, available at: <www.irishtimes.com/newspaper/breaking/2008/0813/breaking180.htm>.

95. In 2005, French students protested against Bologna reforms, causing the University of Paris 8 Vincennes-Saint-Denis to temporarily shut its doors. See Marshall Paris 2005. In 2006, Swedish students protested against the proposal to cut PhD terms. See Schubert 2006. In 2008, numerous protests directed specifically at the Bologna Process as well as the 'commercialization of higher education' in general took place all over Europe, but mostly in Spain. On the 7 May 2008, close to 5,000 students protested against the Bologna Process in Zagreb. On the 19 June students representatives in Austria protested against further restrictions to take up a Master degree, part of the reforms introduced by the Austrian government in relation with the Bologna process. On the 8 May, more than 10,000 students and teachers protested against the Bologna Process in Barcelona, after they had already done so in a huge demonstration with 10,000 participants in Barcelona and more than 3,000 in Sevilla on 6 Mar. 2008. In Grenada, 150 protesting students occupied a faculty on 24 April. See *Estrechno.Indymedia.Org.* Protests also took place in Madrid where students blocked roads. 22 October: protests took place in thirty cities across Spain against the Bologna Process and in defence of public education. The protests were taken up in Italy, where about 5,000 people assembled in Milan. Less than a month later, on the 20 November, thousands of students in several Spanish cities protested again against the Bologna process. See *ThinkSpain.Com, Blip.TV, youtube.com.* In 2009, the Spanish resistance continued. On the 19 March, students occupied the central building of the University of Barcelona in protest against Bologna, and teachers, parents, students, pupils and workers joined a demonstration counting 50,000 participants in the city centre demanding different education policies. On 10 Feb. 2009, professors and researchers in France joined the protest against the Bologna reforms in the nation's major cities. See: Education: Bologna process, sales time in French universities, at *CafeBabel.com: La Rivista Europea.*

amongst politicians, it is this very intergovernmental level bargaining that has produced the reform mechanisms that has left them out of the loop'.[96] Although most of the protests focus on the Bologna Process, some are also directed at the EU and its education policy. For example, on the 6 November 2008, large numbers of university students as well as professors and teachers protested in the streets of the Greek capital and other cities in the country, against the government's plans to grant full recognition to degrees obtained from private colleges in accordance with EU secondary legislation.[97] Furthermore, the misbelief that the Bologna reforms are imposed by the EU is persistent in popular opinion in many countries, meaning that some of the criticism is mistakenly directed at the EU. Although the protests can partly be explained by misinformation, anti-reform attitudes and dissatisfaction with the economic conditions of the countries concerned, they do indicate that Bologna is not simply the bottom-up, well-consulted, transparent and student/teacher-friendly measure it is often claimed to be.

As for the potential benefits to students in terms of recognition of their diplomas and credits and increased options to study at several universities both within one country as in several countries, it should be stated that the Declaration by no means provides them with a mechanism or guarantee that they will be able to reap them. As was pointed out before, the Bologna Declaration does not intend to grant any rights to individuals. As a consequence, for example, there is no guarantee for students that have successfully concluded a Bachelor programme to have it recognized at another university in order to be admitted to a Master programme, unless national legislation grants them that right. Seeing that the specific action lines of Bologna do not include such a legal endorsement of the proposed measures in the national law of the signatories, it is unlikely that countries will adopt such a right to recognition on their own motion. Indeed, as the Bologna with Student Eyes Report shows:

> in many countries, the accessibility of a Master programme for graduates holding a first-cycle qualification presents a major problem. Only in few countries, all Bachelor graduates who wish to study a Master programme have that opportunity. Often Bachelor graduates from the same institution are favoured regarding admission to Master programmes, putting students from other institutions or countries in a worse position.[98]

As Furlong notes, the Declaration is phrased in such general terms that it is difficult to envisage how in this form it could be enforced through national or international courts.[99] However, such things do have a way of ending on the doorstep of judicial bodies. One can imagine a student bringing a claim against a university or maybe even an employer, for failing to recognize or classify their degree in accordance with the Bologna Declaration. Whenever a court is faced with such an argument, it

96. Phillips 2008.
97. *EKathimerini.Com.*
98. *Ibid.*
99. Furlong 2005, 54.

will have to decide on the legal significance of the Bologna Declaration. It is unlikely for any national court to rely directly on the Declaration, but if the Bologna Process has been transposed into national law, the basis of an individual claim might be stronger and a court might consult the Bologna Declaration as a source of interpretation, especially in case of an ambiguity in the relevant national legislation.[100] One interesting case of a graduate bringing a claim on the basis of the Bologna reforms in relation to the Staff Regulations of Officials of the European Communities has come before the European Union Civil Service Tribunal.[101]

Mr Reali, who had obtained the *Laurea in scienze agrarie* (degree in agricultural sciences) at the University of Florence in 1985, had worked for the European Commission for several years before the Commission in 2006 offered him a fixed-term contract as a member of the contract staff, employed in function group IV and classified at grade 14, step 1. In 2007, Reali brought a complaint under Article 90(1) of the Staff Regulations in which he contested his classification and requested a higher grade, taking the view that his professional experience exceeded the twenty years required for classification at grade 16. He maintained that his *Laurea in scienze agrarie* was equivalent, since the integration of the recommendations of the Bologna Declaration in Italian law by the Decree of 5 May 2004 and the Decree of 22 October 2004, to a 'Bachelor's' degree plus a 'Master's' degree. Consequently, as the holder of a 'Bachelor's' degree he would fulfil the minimum conditions in terms of diplomas to be recruited as a member of the contract staff in function group IV, implying that his 'Master's' degree should be regarded as one year of professional experience, enabling him to reach the threshold of twenty years of professional experience required for classification in grade 16. In his argumentation, Reali submitted that 'the Bologna Declaration forms part of the *acquis communautaire*, despite not being a binding measure, in so far as it encourages the signatory countries to reform their higher-education systems in order to create an overall convergence of diplomas at European level'. As a result, he argued, where a qualification or diploma was recognized in one Member State, that recognition was binding on the other Member States and consequently on the Commission, which was 'not entitled to ignore such recognition on pain of infringing the principle of subsidiarity set out in the Bologna Declaration and in the case-law'. In its defence, the Commission pointed out that it was not an addressee of the Bologna Declaration and that the Declaration had no binding legal value. The Commission maintained that the Bologna Declaration did not concern internal decisions by the institutions on the method for calculating professional experience for the purposes of grading an official or member of the temporary or contract staff. The Tribunal did not speak out on the matter in explicit terms, but from the judgment it can be deduced that Reali's arguments were not found convincing. The Tribunal held that even on the supposition that the Italian legislation entailed

100. An example of such a case in the Netherlands is Case *A. v. het college van bestuur van de Open Universiteit*, LJN: AR5729.
101. Case F-136/06, *Enzo Reali v. Commission of the European Communities.*

equivalence as between the applicant's diploma, obtained after four years of studies, and a 'Master's' degree, obtained after five years of studies, it could not be inferred, for the purposes of determining the applicant's grade, that the Commission was under an obligation to treat the applicant's diploma as equivalent.

4. CONCLUSIONS

It should be underlined that *no action* was also an option. The Member States were in absolutely no way forced to yield their education systems to some kind of uniform standard, either binding or guiding. There would be obstacles to student mobility and to the labour force in general left to exist. But the Member States could legitimately consider this a small price to pay for preserving national autonomy and diversity, not only in terms of content but also in cycles, diplomas and credit structures. With the Bologna Process the Member States made a choice. They chose a uniform standard; they chose a two-tier system for reasons of readability and transparency that would by its nature only really work if applied in a consistent and uniform manner in all the participating countries. Thus, by the nature of the objective it intends to achieve, it requires a strong system of enforcement and of uniform interpretation. The point therefore is that the Member States do not have to create and implement a uniform standard in higher education degree-cycles, but if they decide to do so, the EU legal framework constitutes the most effective and transparent way. To say that Member States have straddled the borders of loyal cooperation as laid down in Article 4(4) TFEU (ex Article 10 EC), by embarking on intergovernmental cooperation in the context of Bologna implies far-reaching interpretations of the Treaty, expressing what is probably a minority view. It would meet resistance in the Member States, who since long have perceived educational policy as 'an excellent subject for intergovernmental cooperation in close connection with EU action, but could not the subject of genuine EU action itself'.[102] Still, it is a fair statement that the objectives of the Union should be achieved using its own system of law, its own institutions and its own procedures. With the Bologna Process Member States have rendered inoperative the EU institutions and their further development, by resorting to joint international action. They have avoided the EU law-making process with its institutional safeguards, the rules of the Treaty relating to supervision and implementation of European law and the rules on the judicial protection of legal rights. The increased involvement of the Commission in the Bologna Process might be a positive development, but it is regrettable that the most democratic organ of the EU, the Parliament, remains practically excluded. By proceeding in the way they have done, Member States have chosen the less open, less transparent and less democratic manner to Europeanize higher education, and have obstructed the EU Institutions to do it, and to do it better. Although *stricto sensu* it would be a bridge too far to say that their action was illegal, it was certainly undesirable.

102. De Witte 1989, 14–15.

It is surprising that still today, the competence of the EU in education is often so gravely underestimated. For one, this is because of the underrated potential of Article 165 TFEU itself. Moreover, the potential of other legal bases in the Treaty to affect education is generally neglected, due to the fallacy that the prohibition of harmonization would stand in the way of any type of legal measure affecting the area of education. Uncovering this fallacy puts the intergovernmental projects embarked upon outside the EU framework, such as the Bologna Process, in a different perspective. The EU institutional framework provides for several modes of governance, supranational as well as intergovernmental. Although the foregoing critique lead to the conclusion that governments should not be free to simply pick the solution they deem most fit for the goals they want to achieve, for also the OMC and intergovernmental cooperation in the Council should best be avoided if proper legislative competence exists, the fact that these intergovernmental methods within the EU framework were not even considered, indicates something. To a certain extent, the value of the 'alternatives' lies in the assumption that working through the EU would have provided for a 'better' project, in terms of content and implementation. 'Better', because it would have been easier to coordinate, both internally (the Process itself) as externally (its relation with EU programmes), and hence more efficient. It would have provided Member States with practical institutional facilities to help them achieve their goals. Therefore, intergovernmental cooperation within instead of outside the EU would perhaps have constituted the lesser of two evils. However, the real value of the alternatives is rather that the fact that an intergovernmental declaration outside EU structures was preferred goes to show how badly the Member States wanted to exclude the EU.

Why did the Member States want to avoid the EU at all cost? Defenders of Bologna's intergovernmental character often explain it by the fear of the Member States that giving the Union one inch, it will lead to it taking a whole yard. Indeed, it appears that with the Bologna Process the Member States have tried to avoid the growing influence on higher education by the EU, which is to a certain extent understandable. The case law of the ECJ has necessitated the restructuring of educational systems in several countries to ensure equal access to foreign EU students. Also the Directives relating to the mutual recognition of qualifications have had serious impact as they have led to a harmonization of curricula of the regulated professions concerned. The European Institutions seem to operate with a consistent pro-integration bias. Probably because of this the Member States are mistrustful of the EU, and the European Commission in particular. Although the Commission has always respected the non-harmonization paradigm, the Member States suspected it to do so only *nolens volens.*[103] They suspected that the Commission would show its real face as a 'harmonizer' as soon as it would be provided with the opportunity to do so. Obviously, it would be rather difficult for the Commission to go and 'harmonize' the education sector on its own, without the Member States onboard. The Commission does not pass legislation by itself. It always seems rather curious when Member States allude to the dangers of the EU

103. Wächter 2004, 271.

and accuse it of unwanted intrusion, as they – the Member States – *are* the EU. To some the EU resembles Frankenstein's monster, with competence creep and spill-over left and right, and the terrifyingly extensive and teleological interpretations of the Treaty by the ECJ in the treacherous slipstream of economic integration, but it could be countered that the only thing the EU really does is executing and enforcing what the Member States themselves – at least in majority – have agreed upon.

It is true that the expanding role of the EU gives rise to fear and debate in the Member States no matter what policy field is concerned, let alone if it relates to education. As education is closely connected to cultural identity, and seen as a traditional function of the nation-state, Member States guard their national educational autonomy jealously.[104] It has been argued that adopting the Bologna Process inside EU institutions would have led to a 'top-down, centralized approach resulting in the bureaucratization of the Bologna Process, robbing it of its flexibility, responsiveness and creativity'.[105] It turns out, however, that the complicated administrative procedure of EU law-making would most probably have guaranteed *better law*, from various perspectives applying various norms, and that a degree of centralization would not have been undesirable in order to make sure that what was agreed was actually achieved. This necessarily leads one to question whether it was not precisely because of that, because of the transparent procedures and the efficient enforcement, that the Member States chose to sideline the EU. The foregoing chapters have certainly provided us with some evidence to support this point. But even without adopting this somewhat cynical view, we can draw confidently the conclusion at this point that the Bologna Process has amounted to harmonization by stealth; ill-considered and ill-defined, ill-executed and increasingly ill-received. The Member States have now limited their own autonomy, by less accountable means.

104. Ryba 1992, 11.
105. House of Commons, Education and Skills Committee 2007a, 32.

Chapter 7
Conclusions

1. DAYS OF YORE

Authors and policy-makers in the field of European higher education often refer to the heyday of academic mobility in days of yore. It is claimed that in the time where Europe's first universities were born, roughly between 900 and 1100 AD, students and academics would 'freely circulate and rapidly disseminate knowledge throughout the continent'.[1] Back in those days, universities allegedly strongly encouraged such mobility among teachers and students, deeming this mutual exchange of information essential for the development of knowledge.[2] Erasmus of Rotterdam (1469–1536), whose name was not coincidentally chosen for the EU's successful student mobility programme, is often mentioned in this context.[3] Erasmus studied at the University of Paris, was tutor to the son of King James II of Scotland, gained his doctorate in theology at Bologna, held a readership in theology at Cambridge and worked at a publishing house in Venice. Subsequently he lived in Freiburg and then retired to Basle. In his Opinion to the *Morgan and Bucher* case, Advocate General Colomer declared that 'the legend of Erasmus provides a ray of hope that those [current] barriers [to intra-European student mobility] may be overcome'.[4] The frequent use of this image of unrestrained intellectual mobility to introduce writings and policy documents on European higher education can be easily explained, as it is both inspiring as slightly ironic. It is inspiring to imagine intellectuals all over the European continent commonly sharing knowledge, their cooperation leading to greater progress and development

1. Sorbonne Declaration, second paragraph.
2. Magna Carta Universitatum.
3. A noteworthy example is the Opinion of Advocate General Colomer of 20 Mar. 2007 to Joined Cases C-11/06 and C-12/06, *Morgan and Bucher* [2007] ECR I-9161.
4. *Ibid.*

than could have been achieved without this combining of forces. Academic synergy indeed constitutes one of the reasons to encourage student and teacher mobility also in our time. Slightly ironic, on the other hand, it can be called that in our current age, often characterized as one of globalization, we are striving but struggling to achieve the situation that our ancestors allegedly already established about three-quarters of a millennium ago.

Regardless of whether these references to times long past account for a realistic comparison or should be regarded as mostly empty rhetoric, for promoters of the Europeanization of higher education they constitute a stimulating historical framework in which current European-level initiatives can be placed. The references serve well to endow some degree of historically generated legitimacy on the, often controversial, initiatives to open up the conservative higher education sector. If European level initiatives are construed as a revival of the past, rather than radical progress in the integration process, they might meet less resistance. The traditionally nationalistic attitude, protective of national educational autonomy that dominates the field of higher education, is not difficult to explain if one considers the fact that education goes to the core of the sovereignty of the nation-state.[5] Education serves to pass on society's values to the children of the nation and it is employed by the state to make 'good citizens'.[6] The choice of the values that a society decides to transmit to its future members is intrinsically connected to national identity. Therefore, 'deeply rooted in local, regional and national culture, education takes different forms in each country reflecting the different expectations of our societies'.[7] Education is a firmly established competence of the nation-state. As Leuze et al. note,[8] education has become a 'normative good'[9] of the modern state, and it is this state that prominently decides over the structural set-up of the education systems, arranges the financing of the education for its citizens and is held accountable for the achievements, as well as the pitfalls. It is natural for the state to defend its position as the decider, internally as well as externally.

2. THE EUROPEAN COURT AND NATIONAL AUTONOMY

In that light it is not all that surprising to find national politicians on occasion pitted against the ECJ. Although it is to be applauded that the Court is somewhat reluctant to acknowledge sovereignty claims by the Member States, suspicious of covert protectionism at the cost of individual European citizens and their fundamental free movement rights, it seems that the Court is sometimes blinded by an individual-oriented approach, concerned with maximizing the rights of the

5. See Young 2002, 1670–1677.
6. See Ravitch & Viteritti 2001.
7. As stated by M. Marin, member of the European Commission, in a European Parliament debate on encouraging teacher mobility. *Debates of the European Parliament*, 24 Oct. 1986, OJ Annex No. 2-344/275, at 281. See also Handoll 1989, 31.
8. Leuze et al. 2008, 1.
9. Hurrelmann et al. 2007, 3.

European citizen it finds before it, unaware of long-term backlashing effects that might deteriorate the situation of (larger groups of) the very individuals it tries to protect and benefit. It is remarkable that the European Court attaches so little value to the national autonomy principle as laid down in Article 165(1) TFEU, even more so because the Court has done much to give legal significance to the second paragraph of that very same provision, in order to broaden the scope of EU influence. Member States are granted only a very limited amount of leeway in the implementation of their educational policy whenever it touches upon internal market freedoms, which helps to explain the increasing criticism of politicians directed at the ECJ. It cannot be denied that the overall tone of Article 165 TFEU is one demanding respect for national autonomy and diversity in educational affairs. Responsibility and powers relating to the content and organization of the educational systems lie primarily with the Member States, leaving the EU with the secondary role of facilitating and encouraging cooperation and mobility. This is an important paradigm, and the argument that it should not be hollowed out by overly extensive interpretation of internal market powers and the rights that citizens derive from the fundamental freedoms, especially by a too rigid application of the proportionality test, is a fair one.

The impact of the Court's case law is substantial. Even more so, considering the dynamics of European integration entailing that negative integration often needs to be accompanied by positive integration in the form of coordinating or harmonizing legislation. When national legislation is condemned for incompatibility with European law, its inapplicability leaves a gap, triggering the need for a European solution. This begs the question what should happen if there is no legislative competence in the field in question. Following Handoll: 'One could indeed argue that, where the Court has recognised the intrusiveness of "functional" rules of free movement and non-discrimination into areas of national competence, the Community will have to be competent to take positive action to resolve resulting difficulties.'[10] In many cases, this makes perfect sense. Of course, cooperation is the key to many problems, and it seems that regional and/or European level coordination between the Member States would be desirable to meet the concerns related to several of the previously discussed judgments of the Court. For example, one could argue that a European arrangement dealing with 'who pays what for mobile students' is necessary to solve the current problem of potential double entitlements and some of the financial problems of uneven student mobility.

However, not in all situations harmonization is a desirable answer. When Advocate General Sharpston, in her Opinion to the *follow-up Belgian Education Case,* argued that the new Belgian legislation dealing with its universities overburdened by French students was in breach of EU law, she too quickly brushed away Belgium's problems by presenting harmonization as the solution.[11] She explicitly

10. Handoll 1989, 36.
11. Opinion of Advocate General Sharpston, delivered on 25 Jun. 2009, in Case C-73/08, *Nicolas Bressol and Others and Céline Chaverot and Others v. Gouvernement de la Communauté française.*

invited the EU legislature to start to consider its legislative options on the matter. Although it would trigger an interesting debate on the scope of EU competence in the area of higher education, a matter that has been very pertinent to the present research, to present harmonization as the solution in this particular case not only testifies of a considerable amount of insensitivity, but it also fails to really offer any viable alternative. What kind of measure would deal with the French/Belgian and German/Austrian problems in a satisfactory manner; a harmonization of entry requirements for certain studies all over Europe? What would be the content of those requirements? A European-level imposed *numerus clausus* system for selected studies? Or a European-level imposed 'free access without charge' regime? Although it is perhaps not impossible to find some kind of acceptable system, the fact that Member States would be forced to accept such as the only solution severely impinges on their freedom to organize higher education in the way they see fit.

The ECJ has firmly rejected the proposition that in the area of education, the Treaty allows a Member State from treating its own nationals more favourably because of its special responsibilities towards its own nationals. Many Member States might still be grappling with that conclusion, for they cannot see at what point they have actually legally committed themselves to such a fully fledged free movement of students. Some might fear scholarship tourism, others the overflooding of their universities, and all dread the influence of the EU over educational affairs. The insertion of a specific provision dealing with education in the Maastricht Treaty was generally seen as an attempt of the Member States to call a halt to further EU action in this field. Apparently dissatisfied, or at least worried by the developments that had taken place in the absence of an explicit legal basis, the reaction was to create one, but very limited. On the one hand, therefore, it was supposed to serve as a signal to the Court, by drawing some clear lines in the sand. On the other hand, however, it was also a written endorsement and retroactive legitimization of the interpretations of the Treaty as given by the European Court. Apparently, the Court still benefited from an enormous authority, unrivalled by any other international tribunal, and to some extent, the Member States might have been pleased with the rights of mobility that had been established. This shows the complexity of the relationship between the Court and the Member States. The Member States might not have committed themselves to a fully fledged competence in education, but they did agree on a mobile labour force, and on an integrated labour market. They also agreed that banning nationality-based discrimination was the key to achieving that goal. And moreover, it is the Member States who have so recently confirmed the direction of increased integration in higher education, as they have sought to establish an EHEA, without internal borders and unlimited student mobility. It is the Member States, without any EU pressure, initiative or initial involvement, who have decided to structurally harmonize their entire system of higher education.

The ECJ always has had the difficult task of meandering through the cross-currents of Member States' desires and interests, and has often been so bold as to decide what was best for them in the long run. And it has often gotten away with that. One could suggest that Member States have, perhaps tacitly, accepted the authority of the Court to push integration and to stretch their legal obligations to the maximum, because they knew they needed such a strong institution to achieve what they set out to achieve. Why else would the original Member States have accepted the judgment in *Van Gend en Loos*,[12] which was far beyond activism, and looked more like judicial revolutionism? The Court went against what half of the original Member States explicitly submitted at the hearing and invented a 'new legal order for the benefits of which the states have limited their sovereign rights'. The Member States could have qualified this as an illegitimate power-grab by the Court and could have decided to either ignore its judgments or abolish it altogether. They did not do so. Of course, the history of the integration process shows rebellious (constitutional) courts and defiant Member States, once in a while overtly testing and contesting the authority of the ECJ. But in general, this is a healthy part of the development. However, it is difficult to establish whether or not the Court has overplayed its hand recently, with its controversial rulings in *Bidar* and the *Belgian and Austrian education cases.* It should not be forgotten that the Court has also handed down some other ill-received far-reaching judgments in other areas. The recent criticism directed at the ECJ seems to be of an unparalleled harshness and formulated in a tone of anger and disappointment. Perhaps the more restrictive ruling in the recent *Förster* case, which can be seen as a partial reversal of *Bidar*, signals that the Court is exercising caution because of this political upheaval. In that respect, it will also be very interesting to see how the sequel to the *Belgian Education case* will turn out.

3. MEMBER STATES EUROPEANIZING HIGHER EDUCATION

Notwithstanding the legitimate criticism of the ECJ's intrusive approach, it should be accepted that European law sometimes affects national policy, including educational policy, in a way not planned by the national legislature. Moreover, the cries of the politicians at least partly consist of crocodile tears. Obviously it is not just the ECJ who is responsible for all the educational integration of the past years. As was just pointed out, it is the Member States themselves that have played the most important role in the increased Europeanization of education, both in their Council capacity and outside, most notably of course in the intergovernmental arena of the Bologna Process. As Chapter 5 has shownit is clear that although the Commission currently plays an important role in the Process, it was a bystander in the beginning and has been restricted to a mere facilitative role. The Parliament and the Court remain completely excluded. This is why the Bologna Process is at the same time a *de-nationalization* and a *re-nationalization* of higher education. Explaining the contradictory attitudes of politicians towards European-level action

12. Case 26/62, *NV Algemene Transport- en Expeditie Onderneming van Gend & Loos v. Netherlands Inland Revenue Administration* [1963] ECR 00001.

in this field and the role of the EU is exceedingly difficult and has generally been outside the scope of this book. It does, however, serve us well to reflect a little on the reasons of governments to embark on Europeanization.

Although the preservation of national autonomy does not necessarily stand in the way of European cooperation as such, autonomy – and diversity – are so highly valued that the reasons to 'open up' the sector to international influences need to be strong and convincing. Naturally, this counts even more for the case where the European initiative in question entails the conferral of powers to a supranational level. The most genuine reason for European-level action in higher education, as in most other fields, is to achieve objectives that a single state cannot achieve, or not as good, on its own. One can imagine a plenitude of objectives, educational or broader, for the achievement of which European-level action/cooperation in the field of higher education can constitute a more effective way than mere domestic action. These include the stimulation of knowledge dissemination, the development of a (European) knowledge economy, the increase of employability, the boosting of the competitiveness of Europe's educational systems, the enhancement of the individual's right to education and diploma recognition, the promotion of common cultural understanding, and the creation/strengthening of a European identity. The achievement of some of these objectives necessarily implies some degree of European-level coordination, as they are 'European objectives' in themselves. For the achievement of others, it is a policy choice to engage in cross-border cooperation.

We have seen in Chapters 2 and 6 that apart from these considerations that merit European-level action, policy-makers might be drawn to the European arena for slightly more strategic reasons. As argued by Moravcsik, international cooperation redistributes domestic power in favour of national executives by permitting them to loosen domestic constraints imposed by legislatures, interest groups, and other societal actors.[13] In the area of higher education, politicians might have a particularly strong inclination to employ this political strategy. As we have discussed in Chapter 4, higher education is of increasingly important economic value in the upcoming knowledge-based societies. Every government will have different views and priorities concerning both the organization and content of higher education, and its purposes. Many new governments will have an interest in reforming this rich and versatile policy field according to their political convictions. At the same time, the sector is notoriously difficult to reform, because the strong views and interests of influential educational institutions, which often enjoy extensive autonomy, as well as those of the public at large are to be taken into account. Thus one often finds that in the national educational arena, politicians are at the same time eager and reluctant to push reforms. Embarking on a European project allows the politicians to introduce unpopular national reforms under the cover of 'Europe', hence without having to take the full responsibility.

13. Moravcsik 1994, 1.

Indeed, this appears to have been the strategy employed by Allègre in launching the Sorbonne initiative.[14] As Chapter 2 has shown, the two-level game is in fact characteristic of the entire Bologna Process. A critical attitude is warranted here. If European-level action is resorted to in order to avoid national public scrutiny, severe problems with the democratic legitimacy of the project arise. Such concerns have plagued the EU for a long time, and to a certain extent rightly so. The question whether the EU should possess, exercise and seek to expand its powers in higher education is an important one, and its answer closely relates to these legitimacy questions. As we have seen in Chapter 4, the textual basis upon which many of the educational rights have been granted to individuals is thin, to say the least. If the legitimacy of the entire European integration project is already weak, it seems problematic to pursue increased educational integration if the justification for it cannot even be found in the text of the Treaty. Ever since the beginning, the European Court has been pushing the boundaries in this respect. But instead of the foregoing being a valid argument for the governments of the Member States to embark on the Bologna Process without and outside the EU institutions, it is an argument why it is even more worrisome that they have done so. As has been argued in Chapter 6, the EU for all its democratic defects is still more democratic than the intergovernmental smoke-filled rooms of the Sorbonne and Bologna Declarations.

However, as we have also noted in Chapter 6, this argument is most forceful if one contrasts the Bologna Process with EU hard law, or at least soft law adopted through the Community method. It is in fact only in that case that it can convincingly be claimed that the decision-making mechanisms guarantee a certain level of democracy and legitimacy and that the rule of law is upheld, not the least by the fact that individuals, such as students, have recourse to the European Court. The ever-increasing powers of the European Parliament should compensate for the loss of parliamentary control at the national level, a loss that is partly inherent in international law/policy-making. From this point of view, therefore, the increasing use of soft law in the EU, such as the OMC, can be called as worrisome as the public international soft law making of the Bologna Process outside the EU's institutional framework. As Trubek, Cottrell and Nance note, recent years have indeed seen significant criticism on the use of soft law in the EU, the objections including that soft law lacks clarity and precision needed to provide predictability and a reliable framework for action and that it bypasses normal systems of accountability.[15] Although soft law appears to be less intrusive to national autonomy, and thus more respectful of national preferences and diversity, it in fact proves to be a treacherously powerful policy source. More than it being a relatively unchecked and unlimited method of policy-making, its power actually lies in that it is unchecked and unlimited. This is an important finding, for it lays bare its doubtful legitimacy as well as the underlying problem that apparently what politicians strive to achieve does not concur with what their constituencies believe. This gap

14. Racké 2007.
15. Trubek, Cottrell & Nance 2006, 66.

between citizens and their governors has been often discussed both in an EU and national context.

4. EDUCATION AND ECONOMICS: UNEASY BEDFELLOWS

It remains doubtful that there will soon be a general consensus among the population that educational affairs should be arranged at a European level. The students and teachers, the intended beneficiaries of increased intra-European mobility, seem to have turned *en masse* against the recent surge of Europeanization of higher education.[16] Although the protesting crowds are perhaps not always consistent in what they are protesting against, for sometimes it is the EU, sometimes the Bologna Process and sometimes their national government, it might be possible to distil a common objection against many of the reforms that the educational sectors of the Member States have seen over the past years. The general sense seems to be that despite all the political high talk about how imperative education is for contemporary societies, the sector and its people are continuously subjected to cutbacks and downsizings, and increasing demands of economic efficiency. In that sense, it is probably more the economization than the Europeanization of higher education that is objected to, but there is some truth in conflating the two. The Bologna Process carries a distinct economic flavour, as does the educational policy of the EU. The former introduces the Anglo-Saxon model on the European continent, not only in terms of labels and structures, but also in ideology. The latter has most often dealt with education from an economic perspective, most recently has brought it into the Lisbon Strategy to become the world's most competitive knowledge economy, and the educational rights that have been granted seem to flow more from a labour market logic than anything else. This is a valid objection against increased EU involvement in education, as well as against the Bologna Process. As Karlsen argues:

> The Bologna main objects 'The European Education Area' correspond well to the 'Internal Market'. In particular higher education and knowledge are looked upon and treated more like economic commodities inside a certain area. There is clearly a movement towards a marketization in the field of education (Schostak 1993). The dominant aims for the exchange and mobility of 'human capital' and knowledge are preparations for increasing competition on the global market place and preparation of students for the internationalized labour market. The cultivation of the individual (Bildung) is not absent, but primarily instrumental and not for its intrinsic values.[17]

---

16. For a more detailed account of the protests, see the discussion of the position of the student in the Bologna Process in Ch. 6.
17. Karlsen 2005, 4.

Dealing with educational matters with a fundamentally economically tainted view is not without consequence. If all the internal market freedoms are limitlessly applied to educational actors and their activities, this does not only pose a legal problem in bypassing Article 165(1) TFEU, but it simply does not seem to respect the fact that in education, considerations that are not economic – and that might very well be at odds with economic efficiency – play an important role. Obviously, the European Court has applied a more detailed approach, allowing restrictions of movement if objectively justified. But the national policies in question have to meet a rigorous and strictly applied proportionality test if they even only indirectly hinder a free single market. It is understandable that some, on principle, object to internal market logic being the general rule and aims such as achieving a high quality of education, the exception. Nonetheless, most of the cases before the ECJ cannot easily be characterized as an EU economic interest against a Member State's socio-cultural interest. Often, when governments argue laudable aims before the Court in defence of a national measure, such as 'free access to education for all', they forget a second part of the sentence, such as 'children of taxpayers of this country'. Most of the case law shows that there is simply still a fundamental lack of trust and solidarity between the Member States in matters of higher education, rather than an EU imposed commercialization at the cost of national socio-cultural interest.[18]

It is in fact the Member States who prove so keen to 'economize' higher education. They promote this approach in their capacity as Member States of the EU, most particularly via the Council and its Lisbon Strategy, and they do so outside the EU framework, most notably in the context of the Bologna Process. Although 'the weight of Europe' is deployed to push reforms into this direction, it is not Europe or Europeanization per se, that forces a neo-liberal view on educational affairs. Rather it appears that the governments of most European countries, at the moment, adhere to this philosophy, and that they would also have pursued it without Europe if necessary. It is very well possible to aspire to a strong and unified Europe, without borders for educational mobility and with an active role in educational policy, also for non-economic reasons. Knowledge dissemination, cultural exchange, bundling of intellectual forces, achieving a better allocation of intellectual resources, creating centres of excellence, honouring Europe's intellectual heritage and many other reasons could support the case for a strong Europe in (higher) education affairs, without making this entirely contingent on an economic dimension. A positive synergy can very well exist between Europeanization of education for economic reasons and for quality/social reasons. This is why, in the adoption of the hypothetical Bologna Directive, it would be so desirable to use

---

18. In light of this lack of trust it is remarkable that in the Bologna Process, Member States have suddenly agreed to far-reaching recognition of each other's higher education systems. If there is already a lack of trust between the EU Member States, it is hard to imagine that without any discussion countries such as Russia have been accepted to the Bologna club of countries whose diplomas will be mutually recognized. This is either very inconsistent, or it indicates that the Bologna signatories did not take their mutual commitments to recognition very seriously.

Article 21(2) TFEU (ex Article 18(2) EC) as an (additional) legal basis. It would perhaps be even more desirable to adopt the measure on the basis of a strong education provision (in conjunction with the internal market provisions and the citizenship legal basis), but this has been made impossible by the prohibition of harmonization in Article 165(4) TFEU.

5. TWO PARADOXICAL FALLACIES

Two persistent fallacies exist about the Bologna Process and its relationship with the EU, remarkably contradictory to each other. If anything, the foregoing chapters should have dispelled both. First, contrary to popular belief, the Bologna Process is not an EU law or EU project. As we have seen in Chapters 2 and 5, the entire Bologna enterprise has been enacted outside the institutional framework of the EU. This is not to say that it should not have been an EU law, which has been the argument of Chapter 6. This links in to the second fallacy, namely that the Bologna Process has not been enacted by the EU because it lacked sufficient legal competence to enact the project in the form of a binding measure such as a Directive. As we have seen, also this constitutes a misbelief, one that is more common among politicians and academics, both in political science and law. This second fallacy has indeed been more difficult to dispel, since it has required an extensive analysis of the legal competence of the EU in higher education, in internal market affairs and in general, in Chapter 6. There is some interest for politicians in fostering both fallacies. With regard to the second, politicians themselves would perhaps like to believe the competence of the EC thus limited and secondly, they would perhaps not like to face the consequences of the uncovering of that myth. After all, it makes it a politically sensitive question why then the EU was avoided indeed. The most cynical view is that the EU, ironically enough, was in fact too democratic to achieve what the participating politicians sought to achieve with the Bologna Process: namely to push through reforms in their national higher education sector, resorting to European intergovernmental action to disable national debate and parliamentary scrutiny. Linking back into the first fallacy, it will have suited these politicians very well that many believed it to be an EU project – the air of bindingness has probably allowed them to institute reforms that would otherwise have stranded in parliament.

Bibliography

Abelson, M. A Europe of Knowledge and the Civic Mission of Universities. *Paper presented at the Third Conference on Knowledge and Politics.* Bergen: University of Bergen, 2005.

Adam, S. & V. Gemlich. *ECTS Extension Feasibility Project.* Report for the European Commission, 2000.

Allègre, C. *Toute vérité est bonne à dire. Entretiens avec Laurent Joffrin.* Paris: Robert Laffont & Fayard, 2000.

Alesi, B., et al. *Status of the Introduction of Bachelor and Master Programmes in the Bologna Process and in Selected European Countries Compared with Germany.* Centre for Research on Higher Education and Work Report, 2005.

Amaral, A. & A. Magalhaes. 'Epidemiology and the Bologna Saga'. *Higher Education* 48 (2004): 79–100.

Andersen, S. & A. Glencross. *Pre-Empting the Court: Member State Expectations, Political Oversight and the Nexus of Law and Politics in the EU.* Paper Presented at the EUSA Biennial Conference Montreal, 17–19 May 2007.

Ash, M. 'Bachelor of What, Master of Whom? The Humboldt Myth and Historical Transformations of Higher Education in German-Speaking Europe and the US'. *European Journal of Education* 41, no. 2 (2006): 245–267.

Attali, J. *Pour une modele europeen d'enseignement superieur: rapport a Monsieur le Ministre de l'Education Nationale, de la Recherche et de la Technologie,* Paris: Ministere de l'Education nationale, de la Recherche et de la Technologie, 1998.

Balzer, C. & K. Martens. *International Higher Education and the Bologna Process. What part does the European Commission play?* Paper presented to the epsNet 2004 Plenary Conference, 18–19 June 2004.

Balzer, C. & A. Rusconi. 'From the European Commission to the Member States and Back – A Comparison of the Bologna and the Copenhagen Process'.

In *New Arenas of Education Governance, the Impact of International Organizations and Markets on Educational Policy Making*, edited by K. Martens, A. Rusconi & K. Leuze. Houndmills: Palgrave Macmillan, 2007, 57–75.

Barnard, C. *The Substantive Law of the EU. The Four Freedoms.* Oxford: Oxford University Press, 2004.

Barnier, M. & A. Vitorino. *The Community Method.* CONV 231/02, 3 September 2002.

Belien, P. 'Austria and Denmark Fear American-Style Supreme Court'. *The Brussels Journal*, 13 January 2006.

Belloc, B. The Sorbonne-Bologna Process: A French National and Institutional Point of View. *Paper for the Symposium on 'Constructing the European Education Area'*. University of Wisconsin-Madison, 7–9 April 2005.

Benoit-Rohmer, F. & H. Klebes. *Council of Europe Law. Towards a Pan-European Legal Area.* Strasbourg: Council of Europe Publishing, 2005.

Bergan, S. 'Recognition Issues in the Bologna Process: Background and Outline of the Issues'. In *Recognition Issues in the Bologna Process*, edited by S. Bergan. Strasbourg: Council of Europe Publishing, 2003.

Bergan, S. Representative of the Council of Europe, *Speech to the London Ministerial Conference*, 17–18 May 2007, available online at: <www.coe.int/t/dg4/highereducation/EHEA2010/London2007/London%20speech%20SB%20final%20version_EN.asp#TopOfPage>.

Bergan, S. & A. Rauhvargers. 'The Council of Europe/UNESCO (Lisbon) Recognition Convention – What It Is and How to Use It'. In *Standards for Recognition: The Lisbon Recognition Convention and Its Subsidiary Texts*, edited by Council of Europe. Strasbourg: Council of Europe Publishing, Council of Europe Higher Education Series No. 3, 2005.

Bevc, M. 'Funding, Equity and Efficiency of Higher Education'. *IB revija* 1 (2008): 5–18.

Bompard, P. 'Angry Italians Don't Mince Words over Bologna'. *Times Higher Education*, 11 August 2006, available online at: <www.timeshighereducation.co.uk/story.asp?storyCode=204763&sectioncode=26>.

Bulvinaite, I. 'Union Citizenship and Its Role in the Free Movement of Persons Regimes'. *Web Journal of Current Legal Issues* 5 (2005), available at: <http://webjcli.ncl.ac.uk/2003/issue5/bulvinaite5.html>.

De Búrca, G. & B. De Witte. 'The Delimitation of Powers between the EU and Its Member States'. In *Accountability and Legitimacy in the European Union*, edited by A. Arnull & D. Wincott. Oxford: Oxford University Press, 2002, 201–222.

Charlier, J. & S. Croché. The Bologna Process and Its Actors. *University of Siena Working Paper,* No. 8, 2004.

Charlier, J. & S. Croché. 'The Bologna Process: The Outcome of Competition between Europe and the United States and a Stimulus to This Competition'. *European Education* 39, no. 4 (Winter 2007–2008): 10–26.

Corbett, A. 'Ideas, Institutions and Policy Entrepreneurs: Towards a New History of Higher Education in the European Community'. *European Journal of Education* 38, no. 3 (2003): 315–330.

Corbett, A. Europeanisation and the Bologna Process. *Paper presented to the conference co-sponsored by the ESRC and UACES*, 16 July 2004, 6.

Corbett, A. *Universities and the Europe of Knowledge: Ideas, Institutions and Policy Entrepreneurship in EU Higher Education 1955–2003.* Basingstoke: Palgrave, 2005.

Corbett, A. Higher Education as a Form of European Integration: How Novel Is the Bologna Process? *Arena Working Paper*, No. 15, December 2006.

Cowen, R. 'The Bologna Process and Higher Education in England'. In *Changing Universities in Europe and the 'Bologna Process'*, edited by D. Palomba. Comparative Education Studies, 2008, 47–72.

Craig, P. & G. de Búrca. *EU Law, Text Cases and Materials.* Oxford: Oxford University Press, 2003.

van Crayenest, F. 'La nature Juridique des Résolutions sur la Coopération en Matière d'Education'. In *European Community Law of Education*, edited by B. de Witte. Baden-Baden: Nomos Verlagsgesellschaft, 1989, 127–143.

Confederation of EU Rectors' Conferences & Association of European Universities (CRE) 1999.

European Union Rectors' Conferences & Association of European Universities. *The Bologna Declaration on the European Space for Higher Education: an Explanation*, 1999, available online at: <ec.europa.eu/education/policies/educ/bologna/bologna.pdf>.

Cremona, M. 'The Doctrine of Exclusivity and the Position of Mixed Agreements in the External Relations of the European Community'. *Oxford Journal of Legal Studies.* 2, no. 3 (1982): 393–428.

Cremona, M. 'Defending the Community Interest'. In *EU Foreign Relations Law, Constitutional Fundamentals*, edited by M. Cremona & B. de Witte. Oxford: Hart Publishing, 2008.

Crosier, D., L. Purser & H. Schmidt. *Universities Shaping the European Higher Education Area.* Trends Report V, 2007.

Davies, G. 'Higher Education, Equal Access, and Residence Conditions: Does EU Law Allow Member States to Charge Higher Fees to Students not Previously Resident?'. *Maastricht Journal of European and Comparative Law* 12 (2005): 227–240.

Davies, G. 'Any Place I Hang My Hat, or: Residence Is the New Nationality'. *European Law Journal* 11, no. 1 (2005): 43–56.

Davies*

Davies, H. Higher Education in the Internal Market. *UACES European Studies Online Essays*, available at: <www.Uaces.org>.

Dougan, M. 'Fees, Grants, Loans and Dole Cheques: Who Covers the Cost of Migrant Education within the EU?'. *Common Market Law Review* 32 (2005): 943–986.

Davies, G. The Process and Side-Effects of Harmonization of European Welfare States. *Jean Monnet Working Paper*, 02/06, 2006.

Eberlein, B. & D. Kerwer. 'New Governance in the European Union: A Theoretical Perspective'. *Journal of Common Market Studies* 42, no. 1 (2004): 121–142.

Enders, J. Governing the Academic Commons. About Blurring Boundaries, Blistering Organisations, and Growing Demands, *The Cheps Inaugurals 2002*, University of Twente: CHEPS, 69–105, available online at: <www.utwente.nl/cheps/whats_new/latest_news/archive/chepsboekje.pdf>.

Enders, J. 'Higher Education, Internationalization and the Nation-State: Recent Developments and Challenges to Governance Theory'. *Higher Education* 47, no. 3 (2004): 361–382.

Ertl, H. & D. Phillips. 'Standardization in EU Education and Training Policy. Findings from a European Research Network'. *Comparative Education* 42, no. 1 (2006): 77–91.

Erza, E. & A. Sanchez. 'L 'Auberge espagnole (2002): Transnational Departure or Domestic Crash Landing?'. *Studies in European Cinema* 2, no. 2 (2005): 137–148.

The National Unions of Students in Europe (ESIB). *Bologna with Student Eyes*, 2007.

Eurydice. *Focus on the structure of Higher Education in Europe. National Trends in the Bologna Process.* Brussels: European Commission DG Education and culture, 2003/4.

Eurybase. *The Education System in Germany 2006/7.* Brussels: European Commission DG Education and Culture, 2007.

Fejes, A. 'The Bologna Process. Governing Higher Education in Europe through Standardisation'. In *The Bologna Process and the Shaping of the Future of Knowledge Societies*, edited by T. Halvorsen & A. Nyhagen. Bergen: Department of Administration and Organization Theory, Department of Sociology and Forum for University History at the University of Oslo, 2005, 219–231.

Finaldi-Baratieri, D. The Only European Schools in the European Union? *EUI Working Papers HEC*, No. 6, 2000.

Fitchew, G. European Policy and Legislation on Immigration. *Migration Watch UK Briefing Paper 4.12*, 2009.

Flynn, J. 'Gravier: Suite du Feuilleton'. In *European Community Law of Education*, edited by B. de Witte. Baden-Baden: Nomos Verlagsgesellschaft, 1989, 95–112.

Freier Zusammenschluß von Studentinnenschaften. *Failing Bologna: State of Implementation of the Bologna Objectives in Germany.* Report of the National Union of Students in Germany for the Berlin Summit on Higher Education, Bonn, 2003.

Furlong, P. 'British Higher Education and the Bologna Process: An Interim Assessment'. *Politics* 25, no. 1 (2005): 53–61.

Garben, S. The Bologna Process from a European Law Perspective. *EUI Working Paper*, Law No. 2008/12, 2008.

Garben, S. 'Case C-73/08, Nicolas Bressol and Others, Céline Chaverot and Others v. Gouvernement de la Communauté française, [2010] ECR I-148'. *Common Market Law Review* 47, no. 5 (2010): 1493–1510.

Garben, S. 'The Bologna Process: From a European Law Perspective'. *European Law Journal* 16, no. 2 (2010): 186–210.

Gaviano, M. 'Bologna Process: French Universities React'. *Café Babel.com*, 9 February 2009, available online at: <www.cafebabel.co.uk/article/28618/bologna-process-protest-france-education-system.html>.

van Gerven, W. 'Harmonization of Private Law'. In *A Review of Forty Years of Community Law*, edited by A. McDonnell. The Hague: Kluwer Law International, 2005, 227–254.

Goldirova, R. 'EU Seeks to Close Its Institutional Wrangling'. *EU Observer*, 18 October 2007, available online at: <http://euobserver.com/9/24991>.

Golynker O. 'Student Loans: The European Concept of Social Justice According to Bidar'. *European Law Review* 31, no. 3 (2006): 612–627.

Gomitzka, A. Coordinating Policies for a 'Europe of Knowledge'. Emerging Practices of the 'Open Method of Coordination' in Education and Research, *Arena Working Paper*, No. 16, March 2005.

Gomitzka, A. The Open Method of Coordination as Practice. A Watershed in European Education Policy? *Arena Working Paper*, No. 16, December 2006.

Gori, G. *Towards an EU Right to Education.* The Hague: Kluwer Law International, 2001.

Hablitzel, H. 'Harmonisierungsverbot und Subsidiaritätsprinzip im europäischen Bildungsrecht'. *Die Öffentliche Verwaltung* 10 (2002): 407–414.

Hackl, E. Towards a European Area of Higher Education: Change and Convergence in European Higher Education, *EUI Working Paper*, RSC No. 2001/09, 2001.

Halvorsen, T. & A. Nyhagen. *Welcome Speech to The Third Conference on Knowledge and Politics.* University of Bergen: Conference on The Bologna Process and the Shaping of the Future Knowledge Societies, 18–20 May 2005.

Handoll, J. 'Foreign Teachers and Public Education'. In *European Community Law of Education*, edited by B. de Witte. Baden-Baden: Nomos Verlagsgesellschaft, 1989, 31–50.

Haug, G. & C. Tauch. *Towards a Coherent European Higher Education Space: From Bologna to Prague.* Amsterdam: European Association for International Education, 2000.

Haug, G. & C. Tauch. *Towards the European Higher Education Area: Survey of Main Reforms from Bologna to Prague.* Trends Report II, Executive Summary, 2001.

Henkel, I. 'Rüttgers und der Club'. *Die Zeit* 23 (1997).

Herzog, R. & L. Gerken. Stoppt den Europäischen Gerichtshof, *Frankfurter Allgemeine Zeitung*, 8 September 2008, 8.

Herzog, R. & L. Gerken. *Stop the European Court of Justice.* Freiburg: Centrum für Europäische Politik, 2008, available online at: <www.cep.eu/fileadmin/user . . . /Herzog-EuGH-Webseite_eng.pdf>.

Hoareau, C. Consequential Deliberative Governance? Analysing the Impact of Deliberation on Attitudinal and Policy Change in the European Higher Education Area. *London School of Economics Working Paper,* 2009.

Hochbaum, I. 'Kohesion und Subsidiarität. Maastricht und die Länderkulturhoheit'. *Die Öffentliche Verwaltung* 7 (1992): 285–292.

Hodson, D. & I. Maher. 'The Open Method as a New Mode of Governance: The Case of Soft Economic Policy Co-ordination'. *Journal of Common Market Studies* 39, no. 4 (2001): 719–746.

Hooghe, L. 'EUSA Conference: Can Big Be Beautiful'. *EUSA Review* 20, no. 3 (2007).

Horspool, M. & M. Humphreys. *European Union Law.* New York: Oxford University Press, 2008.

House of Commons, Education and Skills Committee. *The Bologna Process, Fourth Report of Session 2006–7*, 2007.

House of Commons, Education and Skills Committee 2007b

House of Commons Education and Skills Committee. *The Bologna Process: Government Response to the Committee's Fourth Report of Session 2006–07*, 2007.

Huisman, J. & M. van de Wende. 'The EU and Bologna: Are Supra- and International Initiatives Threatening Domestic Agendas?'. *European Journal of Education* 39, no. 3 (2004): 349–357.

Hurrelmann, A., et al. 'The Golden-Age Nation State and Its Transformation: A Framework for Analyis'. In *Transforming the Golden-Age Nation State*, edited by A. Hurrelmann et al. Houndsmill, Basingstroke: Palgrave Macmillan, 2007, 1–23.

International Centre for Higher Education Research, University of Kassel. *The Professional Value of ERASMUS mobility*, Final Report, 2006.

Jacqué, J. *Droit Institutionnel de L'Union Européenne.* Paris: Dalloz, 2004.

Jobbins, D. 'It's Now or Never to Bring on Bologna'. *Times Higher Education*, 28 March 2003, available online at: <www.timeshighereducation.co.uk/story.asp?storyCode=175696&sectioncode=26>.

Jones, H. *Education in the European Community*, Speech at the annual Congress of the Irish Vocational Education Association, 1978.

Jørgensen, S. 'The Right to Cross-Border Education in the European Union'. *Common Market Law Review* 46, no. 5 (2009): 1567–1590.

Juncker, J.C. *Council of Europe – European Union: A Sole Ambition for the European Continent*, Report to the Heads of State and Government of the Member States of the Council of Europe, 11/04/2006.

Kahn, S. The European Higher Education Area at the Crossroads, *Revue en ligne 'Etudes Europeennes'*, available online at: <www.cees-europe.fr/en/etudes/revue3/r3actu1.PDF>.

Kälvemark, T. & M. van der Wende. *National Policies for the Internationalization of higher Education in Europe.* Stockholm: National Agency for Higher Education, 1997.

Kapteyn, P.J.G. & P. VerLoren van Themaat. *Inleiding tot het Recht van de Europese Gemeenschappen: Na Maastricht.* Deventer: Kluwer, 1995.

Karlsen, G. *The Bologna Process – A Judicial Confirmation of EU's Policy of Education?* Paper for the 3rd Conference of Knowledge and Politics at The University of Bergen, 18–20 May 2005.

Keeling, R. 'The Bologna Process and the Lisbon Research Agenda: The European Commission's Expanding Role in Higher Education Discourse'. *European Journal of Education* 41, no. 2 (2006): 203–223.

Kilpatrick, C. & K. Armstrong. 'Law, Governance and New Governance: The Changing Open Method of Coordination'. *Colombia Journal of European Law* 13 (2007): 649–678.

Kirkwood-Tucker, T. 'Toward a European Model of Higher Education'. *European Education* 36, no. 3 (2004): 51–69.

Knudsen, I. *Project Report: Trends in Learning Structures in Higher Education*, 1999.

Koutrakos, P. *EU International Relations Law*. Oxford: Hart Publishing, 2006.

Krücken, G. 'Organizational Fields and Competitive Groups in Higher Education: Some Lessons from the Bachelor/Master Reform in Germany'. *Management Revue* 18, no. 2 (2007): 187–203.

Kuptsch, C. 'Students and Talent Flow. The Case of Europe: From Castle to Harbour?'. In *Competing for Global Talent*, edited by C. Kuptsch & E. Pang. Geneva: International Institute for Labour Studies, 2006, 33–63.

Kwiek, M. 'The Emergent European Educational Policies under Scrutiny: The Bologna Process from a Central European Perspective'. *European Educational Research Journal* 3, no. 4 (2004): 759–776.

Lambers, H. 'Subsidiarität in Europa – Allheilmittel oder juristische Leerformel?'. *Europarecht* (1993): 229–242.

Lenaerts, K. 'ERASMUS: Legal Basis and Implementation'. In *European Community Law of Education*, edited by B. de Witte. Baden-Baden: Nomos Verlagsgesellschaft, 1989.

Lenaerts, K. 'Education in European Community Law after Maastricht'. *Common Market Law Review*, 31 (1994): 7–41.

Lenaerts, K. & P. van Ypersele. 'Le principe de subsidiarité et son contexte: étude de l'article 3B du traité CE'. *Cahiers de Droit Européen* (1994): 3–83.

Leuze, K., et al. Transformations of the State, *TranState Working Paper, No.* 72, Bremen, 2008.

Lohmar, B. & T. Eckhardt (eds) *The Education System in the Federal Republic of Germany 2007, A Description of the Responsibilities, Structures and Developments in Education Policy for the Exchange of Information in Europe*. Bonn: Secretariat of the Standing Conference of the Ministers of Education and Cultural Affairs of the Länder in the Federal Republic of Germany, 2009.

Lonbay, J. 'Education and the Law: The Community Context'. *European Law Review* 14, no. 6 (1989): 363–387.

Lonbay, J. 'The Mutual Recognition of Professional Qualifications in the EC'. In *Professional Liability Law and Insurance*, edited by R. Hodgin. London: LLP, 1999, 1–40.

Lonbay, J. 'Reflections on Education and Culture in EC Law'. In *Culture and European Union Law*, edited by R. Craufurd Smith. Oxford: Oxford University Press, 2004, 243–276.

Lourtie, P. *Furthering the Bologna Process, Report to the Ministers of Education of the signatory countries*, Report commissioned by the Follow-up group of the Bologna Process, Prague, 2001.

Marshall Paris, J. 'French Protest over Bologna'. *Times Higher Education*, 29 April 2005, available online at: <www.timeshighereducation.co.uk/story.asp?storyCode=195681&sectioncode=26>.

Martens, H. & F. Zuleeg. 'Where Would We Be Now without the Euro?'. *EUobserver*, 15 October 2008, available online at: <http://euobserver.com/9/26933>.

Martens, K. & K. Wolf. 'Boomerangs and Trojan Horses: The Unintended Consequences of Internationalizing Education Policy through in the EU and the OECD'. In *European Integration and the Governance of Higher Education and Research.* edited by A. Amaral et al. Dordrecht, Netherlands: Springer, 2009, 81–108.

Mayntz, R. New Challenges to Governance Theory, *EUI Working Paper*, 1998.

Meek, V. 'Changing Patterns in Modes of Co-ordination of Higher Education'. In *Higher Education in a Globalizing World. International Trends and Mutual Observations*, edited by J. Enders & O. Fulton. Dordrecht: Kluwer, 2002, 53–72.

van der Mei, A.P. *Free Movement of Persons within the European Community, Cross-Border Access to Public Benefits.* Oregon: Hart Publishing, 2003.

van der Mei, A.P. 'EU Law and Education: Promotion of Student Mobility versus Protection of the Education Systems'. In *Social Welfare and EU Law*, edited by M. Dougan & E. Spaventa. Oxford: Hart Publishing, 2005, 219–240.

van der Mei, A.P. 'Freedom of Movement for Students: In Search of a More Satisfactory Balance between the Goal to Promote Student Mobility and the Need to Protect Education Systems'. In *Migration, Integration and Citizenship, A Challenge for Europe's Future*, edited by H. Schneider, vol. I. Maastricht: Forum Maastricht, 2005.

Miller, V. & C. Taylor. The Treaty of Lisbon: amendments to the Treaty on European Union, *Research Paper 08/09*, International Affairs and Defence Section, House of Commons Library, 2008.

Moravcsik, A. Why the European Union Strengthens the State: Domestic Politics and International Cooperation, *Harvard University Centre for European Studies Working Paper Series,* No. 52, 1994.

Murphy, M. 'Covert action? Education, Social Policy and Law in the European Union'. *Journal of Education Policy* 18, no. 5 (2003).

Muller, P. & P. Ravinet. 'Construire l'Europe en résistant à l'UE ? Le cas du processus de Bologne'. *Revue Internationale de Politique Comparée* 15, no. 4 (2008): 653–665.

Nokkala, T. Discursive construction of the role of the universities as national and international institutions in the European Higher Education Area. *Paper presented at the 1st International Euredocs Conference.* Paris, 2004, available online at: <http://euredocs.sciences-po.fr/en/conference/2004/terhi_nokkala.pdf>.

O'Leary, S. *The Evolving Concept of Community Citizenship.* London: Kluwer Law International, 1996.

Olsen, J. 'The Many Faces of Europeanization'. *Journal of Common Market Studies* 40, no. 5 (2002): 921–952.

Oostlander, A. *Report on the Proposal for a Council Decision on the conclusion by the European Economic Community and the European Atomic Energy Community of the Convention defining the Statute of the European Schools*, COM (93) c3 – 0142/93.

Orivel, F. 'The Bologna Process in France: Origin, Objectives and Implementation'. In *Changing Universities in Europe and the 'Bologna Process'*, edited by D. Palomba. Comparative Education Studies, 2008, 125–148.

Palayret, J. *A University for Europe, Prehistory of the European University Institute in Florence (1948–1976).* Rome: Presidency of the Council of Ministers, 1996.

Papatsiba, V. 'Making Higher Education More European through Student Mobility? Revisiting EU Initiatives in the Context of the Bologna Process'. *Comparative Education* 42, no. 1 (2006): 93–111.

Paris, J. 'French protest over Bologna'. *Times Higher Education*, 29 April 2005, available online at: <www.timeshighereducation.co.uk/story.asp?storyCode=195681&sectioncode=26>.

Parker, G. 'Austrian Chancellor Urges EU Court to Heed National Feelings'. *Financial Times*, 20 April 2006.

Pépin, L. 'The History of EU Cooperation in the Field of Education and Training: How Lifelong Learning Became a Strategic Objective'. *European Journal of Education* 42, no. 1 (2007): 121–132.

Pertek, J. *La Reconnaissance des qualifications dans un espace europeen des formations et des professions.* Brussels: Bruylant, 1998.

Phillips, L. 'Anti-Bologna Movement Spreads in Spain'. *EU Observer*, 15 December 2008, available online at: <euobserver.com/881/27303>.

De la Porte, C. 'Is the Open Method of Coordination Appropriate for Organising Activities at European Level in Sensitive Policy Areas?'. *European Law Journal* 8, no. 1 (2002): 38–58.

Racké, C. The Bologna Process and the EU: Neither within nor without. *Paper presented at the Third International EUREDOCS Conference.* Kassel: International Centre for Higher Education Research, 2006.

Racké, C. 'The Emergence of the Bologna Process: Pan-European Instead of EU Governance'. In *Dynamics and Obstacles of European Governance* edited by D. De Bièvre & C. Neuhold. Cheltenham: Edward Elgar Publishing, 2007, 29–49.

Rauhvargers, A. 'Improving the Recognition of Qualifications in the Framework of the Bologna Process'. *European Journal of Education* 39, no. 3 (2004): 331–347.

Rauhvargers, A. & S. Bergan. *Challenges in Recognition*, Council of Europe Higher Education Series No. 10, Strasbourg: Council of Europe Publishing, 2008.

Ravitch, D. & J. Viteritti. *Making Good Citizens. Education and Civil Society.* New Haven: Yale University Press, 2001.

Ravinet, P. 'From Voluntary Participation to Monitored Coordination: Why European Countries Feel Increasingly Bound by Their Commitment to the Bologna Process'. *European Journal of Education* 43, no. 3 (2008): 353–367.

Ravinet, P. Analyzing the Institutionalization of Europe: Back to the Classics. The Case of the Bologna Process, *ARENA Working Paper,* 2008.

Regent, S. 'The Open Method of Coordination: A New Supranational Form of Governance?'. *European Law Journal* 9, no. 2 (2003): 190–214.

Reed-Danahay, D. 'Citizenship Education in the "New Europe": Who Belongs?'. In *Reimagining Civic Education*, edited by B. Levinson & D. Stevick. Rowman & Littlefield, 2007, 197–215.

Reichert, S. & C. Tauch. 'Bologna Four Years After: Steps toward Sustainable Reform of Higher Education in Europe'. *European Education* 36, no. 3 (2004): 36–50.

Rothblatt, S. & B. Wittrock. 'Introduction: Universities and "Higher Education" '. In *The European and American University since 1800*, edited by S. Rothblatt & B. Wittrock. Cambridge: Cambridge University Press, 1993.

Roy, J. 'Between Cherry-Picking and Salvaging the Titanic: Spain and the Rescuing of the Essence of the EU Constitution'. In *The Rise and Fall of the EU's Constitutional Treaty*, edited by F. Laursen. Brill Academic Publishers, 2008, 123–144.

Rugaas, B. 'Foreword'. In *Recognition Issues in the Bologna Process*, edited by S. Bergan. Strasbourg: Council of Europe Publishing, 2003.

Runner, P. 'Financial Crisis Builds Polish Euro-Entry Momentum'. *EurActiv*, 28 October 2008, available online at: <http://euobserver.com/9/27004>.

Ryba, R. 'Toward a European Dimension in Education: Intention and Reality in European Community Policy and Practice'. *Comparative Education Review* 36, no. 1 (1992): 10–24.

Schermers, H. & N. Blokker. *International Institutional Law.* Leiden: Brill Academic Publishers, 2003.

Schmidt, V. 'European "Federalism" and Its Encroachments on National Institutions'. *The Journal of Federalism* 29, no. 1 (1999): 19–44.

Schneider, H. *Die Anerkennung von Diplomen in der Europäischen Gemeinschaft.* Antwerp: Intersentia, 1995.

Schneider, H. & S. Claessens. 'The Recognition of Diplomas and the Free Movement of Professionals in the European Union'. In *Migration, Integration and Citizenship, A Challenge for Europe's Future*, edited by H. Schneider, vol. I. Forum Maastricht, 2005.

Schneider, H. & S. Claessens. 'The Recognition of Diplomas and the Free Movement of Professionals in the European Union: Fifty Years of Experiences'. In *Conference Proceedings IALS*, edited by International Association of Law Schools. Montreal: IALS, 2008, 5–90.

Schriewer, J. '"Rationalized Myths" in European Higher Education: The Construction and Diffusion of the Bologna Model'. *European Education* 41, no. 2 (2009): 31–51.

Schubert, C. 'Swedish Students Protest Proposal to Cut PhD Terms'. *Nature Medicine* 12, no. 4 (2006): 373–373.

Schüttemeyer, S. 'The Current State of Political Science in Germany'. In *The State of Political Science in Western Europe*, edited by H. Klingemann. Opladen & Farmington Hills: Barbara Budrich Publishers, 2007, 163–186.

De Schutter, O. 'Two Europes of Human Rights: The Emerging Division of Tasks between the Council of Europe and the European Union in Promoting Human Rights in Europe'. *Columbia Journal of European Law* 14 (2007–2008): 509–562.

Schwartz, I. 'Article 235 and Law-Making Powers in the European Community'. *International and Comparative Law Quarterly* 27 (1978): 614–628.

Scott, C. 'The Governance of the European Union: The Potential for Multi-level Control'. *European Law Journal* 8, no. 1 (2002): 59–79.

Scott J. & D. Trubek. 'Mind the Gap: Law and New Approaches to Governance in the European Union'. *European Law Journal* 8, no. 1 (2002): 1–18.

Senden, L. *Soft Law in European Community Law.* Portland: Hart Publishing, 2005.

Shaw, J. 'Education and the Law in the European Community'. *Journal of Law & Education* 21, no. 3 (1992): 415–442.

Shaw, J. 'From the Margins to the Centre. Education and Training Law and Policy'. In *The Evolution of EU Law*, edited by P. Craig & G. de Búrca. Oxford: Oxford University Press, 1999, 555–595.

Skouris, W. 'La Liberté d'établissement et de prestation de services en matière d'enseignement'. In *European Community Law of Education*, edited by B. de Witte. Baden-Baden: Nomos Verlagsgesellschaft, 1989.

Smith, A. 'Joint Programmes of Study – An Instrument of European Cooperation in Higher Education'. In *Collection of Studies of the EEC Commission*, Education Series No. 7. Luxembourg: Office for Official Publications, Commission of the European Communities, 1979.

Snyder, F. Soft law and institutional practice in the European community, *EUI Working Paper*, No. 93/5, 1993.

Snyder, F. 'Soft Law and Institutional Practice in the European Community'. In *The Construction of Europe: Essays in Honour of Emile Noël*, edited by S. Martin. Dordrecht: Kluwer Academic Publishers, 1994.

Strumia, F. 'Citizenship and Free Movement: European and American Features of a Judicial Formula for Increased Comity'. *Columbia Journal of European Law* 12 (2005–2006): 713–750.

Teichler, U. 'The Changing Debate on Internationalization of Higher Education'. *Higher Education* 48, no. 1 (2004): 5–26.

Terry, L. 'Living with the Bologna Process: Recommendations to the German Legal Education Community from a U.S. Perspective'. *German Law Journal* 7, no. 11 (2007): 863–905.

Terry, L. 'The Bologna Process and Its Impact in Europe: It's So Much More than Degree Changes'. *Vanderbilt Journal of Transnational Law* 41, no. 1 (2008): 107–228.

Toth, A.G. 'The Principle of Subsidiarity in the Maastricht Treaty'. *Common Market Law Review* 29 (1992): 1079–1105.

Treib, O., H. Bähr & G. Falkner. Modes of Governance: A Note towards Conceptual Clarification', *European Governance Papers (EUROGOV)*, No. N-05-02, 2005.

Trubek, D., P. Cottrell & M. Nance. ' "Soft Law,", "Hard Law" and EU Integration'. In *Law and New Governance in the EU and the US*, edited by G. de Búrca & J. Scott. Portland: Oxford, 2006, 65–96.

United Kingdom Higher Education Europe Unit. *Submission to the House of Commons Inquiry on the Bologna Process*, 2006.

Verbruggen, M. *Tussen Subsidiariteit en Harmonisatie: Een onderzoek naar de instrumenten voor het voeren van een Europees onderwijsbeleid.* Unpublished PhD Thesis, University of Leuven, 2001.

Verbruggen, M. 'De Bolognaverklaring en het Europees Onderwijs: Enkele Juridische Kanttekeningen'. In *Europa en het Onderwijs*, edited by Onderwijsraad. Den Haag, 2002, 27–55.

Verbruggen, M. 'De Bolognaverklaring kritisch getoetst aan het Europees onderwijsbeleid'. *Sociaal Economische Wetgeving* (2003): 199–212.

Vogel, M. 'Diversity and Comparability – Towards a Common European Higher Education Area'. *Analytical and Bioanalytical Chemistry*. 387, no. 1 (2007).

Wächter, B. 'The Bologna Process: Developments and Prospects'. *European Journal of Education* 39, no. 3 (2004).

Walker, N. & G. de Búrca. 'Reconceiving Law and New Governance'. *Colombia Journal of European Law* 13 (2007): 519–537.

De Witte, B. 'The Scope of Community Powers in the Field of Education and Culture in the Light of Subsequent Practice'. In *The Dynamics of EC-Law*, edited by R. Bieber & G. Ress. Baden-Baden: Nomos Verlagsgesellschaft, 1987, 261–281.

De Witte, B. 'Introduction'. In *European Community Law of Education*, edited by Bruno De Witte. Baden-Baden: Nomos Verlagsgesellschaft, 1989, 9–18.

De Witte, B. 'Higher Education and the Constitution of the European Community'. In *Higher Education in Europe*, edited by C. Gellert. London: Kingsley Publishers, 1993, 185–202.

De Witte, B. 'Internationale verdragen tussen lidstaten van de Europese Unie'. In *De plaats van de Europese Unie in het veranderende bestel van de volkenrechtelijke organisatie*, edited by R. Wessel & B. de Witte, Mededelingen van de Nederlandse Vereniging voor Internationaal Recht, Nr. 123. Den Haag: Asser Press, 2001.

De Witte, B., A. Geelhoed & J. Inghelram. 'Legal Intruments, Decision-Making and EU Finances'. In *The Law of the European Union and the European Communities*, edited by P. Kapteyn & P. VerLoren van Themaat. Alphen aan den Rijn: Kluwer Law International, 2008, 273–419.

Witte, J. 'The Introduction of Two-Tiered Study Structures in the Context of the Bologna Process: A Theoretical Framework for an International Comparative Study of Change in Higher Education Systems'. *Higher Education Policy* 17, no. 4 (2004): 405–425.

Witte, J. *Changes of Degrees and Degrees of Change.* Enschede: CHEPS, 2006.

Wolinetz, S. 'Trimming the Sails: The Dutch and the EU Constitution After the Referendum'. In *The Rise and Fall of the EU's Constitutional Treaty*, edited by F. Laursen. Brill Academic Publishers, 2008, 181–200.

Young, E. 'Protecting Member State Autonomy in the European Union: Some Cautionary Tales From American Federalism'. *New York University Law Review* 77 (2002): 1670–1677.

Zgaga, P. *The Bologna Process: From Prague to Berlin and After.* Paper on the basis of author's engagement in the Bologna follow-up group as rapporteur for the Berlin conference in September 2003.

Zgaga, P. Looking Out: The Bologna Process in a Global Setting. Oslo: Norwegian Ministry of Education and Research, *Report presented to the Ministerial Meeting of the Bologna Process*, London, May.

Zilioli, C. 'The Recognition of Diplomas and Its Impact on Educational Policies'. In *European Community Law of Education*, edited by B. de Witte. Baden-Baden: Nomos Verlagsgesellschaft, 1989, 51–70.

Appendix 1

Sorbonne Joint Declaration*

Joint Declaration on Harmonisation of the Architecture of the European Higher Education System

by the four Ministers in charge for France, Germany, Italy and the United Kingdom

Paris, the Sorbonne, May 25 1998

The European process has very recently moved some extremely important steps ahead. Relevant as they are, they should not make one forget that Europe is not only that of the Euro, of the banks and the economy: it must be a Europe of knowledge as well. We must strengthen and build upon the intellectual, cultural, social and technical dimensions of our continent. These have to a large extent been shaped by its universities, which continue to play a pivotal role for their development.

Universities were born in Europe, some three-quarters of a millenium ago. Our four countries boast some of the oldest, who are celebrating important anniversaries around now, as the University of Paris is doing today. In those times, students and academics would freely circulate and rapidly disseminate knowledge throughout the continent. Nowadays, too many of our students still graduate without having had the benefit of a study period outside of national boundaries.

We are heading for a period of major change in education and working conditions, to a diversification of courses of professional careers with education and training throughout life becoming a clear obligation. We owe our students, and our society at large, a higher education system in which they are given the best opportunities to seek and find their own area of excellence.

---

* *Source*: <www.bologna-berlin2003.de/pdf/Sorbonne_declaration.pdf>.

An open European area for higher learning carries a wealth of positive perspectives, of course respecting our diversities, but requires on the other hand continuous efforts to remove barriers and to develop a framework for teaching and learning, which would enhance mobility and an ever closer cooperation.

The international recognition and attractive potential of our systems are directly related to their external and internal readabilities. A system, in which two main cycles, undergraduate and graduate, should be recognized for international comparison and equivalence, seems to emerge.

Much of the originality and flexibility in this system will be achieved through the use of credits (such as in the ECTS scheme) and semesters. This will allow for validation of these acquired credits for those who choose initial or continued education in different European universities and wish to be able to acquire degrees in due time throughout life. Indeed, students should be able to enter the academic world at any time in their professional life and from diverse backgrounds.

Undergraduates should have access to a diversity of programmes, including opportunities for multidisciplinary studies, development of a proficiency in languages and the ability to use new information technologies.

International recognition of the first cycle degree as an appropriate level of qualification is important for the success of this endeavour, in which we wish to make our higher education schemes clear to all.

In the graduate cycle there would be a choice between a shorter master's degree and a longer doctor's degree, with possibilities to transfer from one to the other. In both graduate degrees, appropriate emphasis would be placed on research and autonomous work.

At both undergraduate and graduate level, students would be encouraged to spend at least one semester in universities outside their own country. At the same time, more teaching and research staff should be working in European countries other than their own. The fast growing support of the European Union, for the mobility of students and teachers should be employed to the full.

Most countries, not only within Europe, have become fully conscious of the need to foster such evolution. The conferences of European rectors, University presidents, and groups of experts and academics in our respective countries have engaged in widespread thinking along these lines.

A convention, recognising higher education qualifications in the academic field within Europe, was agreed on last year in Lisbon. The convention set a number of basic requirements and acknowledged that individual countries could engage in an even more constructive scheme. Standing by these conclusions, one can build on them and go further. There is already much common ground for the mutual recognition of higher education degrees for professional purposes through the respective directives of the European Union.

Our governments, nevertheless, continue to have a significant role to play to these ends, by encouraging ways in which acquired knowledge can be validated and respective degrees can be better recognised. We expect this to promote further inter-university agreements. Progressive harmonisation of the overall framework of our degrees and cycles can be achieved through strengthening of already existing experience, joint diplomas, pilot initiatives, and dialogue with all concerned.

We hereby commit ourselves to encouraging a common frame of reference, aimed at improving external recognition and facilitating student mobility as well as employability. The anniversary of the University of Paris, today here in the Sorbonne, offers us a solemn opportunity to engage in the endeavour to create a European area of higher education, where national identities and common interests can interact and strengthen each other for the benefit of Europe, of its students, and more generally of its citizens. We call on other Member States of the Union and other European countries to join us in this objective and on all European Universities to consolidate Europe's standing in the world through continuously improved and updated education for its citizens.

Claude ALLEGRE	**Luigi BERLINGUER**	**Tessa BLACKSTONE**	**Jürgen RÜTTGERS**
Minister for National Education, Research and Technology (France)	Minister for Public Instruction, University and Research (Italy)	Minister for Higher Education (United Kingdom)	Minister for Education, Sciences, Research and Technology (Germany)

Appendix 2

The Bologna Declaration of 19 June 1999*

Joint Declaration of the European Ministers of Education

The European process, thanks to the extraordinary achievements of the last few years, has become an increasingly concrete and relevant reality for the Union and its citizens. Enlargement prospects together with deepening relations with other European countries, provide even wider dimensions to that reality. Meanwhile, we are witnessing a growing awareness in large parts of the political and academic world and in public opinion of the need to establish a more complete and far-reaching Europe, in particular building upon and strengthening its intellectual, cultural, social and scientific and technological dimensions.

A Europe of Knowledge is now widely recognised as an irreplaceable factor for social and human growth and as an indispensable component to consolidate and enrich the European citizenship, capable of giving its citizens the necessary competences to face the challenges of the new millennium, together with an awareness of shared values and belonging to a common social and cultural space.

The importance of education and educational co-operation in the development and strengthening of stable, peaceful and democratic societies is universally acknowledged as paramount, the more so in view of the situation in South East Europe.

The Sorbonne declaration of 25th of May 1998, which was underpinned by these considerations, stressed the Universities' central role in developing European cultural dimensions. It emphasised the creation of the European area of higher education as a key way to promote citizens' mobility and employability and the Continent's overall development.

---

* *Source*: <www.magna-charta.org/pdf/BOLOGNA_DECLARATION.pdf>.

Several European countries have accepted the invitation to commit themselves to achieving the objectives set out in the declaration, by signing it or expressing their agreement in principle. The direction taken by several higher education reforms launched in the meantime in Europe has proved many Governments' determination to act.

European higher education institutions, for their part, have accepted the challenge and taken up a main role in constructing the European area of higher education, also in the wake of the fundamental principles laid down in the Bologna Magna Charta Universitatum of 1988. This is of the highest importance, given that Universities' independence and autonomy ensure that higher education and research systems continuously adapt to changing needs, society's demands and advances in scientific knowledge.

The course has been set in the right direction and with meaningful purpose. The achievement of greater compatibility and comparability of the systems of higher education nevertheless requires continual momentum in order to be fully accomplished. We need to support it through promoting concrete measures to achieve tangible forward steps. The 18th June meeting saw participation by authoritative experts and scholars from all our countries and provides us with very useful suggestions on the initiatives to be taken.

We must in particular look at the objective of increasing the international competitiveness of the European system of higher education. The vitality and efficiency of any civilisation can be measured by the appeal that its culture has for other countries. We need to ensure that the European higher education system acquires a world-wide degree of attraction equal to our extraordinary cultural and scientific traditions.

While affirming our support to the general principles laid down in the Sorbonne declaration, we engage in co-ordinating our policies to reach in the short term, and in any case within the first decade of the third millennium, the following objectives, which we consider to be of primary relevance in order to establish the European area of higher education and to promote the European system of higher education world-wide:

> Adoption of a system of **easily readable and comparable degrees,** also through the implementation of the Diploma Supplement, in order to promote European citizens employability and the international competitiveness of the European higher education system
>
> Adoption of a system essentially based on **two main cycles,** undergraduate and graduate. Access to the second cycle shall require successful completion of first cycle studies, lasting a minimum of three years. The degree awarded after the first cycle shall also be relevant to the European labour market as an appropriate level of qualification. The second cycle should lead to the master and/or doctorate degree as in many European countries.

Establishment of a **system of credits** – such as in the ECTS – as a proper means of promoting the most widespread student mobility. Credits could also be acquired in non-higher education contexts, including lifelong learning, provided they are recognised by receiving Universities concerned.

Promotion of **mobility** by overcoming obstacles to the effective exercise of free movement with particular attention to:

- for students, access to study and training opportunities and to related services
- for teachers, researchers and administrative staff, recognition and valorisation of periods spent in a European context researching, teaching and training, without prejudicing their statutory rights.

Promotion of **European co-operation in quality assurance** with a view to developing comparable criteria and methodologies.

Promotion of the **necessary European dimensions in higher education,** particularly with regards to curricular development, inter-institutional co-operation, mobility schemes and integrated programmes of study, training and research.

We hereby undertake to attain these objectives – within the framework of our institutional competences and taking full respect of the diversity of cultures, languages, national education systems and of University autonomy – to consolidate the European area of higher education. To that end, we will pursue the ways of intergovernmental co-operation, together with those of non governmental European organisations with competence on higher education. We expect Universities again to respond promptly and positively and to contribute actively to the success of our endeavour.

Convinced that the establishment of the European area of higher education requires constant support, supervision and adaptation to the continuously evolving needs, we decide to meet again within two years in order to assess the progress achieved and the new steps to be taken.

Signatories:

Caspar EINEM Minister of Science and Transport (Austria)	
Jan ADE Director General Ministry of the Flemish Community Department of Education (Belgium)	Gerard SCHMIT Director General of French Community Ministry for Higher Education and Research (Belgium)

Eduard ZEMAN Minister of Education, Youth and Sport (Czech Republic)	Anna Mmia TOTOMANOVA Vice Minister of Education and Science (Bulgaria)
Tonis LUKAS Minister of Education (Estonia)	Margrethe VESTAGER Minister of Education (Denmark)
Claude ALLEGRE Minister of National Education, Research and Technology (France)	Maija RASK Minister of Education and Science (Finland)
Ute ERDSIEK-RAVE Minister of Education, Science, Research And Culture of the Land Scheswig-Holstein (Permanent Conference of the Ministers of Culture of the German Länders)	Wolf-Michael CATENHUSEN Parliamentary State Secretary Federal Ministry of Education and Research (Germany)
Adam KISS Deputy State Secretary for Higher Education and Science (Hungary)	Gherassimos ARSENIS Minister of Public Education and Religious Affairs (Greece)
Pat DOWLING Principal Officer Ministry for Education and Science (Ireland)	Gudridur SIGURDARDOTTIR Secretary General Ministry of Education, Science and Culture (Iceland)
Tatiana KOKEK State Minister of Higher Education and Science (Latvia)	Ortensio ZECCHINO Minister of University and Scientific And Technological Research (Italy)
Erna HENNICOT-SCHOEPGES Minister of National Education and Vocational Training (Luxembourg)	Kornelijus PLATELIS Minister of Education and Science (Lithuania)
Loek HERMANS Minister of Education, Culture and Science (the Netherlands)	Louis GALEA Minister of Education (Malta)

Wilibald WINKLER Under Secretary of State of National Education (Poland)	Jon LILLETUN Minister of Education, Research and Church Affairs (Norway)
Andrei MARGA Minister of National Education (Romania)	Eduardo Marçal GRILO Minister of Education (Portugal)
Pavel ZGAGA State Secretary for Higher Education (Slovenia)	Milan FTACNIK Minister of Education (Slovak Republic)
Agneta BLADH State Secretary for Education and Science (Sweden)	D. Jorge FERNANDEZ DIAZ Secretary of State of Education, Universities, Research and Development (Spain)
Baroness Tessa BLACKSTONE of Stoke Newington Minister of State for Education and Employment (United Kingdom)	Charles KLEIBER State Secretary for Science and Research (Swiss Confederation)

Table of Cases

Table of Legislation

Index

EUROPEAN MONOGRAPH SERIES

1. Lamm Betten (ed.), *The Future of European Social Policy*, 1991 (ISBN 90-654-4585-4).
2. Annemarie Loman, Kamiel Mortelmans, Harry H.G. Post & Stewart Watson, *Culture and Common Law: Before and After Maastricht*, 1992 (ISBN 90-654-4638-9).
3. John A.E. Vervaele, *Fraud against the Community: The Need for European Fraud Legislation*, 1994 (ISBN 90-654-4634-6).
4. Philip Raworth, *The Legislative Process in the European Community*, 1993 (ISBN 90-654-4690-7).
5. Jules Stuyck, *Financial and Monetary Integration in the European Economic Community*, 1993 (ISBN 90-654-4718-0).
6. Jules Stuyck & A.J. Vossestein (eds), *State Entrepreneurship, National Monopolies and European Community Law*, 1993 (ISBN 90-654-4773-3).
7. Jules Stuyck & A. Looijestijn-Clearie (eds), *The European Economic Area EC-EFTA*, 1994 (ISBN 90-654-4815-2).
8. Rosita B. Bouterse, *Competition and Integration: What Goals Count?*, 1995 (ISBN 90-654-4816-0).
9. René Barents, *The Agricultural Law of the EC: An Inquiry into the Administrative Law*, 1994 (ISBN 90-654-4867-5).
10. Nicholas Emiliou, *Principles of Proportionality in European Law: A Comparative Study*, 1996 (ISBN 90-411-0866-1).
11. Eivind Smith, *National Parliaments as Cornerstones of European Integration*, 1996 (ISBN 90-411-0898-X).
12. Jan H. Jans, *European Environmental Law*, 1996 (ISBN 90-411-0877-7).
13. Síofra O'Leary, *The Evolving Concept of Community Citizenship: From the Free Movement of Persons to Union Citizenship*, 1997 (ISBN 90-411-0878-5).
14. Laurence W. Gormley (ed.), *Current and Future Perspectives on EC Competition Law*, 1983 (ISBN 90-411-0691-X).
15. Simone White, *Protection of the Financial Interests of the European Communities: The Fight against Fraud and Corruption*, 1998 (ISBN 90-411-9647-1).
16. Morten P. Broberg, *The European Commission's Jurisdiction to Scrutinize Mergers*, 3rd Edition, 2006 (ISBN 978-90-411-2474-6).
17. Doris Hildebrand, *The Role of Economic Analysis in the EC Competition Rules: The European School*, 2nd Edition, 2002 (ISBN 90-411-1706-7).
18. Christof R.A. Swaak, *European Community Law and the Automobile Industry*, 1999 (ISBN 90-411-1140-9).
19. Dorthe Dahlgaard Dingel, *Public Procurement: A Harmonization of the National Judicial Review of the Application of European Community Law*, 1999 (ISBN 90-411-1161-1).
20. John A.E. Vervaele (ed.), *Compliance and Enforcement of European Community Law*, 1999 (ISBN 90-411-1151-4).

21. Martin Trybus, *European Defence Procurement Law: International and National Procurement Systems as Models for a Liberalized Defence Procurement Market in Europe*, 1999 (ISBN 90-411-1167-0).
22. Helen Staples, *The Legal Status of Third Country Nationals Resident in the European Union*, 1999 (ISBN 90-411-1277-4).
23. Damien Geradin (ed.), *The Liberalization of State Monopolies in the European Union and Beyond*, 1999 (ISBN 90-411-1264-2).
24. Katja Heede, *European Ombudsman: Redress and Control at Union Level*, 2000 (ISBN 90-411-1413-0).
25. Ulf Bernitz & Joakim Nergelius (eds), *General Principles of European Community Law*, 2000 (ISBN 90-411-1402-5).
26. Michaela Drahos, *Convergence of Competition Laws and Policies in the European Community*, 2002 (ISBN 90-411-1562-5).
27. Damien Geradin (ed.), *The Liberalization of Electricity and Natural Gas in the European Union*, 2001 (ISBN 90-411-1560-9).
28. Gisella Gori, *Towards an EU Right to Education*, 2001 (ISBN 90-411-1670-2).
29. Brendan P.G. Smith, *Constitution Building in the European Union*, 2001 (ISBN 90-411-1695-8).
30. Friedl Weiss & Frank Wooldridge, *Free Movement of Persons within the European Community*, 2nd Edition, 2007 (ISBN 978-90-411-2545-3).
31. Ingrid Boccardi, *Europe and Refugees: Towards an EU Asylum Policy*, 2002 (ISBN 90-411-1709-1).
32. John A.E. Vervaele & André Klip (eds), *European Cooperation Between Tax, Customs and Judicial Authorities*, 2001 (ISBN 90-411-1747-4).
33. Wouter P.J. Wils, *The Optimal Enforcement of EC Antitrust Law: Essays in Law and Economics*, 2002 (ISBN 90-411-1757-1).
34. Damien Geradin (ed.), *The Liberalization of Postal Services in the European Union*, 2002 (ISBN 90-411-1780-6).
35. Nick Bernard, *Multilevel Governance in the European Union*, 2002 (ISBN 90-411-1812-8).
36. Jill Wakefield, *Judicial Protection through the Use of Article 288(2) EC*, 2002 (ISBN 90-411-1823-3).
37. Sebastiaan Princen, *EU Regulation and Transatlantic Trade*, 2002 (ISBN 90-411-1871-3).
38. Amaryllis Verhoeven, *The European Union in Search of a Democratic and Constitutional Theory*, 2002 (ISBN 90-411-1872-1).
39. Paul L.C. Torremans, *Cross Border Insolvencies in EU, English and Belgian Law*, 2002 (ISBN 90-411-1888-8).
40. Malcolm Anderson & Joanna Apap (eds), *Police and Justice Cooperation and the New European Borders*, 2002 (ISBN 90-411-1893-4).
41. Christin M. Forstinger, *Takeover Law in EU and USA: A Comparative Analysis*, 2002 (ISBN 90-411-1919-1).

42. Antonio Bavasso, *Communications in EU Antitrust Law: Market Power and Public Interest*, 2003 (ISBN 90-411-1974-4).
43. Fiona G. Wishlade, *Regional State Aid and Competition Policy in the European Union*, 2003 (ISBN 90-411-1975-2).
44. Gareth Davies, *Nationality Discrimination in the European Internal Market*, 2003 (ISBN 90-411-1998-1).
45. René Barents, *The Autonomy of Community Law*, 2003 (ISBN 90-411-2251-6).
46. Gerhard Dannecker & Oswald Jansen (eds), *Competition Law Sanctioning in the European Union*, 2004 (ISBN 90-411-2100-5).
47. Nauta Dutilh (ed.), *Dealing with Dominance: The Experience of National Competition Authorities*, 2004 (ISBN 90-411-2211-7).
48. Stefaan van den Bogaert, *Practical Regulation of the Mobility of Sportsmen in the EU Post Bosman*, 2005 (ISBN 90-411-2327-X).
49. Katalin Judit Cseres, *Competition Law and Consumer Protection*, 2005 (ISBN 90-411-2380-6).
50. Philipp Kiiver, *The National Parliaments in the European Union: A Critical View on EU Constitution Building*, 2006 (ISBN 978-90-411-2452-4).
51. Alexander Turk, *The Concept of Legislation in European Community Law*, 2006 (ISBN 978-90-411-2472-2).
52. Dimitrios Sinaniotis, *The Interim Protection of Individuals before the European and National Courts*, 2006 (ISBN 978-90-411-2498-2).
53. M. Holoubek & D. Damjanovic, M. Traimer (eds), *Regulating Content: The European Regulatory Framework for the Media and Related Creative Sectors*, 2006 (ISBN 978-90-411-2597-2).
54. Anneli Albi & Jacques Ziller (eds), *The European Constitution and National Constitutions: Ratification and Beyond*, 2006 (ISBN 978-90-411-2524-8).
55. Gustavo E. Luengo, *Regulation of Subsidies and State Aids in WTO and EC Law: Conflicts in International Trade Law*, 2007 (ISBN 978-90-411-2547-7).
56. Eniko Horvath, *Mandating Identity: Citizenship, Kinship Laws and Plural Nationality in the European Union*, 2007 (ISBN 978-90-411-2662-7).
57. Rass Holdgaard, *External Relations Law of the European Community: Legal Reasoning and Legal Discourses*, 2007 (ISBN 978-90-411-2604-7).
58. Jill Wakefield, *The Right to Good Administration*, 2007 (ISBN 978-90-411-2697-9).
59. Dimitry Kochenov, *EU Enlargement and the Failure of Conditionality: Pre-accession Conditionality in the Fields of Democracy and the Rule of Law*, 2008 (ISBN 978-90-411-2696-2).
60. Despina Mavromati, *The Law of Payment Services in the EU: The EC Directive on Payment Services in the Internal Market*, 2008 (ISBN 978-90-411-2700-6).
61. Anne Meuwese, *Impact Assessment in EU Lawmaking*, 2008 (ISBN 978-90-411-2720-4).

62. Ulf Bernitz, Joakim Nergelius & Cecilia Cardner (eds), *General Principles of EC Law in a Process of Development*, 2008 (ISBN 978-90-411-2705-1).
63. Johan van de Gronden (ed.), *The EU and WTO Law on Services: Limits to the Realisation of General Interest Policies within the Services Markets?*, 2008 (ISBN 978-90-411-2809-6).
64. Alina Tryfonidou, *Reverse Discrimination in EC Law*, 2009 (ISBN 978-90-411-2751-8).
65. Mikael Berglund, *Cross-Border Enforcement of Claims in the EU: History Present Time and Future*, 2009 (ISBN 978-90-411-2861-4).
66. Theodore Konstadinides, *Division of Powers in European Union Law: The Delimitation of Internal Competence between the EU and the Member States*, 2009 (ISBN 978-90-411-2615-3).
67. Mattias Derlén, *Multilingual Interpretation of European Union Law*, 2009 (ISBN 978-90-411-2853-9).
68. René Barents, *Directory of EU Case Law on the Preliminary Ruling Procedure*, 2009 (ISBN 978-90-411-3150-8).
69. Yan Luo, *Anti-dumping in the WTO, the EU and China: The Rise of Legalization in the Trade Regime and its Consequences*, 2010 (ISBN 978-90-411-3207-9).
70. Patrick Birkinshaw & Mike Varney (eds), *The European Union Legal Order after Lisbon*, 2010 (ISBN 978-90-411-3152-2).
71. Thomas Gr. Papadopoulos, *EU Law and Harmonization of Takeovers in the Internal Market*, 2010 (978-90-411-3340-3).
72. Bas van Bockel, *The* Ne Bis In Idem *Principle in EU Law*, 2010 (978-90-411-3156-0).
73. Veljko Milutinović, *The 'Right to Damages' under EU Competition Law: From* Courage v. Crehan *to the White Paper and Beyond*, 2010 (978-90-411-3235-2).
74. Amandine Garde, *EU Law and Obesity Prevention*, 2010 (978-90-411-2706-8).
75. Leonard Besselink, Frans Pennings & Sacha Prechal (eds), *The Eclipse of the Legality Principle in the European Union*, 2011 (978-90-411-3262-8).
76. Sacha Garben, *EU Higher Education Law: The Bologna Process and Harmonization by Stealth*, 2011 (978-90-411-3365-6).

www.ingramcontent.com/pod-product-compliance
Lightning Source LLC
Chambersburg PA
CBHW071241230926
51849CB00001B/188
9789041133656